Women of Fire and Spirit

Women of Fire and Spirit

History, Faith, and Gender
in Roho Religion in Western Kenya

CYNTHIA HOEHLER-FATTON

New York Oxford
OXFORD UNIVERSITY PRESS
1996

Oxford University Press

Oxford   New York
Athens   Auckland   Bangkok
Calcutta   Cape Town   Dar es Salaam   Delhi
Florence   Hong Kong   Istanbul   Karachi
Kuala Lumpur   Madras   Madrid   Melbourne
Mexico City   Nairobi   Paris   Singapore
Taipei   Tokyo   Toronto

and associated companies in
Berlin   Ibadan

Copyright © 1996 by Cynthia Hoehler-Fatton

Published by Oxford University Press, Inc.
198 Madison Avenue, New York, New York 10016

Oxford is a registered trademark of Oxford University Press, Inc.

Library of Congress Cataloging-in-Publication Data

Hoehler-Fatton, Cynthia Heyden.
    Women of fire and spirit : history, faith, and gender in Roho
religion in Western Kenya / Cynthia Hoehler-Fatton.
        p.   cm.
    Includes bibliographical references (p.   ).
    ISBN 0–19–509790–4; ISBN 0–19–509791–2 (pbk.)
    1. Independent churches—Kenya—Nyanza Province—Case studies.
2. Christian sects—Kenya—Nyanza—Case studies.   3. Ruwe Holy Ghost
Church of East Africa.   4. Musanda Holy Ghost Church of East Africa.
5. Women in Christianity—Kenya—Nyanza Province—Case studies.
6. Luo (African people)—Religion.   7. Nyanza Province (Kenya)—
church history.   I. Title.
BR1443.K4H64   1996
289.9—dc20   95–11563

9 8 7 6 5 4 3 2 1

Printed in the United States of America
on acid-free paper

To Robert

ACKNOWLEDGMENTS

Many people have made this study possible. I could not have conducted my field research without the interest of members of Roho congregations throughout Nyanza Province, Kenya, especially in Ruwe, Musanda, Masumbi, Sinaga, Kisumu, and Mirunda. Recognition must go, first and foremost, to the late Anna Inondi (1907–1992), daughter of Odhialo. Despite her illness, "Soso" Anna spent many hours with me, recounting the history of the Ruwe Holy Ghost Church. Thanks are also due her son, Meshak Ogola, whose thoughtful arrangement of interview sessions with church elders and commitment to accuracy greatly facilitated the chronological organization of this material. Bishop Ibrahim Owuor Mango of the Musanda Holy Ghost Church was welcoming and forthcoming with biographical information about his late father, the Reverend Alfayo Odongo Mango. Jacob Zadock Ochoma, the general secretary of the Ruwe Holy Ghost Church, was most helpful in providing church lists and records.

I am humbly indebted to many remarkable Luo women who shared with me their religious experiences and their views on life, womanhood, and faith. Among those deserving special mention are Esta Songa, *Laktar* Nereya "Jakinda" Owuor, *Laktar* Nereya Auma, the late Dibora Onyango, *Laktar* Joan Akello, Margaret Uba, Anna Ayoo, Sarah Odenyo, Syprose Akinyi Odero, and Sister Seraphine Oweggi. I am also grateful to Teacher Morris Akeich Opiyo, who facilitated all my research in Masumbi, and to Pastor Joel Muudo Okwany. Thanks also go to Pastor Elisha Eliakim Ndong'a of Sinaga; the Reverend Peter Asava, the Reverend Alfred Sagida, and Pastor Dishon Osore of the Holy Spirit Church of East Africa, Bukoyoni; and Bishop Elijah Ayodo of the Mother Spirit Church, Kisumu.

This project could not have been completed without the tireless dedication of my skilled research assistant, John M. Haung Godia. Henry Osodo helped with the transcription of Roho hymns and liturgies, and Lebaus Onyango was of great assistance with interviews in Mirunda. Former Curator Meshak Kokwaro and Assistant Curator Peter Nyamenya of the Kisumu Museum helped me make initial contacts with Roho congregations. I similarly thank the Reverend Daniel Ogusu, Haggai Nundu, and John Padwick for their contacts, advice, and guidance.

Many people opened their homes and hearts to me. I am indebted to David and Anna Opiyo and their children for their hospitality and caring concern. I am likewise grateful to Procrus Odhiambo Godia, Mary Odhiambo, Helidah, and their entire family. I thank Bishop Joseph and Jenipha Wasonga for their warm encouragement. My sincere gratitude also goes to the School Sisters of Notre Dame at Ojolla, Kisumu, and Kisii, especially to Sister Eunice Silkey for many years of friendship and good counsel. Finally, deepest thanks go to my family away from home, Peter and Vicky Nyamenya and their children, Lorrine, Ken, Noel, and Tom Joel.

Several institutions have supported this project. The Carter G. Woodson Institute for Afro-American and African Studies at the University of Virginia provided a substantial portion of my initial fieldwork funding and later awarded me a generous dissertation fellowship. To Director Armstead Robinson, Associate Director William Jackson, and the Institute staff, I am truly grateful. I also wish to thank the Office of the President of Kenya for granting me clearance to conduct this research, which I carried out under the kind auspices of the Institute of African Studies at the University of Nairobi. I am indebted to Richard Ambani and the rest of the staff at the Kenya National Archives for their invaluable help. I also express my gratitude to Stan Nussbaum at the Center for New Religious Movements, who arranged for my use of the Harold Turner Collection; to the curator of the Church Missionary Society Archives at the University of Birmingham, England; and to Carolyn Davis at the George Arents Research Library for Special Collections at Syracuse University.

As one would expect, the methodology and analyses presented in this book bear the marks of my teachers at the University of Virginia. I am indebted to Professor Abdulaziz Sachedina for his insight into religious devotion and piety. I owe a great deal to Professor Gianfranco Poggi for instruction in sociological theory; to Professor Joseph Miller for his course on historiography and his comments on my dissertation proposal; and to Professor Susan McKinnon for a grounding in the anthropological classics on the Nilotes and advice on gender issues. My dissertation advisor, Professor Benjamin Ray, has offered steady guidance in the history of religions discipline while allowing me freedom to pursue my own intellectual interests. For his encouragement and mentoring, I shall always be grateful.

The arguments delineated in these pages have benefited from my discussions with scholars in Kenya and in the United States. My sincere thanks to all of the following: E. S. Atieno Odhiambo, Hannah Kinoti, Daniel Nthamburi, D. A. Masolo, Duncan Okoth-Okombo, H. Odera Oruka, Asenath Bole Odaga, Nancy Schwartz, Parker Shipton, Paul Robinson, Tessa Bartholomeusz, Tracy Fessenden, and Jim Ceaser. A special word of gratitude goes to Blaire French, who has expressed continued enthusiasm for this project from the very start and who generously volunteered her time and expertise in editing the manuscript. George O. Ndege's assistance with translation is likewise appreciated. I also wish to express my thanks to Cynthia Read, Peter Ohlin, and Cynthia Garver at Oxford University Press, along with Joy Matkowski, the copy editor.

Last but not least, I acknowledge my family. My late grandmother Eva Anderson, a great believer in women's education, left me the funds that enabled me to complete my fieldwork. My parents, Harry and Judith Hoehler, and my sisters, Carolyn and Kristen, have offered support throughout. Vanessa, my stepdaughter, and Luc, my infant son, sources of such happiness, have helped me keep my academic work in perspective. Finally, I owe more to my husband, Robert Fatton, than I could ever say. He has applied his scrutinizing eye and critical mind to every stage of my project and forced me to clarify my thinking on numerous points. It is to him that I lovingly dedicate this book.

CONTENTS

INTRODUCTION

In 1983, while teaching at Ojolla Secondary School on the grounds of one of the oldest Catholic mission stations in western Kenya,[1] I witnessed my first *juogi* (spirit) attack. It was late in the afternoon and the only students left in the compound were a few girls who had begun boarding in the new dormitory. Suddenly, there was a commotion on the southern side of the dormitory. Rounding the corner, I found Cornelia A., one of our Form One students, in distress. She was shaking and hyperventilating, her eyes wide with terror, as she pointed at the air, gasping, *Obiro! Obiro!* (He/She is coming!) Somehow I managed to quiet Cornelia as the headmistress shooed the other students away. She didn't want to run the risk of allowing Cornelia's condition to spark an episode of "mass hysteria," as had been known to happen at other girls' boarding schools. Cornelia did not return to Ojolla the following term, so I don't know what ever became of her. I was surprised to learn that her classmates did not find her encounter with what they termed "evil spirits" or "satans" to be particularly extraordinary.

During the remainder of my two-year stint as a teacher among the Luo people in Nyanza Province, I gradually came to appreciate the pervasiveness of belief in *juogi*. In numerous ritualized and mundane ways, Luos express their assumption that spiritual entities are real presences. *Juogi* can be both kind and cruel, and their power can be tapped for constructive or destructive purposes. When wronged or neglected, ancestral *juogi*—known as *kwere*—can afflict their living descendants with illness or misfortune until appropriate propitiatory offerings are made.[2] Particularly vengeful *juogi* may be classified as *jochiende* (demons or malevolent ghosts), and stronger ritual measures must be employed to stem their harmfulness (Ocholla-Ayayo 1976; Owuor Anyumba 1974, 5). Certain divinities can be called "free spirits," for they are believed capable of striking anyone, irrespective of lineage or clan. Most of these free *juogi* (e.g., *juok nam*, *juok Mumbo*, and *juok yie*)[3] are believed to possess[4] individuals, who, once initiated into the cult of that particular divinity, function as its mediums and are able to capitalize on its power.

It appears that the way in which Luos classify spiritual entities, however, is gradually changing. In the past, judging from the investigations of researchers such as Michael Whisson and Henry Owuor Anyumba in the 1950s and 1960s, the distinctive characteristics of each class of free *juogi* and their corresponding cults were fairly widely known. In the minds of most younger Luos today, however, *juogi* have lost their individuality and tend to blur together. Moreover, the very term *juogi* has taken on somewhat negative overtones. The old category of positive *juogi* seems to be increasingly occupied by the Holy Spirit (*Roho Maler* or *Chuny Maler*) or by angels who send messages and blessings from heaven. Whereas in the past people would turn to their *kwere* (or other *juogi*) for help in difficult times, Christians—who make up nearly 90 percent of the Luo population[5]—now frequently turn to the Holy Spirit.

This does not mean that traditional diviner-doctors (*ajuoke*) are no longer consulted. Indeed, people often consult a variety of practitioners in their search for cures (Cohen and Odhiambo 1989, 89). But Roho is generally considered one of the superior forces. I have known staunch members of noncharismatic religions (e.g., Catholics, Anglicans), who, upon failing to clear their home of some misfortune, turn to healers or seers from indigenous churches for help. In such circumstances, the woman or man of the house may look for "people of heaven" (*jopolo*)—as the white-robed members of independent churches are often addressed—who are known to be strong in the Spirit. The individual then invites the group of *jopolo* to stage an all-night prayer session in his/her home in hopes that their Roho will expunge the evil.

This study concentrates on one such community of *jopolo*, the Ruwe Holy Ghost Church of East Africa. The Ruwe denomination is one of a number of Spirit (Roho) churches historically tied to an ecstatic Holy Spirit movement that crystallized under the leadership of Alfayo Odongo Mango of Musanda in the 1930s. Like most Kenyan independent churches, the Ruwe Roho church is smaller and poorer than its neighboring mission-derived churches, comprising only sixteen to twenty thousand active members,[6] most of whom are peasants. The history of the Roho movement is told largely from the point of view of Ruwe members, but I have also included testimonies from members of the closely related Musanda Holy Ghost Church of East Africa, which is headed by Ibrahim Owuor Mango, Odongo Mango's son. In addition, I have incorporated material on some Luo Roho congregations in Siaya and Gem that have recently affiliated with the Holy Spirit Church of East Africa, headquartered in Bukoyoni, Maragoli.[7] Brief remarks on the fledgling Spirit Mother Church founded in Kisumu by former Roho Musanda member Elijah Ayodo appear in the final chapter. Members of all these Roho churches view themselves as custodians of the Spirit. They carry on a tradition of spirit possession and mediumship that is still an important aspect of Luo culture. Indigenous religious conceptualization and terminology may be changing, but belief in spiritual agency remains a cornerstone of the worldview of most Luos.

It is far more difficult to make sense of Roho religion within the constructs of secular scholarship than within an environment where the factuality of spiritual forces is a given. In the past, historians of religion have posited the category of the Sacred (Eliade 1959) or the Numinous (Otto 1923) as an objective reality. Drawing on the phenomenological tradition, scholars simply assumed the authenticity of religious experience alongside aesthetic, emotional, and mental experience. In their view, whatever else humanity was, it was inherently religious, a notion encapsulated in the phrase *homo religiosus* (Eliade 1959). The phenomenological approach of Gerhardus van der Leeuw, Joachim Wach, Mircea Eliade, and their disciples is one that "commits the investigator to an affirmation of the existence of a transcendent sacred" (Ray 1991a, 12). In their interpretive work, they applied their paradigm of the Sacred—a concept that naturally reflected their own theological leanings—onto the religious systems of other peoples.

Since Mircea Eliade's death in 1986, a spate of articles and books have reevaluated the legacy of the master and his school (Paus 1989; Rennie 1992; Smith 1987; Rudolph 1989; Ryba 1991; Segal 1989; Segal and Wiebe 1989; Valk 1992; Werblowsky 1989; Christ 1991). Many scholars of religion acknowledge the significant comparativist contributions Eliade has made to the field, but they reject the essentialist, phenomenological underpinnings of this thought (Penner 1986). They test and revise Eliadian categories for use as interpretive tools, but not as causal, sui generis phenomena (Smith 1978, 1987; Carrasco 1987; Ray 1987, 1991a). These scholars are representatives of a major "humanistic" trend which has been cultivated within the history of religions discipline. Proponents of the humanistic approach seek to "study religion without making any assumptions about its metaphysical grounds or object" (Ray 1991a, 12). As far as possible, they aim to understand and elucidate what religious systems mean for the believers themselves, in the particular context and explanatory terminology of the communities they study.

My own interpretive project is conducted on several overlapping planes. Like many of the recent "humanistic" studies in the history of religion, this book seeks to present Roho members' understanding of their symbols and liturgy within the framework of their own history and theological ideas. In addition, it considers the ramifications of the Roho movement against a backdrop of rapid socioeconomic change. Finally, it examines the impact of wider social processes on Roho members, women in particular, and, in turn, discusses women's influence on Roho religious formation and history. Thus, this analysis not only approaches Roho religion as a meaningful interpretation of the world but also takes seriously the role of members' faith in making local history.

My conclusions and interpretations are drawn from eight months of intensive fieldwork in Nyanza Province, carried out between April 1990 and March 1991. The chapters also integrate information collected in 1983 by my Ojolla students during their year-long study of Luo traditions. My firsthand familiarity with the practices of other Kenyan independent churches derives in part from a field project conducted in Maragoli and Nairobi in 1981, as well as from interviews conducted in 1990–1991. Finally, to obtain primary source material on British responses to the Roho movement, I have made great use of district and provincial files housed at the Kenya National Archives, as well as the records of the Church Missionary Society in Birmingham, England.

While in the field, I collected my information through a mix of participant observation at Roho gatherings, interviews, informal discussion, and the simple sharing of the rhythms of day-to-day village life. I make no pretensions to objectivity and certainly did not follow the classic social scientific interview protocol, which requires emotional distance and frowns on the interviewer who responds to questions from interviewees (Oakley 1981). Rather, I adopted a qualitative approach consistent with recent feminist methodology (Jacobs 1991; Jayaratne and Stewart 1991), through which I sought to develop a trusting relationship with the women and men among whom I lived. As an investigator, I naturally hoped that this trust would encourage women to open up, but it also required that I be open with them. For me, participating meant that when Roho members asked questions about my family, aspirations, and religious experiences, I responded in good faith, just as I was asking them to do. It also means that the researcher is pulled in many directions by the troubles and material needs of the people. Thus, although some fieldworkers are reluctant to pay informants as a matter of principle, I frequently assisted my interviewees with small amounts of cash, food, or whatever else I had to share.[8]

In its original form, my research design entailed far less emphasis on oral history. When I began spending time with members of the Ruwe denomination, however, it soon became clear that the story of their founding was at the very heart of their collective religious identity. I was deeply impressed by one church member in particular, Anna Inondi, who desired to tell me the story of her congregation. It is partly as a result of my promise to her that I have devoted so much space to painstakingly recounting the church's history.

I should make an additional comment with respect to my handling of Inondi's testimony. I chose to integrate all the relevant written documentation I could find. My purpose was to achieve the fullest reconstruction of the Roho past as was possible. This objective, I feel, would have been consistent with Inondi's wishes. The process of integrating written and oral sources has been less daunting than might be imagined, for Inondi had a formidable memory for sequence; other elders helped recollect key dates. When placed alongside archival documentation, the oral narrative has proved remarkably consistent chronologically. The viewpoints contained in the oral and written sources are, of course, vastly divergent. I should add that, when I interviewed Anna, I had no prior knowledge of the existence of Ogot's biographical essay on Mango or of the wealth of material contained in colonial administrative records. Therefore, existing written documentation did not influence my recording of Inondi's narrative.

The first three chapters of this book deal primarily with the historical evolution of the Roho church. I have chosen to divide the story of the Ruwe Holy Ghost Church into three phases for thematic purposes, as well as for the sake of manageability. The first phase (1912–1933) encompasses the growth of the charismatic Roho movement in the Ruwe locality and the emergence of Mango as a key religious and political personality in the region. The second phase (April

1933–January 1934) is brief but significant, for during these ten months Mango and his followers were pushed out of the Anglican church and rejected by the surrounding Wanga community. This hostility and ostracism from a number of fronts had the effect of accelerating the crystallization of a new Luo-Christian synthesis as the Joroho were suddenly forced to install their own religious rites. The third phase of Roho history, outlined in chapter 3, begins with the aftermath of Mango's death in 1934 and extends through the official registration of the Roho church with the Kenyan government in 1966. During this period, the Joroho consciously devoted themselves to shaping and transmitting a new African Christianity based on the agency of the Holy Spirit. The 1930s and 1940s were thus characterized by energetic proselytizing, expansion, and innovation. The 1950s and 1960s, however, saw the gradual solidification and institutionalization of Roho religion, a process that inevitably altered the character of the Roho movement while ensuring its survival in postcolonial Kenya.

In each chapter, I have addressed thematic and theoretical issues raised by the particular period covered. Thus, the conclusion of chapter 1 considers the increasing religious significance of land among the Luo during the colonial era, the conclusion of chapter 2 analyzes the paradigm of schism in light of the foregoing information on the Roho movement, and the conclusion of chapter 3 proposes a framework for understanding the changes Roho women's roles have undergone between 1934 and 1960. Chapters 4 and 5 address aspects of contemporary Roho religion. The former examines the Roho worldview with special attention to the way in which the founding myth is both recapitulated and recast through liturgy and ritual. The latter privileges Roho women's voices, as I attempt to interpret the meaning and power of their faith.

It is a felicitous fact of fieldwork that most students come away from their encounters with other communities' systems of belief indebted to their hosts for newfound insights. Anna Inondi and the other Roho women and men I had the good fortune to meet have taught me a great deal. They have instructed me not only about the Roho worldview but also about the Christian way of life. I hope that this study will therefore be a contribution to the study of vernacular Christianity[9] as much as it is a study of contemporary Luo religious modes of expression.

NOTE ON ORTHOGRAPHY

Given the wide variation in renderings of Luo collective nouns, group names, and place names, my orthographic choices are, by necessity, somewhat arbitrary. I have sought to strike a balance between internal consistency and employing forms familiar to most readers. To this end, my spelling of all religious groups is patterned after the common Dholuo rendering of 'Joroho' (*Jolang'o*, *Jokiristo*, *Joanglikan*). For subethnic and clan groupings that are constructed around an ancestral or regional name, I have used an internal capital (JoUgenya, JoAlego). I have thus avoided the use of hyphens, as increasingly appears to be the trend, with the exception of terms incorporating the locative marker 'ka' (*Jo-kaLawi*, *Jo-k'Aloo*), again because this is a common form. I request the indulgence of readers for any awkwardness caused by these and all other stylistic decisions.

NOTE ON THE ROHO (HOLY SPIRIT) LITURGICAL LANGUAGE

In his description of Alfayo Odongo Mango's Roho movement, D. H. Rawcliffe states "one of their 'chief priests' wrote copiously in an 'unknown tongue' during a state of trance which, he claimed, was inspired by the Holy Ghost: the [Roho adherents] said they could understand what was written and carefully preserved the writings" (Rawcliffe 1954: 27–28). This secret or special language is a feature of Roho religion that has continued to intrigue observers, but surprisingly little is known about it. The language is called Dhoroho, which literally means "language of the spirit." The 'chief priest' mentioned by Rawcliffe was in fact Roho prophet Paulo Rang'eng'a, one of Mango's followers from Ruwe in Ugenya. Roho members believe that shortly after Mango's death in 1934, Rang'eng'a was selected by God to reveal a unique, sacred tongue as proof of the Roho community's divine selection. Inspired by the Holy Spirit, Rang'eng'a devoted all his time to translating Scripture and song into a new tongue, but his associates soon protested that the words sounded too much like English, the language of their colonial and missionary oppressors. Rang'eng'a prayed over the matter and tradition has it that a year later, in 1935, the Holy Spirit gave him another language— the current Dhoroho—that did not at all resemble a European tongue and was therefore acceptable.

In the strict sense, Dhoroho is not a language at all but rather an encoding of Dholuo. Every discrete sound in Dholuo has a corresponding sound in Dhoroho. Vowels correspond to other vowels, consonants to other consonants. For example, *a* in Dholuo is *o* in Dhoroho; *o* is *i*, *ny* is *j*, *y* is *sh*, and *l* is *r*. Words are therefore translated letter for letter. Thus *Nyasaye* ("God" in Dholuo) becomes *Jongoshu* in Dhoroho; *polo* ("heaven" in Dholuo) becomes *biri*.

The founders of the Roho community emphasized the importance of learning Dhoroho. From the late 1930s through the early 1950s, Roho adherents from various regions sent their children to stay in Ruwe—the headquarters for one branch of the Roho church—for extended periods in hopes of exposing them to the fundamentals of Roho religion, including Dhoroho. The young people would assist their host families in farm work and domestic chores in return for instruction in the basics of the Bible, rudimentary reading and writing skills, and the "language of the Spirit." Over the years Paulo Rang'eng'a, Isaya Goro, and others produced collections of hymns and biblical verses translated into Dhoroho, which were housed in their homes (unfortunately, most of these compilations have since disappeared). In Ruwe, the new language was not reserved solely for ritual but was used in mundane contexts as well. Elderly members of the Ruwe congregation can still occasionally be heard greeting one another in Dhoroho along the paths. However, it seems that this was not the case elsewhere. If the revealed tongue was ever successfully propagated in other parts of Luoland, there is little evidence left to that effect. For the vast majority of the current Roho population, Dhoroho has the status of liturgical Latin. Members can generally recite the Apostles' Creed and the Lord's Prayer in Dhoroho, and they can probably understand key vocabulary such as *Jongoshu* (God) and *Shunga* (Jesus), but that is all. Recently, there has been much talk of organizing several week-long seminars at Ruwe for the express purpose of teaching Dhoroho to church members. Such seminars, however, are difficult to finance and difficult to schedule. Members have to raise the fare to travel to the headquarters, and someone has to provide food for them while they are there. During school vacations, children are either needed to help at home or expected to study for their exams, So, despite much concern about the decline in knowledge of Dhoroho, steps to remedy the problem are not being taken.

Below is a chart of Dholuo sounds and their corresponding codes in Dhoroho, compiled with the help of Ruwe Roho elder and teacher, Meshak Ogola.

Vowels		Consonants			
Dholuo	Dhoroho	Dholuo	Dhoroho	Dholuo	Dhoroho
a	= o	b	= p *or* b	n	= nd
e	= u	ch	= dh *or* ph	nd	= m
i	= e	d	= th	ng	= f
o	= i	dh	= d	ng'	= g
u	= a	f	= n	ny	= j
		g	= t	p	= b *or* p
		h	= nz *or* ndh	r	= mb *or* mp
		j	= w	s	= ng'
		k	= ch	t	= v
		l	= r	th	= k
		m	= s	w	= nj
		mb	= y	y	= sh

Some Common Words and Phrases

Dholuo	Dhoroho	English
Wuonwa	Njanindnjo	Our Father
Yesu Kiristo	Shunga Chempengvi	Jesus Christ
Ruoth	Ompaik	Lord
Nyasaye	Jongoshu	God
Wapako nyingi maler	Njobochi jefe sorump	We praise your name [which is] holy
Amin	Osend	Amen
Ji duto	We thavi	All the people
E piny kaka e polo	U bej chocho u biri	On earth as it is in heaven
Richowa	Mpephijno	Our sins
Jakony	Wochij	Helper
Ayie	Osheu	I believe
Misawa	Song'onjo	Hello
Ungima	Afeso	Are you well?

KEY FIGURES IN THE
ROHO HISTORICAL NARRATIVE
(In alphabetical order by last name)

Mariam Abonyo   A leading woman Roho missionary from Ruwe; recipient of many hymns from the Holy Spirit.

Abwodha   One of Mango's Luyia neighbors whose confrontation with the Roho women soldiers resulted in his death and sparked the fighting that led to the Musanda massacre in 1934.

Elizabeth Adhiambo   A young convert from Sira Buholo who testified during the official investigation that the Joroho were not the agressors, but were on the defensive when fighting broke out in Musanda.

Persila Adongo   One of the Musanda martyrs; a girl under 10 years of age who died in Mango's burning house.

Sarah Agot   Roho prophetess, whose home in Mirunda, South Nyanza, became a center for faith healing and Roho activity in the 1940s. Since her death in 1986, she has been revered by some as the Holy Spirit incarnate.

Roslida Ajanja   An early convert from Usenge who helped establish the Roho congregation at Yimbo.

Turfosa Aloo   A leader of the Roho women soldiers and Musanda martyr who died of a spear wound.

Patricia Amis   A girl from Alego Nyajuok who was cured of *chira* by Lawi Obonyo.

Lieutenant Colonel E. L. B. Anderson   District Commissioner of North Kavirondo during the Musanda affair.

Nora Anyango   A pioneering follower of Mango from Goye, Yimbo; later married Nicholas Odongo of Ruwe.

Zadok Aol   One of the young Musanda martyrs who burned to death alongside Mango.

Daudi Arinda   Ardent supporter of Mango and Lawi who, together with his brother, Isaya Goro, provided the land for the Ruwe Holy Ghost Church; husband of Nora Nyadero.

Elias Awanda   One of the so-called "Luo agitators" who was banished from his homestead in North Kavirondo in 1931.

Jakobo Buluku   Charismatic Quaker and founder of the Holy Spirit Church of East Africa at Bukoyoni, near Mbihi in Western Province.

Canon Burns   An Anglican missionary who, according to Roho tradition, witnessed Mango's miraculous prayer in Nairobi in the mid-1920s.

Walter Chadwick   Owen's predecessor and founder of the C.M.S. mission station at Butere. Remembered by the Joroho as the man who took an interest in the young Mango and sent him to school.

R. R. Evison   A Kisumu lawyer hired by Mango and fellow Kager leaders to determine the viability of their lost lands case.

Abdallah ("Wamdala") Gangla   One of the Kager ordered in December 1931 to quit his home in North Kavirondo for refusing to acknowledge tenant status.

Lazaro Gombe   An Anglican who was opposed to Roho missionaries entering his *boma*; cousin of Isaya Goro.

Isaya Goro   A pioneering Roho missionary whose home was the focus of Roho religion in Ruwe for many years; husband of Anna Inondi.

Captain Hislop   The District Officer of North Kavirondo who conducted the investigation into the 1934 "disturbances at Musanda" and compiled an extensive report.

C. W. Hobley   The Provincial Commissioner of Kavirondo (Nyanza), chiefly remembered by Joroho as the man who, in the late 1890s, led the Wanga in wars against the Luo, enabling the former to drive the latter out of territory the Luo had earlier conquered.

Anna Inondi   A Roho soldier and *laktar* (healer), known to many as "Soso" (Mama), honored for her important role in establishing Roho religion in Ruwe; wife of Roho missionary Isaya Goro.

Dorsila Kinyou   A leader of the Roho women *askeche* (soldiers).

Reverend Leech ("Alichi")   A missionary in charge of Butere diocese at the time of Mango's death; remembered as a compassionate man, in contrast to Owen.

Alfayo Odongo Mango   The patriarch and savior of the Musanda-derived Roho churches; martyred in January 1934; husband of Rael Oloyo.

Ibrahim Owuor Mango   A schoolboy at the time of the death of his father, Alfayo Odongo Mango. Current bishop of the Musanda Holy Ghost Church.

Paulo Mboya   A Luo chief in South Nyanza, remembered by Roho elders as friendly, but administrative records indicate that he was suspicious of the movement.

Muhwana   A Wanga neighbor of Mango who was killed by the Roho women *askeche* in the Musanda *Iweny* (battle) of 1934.

Mulama   A Wanga chief of Marama location, half-brother to Mumia and close associate of Owen.

Mumia   A Wanga Paramount chief, opponent of Mango's clan (Kager) and his Roho movement.

Abisage Muriro   An early covert and hymnist; wife of the first Ruwe Roho Bishop, Barnaba Walwoho.

Musa Muga   A youth who was one of the Musanda martyrs; he died from a spear wound obtained during the Wanga attack.

Daniel Musigo   A founding member of the Ugenya Kager Luo Clan Association and an Anglican evangelist.

Fanny (Miss) Moller ("Musmula")   An Australian missionary and school-teacher; found Ng'iya Girls School in 1923. Remembered as an ally of Owen and for her heated verbal exchange with Lawi.

Salome Ndiany   Mango's eldest daughter, originally designated to succeed him.

Antipa Ngutu   One of the four Kager agitators banished from their homes, who subsequently became a member of the Roho group and set up residence in Mango's compound.

Nora Nyadero   An active Roho missionary who first joined the movement after Lawi cured her of possession by demons; the wife of Daudi Arinda.

Leah Nyalwal   An early Roho convert from Ugenya who took a vow with other women to delay marriage in order to serve the Holy Spirit.

Silvano Nyamogo   A fiery spirit-filled preacher and close associate of Lawi Obonyo.

Isaka Obayo   An elderly blind man who was in charge of children during the Musanda retreat; martyred in the *mach* (fire).

Lawi Obonyo   Carpenter, charismatic miracle-worker, and nephew of Mango, Lawi is remembered as "the helper" (*jakony*) designated by God to assist the fledgling Roho community. He was killed by Wanga warriors the morning after the *mach*, making him one of the Musanda martyrs.

Nicholas Odongo   A senior Anglican evangelist at Ruwe known for his angry temper who protected Mango from harassment; husband of Nora Anyango.

Meshak Ogola   A Ruwe Roho elder and teacher; survivor of the *mach*; son of Anna Inondi and Isaya Goro.

Jeremiah Ogutu   A Ruwe Roho member, baptized as a baby by Mango; survivor of the *mach*.

Konya Ojanja   Mango's father, killed in "the Hobley wars."

Rael Oloyo   Active in the Roho church in the 1930s and 1940s; wife of Alfayo Odongo Mango.

Elijah Oloo   An ex-army sergeant who was crowned *Kingi* of the Joroho in January 1934.

Johana Omina   A Ruwe Roho elder and *laktar*; survivor of the *mach*.

Salome Omondi   One of the Musanda martyrs, a teenaged girl who died of burns.

Matthayo Opiyo   Converted by Isaya Goro after Mango's death; his home in Uyoma was the first to join the Ruwe Roho denomination.

Ibrahim Osodo   According to tradition, Osodo was the first person in the Ruwe area to be possessed by the Holy Spirit when it entered his chest around 1914. Osodo's small band of youthful Christians disbanded when many were conscripted into the colonial forces.

Mariam Otira   A former witchdoctor and one of the foundresses of the Roho church in Yimbo.

Walter Edwin Owen   Archdeacon of Kavirondo from 1918 to 1945; Owen oversaw all the C.M.S. work among the Luo and Abaluyia and was Mango's superior; he is not remembered kindly by the Joroho.

Joel Owino   Lawi's son and one of the young Musanda martyrs who died inside Mango's burning house.

Canon Pleydell   Known as "Bwana Orengo" (Mr. Fly Whisk); taught Mango and was a pastor at Ng'iya at the time of the Musanda tragedy.

Paulo Rang'eng'a   Best known as the recipient and scribe of Dhoroho, the Roho liturgical language.

Esta Songa   Joined the Roho movement as a young woman; postponed marriage in order to serve the Spirit as a missionary.

Zakayo Wandeyi   A former Anglican catechist, Wandeyi at first resisted Mango's call to repentance in Uriya forest in 1916, but later became a Roho convert; credited with exposing Mulama's polygyny to Archdeacon Owen.

Barnaba Walwoho   An assistant catechist at Ruwe in the 1930s became the first Bishop of The Ruwe Holy Ghost Church; husband of Abisage Muriro.

Leah Were   An early covert to Roho religion and active member of the Ruwe church.

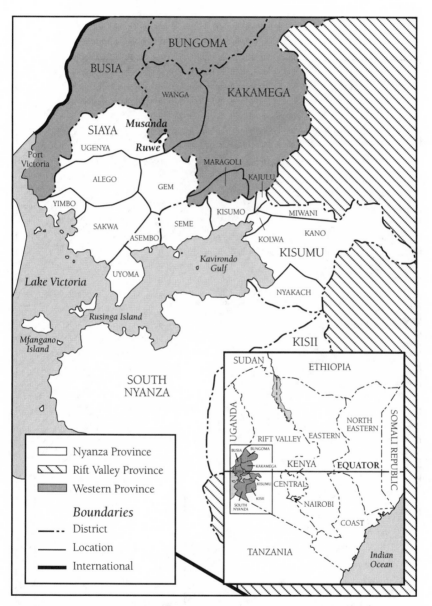

The Kavirondo Gulf region (predominantly Luo) and lower Western Province (predominantly Luyia) in Western Kenya; administrative districts and selected locations. Ruwe and Musanda in Ugenya and Wanga locations, respectively. Inset of the area in East Africa.

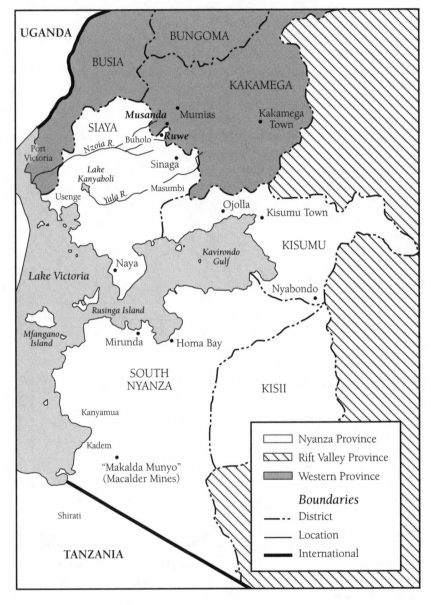

Important sites in the Roho historical narrative.

Women of Fire and Spirit

1

The Early Phase of the Roho Movement

Different Perspectives on Roho History

The Musanda Holy Ghost Church of East Africa, the Ruwe Holy Ghost Church of East Africa, and the Cross Church of East Africa share common roots. All trace their origin to the Roho (Spirit) movement that emerged in western Kenya among the Luo and culminated in the death of charismatic preacher Alfayo Odongo Mango in 1934. These three main Roho branches, with their respective headquarters all in Nyanza Province, number among the more than two hundred twenty registered independent churches in Kenya. According to my estimates, in 1991 their collective membership was between fifty and seventy-five thousand.[1]

For the members of these churches, the life and death of Alfayo Odongo Mango is of central importance. Within the Ruwe Holy Ghost churches—in which I conducted most of my research—an outsider is immediately struck by the frequent mention of Mango and his assistant, Lawi Obonyo. One also cannot help but note the eagerness with which members recount episodes in the history of the Roho church. On a symbolic and theological level, the story of Mango's struggle against the Europeans has taken on a life of its own. The prophecies Mango made, the miracles Lawi performed, the battle their followers bravely fought, and the fire that killed them are all elaborated through interwoven layers of biblical and indigenous metaphor. In the minds and hearts of Roho Christians, the sacrifices of the early Roho community at Musanda are salvific; in the person of Mango, God fulfilled his promise to provide Africans with a savior of their own, and Mango's martyrdom has ushered in a new age of the Holy Spirit in the church in Africa.

Perhaps because of the centrality of the founding story in the church's spiritual and moral orientation, many members stress the need for accuracy in the oral transmission of their history. During weekly sabbath services and particularly during the large annual Celebration of Remembrance (*Sikukuu mar Rapar*),[2] elderly eyewitnesses (*jomoneno*) are called on to recount what took place at

3

Musanda. At the *Sikukuu,* which marks the anniversary of Mango's death, members perform a dramatization of the fire (*mach*) in which he died and sing hymns about the beginning of Roho religion. Over the years, the result has been the gradual development of a quasi-canonical oral tradition that is celebrated and disseminated throughout approximately three hundred sixty Ruwe congregations. [3]

When conducting my inquiries, I was continually referred by members to respected church elders—both male and female—who had known Mango personally. My primary informant was a Luo woman named Anna Inondi. Born around 1907, Anna joined the Roho movement as a young woman and devoted her entire life to the faith. In the spring of 1990, she was very frail and sick but was still visited and honored by Ruwe Roho Christians who had given her the title *Mama Kanisa* (Mother of the Church). In a series of interviews, Anna offered me a lengthy and detailed history of her church. It is Inondi's account—corroborated and modified by other elders—that forms the bulk of the oral material contained here and in the next two chapters. In this testimony, Mango appears as a strong-willed individual. Imbued with the Holy Spirit, he was able to heal people, foresee the future, and assert the need for an African-run church in the face of foreign domination.

Like the cult of Mumbo in Kisii and Elijah Masinde's *Dini ya Masambwa* in Kitosh (Wipper 1977; DeWolf 1983; Shimanyula 1978), the Roho movement was carefully watched by colonial officials in Nyanza. There is, therefore, a considerable amount of information on Mango and the Joroho (people of the Spirit) contained in district and provincial records. [4] The most detailed information concerns Mango's political activities during the three years prior to his death in the Musanda disturbances. Other useful documentation includes a record of the testimonies made by Wanga and Roho witnesses during the inquiry conducted by the District Office of North Kavirondo immediately following the disturbances (also known as the Musanda massacre). Finally, there is a carefully compiled report on the Roho movement by Captain Hislop, the district officer in charge of the investigation, who includes his conclusions and personal insights. At least one historian has relied heavily on this archival material in documenting Mango's leading role in Kager clan agitation in Buholo (Ogot 1971).

The picture of Alfayo Odongo Mango that emerges from this body of colonial documentation is one of an angry, stubborn individual involved in a long-standing, bitter land dispute between the Kager Luo and the Wanga. The Wanga are a Bantu clan whose strength and landholdings increased considerably with the arrival of the British, who repeatedly backed Wanga military campaigns against their neighbors. Resentful of being classified by the government as a tenant on land he considered rightfully his own, Mango joined forces with other Kager in Buholo and Ugenya to press claims for their "lost lands." He openly opposed the British policy of appointing Wanga headmen over Luo communities and led a campaign to have the South Wanga–Buholo boundary redrawn so that his and other Kager settlements would all fall within the same district (Central Nyanza). The Kager leaders felt that if the boundary were redrawn, the clan would be better able to put forth a unified resistance to the hegemony of the despised Wanga Paramount Chief Mumia, his brothers, and sons.[5] In short, Alfayo Odongo Mango had been a thorn in the side of the British for a number of years. When he emerged as a primary leader of the growing Roho cult, British authorities naturally tended to perceive his involvement as politically motivated. The cult was seen as a last-ditch attempt to rally support through the vehicle of religious organization.

A second, more colorful source of written information on the history of the Roho movement is the correspondence of Anglican missionaries in Kavirondo (now Nyanza) during this period. Of particular relevance are the letters of Archdeacon Walter Edwin Owen to Church Missionary Society (C.M.S.) officers in Nairobi and London and to colonial officials posted in Kakamega and Kisumu in the 1930s and 1940s. Owen was a complicated and controversial figure. In 1918, after fourteen years in Uganda, the Irish pastor had been sent by Bishop Willis to Kavirondo (then still part of the Uganda diocese) to head the C.M.S. mission there. A staunch proponent of native rights, Owen oversaw the growth of a vigorous, self-supporting, lay-run Anglican church, and encouraged the same level of indigenous initiative in political matters (Welbourn and Ogot 1966, 26–27; Atieno Odhiambo 1973, 7). For instance, the organizers of the Young Kavirondo Association—the first independent political body established in Luoland—were all closely affiliated with Owen's C.M.S. center at Maseno. When the government was on the verge of banning the association in 1923, Owen prevailed upon the provincial commissioner not to do so. Instead, the archdeacon himself became the president of the organization under its new name, the Kavirondo Taxpayers' Welfare Association. The association proved a vital and effective vehicle for voicing local protest against a wide array of exploitative colonial policies. Needless to say, Owen's activities did not win favor among settlers and officials, who consequently dubbed him "the Archdemon of Kavirondo" (Lonsdale 1970, 607–608). Nor was he popular among his more conservative colleagues in the Mombasa diocese, who felt that Owen's insistence on African-run parishes was dangerously premature.

Owen was exceptionally outspoken in his criticism of Europeans' patronizing attitudes toward Africans (Welbourn and Ogot 1966, 27). Yet his own Christian liberalism, like that of many other C.M.S. missionaries of his day, was itself "laced with paternalism" (Strayer 1978, 107).[6] When he was flouted, Owen's attitude of active service could transform into an angry vindictiveness, as is apparent in Owen's letters about the Roho movement. Alfayo Odongo Mango was well known to Archdeacon Owen. Mango had been one of the first Luos chosen by Owen's predecessor, Archdeacon Walter Chadwick, to train as a catechist at the C.M.S. Normal School in Maseno. In his capacity as evangelist, Mango later openly challenged some of Owen's decisions, such as the archdeacon's attempt to make Luhanga (the Wanga tongue) the official language of worship in Butere pastorate (Ogot 1971, 95). Despite their differences, Owen nevertheless appointed Mango in 1927 to be deacon of a large, predominantly Luo area that included South Wanga, Buholo, South Ugenya, Marama, and Gem locations (Ogot 1971, 101). However, when Mango refused to desist from leading the Kager in their agitation over "lost lands," Owen's dealings with his appointee became increasingly strained.

Owen and his colleagues the Reverend A. J. Leech at Butere and Canon Pleydell at Ng'iya believed that Silvano Nyamogo and Lawi Obonyo of Musanda were the initiators of the Roho movement and the ones responsible for introducing it to Alego and other parts of Central Kavirondo. Lawi, who according to Owen had a history of "dementia,"[7] had led a series of "'Holy Ghost' revival and evangelistic meetings" in Alego and Gem. These sessions, in Owen's words, "had been characterised by the most extravagant forms of hysteria."[8] As Mango became involved with Lawi's group, he started ignoring Owen's summons and began baptizing people on his own. On January 17, 1934, five days before Mango was murdered, the Archdeacon reported to the district commissioner:

> Alufayo Odongo has broken away from the Anglican Church, repudiated the authority of myself and the Bishop, refuses to have any communication with us thus, incidentally, breaking No. 4 of the terms of agreement come to before you on April 10th, 1933 with the Bantu authorities.[9]

Then, as a kind of explanation for behavior that Owen clearly found otherwise inexplicable, he reports that Mango's eldest son was "convinced that his father was mentally unhinged and abnormal."[10]

Archdeacon Owen's depiction of Mango thus basically agrees with the perspective of the colonial officials. The Anglican cleric did, in fact, view Mango and Lawi as trying to "make a cat's paw of the Church to further their clan and tribal aims."[11] But Owen's comments convey an added sense of personal affront tinged with incredulity, as he watched his deacon grow increasingly committed to a strange form of religion that Owen found both repulsive and baffling.[12] By the end of 1933, Owen seems to have established a fixed dichotomy in his mind between those Christians "loyal to us" and Mango's Roho group, despite the fact that the followers of Mango and Lawi continued to consider themselves part of the Church Missionary Society for several more years.

Throughout his tenure in Nyanza, Owen had struggled to plant a church that could take deep indigenous root, as the C.M.S. had succeeded in doing in Uganda. Moreover, it is clear that Owen perceived himself to be a true friend and champion of the native against colonial oppressors (Lonsdale 1970, 608; Greaves 1969, 87). Thus, Owen could not comprehend a movement in which poor Africans appeared to want emancipation from *him!*[13] He explained the cult as a collection of ignorant, uneducated folk who had fallen under the sway of two frauds. On the one hand, then, he describes Mango and Lawi as mad people who believe themselves divinely inspired. On the other hand, he depicts them as shrewd, calculating individuals hiding their political agenda behind a veil of religious fervor. The fundamental incompatibility of these two images of Mango, Lawi, and their motives did not seem to occur to Owen.

Colonial, missionary, and oral sources are all useful in reconstructing the history of the Roho movement. To be sure, each contains a distinctive interpretation and thus offers a different picture of Alfayo Odongo Mango and his motives. Governmental officials saw the Roho group as subversive and troubling. Mango's movement was a painful reminder of the administration's failure to quell tribal conflict and settle land disputes in south Wanga. Local C.M.S. missionaries were equally alarmed by the vitality of the Roho cult, which suggested that Christianity in western Kenya was fast outgrowing their control. They saw the sapling so carefully planted by the C.M.S. being twisted by unscrupulous nominal converts who were able to manipulate peasants lacking sufficient exposure to true Christian teachings.

Today's Roho members offer yet a third perspective. For them, Mango is an exclusively positive figure. He is portrayed as both temporal and spiritual liberator; he established the first truly African church, and his death atoned for the sins of black people, giving them entry into heaven.

The historical sources that chroniclers privilege naturally shape their analyses of the movement as a whole. My study takes as its foundation the oral tradition preserved within the Ruwe Holy Ghost church. I then employ colonial and missionary records as a supplement to that basic narrative and point out discrepancies where they occur.

I have adopted this method for two reasons. First, irrespective of whatever else it may have once been, today's institutionalized Roho movement is essentially religious. Inondi's account highlights this religious dimension, enabling us to see the continuity and gradual evolution of the Roho faith since the 1930s. By "religious," I mean phenomena arising from a culturally conditioned response to a perceived transcendent reality that is affirmed by a community, codified within myth or scripture, and enacted in ritual and through which people attempt to act in ways that bring daily existence into closer alignment with their sense of spiritual reality. Such a definition encompasses those political projects and goals that are anchored within a value system whose ultimate referent is transcendent. For instance, in the eyes of Roho elders, Mango's political activities were an integral part of his religious program. When asked, elders acknowledge that Mango was involved in a land dispute, but they see his activities within the context of securing freedom for the young Roho community to flourish and spread God's word. In other words, Mango is not remembered by contemporary Roho Christians as a Luo nationalist but as a religious rebel. Most of the conflicts he was engaged in are not recorded in Roho oral tradition as interethnic struggles but as problems resulting from persecution by other Anglicans who were backed—if not incited—by the missionaries.

Some outsiders and historians may challenge this perception of Mango as a "mythicized" gloss, a distorted picture of a man whose aims were actually political and material. However, the data on which such a critique would be based— the records of colonial officials and European missionaries—are, again, no more sound than the testimony of Mango's religious followers. The task of the chronicler who wishes to tell the story of Mango and the Roho movement in as balanced a fashion as possible is not a matter of embracing either the religious or the political viewpoint to the exclusion of the other. Rather, the chronicler must decide which of the two reified categories—religion or politics—will *encompass* the other in the historiography of the Roho denomination. In following the lead of the church members themselves, I have chosen to understand Roho religion as the matrix out of which Mango's political struggles arose, rather than depict the Roho church as a by-product of these disputes. The overall historical picture that emerges is not simply more in keeping with the Roho point of view, but makes the character of Mango's overall legacy more comprehensible.

The second reason for privileging oral tradition in the reconstruction of Roho history concerns the role of women. Only in members' oral accounts are the contributions of Roho women documented. Although colonial and missionary reports may be more reliable as far as basic chronology is concerned, they highlight the activities of male leaders exclusively. When women are mentioned in these written texts, it is usually in collective (and dismissive) terms. As we will see, women have always been the backbone of this popular religion. A history that is silent with respect to their activities would be seriously skewed.

According to the testimony of Inondi and other Roho elders, women were critical to the emergence of the Roho movement. In the 1930s, women endured beatings and sacrificed their reputations in order to attend prayer sessions in people's homes. When necessary, as in the "war" of 1934, women formed bands of *askeche* (soldiers) to defend themselves and their menfolk against persecution. After the death of Mango and Lawi, Chief Murunga of South Wanga, backed by the Local Native Council and the district officer, banned Wanga women from attending Roho meetings. Adherents were forced to gather secretly in other villages, worshiping in whispers. Elders explain that this was a time of trial and hardship for the Roho community; many men were inclined to drop out. The religion was kept alive primarily by women. "When women have decided something," one informant told me with reference to this period, "they don't change their minds easily the way men do."

In the late 1930s and 1940s, women undertook long, arduous missionary journeys, often with men and occasionally alone. At times they were imprisoned for their activities. They founded congregations and presided over local branches. Some women took an oath among themselves to postpone marriage so that they could devote their lives exclusively to spreading the Roho faith. The well-loved hymn that Roho women sing during the Celebration of Remembrance commemorates women's involvement at Musanda and encapsulates their view of themselves as warriors for the faith:

Wan nyi kedo, wan nyi mach;
(We are women of war, we are women of fire;)

Wan nyi loyo, wan nyi tong;
(We are women of victory, we are women of spears;)

Wanamor, wanamor ei polo!
(We will be happy, we will be happy in heaven!)

British observers, and missionaries in particular, did take notice of the predominance of women in Mango's circle.[14] Unlike Roho oral tradition, which treats the pivotal role of women in the early movement as a sign of strength, British missionaries considered women's predominance in the Roho cult as indicative of its devious nature. Some telling excerpts from a lengthy letter written by Archdeacon Owen to the secretary of the Church Missionary Society in Nairobi describe the former's experience at one of Lawi's prayer meetings in 1933:

> Lawi was holding forth. He [Canon Pleydell] could not hear what he said . . . but in a short time Lawi stopped dead and fixed his eyes on a decent looking woman seated on the floor (as were all of them) in front of him. He kept his eyes fixed on the woman, without saying a word for about three minutes, when the woman began to tremble and shake all over, and set up a hysterical yelling. At this juncture, Miss Moller and I arrived. I heard yells rising on the night air, and boldly pushed the door and went in. The hut was packed to suffocation with people about 80. The vast majority women and girls, though there were children too. As soon as I entered, and they had realized who I was in the dim light of the one hurricane lamp which provided illumination, Lawi motioned the people to rise, whereupon a woman who had been trembling and shaking and elaculating . . . put her baby on the floor and executed a mad hysterical dance in front of me, raising her arms to heaven and behaving in a most embarrassing way.[15]

Roho churches cultivate an atmosphere in which people can let go and experience spiritual power in a variety of ways. Some believers speak in tongues, some jump up and down, some collapse in trance. Women known as *laktache* (healers or doctors) are ready to restrain ecstatic dancers who are out of control. They also guard unconscious individuals whose souls are believed to have temporarily left their bodies. The archdeacon witnessed two participants in a deep trance, each tended by a woman, but just as he could make no sense of the "hysterical" dances before him, neither could he comprehend this situation:

I had noticed as soon as I approached the table, two youths lying in a huddled fashion apparently in a deep sleep with their heads and shoulders lying on the laps of a couple of hefty wenches who were squatting on the floor, evidently in charge of the sleeping beauties.[16]

Upon later examination, Owen himself admitted that the boys were not asleep but, in fact, in a strange coma. Yet the archdeacon still saw something decidedly provocative and illicit about the practice of women or girls guarding the boys, as he makes clear in his closing remarks:

Well, it has been one of the weirdest experiences of my life, and it gives rise to much thought. An outstanding lesson is the peril of leaving girls uneducated to an equal level with the boys. It is the girls, maturing and matured physically, and to a lesser degree the married women, who form the large bulk of the "converts" to the cult. . . . Curiously enough, I have recently said over and over again in pressing the claims of girls education that an unscrupulous Maseno school boy could twist unsophisticated girls round his fingers. . . . The dangers of the movement are obvious. In spite of the fact that it is done under the cloak of religion and evangelism I am convinced that there is deception which must have an element of consciousness in it, on the part of Lawi. . . . The sex dangers are obvious. Those two lads with their heads and shoulders pillowed on the willing laps of hefty, lusty wenches, when they came round would be able to twist those same wenches round their fingers. Sex passions must be aroused under circumstances of darkness . . . which present every opportunity to grave temptation.[17]

Owen's comments convey the prevailing attitude of European missionaries at that time toward women in general and toward African women in particular. The popular eighteenth-century European view of women as hysterical, irrational, and "more obedient to nature's impulses" than men had become even more exaggerated when applied to so-called primitive women of the tropics, whom traveler-writers depicted as happy in their natural state, sharing men freely and spontaneously (Bloch and Bloch 1980, 34; Jordanova 1980, 49; Comaroff and Comaroff 1991, 104–106; Stocking 1987, 199–202; Beidelman 1982, 133). Owen's correspondance indicates that he, like so many of his colleagues, perceived among his flock an ever-present tendency toward illicit sex and promiscuity that required vigilant control.

British missionaries drew on such widespread stereotypes to justify their imposition of the countervailing Victorian ideal of feminine virtue—the moral, sweet, passive homemaker—upon their converts (Stocking 1987, 199). Nineteenth- and early twentieth-century missionaries encouraged their wives to instruct local women in sewing, hygiene, deportment, first aid, and other tasks related to the domestic sphere, which together with basic lessons in Scripture were considered crucial to turning African women into "good Christian wives and mothers" (Pirouet 1978, 16–17; Beidelman 1982, 70, 158). Nevertheless, prior to the 1930s, the commitment of the C.M.S. to its female volunteers and to work among African women was slight. Most women serving under society auspices had to secure independent funding and were left to initiate their own projects once in the field. Few schools, programs, or services for native women were yet established, and, as Strayer points out, the subordinate position of women in the missions "had no small effect on the mission's efforts among the African female population" (Strayer 1978, 6).[18]

In sum, one can argue that, during this period, male C.M.S. missionaries tolerated women, European and African, only as long as they did not interfere with the primary work of the mission: converting African men—in particular, chiefs and their sons. Women were to help their menfolk when needed; otherwise, they ought to keep to themselves and pursue their own home-related projects.[19] The missionary enterprise, despite its avowedly nonconformist attitude toward many Victorian values, rarely questioned entrenched assumptions about the sexes and, instead, sought to reproduce European gender spheres within their mission station communities.[20]

It is not surprising, then, that missionaries who were aware of the Roho movement did not perceive women to play a pivotal role. There was no doubt in Archdeacon Owen's mind that Mango and Lawi were the cult's primary movers. Roho women were its victims. Nameless, excitable, and ignorant, the Roho "wenches" were easily misled by men. The primary picture that emerges from missionary and colonial documents of women's participation in the Roho movement—as in other Nyanza cults—is of an involvement that was both sexually deviant[21] and feebleminded.

Owen's remarks on the vulnerability of the women and girls who were attending the Roho service are consistent with the archdeacon's lifelong campaign to alleviate some of the "sorrows and helplessness of African womanhood" (Richards 1947, 7). Despite their failure to see how their own organization discriminated against women, Archdeacon Owen and other C.M.S. missionaries were keenly sensitive to instances of African men oppressing women. They were highly critical of "tribal" practices they considered abusive of women: clitoridectomy, bride-price, polygyny, arranged marriages, and the levirate were all condemned.[22] Owen pressured his male converts to take the lead in rejecting these institutions[23] and was equally persistent in his protests against colonial policies that he felt to be demeaning and burdensome to women, such as the hut tax and the forced labor of young women on government construction projects and settlers' farms.[24] Whereas Owen's concern for victimized native women may have been sincere, it also justified his elevated role as rescuer, and it continued to be qualified by his suspicion of their wantonness. We can conclude that Owen's perception of African women and of his own response to their plight prevented him from seeing the participation of Roho women clearly. His sectarianism and his discomfort with ecstatic forms of worship compounded his inability to see Roho members as persons involved in a constructive undertaking.

Were Roho women misguided souls, as missionary and colonial documents suggest, or clear-minded, determined individuals, as Inondi and other Roho members maintain? Were they ignorant wenches or resolute warriors—how can one reconcile these dichotomous images? One obviously cannot. As we have seen, the C.M.S. of the nineteenth and early twentieth centuries and the administration of Kenya were sexist organizations. Missionaries—and the government officials who often depended on them for insights into indigenous culture—generally espoused pejorative views of African women. It is, therefore, not surprising that records written by the former simply do not contain useful information on the latter. One must rely on the memories of participants themselves to fill the void. This approach, as I hope will become clear in the next few chapters, is not simply a matter of presenting "the female point of view" on the history of a particular church; it is essential to reconstructing a more accurate history in the first place.

The Roho Narrative: Emergence of the Roho Movement (1912–1933)

Unlike the colonial records, Anna Inondi's account of the Roho movement does not begin in the 1930s with the activities of Alfayo Odongo Mango and Lawi Obonyo, the recognized founders of the Holy Ghost church. Rather, she and other elders of the Ruwe Holy Ghost Church trace the movement's beginnings to 1912, the year in which the Holy Spirit (*Roho Mtakatifu* in Swahili or *Roho/ Chuny Maler* in Luo) made its initial appearance in Ruwe sublocation. According to Inondi, the Spirit first came in the form of a voice, moving through the eaves of people's homes.[25] Then one day it struck a group of (C.M.S.) converts. People were gathering outside, under the trees on a knoll where an unfinished cinder block church belonging to the Church of the Province of Kenya (C.P.K.) now stands. Jeremiah Otang'a, an Anglican catechist and church elder, was to lead the service. As people arrived, they were expected to confess their sins before joining in the hymn singing. When confessing, several people suddenly fell down. Others were scared and tried to run away but were restrained by onlookers. Everyone was then shocked to see the tongues of those who had fallen down growing longer and longer. The victims were crying out in panic, "Ouch, my mouth, my mouth!" (*Ay dhoga, ay dhoga!*) Jeremiah Otang'a prayed for them, and, as they confessed their sins, their tongues shrank to normal size.

According to Inondi's account, the Holy Spirit continued to move about the countryside for a very long time. It then entered the chest of one of the Christians, a young man named Ibrahim Osodo. Osodo had built a small prayer house of his own accord "so that Christians could gather together and their hearts would be one in following the Lord" (*mondo jokanisa ochokore mondo chuny ji obed achiel mar rito Nyasaye*). Inondi explained that the spirit used to speak to people gathering in Osodo's prayer house and enabled them to prophesy and perceive the truth about others (much as a medium [*ajuoga*] would be given enhanced powers by his or her patron spirit):

> [From about 1912 to 1914 or 1915] it [Roho] was talking to us saying things like: "Can't you see, somebody is coming, drinking beer; he is the one coming from that direction over there." When [the person] arrived, you would discover that it was true.
>
> (*Ema owuoyo kodwa ka owacho kaka ok inene, ngato echago biro, ma madho kong'o; echago oa lokacha obiro ka. Kobiro to inene mana ni en adier.*)

After entering Ibrahim Osodo, the Spirit no longer possessed others but spoke to the community from within Osodo's chest.[26] Osodo visited many Christian gatherings and prophesied. Some Christians—particularly C.M.S. church elders such as Jeremiah Otang'a—became fed up with Osodo's activities and urged him to pester people elsewhere. As Inondi expressed it, Otang'a ordered Osodo and his spirits to leave:

> The catechist told them, "Go somewhere else." . . . He said to Ibrahim, "We are fed up with you, your words of the spirit are just too much now. It is only in Ruwe that these things appear; go someplace else. There are many churches, go to another one and talk with the people there."
>
> (*Japuonj wacho nigi, dhiye uru kamoro. . . . Owacho ni Ibrahim ni, da, ise jonyo wa, wecheni mag roho gi ojonyo wa. Ruwe kani kende ema gigi biro gaye; dhiye kama—chielo. Sikunde ng'eny, dhiye emoro mondo iwuoye ko-dgi.*)

Although many thought Ibrahim was crazy or possessed by demons, others listened and believed the voice within him to be truly the Holy Spirit.[27]

A small band of young followers, both women and men, collected around Osodo. Among them were Isaya Goro, Tang're Odemba, Andrea Ogode, Philip Olum, Zacharia Oloo, Anna Inondi, Ada Agola, Elizabeth Kalangwe, and Jacobet Matiro. There were others, too—Inondi could no longer recall their names—some of whom came from Alego. Most were in their teens and early twenties. Osodo and his followers used to gather on the same knoll where Otang'a held worship services, where they would march and sing hymns with great vigor.

Osodo's corps of inspired Christians were soon forced to disperse as a result of the First World War. Paramount Chief Mumia assigned his chiefs the task of finding recruits for the colonial branch of the British Armed Forces fighting the Germans in Tanganyika. The Wanga chief in charge of Ugenya, where Ruwe is located, knew of Osodo's band of energetic, disciplined, healthy youths "with smooth bodies" (*dendgi poth apotha*) who were regularly seen marching to Christian songs. He decided to have them rounded up for military service, together with many Luo Anglican leaders. As Inondi put it:

> The Abaluyia saw that [the marching and singing] as something bad. "The war is advancing and these folk are just enjoying themselves. Let's arrest them and send them to war, instead of leaving them [idle and] happy."
>
> (*Koro nene richo obetie ni Joabaluyia. "Jogi mor to lweny biro, gin ema wadhi wa makgi mondo otergi e lweny. Kar mor gini."*)

However, Walter Chadwick, the archdeacon at the time, protested to Mumia, arguing that the removal of dedicated young Christians from the reserve would threaten the future success of the church in that area. At first, Mumia relented and had only three of the youths in the group conscripted: Isaya Goro, Tang're Odemba, and Ibrahim Osodo himself. However, many other adult males in Ruwe were later forced to enlist.

> After they [the Wanga] arrested [lit., caught] them [Osodo, Isaya, and Odemba] they returned and arrested almost everybody. No man could be seen. . . . Even if you were met [i.e., men encountered on the road were captured on the spot]. . . . They were all taken, even the church elders.
>
> (*Jogo ka nene gisemako, koro eka gichako giduogo me omak amaka piny duto ma kata chwo nene onge. . . . Kata orom kodi. . . . Otergi te, nyaka kata jodong kanisa.*)

I could find no reference to Ibrahim Osodo or his group in colonial records. However, missionaries' writings and historical studies suggest that Osodo's grass-roots band of Christian soldiers was not unique. It was not uncommon for the early Anglican congregations in Kavirondo to march in drill formation.[28] In the following excerpt from an article published in 1916, the Reverend J. J. Willis comments on the individualism and independence of the C.M.S. churches in Luo country:

> As a Missionary district . . . it so happens that Kavirondo occupied a peculiarly independent position. Geographically, politically, linguistically it forms part, and a most important part, of British East Africa. Ecclesiastically and educationally it is linked with Uganda. Regulations drawn up for the Mombasa diocese do not apply to Kavirondo: rules which govern Uganda may prove inapplicable to the very different conditions obtained in Kavirondo. Hence the country occupies a position aloof in a large measure from either.
>
> And as its ecclesiastical position is peculiar so too has been its method of evangelization. Without exception every other part of the Uganda diocese

has drawn, for its pioneer evangelists, directly or indirectly on the Kingdom of Buganda. . . . Nilotic Kavirondo alone has depended on its own resources. With two or three exceptions the entire work of evangelization and education, so far as it has gone, has been the work of native teachers, Kavirondo born. In this matter Kavirondo independence has asserted itself.

And in the method of its working the same spirit has repeatedly been seen. Elsewhere the initiative rests wholly with the European missionary. It is he who first recognizes the need, chooses the agent, and duly sends him out to work. In Kavirondo in not a few cases it is the native who takes the initiative into his own hands. Trained or half-trained, in a Mission School, the Convert returns to his native village and is lost to sight.

Next time the missionary meets him he is in self-imposed charge of a little congregation of Readers, from which in due course a little group of candidates for the catechumenate emerges. So the work grows, but much of it in its initial stages, is carried on in entire independence of the European.

Again the visitor on any Sunday to the native congregation in Kisumu will see what he will see nowhere else but in Kavirondo, a drilled and uniformed congregation. Not all, but some hundreds of them will be found clothed in a short shirt of white, with dark blue facings and a dark blue spine pad; the letters, roughly worked C.M.S.K. across the breast; and on the red fez cap a blue cross on white shield.

A closer inspection will reveal mysterious buttons and stripes showing that from a corporal to a colonel every rank is represented. Two little red buttons on the shoulder indicate a lieutenant, three are a Captain and so on. Even the Red Cross contingent finds its place. Each section of the town has its own Company, and is lined up, with its own officers, outside the building before church. And throughout Kavirondo, in all centres where groups of Readers are to be found, may be seen, in the varying degrees of efficiency, the same thing. The colours vary, the shape of the cross on the cap differs with the different district, but the same general idea is to be seen everywhere. The interesting part of the organization is that it is entirely the native Christian's own idea. They have designed and paid for their own uniforms. They drill and organize themselves without instructions or intervention from any white man; a clearer proof of natural independence it would be difficult to find. Certainly the effect when a large number are gathered together is most striking. (Willis 1916, 20–23, as quoted in Welbourn and Ogot 1966, 24–25, reprinted by permission of Oxford University Press.)

The Reverend John Jamieson Willis was the first Anglican missionary sent by the C.M.S. mission in Uganda to work among the Luo. In 1906, he founded the station at Maseno, where he worked until he was called back to Kampala as bishop in 1912. As is evident from just-quoted text, Willis was a strong believer in the need for a fully indigenized Christianity, a belief, it would seem, that coincided with the inclination of many Luo converts to take control of their newfound religion. Kavirondo was at this time part of the Uganda diocese,[29] so the liberal organizational structures and evangelization policies employed in Uganda were applied to the new mission field as well. Lonsdale writes that "Nyanza Anglicans were early given considerable local responsibility, Willis having formed a church council while all the council members were still schoolboys" (1970, 594).

As had occurred throughout Buganda and its neighboring kingdoms, Christian converts in Kavirondo often constructed their own prayer houses or churches, which also served as schools. Local people called these small buildings *synagogi*, as they were known in Buganda,[30] *sikunde* (schools), or *od mar lemo* (prayer houses) in Dholuo. Inondi and two other Roho church leaders, Daniel Were and Meshak Ogola (Inondi's son), explain that Osodo's initiative in constructing his own prayer house evoked jealousy among his neighbors. According to Luo tradition, a young man builds his first house in preparation for marriage. After marriage, he may add granaries, cattle kraals, and other dwellings. It was not proper for a single youth to construct a house in which he welcomed large groups of visitors, thereby appropriating status and prestige that were generally the preserve of older men. To make matters worse, Osodo built a number of small houses for his followers. In creating a kind of Christian commune, he alienated members of the local community, who saw him building a counterfeit home, without the bride-wealth, seniority, or approval of his elders.

Although clan elders may not have objected to Osodo's temporary removal from the community, Inondi implied that interethnic animosity prompted the chief to have Osodo, Odemba, and Isaya conscripted into the colonial forces. Luyia-Luo friction in this region of western Kenya was rooted in a long-standing struggle over land.

It is necessary at this point to provide more background on the land conflict that most likely contributed to Osodo's conscription and became a primary focus of Alfayo Odongo Mango's energies during the 1920s and 1930s. According to the Luo historian Professor B. A. Ogot, the controversy dates back to the mid-nineteenth century, when the JoUgenya (a Luo subtribe) conquered much of modern Buholo, as well as a considerable portion of South Wanga. After evicting the Waholo (the Luyia subtribe inhabiting the Buholo region), the JoUgenya "conquered the whole region between the rivers Nzoia and Viratsi up to Inaya and Bukura" (Ogot 1967, 229). Their intent was to push the Abaluyia (the Luyia people) all the way up to Mount Elgon.[31] Only the powerful Wanga clan, led by Nabongo (King) Shiundu, had been able to stop the further northeastward expansion of the JoUgenya. It was during Shiundu's reign (ca. 1841–1880) that the Ugenya Kager settled permanently in Buholo "right on the doorstep of the Abawanga with ominous implications"; the situation was "extremely fluid," with the Ugenya making repeated incursions into adjacent Luyia lands, only to be pushed back again by Shiundu's forces (Were 1967, 126–127). By this time the Wanga had access to Swahili rifles and ammunition and were aided by Masai mercenaries.

The year 1894 marked the beginning of what has been called the age of Wanga subimperialism. In that year, the British Foreign Office recruited C. W. Hobley, formerly of the Imperial British East Africa Company, to go to Chief Mumia's village to set up British administration in Kavirondo. Mumia's village (later known simply as Mumias) was chosen largely because of Mumia's ingratiating posture toward Europeans:

> The Chief Mumia had always been friendly, first to traders, later to the I.B.E.A. Co., and then to the Government. As his village had been, from the time of his father Sundu, a trading centre on the main route to Uganda, it offered a convenient place for the foundation of an administrative station. (Hobley 1970, 81)

Mumia's ready collaboration with the British in "pacifying" "the turbulent collection of tribes" in Nyanza was rewarded in kind by the white overlords (Hobley 1970, 80). Thus, in 1896, Mumia, with Hobley's backing, attempted to drive the Kager out of Buholo and South Wanga. Amazingly, Mumia's forces were defeated. Ogot explains that in the following year, Hobley helped Mumia retaliate by organizing a "punitive expedition" against the Kager:

> Two hundred Luo soldiers were killed with a machine gun in one battle, and the rest fled in all directions and took refuge in neighboring areas, especially in Alego and Bunyala. And many of these refugees settled permanently as minority groups in different parts of Central and North Nyanza. (Ogot 1971, 90)

With the British seeking to establish themselves by ensuring Wanga hegemony, there was little the Kager could now do to regain the territory their fathers had wrested from the Abaluyia decades earlier. However, the Ugenya Luo never forgot Hobley's brutal expedition. The battle would be bitterly invoked over the next thirty years as the Kager repeatedly petitioned the government to restore their "lost lands."[32] Alfayo Odongo Mango's father was one of the nine Luos killed in Mumia's initial attack on Buholo in 1896 (Ogot 1971, 90). Mango and his mother, who had fled during the battle, eventually returned to Buholo, but they were never recognized as anything more than tenants on the land.

At the time that Ibrahim Osodo was conscripted, the country of the Ugenya and the country of the Waholo were ruled by one Wanga chief, Mumia's brother Were Shiundu. Over the years, Luo refugees—such as Mango's family—had trickled back to their previous homes, and trouble was beginning again. In 1915, the government made an attempt to quell these land squabbles by stopping migration. District commissioner Spencer divided Were's territory into two separate administrative units, South Ugenya and Buholo. The administration gave Kager headman Mugenya Agaya authority over South Ugenya, while the Waholo Luyia remained under Were's jurisdiction. "The Waholo were forced to evacuate their bomas in South Ugenya and came to Buholo and similarly the

Kager were returned to South Ugenya."[33] This ruling did little to stop migration, however, and the Luo continued to practice what one official termed "peaceful penetration" across the border well into the 1930s.[34]

Given the tense political climate in 1914–1915, it is easy to see why the Wanga authorities might have been made anxious by the presence of a group of strong Luo youths holding drill sessions in Ruwe. Better to send them off to fight in Tanganyika than run the risk of their agitating against the Wanga.

Anna Inondi recounts that after Ibrahim Osodo and the others left for the army, the activity of the Spirit diminished in Ruwe:

> Now it [Roho] quieted down; those who had it were content, keeping to themselves since that one [Osodo] had been the one working with it. So after his arrest, the spirit returned to silence.
>
> (*Koro oling'; koro ji man kode ong'eyo ang'eya kendgi nikech jalno ema nene tiyo ga kode. Koro ka nene osekawgi to roho koro oduogo oling'.*)

Then, in 1916 the Spirit reappeared in Alego, where it entered a young catechist who was preaching there. The catechist was Alfayo Odongo Mango.

Alfayo Odongo Mango

Childhood, Conversion, and Early Education

Alfayo Odongo Mango was born to Konya Ojanja and Ndiany, the daughter of Ogala Ndoya, in approximately 1884.[35] Sources differ as to the place of Mango's birth. Among the Joroho, it is commonly believed that Mango was born in Musanda on the very land where he was eventually burned to death. Bishop Ibrahim Owuor Mango of the Holy Spirit Church of East Africa attests that both his father and his grandfather, Konya Ojanja, died on their own land at Musanda Iwinda. He maintains that Konya had succeeded in pushing the Wanga inhabitants off the land over a hundred years ago and settled his own family there, building a large fortified homestead (*gunda*) that can still be seen today.

Professor Ogot's research in the 1970s, by contrast, found that Mango was actually born at "Uchirinya in Buholo" where Konya Ojanja's family had settled sometime during the second half of the nineteenth century (1971, 90–91). When Mumia's army attacked Buholo in 1896, Ndiany escaped with her son to her birthplace in Gem Ulumbi. After Konya's death, Mango and his mother returned briefly to Buholo, only to flee back to Gem when Mumia's forces attacked a second time. Ogot goes on to explain:

> But by the beginning of 1899, when Hobley was satisfied that the area was "pacified," he asked Chief Mumia to allow the Kager refugees to return to

their former homes in Buholo. When Mango and his mother returned to their home at Uchirinya, they found it occupied by a Wanga clan called Wakolwe, and they therefore went to live with a relative, Opondo Komo, at Uuas village on the opposite bank of Kisama River. (1971, 90)

According to my informants, Uchirinya and Uuas, like Musanda, were technically part of the colonial administrative region known as South Wanga (as distinct from Buholo), but writings from the period suggest that many local people considered South Wanga to be part of Buholo and used the latter designation in a broad sense. Uchirinya is said to be at the base of Musanda Luo hill, only about a kilometer from Iwinda. Uuas is a little farther to the northwest, along a small road that branches off the Musanda-Mumias road. If Ogot is correct, Mango was not born in Musanda Iwinda (the homestead where the 1934 massacre occurred to the east of Musanda hill) but settled there as a youth with his mother.

In 1931 Archdeacon Owen had also inquired into Mango's background and produced yet another version:

So I began then an investigation into the status of Odongo in the community clamouring that he be evicted. I ultimately dug out that he had come with an elder male relation some twenty years ago, when Mumia brought certain men of the Kager clan to help with the transport of Government loads to Mumias station. This relation was a Jadak [tenant]. In due time Odongo grew up, became baptized, then an evangelist. [36]

This account of Mango's roots conveniently bolstered Owen's insistence that the former was a troublesome outsider who ought to acknowledge his tenant status and adopt an accordingly obedient posture toward local authorities.

The question of Alfayo Odongo Mango's birthplace remains a highly charged issue, both symbolically and politically. For the Roho faithful, who refer to the site of Mango's compound as "our home" (*dalawa*), Musanda constitutes the locus of an interlocking chain of ultimate significances. On that sacred spot, the paradigmatic cycle of birth, death, and renewal was enacted for Roho members by their own African prophet-savior. This cycle is continually recapitulated in the rituals of the church and in members' individual lives. For them, the locus of this central story is Musanda, and they honor its auspiciousness in their annual pilgrimage. That Musanda is the place where both their savior and their faith was born is an existential reality for Joroho, irrespective of what historians and others might say.

For Mango's lineal descendants, the matter of his birthplace bears directly upon the legitimacy of their claims on Musanda Iwinda. Since the 1934 massacre, the land has remained in the hands of the government, but various local factions continue to vie for it. Even if there were some way to determine where Mango was actually born, the effort would be irrelevant in the case of the Roho community, and presumptuously meddlesome in the case of Mango's family, so it is best if we leave this sensitive matter unresolved.

Most of my oral sources jump from Mango's birth to the beginning of his schooling at Butere in 1913. As far as I know, only B. A. Ogot's article documents the intervening years (1971, 91–92). According to Ogot, Mango lost his mother while he was still small and was therefore raised by friends and relatives. He married and shortly thereafter departed to work as a farm laborer in the White Highlands. Ogot explains that Mango learned some European farming techniques, which he later implemented to great advantage in his own garden in Musanda.

On the matter of Mango's wives, our sources again differ. Ogot states that on his return to Musanda, Mango found his brother had appropriated his wife,[37] so he took a new wife named Oloyo from Alego Kanyiek (1971, 91). With the profits gleaned from his successful garden, Mango soon married yet another wife, Aduol, from Buholo. According to Ogot, when Mango converted to Christianity, Oloyo would have nothing to do with the new religion, whereas Aduol was supportive. Yet because the Anglican church recognized only the senior wife as legitimate, Mango was eventually forced to send Aduol away (92).

Although the Ruwe elders did not volunteer information about Mango's pre-conversion polygyny, when I questioned them about Mango's family and offspring, they did acknowledge that Mango had two wives early on and that, as he grew in the Christian faith, he himself realized he should not have more than one. The second wife (her name has been forgotten) had attended Bible readings with him, and they reached the understanding that it would be best if she and her son departed, leaving Rael Oloyo as Mango's only wife. In response to my queries, Mango's son Ibrahim Owuor Mango offered yet a third version. He states that his father married only twice. Mango divorced the first wife, but kept their small son, who died shortly thereafter. Mango was then left with his second wife, Rael Oloyo, a woman who became one of the female leaders in the Roho movement. Mango and she had two sons, Jacob Konya and Ibrahim Owuor, and three daughters, Salome Ndiany, Abigael Atieno, and Fibbi Adhiambo.[38]

The issue of Mango's early marital history should not overly preoccupy us. For the Roho community, what matters is that, as a Christian, Mango embraced the monogamous ideal, establishing a model that all subsequent Roho officials are expected to emulate. What is of interest about these accounts for outsiders trying to reconstruct the roots of the Roho movement, however, is the witness they bear to the divisive impact that Christianity had on polygynous Luo families. Moreover, these accounts of Mango's marriages collectively point to an episode in Mango's life generally downplayed—if not ignored—in Roho oral tradition: Mango's original conversion. Today's Roho members tend to take for granted that Mango was Christian; it is his later reception of the Holy Spirit that is of interest to them. Drawing on material from an unpublished manuscript by H. R. Mudany,[39] Ogot, by contrast, devotes a long paragraph to Mango's conversion to Christianity by African evangelists. According to Ogot (from Mudany), Mango's first exposure to the religion occurred during a visit to Gem Ulumbi: "In his uncle's house, he found some people with strange-looking objects (the [B]ible and prayer book) praying. They invited him to join the congregation and he agreed to do so" (1971, 92). On his return to Musanda, Mango was struck by a terrible illness and seizures and was "haunted by the books he had seen."[40] Traditional healers were called in to cure him, without success. Once he had recovered, Mango went to Madungu in Buholo to visit two prominent leaders of the Kager clan.

> Much to [Mango's] surprise, he found his friends using similar books to the ones he had seen at Ulumbi. He was again invited to join the congregation in prayer, and with some reluctance, he agreed to do so. But, this time, he left the prayer meeting to return home with a profound peace of mind. And on four successive mornings, Mango came back to Madungu to pray without disclosing anything to his wives. On the fourth day, however, he returned with a copy of the First Reader, and jubilantly declared to his stunned wives that he had been converted to Christianity. (Ogot 1971, 92)

There is no mention of this conversion in the oral material I collected, except indirectly through references to Mango's divorce. It is thus difficult to know when it took place, but by the end of 1912[41] Mango had built a grass-thatched mud church not far from Musanda market on a prominent hill known as Musanda Luo, where St. Paul's C.P.K. church today sits.

In that same year, the Reverend Walter Chadwick and his Ganda assistants arrived in Wanga country from Entebbe to open a mission among the Bantu Kavirondo (Abaluyia). According to Ogot, Chadwick met Mango and was impressed by him but was troubled that the eager young Christian leader was not baptized and lacked formal schooling. He thus arranged for Mango—together with three other Luo converts from the area—to attend the C.M.S. Normal School at Maseno in 1913 (Ogot 1971, 93). Ibrahim Owuor Mango maintains that his father first trained as a catechist at Butere in 1913 or 1914 before going to Maseno,[42] but the sequence of Mango's courses is immaterial. It is clear that he studied at Maseno and probably trained, in some form or another, at Butere. He was well known to the missionaries in both places and, in the beginning of his career at least, was supported and encouraged by them.[43] Mango was one of the first Luos from the Buholo and South Wanga regions to go to school (Nundu 1982, 24). He and his Maseno classmates learned reading, writing, and arithmetic, as well as carpentry and brick making—manual skills that Mango would later utilize when replacing the mud-and-dung church on Musanda Luo hill with a permanent brick building. Mango's church on the hill is remembered to have flourished for many years as Luo and Luyia Anglicans worshiped peacefully together within its walls.

Possession by Roho

In his capacity as an authorized Anglican evangelist, Mango undertook a number of preaching safaris—journeys into neighboring areas to spread the gospel. At this point, Roho oral tradition takes up Mango's biography in earnest. Ruwe Roho elders explain that Mango was first possessed of the Holy Spirit in 1916, while he visited a fledgling Christian congregation in Alego Nyadhi[44] accompanied by five fellow Christians, four women and one man: Leah Ohowa, Deborah Muganda, Anna Inondi, Salome Bwagra, and Zakayo Wandeyi. In the Alego church, Mango had a vision in which he saw "something black but shining brightly" (*gimoro marateng to nenore maler ahinya*) coming toward him. Mango's son, Ibrahim Owuor Mango, vigorously rejects the Ruwe version, stating that it was not something black that appeared to his father but "a bright light" (*ler maduong*). In any event, a voice said to Mango: "Odongo, remember what I told you; the warning I have given my followers is this" (*Odongo, par gima nene awachoni; siem mane asiemo jopuonjrena kamae*). The voice then referred Mango to the Gospel of Matthew, chapter 24, verses 24–28. In this passage Jesus tells his disciples that when the Son of man arrives at the end of the time, people will be able to distinguish him from false prophets for he will come "as the lightning comes, from the east and shines as far as the west." The Joroho I spoke with point out that Mango had just traveled westward from Musanda to Alego, and they interpret his vision as a divine confirmation of his messianic calling.

Mango did not at first mention this unusual experience to anyone but thought about the message he had received as he and his small party left Alego. The journey back to Musanda took them through Uriya forest, where they were suddenly knocked down by the Spirit. Through the power of the Spirit, Mango was able to see the sins of his traveling companions, and he demanded that they confess: "Confess your sins; you young women have sins. . . . Gather together and I will pray for you. You have sins; confess your sins!" (*Ful uru richo; nyigi un kod richo. . . . Chokore uru alemnu. Un kod richo; ful uru richo!*)

Three of the women traveling with Mango were Luo. The fourth, Deborah Muganda, was Luyia. The Luo women—who were also relatives of the catechist (*nyigi* [lit., sisters] *japuonj*)—looked down on Muganda and forced her to carry the group's reed mat[45] all the way from Musanda to Alego. They considered themselves above[46] such a task. When asked to confess, it was this sin of pride that they admitted. Zakayo Wandeyi was guilty of the same thing, but refused to confess, saying that he had not done anything wrong: "I cannot join you, because I have not sinned" (*Ok anyal bet kodu nikech ok atimo richo*). At this point, an angel spoke to Mango:

> Now I am going but I will return. Just be peaceful. Your children are still immature. You cannot preach about the law in such a way that your children will understand the word.

(Koro an adhi to ana duog'. Koro bed uru abeda kod kwe. Pod nyithindu yom, onge dak unyal yalo bura, munyalo miyo kodo nyithindo owinj wach.)[47]

After his return to Musanda, Mango continued to preach and perform the duties of a church catechist. The Spirit was now with him, yet Mango kept a low profile, for he did not want to arouse resentment.[48] Moreover, the angel had told him to be patient, so he remained calm and waited for the Holy Spirit to come back with active force.

A brief remark contained in a letter written in 1934 by Archdeacon Owen serves to corroborate that Mango had led a charismatic movement at just about the time that Roho members say Odongo received the Spirit. It also suggests that there was indeed a long hiatus between Mango's initial involvement in this type of religion and the later surfacing of the Roho movement in the 1930s, a chronology consistent with members' accounts.

> Alufayo Odongo, questioned by Canon Pleydell as to whether he were privy to the itinerant activities of Lawi, or had sent him forth, denied this. Canon Pleydell in 1917, before I was sent to Kavirondo had had experience of a movement characterized by much hysteria and visions of which Alufayo was the inspirer and mainstay. Hence his question, for Lawi was living in the same village with Alufayo, and their association together was very close, and Canon suspected that Alufayo was behind Lawi.[49]

Inondi explains that, after his mystical experience in Alego, Mango began to preach against certain widely practiced customs. For instance, there was a Luo prohibition against married women eating chicken, but Mango, through the guidance of the Holy Spirit, revealed that women were now free to do so. He also criticized the traditional attitude toward death. According to his teachings, one should not mourn excessively when a relative dies. If a woman loses her husband, she should not mourn "in a bad way," blaming someone for the death, for God is the one who has taken him.[50]

Mango often walked to Ruwe to preach and to visit his cousin Isaya Goro (Inondi's husband). Many of Ruwe's landowning Luo and Wanga (*jopiny*) felt that Mango's real reasons for visiting Ruwe were not religious but political. They accused him of coming to be shown the ruins of the old fortified Kager homesteads in order to bolster his lost lands case with the government. In Inondi's words, Mango responded, "I am not here for ancestral land; I am only worshiping my Lord" (*An ok achung' ni gunda; an alamo mana Nyasacha*).

A number of other events indicate that in the years following his vision in Alego, from about 1917 to 1920, Mango began to face local opposition, primarily from the Wanga community. Most of my informants maintain that this interethnic friction was fueled by the arrival of Owen, who displayed an open preference for Bantu-speaking groups over the Nilotic Luo. Owen's letters reveal that he repeatedly used his influence to reinforce the administration's utilitarian support of Wanga land claims against those of the Luo community. This bias is not surprising. After all, the mission at Butere was located on land offered to the C.M.S. by Mulama. Ogot writes that, when Owen arrived in 1918, he was "highly impressed" by the chief: "They soon became good friends and stuck together in the many inter-tribal and religious conflicts that Owen's activities sparked off in Western Kenya" (1971, 92).

Mango's son recounts an instance in which Zakayo Wandeyi—the teacher who had reportedly refused to make confession in the Uriya forest—dared to speak out against Mulama and received harsh treatment from Owen for making trouble. Mulama was one of the first Wanga chiefs to convert to Christianity. He frequently partook of Holy Communion, and Owen was fond of holding him up as a model for the rest of the community. One day Wandeyi approached Owen and asked why Mulama was permitted to take communion whereas other polygynists were denied that privilege. Owen refused to believe that Mulama had more than one wife. Mulama lived at Butere with his first wife, and Owen had constant contact with them; they had had a church wedding, and all their children had been baptized. Everyone but Owen knew, however, that in reality Mulama had more than thirty wives. The missionary wanted to investigate, so Wandeyi secretly took him to visit several of Mulama's other wives. When asked, each woman replied that chief Mulama was her husband and that the children the visitors could see running around the compound were all his. Thus, Owen "learned Mulama's secret and the chief was promptly removed from his V.I.P. place in the church."[51]

According to Ibrahim Mango, Wandeyi's action infuriated Mulama. He and his assistant chiefs began to plot revenge. As we have seen, Wandeyi and Mango were closely associated: both were teachers in "the church on the hill," and Wandeyi was related to Mango. In an attempt to punish Wandeyi, Mulama incited a group of Wanga to burn down Mango's grass-thatched church. The perpetrators tried to make it appear as if Wandeyi had set the fire, but, of course, most people knew the truth. The district commissioner held a *baraza* (community forum) in Musanda to determine who burnt the church. All who testified were forced to swear that their statements were true. Alfayo and Zakayo swore on the Bible. The rest took *mbira*, a traditional oath that entails holding a (supposed) human skull. The district commissioner found that the Luyia's accusation of Zakayo Wandeyi made no sense, for why would a church teacher wish to burn down his place of work? A few years later, according to Roho elders, all the people who had sworn on the skull died, which proved that they had, in fact, committed the crime themselves.

Ogot's account of this 1919 burning of the Musanda Luo church is slightly different; Ogot states that it was the church tailor, Michael Akoth, whom the Wanga tried to frame. In any event, Archdeacon Owen saw to it that the district commissioner had both Akoth and Wandeyi deported, the former to South

Ugenya and the latter to Gem, a location in Central Kavirondo. Ogot remarks that "the Luo community in Buholo was becoming seriously concerned about the bias Owen showed in his handling of Luo-Luyia problems" (1971, 98).

In addition to Owen's personal friendship with Mulama, many of my informants felt that Owen's obvious tendency to side with the Luyia against the Luo stemmed from the archdeacon's familiarity with Bantu culture and languages. While in Uganda, he had become fluent in Luganda; after being transferred to Kavirondo, he had little trouble picking up Luhanga. Not long after his arrival, Owen was able to speak directly with the Wanga people about their problems and concerns. Among the Nilotic Luo, however, Owen had to work through interpreters for at least several years, for "the Owens were too much occupied in their first days to acquire an entirely new language" (Richards 1947, 11). A Luganda translation of the Bible "beaten out . . . by the best brains of the Waganda themselves" had already been in use in the Uganda diocese for many years (Pilkington quoted in Pirouet 1978, 31). One can imagine that Owen's teaching of Christian doctrine among the Wanga people was facilitated by the fact that religious terms in Luganda frequently had close correlates in Luhanga. Owen was slow, however, to promote the translation of Scripture into Dholuo. In fact, he actually discouraged the translation of the Old Testament—much to the dismay of Luo members of the African Church Council—"as he feared that it would only provide justification for 'backsliding' into the 'polygamy of the surrounding pagan society'" (Strayer 1978, 86). Not until the late 1930s and early 1940s, when he was in ill health, did Owen finally turn to the task of translating substantial sections of the Old Testament into Dholuo.

Between 1925 and 1928, Mango occasionally traveled to Nairobi for Anglican meetings and seminars. On one occasion, Canon George Burns, who was stationed there, asked Mango to assist in leading a worship service for Anglican representatives from all over the colony. As the story goes, when Mango stood up in front of the assembly and began to pray, his body grew to a huge size, such that his head touched the sky while his feet remained on the ground. Burns, who had never seen a black man deliver such a powerful prayer before, reportedly tried to record Mango's words on the door of the church but was ordered (presumably by his superiors) to erase the prayer. According to oral sources, Chief Mulama was in attendance as a representative from Butere parish and also witnessed the event.

This episode appears to be a favorite among Roho members and was often mentioned to me. The image of Mango with his head in the sky resonates with Luo notions of spiritual power. Traditional gargantuan snake divinities, such as Mumbo or Nyang'idi, were often depicted standing erect, with their tails in lakes (Victoria and Kanyaboli, respectively) and their heads in the clouds. Individuals possessed by these divinities sometimes described themselves as being carried aloft on their patrons' heads. When such people returned to earth, they were known to have acquired amazing powers (Whisson 1962, 12–13; Onyango-Ogutu and Roscoe 1974, 22; Nyangweso 1930, 13–17). Similarly, church mem-

bers interpret Mango's taking on a gigantic form as undeniable proof that the
Holy Spirit had seized him—proof that even Europeans were forced to concede.
One Roho adherent, Elijah J. O. Ayodo, asserted that Archdeacon Owen, who
also witnessed Alfayo assuming this immense form in prayer, "bitterly complained to God for sending the Holy Spirit to the Black Africans when [Owen]
had come to teach instead of giving it to the white missionaries who had served
him for so long" (1990, 1).

Padri Alfayo

In 1927 Archdeacon Owen appointed Alfayo Odongo Mango to serve as deacon
over a number of predominantly Luo churches within the Butere pastorate:
Musanda, Ruwe, and Mahondo in South Wanga; Madungu, Got Osimbo,
Konjra, and Ulwan in Buholo; Yiro Mudhiero in Marama; Sidindi in South
Ugenya; and Murumba in Gem (Ogot 1971, 101). In 1928, Mango was selected
by Owen to study theology at St. Emmanuel's Divinity School in Freretown, so
he and his family moved to Mombasa for the duration of the two-year course.

Since his childhood, Mango had had considerable contact with people from
outside western Kenya. Mumias, not more than six-and-a-half kilometers from
Musanda, was an important trading center and meeting place, a crossroads for
travelers making their way back and forth from the coast to the Uganda interior.
In the nineteenth century, caravans of Swahili and Arab traders made Mumias
(then Elureko) the base from which they launched their up-country slaving and
ivory expeditions (Were 1967, 161). Some of these coastal traders settled at
Mumias, as did contingents of the Uasin Gishu Maasai mercenaries employed by
Nabongo Mumia (Ogot 1967, 231). The British administration later introduced
Sudanese soldiers and porters of other African backgrounds (Hobley 1970, 82); all
these groups left their mark on the increasingly heterogeneous center, where
people from Mango's home area went to barter goods.

Mango's involvement in the church also brought him into contact with a
wider world. Ganda evangelists played a crucial role in the missionization of
Nyanza. A number of the first Luo converts actually visited the C.M.S. diocesan
headquarters located in the heart of the Buganda Kingdom. Those who did not
have that opportunity were nevertheless exposed to Ganda nationalism and notions of ecclesiastical self-sufficiency through the Ganda missionaries (Lonsdale
1970, 595–596; Ochieng 1971, 75). Walter Chadwick's pioneering team at
Butere included three Ganda evangelists: Zachariah Nakakongo, John Diba, and
a man called Festus. There was also one Luo convert who had traveled to
Uganda, Paul Ochieng (Ogot 1971, 91). The development of Mango's faith and
thought was no doubt influenced by his contact with these individuals, as well as
by his interaction with Ganda teachers at Maseno.

We can assume that when Mango later went to work in the "White Highlands," he met laborers from other ethnic groups. His trips to Nairobi on church business no doubt exposed him to a still broader mix of nationalities and ethnicities—Indian, Ugandan, Tanganyikan, Zanzibari, Kikuyu, Arab, Maasai. At this time, people of numerous backgrounds were forming semiurban settlements outside Nairobi that, "quite unplanned by the administration contained the seeds of a pan–East African community"; after the war, political associations representing the interests of various native groups began to spring up throughout the colony, creating what Kenneth King has called a "protest mosaic" (1971, 159, xiii).

Freretown, where St. Emmanuel's Divinity School was located, was established by the C.M.S. in 1875 as a colony for freed slaves. Named for Sir Bartel Frere, who negotiated the Treaty of Abolition with the sultan of Zanzibar, the colony was founded by a group of one hundred fifty Africans from what are today Mozambique, Malawi, and Tanzania. They had been rescued from slave dhows by the British, taken to mission stations in Bombay, and then returned to East Africa—hence their popular name the "Bombay Africans." On the whole highly educated, these original settlers and their descendants persistently challenged mission authorities. They called for greater degrees of participation in the colony's administration, fuller representation and respect within the C.M.S., and the freedom to shape their lives as they saw fit (Strayer 1978, 14–28, 70; Ogot 1971, 99). By the time Mango entered divinity school in 1928, tension between the African Church Council (ACC) and the C.M.S. administration was mounting. Ostensibly designed to give Africans some voice in running the church, the ACC was a centralized institution that represented the very first step "toward the formation of an ecclesiastical province independent of Canterbury" (Strayer 1978, 68). The ACC called for more control over church resources and a greater voice in decision making in such matters as the selection and ordination of African pastors. Yet the local missions, headed by Europeans, refused to relax their tight control over funds and had no confidence in the judgment of the ACC on policy matters (68–70). For Anglican deacons and pastors in training such as Mango and his classmates, all of these power-sharing struggles would have been of keen interest. In addition to issues of church control, the students would have exchanged ideas on the growing movements of resistance to colonialism:

It was to [St. Emmanuel's Divinity School] which recruited students from all parts of Kenya, that Mango went. One of his classmates was a Kikuyu, Elijah Gacanja, now Canon Gacanja. It was from fellow students like Gacanja that he obtained valuable information about the struggle between Harry Thuku and the colonial administration. In February 1929, he met Jomo Kenyatta who was then on his way to England as an emissary of the Kikuyu Central Association. The more he heard of Kikuyu land grievances the more he discerned a similarity between the Kikuyu case and the Kager case in Wanga. (Ogot 1971, 99)

Mango's second son, Ibrahim, was only ten years old when he moved with his father, mother, and siblings to Mombasa. He cannot recall much about his father's life there, except that people were amazed by Mango's preaching ability. He remembers clearly that one missionary named Reverend Beecher used to marvel at Mango's presence in the pulpit and commented on the way in which his facial features appeared transformed whenever he prayed. The Ruwe church elders say that one day, as Mango was praying inside the Kisauni church, the Holy Spirit knocked him down and instructed him to return to serve his people suffering in the reserve. When he did return home, after he completed his divinity course in 1930, Mango found the Musanda congregation divided.

During the two years Alfayo Odongo Mango had spent in Mombasa, things had not gone well for the C.M.S. churches in South Wanga. There were not enough pastors to go around, and the rift between Luyia members (primarily Wanga) and Luo members (primarily Kager) had grown. Chief Mulama warned his fellow Wanga to watch out for Mango. According to Roho elders, Mulama concluded that, given the powerful way Mango had preached in Nairobi, the latter would prove a formidable foe who might use his influence with the missionaries to further the Kager lands cause. Inondi recounts that Luos therefore could not get Luyia pastors to baptize their babies. Heeding Mulama's warnings, the Wanga members of the Mango's "church on the hill" seceded from the congregation that they had for years shared with Luos. They then constructed their own Anglican church in 1928–1929, down the slope and across the road on the opposite side of the marketplace. This new church was dubbed "Musanda Bantu"; the original church (which Mango had begun rebuilding in stone) came to be known as "Musanda Luo."

Once back in Musanda, Mango baptized the Luo children who had been rejected by Luyia pastors. Inondi indicated that people from her community were extremely relieved to have someone finally among them who was authorized to baptize (*jabatiso*). The material I have collected renders Mango's ecclesiastical rank unclear, however. When Mango was promoted from evangelist to the post of deacon, members of his congregations began calling him *Padri* (Pastor). From about 1930 on, most archival sources and documents refer to Odongo as "Reverend" or "Pastor." Yet in a letter written in 1934, a month after Mango's death, Archdeacon Owen asserted that Mango was technically never more than a deacon, unable to preside at communion: "Alufayo was a deacon not a priest, but Lawi had announced in October (1933) that if we did not recognize his 'laying on of hands' he would institute his own rites of Holy Communion."[52] This disjuncture between the recognition that Mango's congregations gave him and the actual authority that the church had vested in him would to lead to increasing misunderstanding, and Mango, whose resolve was no doubt strengthened by his exposure to currents of protest in Freretown and Nairobi, was not about to shy away from conflict.

Mango and the Lost Lands

Mango did not let the limitations of his office impede his persistent attempts to improve the position of Luos in North Kavirondo, both within the church and without. He had hardly been back in Musanda one year before he and other Kager leaders began taking definite steps to secure their lost lands. Two other key agitators were Elijah Oloo, an ex-police sergeant, and Shadrack Awelu, the brother of Omoro Omolo, who had led the Kager in an earlier phase of the land rights struggle from 1913 to 1919.

In early April 1931,[53] the group hired Kisumu lawyer R. R. Evison to examine the Central Kavirondo–North Kavirondo boundary and determine the viability of the Kager case. When the local chiefs learned of the consultation[54] and the fact that Mango had received Evison in his home, the already marked man was further penalized with a fine of 300 shillings—a huge sum in those days. Evison was outraged when he heard that Mango had been punished for seeking his counsel and wrote the district commissioner, E. L. B. Anderson, demanding the suspension of the local chief.[55] In Evison's estimation, the Kager had legitimate grounds for wanting the district boundary altered, but his professional opinion was dismissed by Acting Provincial Commissioner Thompson, who stated bluntly that he had "no sympathy with" Kager claims.[56] Several months later, when the Kager again approached Evison, Thompson warned that he did not want the lawyer "precipitating a crisis" by making another appearance in Buholo.[57] In the end, Evison and his clients were told by the administration that "land rights were governed by Customary Law and that the Supreme Court had disclaimed any jurisdiction in such cases" (Ogot 1971, 100).

The district commissioner automatically reduced Mango's fine to 150 shillings—the maximum amount that a *baraza* was permitted to inflict. Anderson then temporarily suspended the fine pending word from headquarters on the legality of natives collecting money to hire a lawyer.[58] It may be that the *baraza's* decision was eventually overruled altogether. A note from Thompson to Anderson in September indicated that "H.Q." had stipulated that Africans "could not be stopped collecting [money] if they wished to."[59]

This affair with Evison ultimately hurt the Kager cause by alerting the administration to the severity of the lands conflict. As Anderson indicated in a letter to Canon A. J. Leech,[60] colonial authorities had simply not been aware of "the extent of the [Kager] movement nor of the harm being done by it."[61] The incident also prompted Archdeacon Owen to conduct a series of investigations in November 1931 "into the reasons why there was such a widespread and strong demand that the Rev. Alufayo Odongo should be evicted from Musanda." Interviews with Luyia inhabitants in Buholo revealed that Mango "was at the back of agitation by members of the Kager Clan to be given possession of thirty-seven holdings throughout Buholo, Yiro and Wanga." Owen informed the district commissioner that Mango was a mere *jadak* (tenant, land client) who had "flouted every right" of his landlords and "gathered around his house seventeen other families . . . without asking sanction from the agelong clan owners of the land." The report concluded with Owen's promise that he would advise the church council "to raise no objections to [Mango's] being evicted" by the Wanga *baraza*. However, the missionary far preferred that the district commissioner force Odongo and his cohorts to make official acknowledgment of their subordinate tenant status.[62]

Anderson promptly followed Owen's suggestion, holding a *baraza* for representatives from both sides on December 13. He urged the Kager to "own themselves tenants"; those who did not would be subject to eviction at the wish of their landlords. The Kager representatives vehemently resisted the government's ruling, arguing that it was Hobley, not the Wanga, who had driven them off their ancestral *bomas*, lands that they had successfully conquered more than a generation ago. Had there been no Hobley, they persisted, they would still be on their land, for they had been "the *Wazungu* [Europeans—i.e., the dominant group] of this country" before the Europeans arrived.[63] Their arguing was to no avail. Mango, Elijah Oloo, Antipa Ngutu, Elias Awanda, and Abdalla Gangla were all deemed "unacceptable to their landlords"[64] and given notice by the Wanga Council of Elders that their permission to remain on Wanga land was terminated.[65]

By March 31, 1932, the council's notice expired, yet neither Mango nor any of the others had quit their homesteads. Abdalla Gangla had died, and his widow, Mwana Arabu, likewise refused to leave. According to Anna Inondi, Abdalla—or "Wamdala," as his name has been preserved in Ruwe oral tradition—had in truth been murdered by the Abaluyia before he was able to arrange a move. Afterward, it is said that his enemies danced on his grave until it was completely flat. In April, Mango and the other three Kager men were brought before the Wanga Tribunal, fined 10 shillings each for contempt of court, and forced to vacate their compounds. Mango took his family to Gem Ulumbi, where his mother and wife were from and where he had fled as a child during the Hobley wars. Elijah Oloo and his family went to stay in Ugolwe in South Ugenya. Exile did not silence them, however.

Ibrahim Owuor Mango explains that, while his father was away, many people wrote letters to the Colonial Office protesting his eviction. Kager leaders in Musanda drafted letters and then traveled to Gem to obtain Mango's signature. Ibrahim and other Roho elders maintain that Mango had so much support in Musanda that people threatened not to pay taxes and even to revolt if Mango were not allowed to return to his home. Indeed, the colonial records indicate that 1932 was a year of increased and better organized agitation by the Kager clan in Wanga and Marama. Despite the district commissioner's warnings, Kager elders again sought attorney Evison's assistance in writing to the chief native commissioner on behalf of the four Kager evictees. Two months later, in April 1932, a deputation of Kager from Yiro and Musanda requested leave to go before the chief native commissioner to plead their case in person. They were granted permission by the new provincial commissioner of Nyanza, H. R. Montgomery, but their appeal nevertheless failed. Sometime before August, these individuals, led by Tosia Obala and Dimo Ndeda from South Marama, Mudembi Ogada from Buholo, and Daniel Musigo from Wanga, formed the Ugenya Kager Luo Clan Association (UKA). After all their previous appeals had fallen on deaf ears, the UKA wrote directly to the governor and outlined their grievances.[66] The North Kavirondo Annual District Report for 1932 contains the official response: "An answer was received that His Excellency saw no reason to alter the decision already arrived at by the Provincial Administration which confirmed the Bantu in their position as the owners of the land."[67] The Ugenya Kager filed a second petition, but again the answer came back that "the Governor's decision was final."[68]

Mango remained in Gem Ulumbi for about a year. Inondi reports that one morning, as Mango was praying, he heard a voice:

> Odongo, you have been chosen together with your home area Musanda as the place where my bright light will reveal itself for thousands and thousands of those living on earth. Stop wasting time and go back to Musanda.
>
> (*Odongo ise yieri gi dalani Musanda kaka ekuma kitunda maler nofwenyre ni ji tara gi tara modak e piny. We ketho kinde to dog Musanda.*)

Mango's son recalls that in 1933, the Colonial Office in England instructed the district commissioner to allow Mango to return to Musanda; I did not find any document to this effect, however. It is clear that on April 10, 1933, Mango and the four other deported Kager attended a meeting at Kakamega and, in front of Chiefs Mumia, Murunga, Mulama, and Osundwa, agreed that they would acknowledge themselves tenants in exchange for permission to return to their former residences. The document they signed included the condition that they were "not to bring other Kager or strangers into their lands without leave of the local Elders" and that Mango agreed "to confine himself entirely to Church and other work connected with his calling as given him by Archdeacon Owen and the Bishop."[69]

Return from Exile

After signing the agreement in April 1933, Mango and his family returned to their former *boma*, which had remained undisturbed during their absence. His fellow Ugenya Kager were apparently encouraged by the government's decision to allow him to return, for in summer 1933, Provincial Commissioner Montgomery received yet another deputation of clan elders—followed by a petition—restating their wish to reside in "the land of [their] fathers," which Hobley had annexed. The signatories agreed to live peaceably under Wanga headmen "until such time as [they were] numerically strong enough to warrant our receiving a chief of our own, a Luo."[70] In his remarks to Montgomery, District Commissioner Anderson commented, "Their effort at diplomacy is so transparent as to be pathetic" and urged the provincial commissioner to warn the Wanga against any concessions to the Kager.[71]

Inondi explained that life for Mango and his family was difficult after their return. They were frequently harassed. Whenever Mango went out, youths were sent by his enemies to ambush him with sticks and stones. In addition, he was repeatedly arrested by the local authorities. Yet he could never really be charged with anything and was always released quickly:

> Day after day, *askaris*[72] would come for him and tell his wife, "cook for us [quickly] so we can be off." But when they would reach [the police camp] they couldn't find any reason to jail him. Things just continued like that.
>
> (*Kiny ka kiny to waskar oom, to iwacho ni dhako ni ted kuon wadhi. To ka gidhi to ok nwang' gima itweyone. Odhi adhiya kamano.*)

In his professional capacity, Mango continued to visit the Anglican churches in his pastorate and to baptize people. Some churches did not receive him warmly, however. Inondi recounts one instance, when Mango arrived in Mudhiero to baptize some new members and was not even allowed to stand at the front of the church—let alone perform baptism—but was forced to sit with the rest of the congregation. After the service, he was on his way back from Mudhiero when it began to rain. Some youths and children had again been sent to cane him. The children's parents were hiding in the bushes in hopes that Mango would be provoked to strike back, at which point the adults would have had just cause to attack the pastor. Instead, when the youths began harassing him, Mango evaded them and hurried to the home of the senior evangelist at Ruwe, Nicholas Odongo, who was related to Rael Oloyo, Mango's wife.

Elkanah Wamira, also an Anglican catechist at Ruwe and a rival, accused Mango of having corrupted the people (*ketho ji*). He had sent an additional party from Yiro to beat up Alfayo on the Mudhiero road, and they had trailed Mango to Nicholas Odongo's home. When they arrived, Odongo blocked their way, saying, "If you want to kill Mango, you will have to kill me first!" Nicholas Odongo was known to be a fierce man, and the crowd was intimidated by his anger, so they left quickly.

While Odongo's wife, Nora Anyango, prepared a meal for their guest, Odongo went out to summon two men to escort Mango home safely. Barnaba Walwoho, an assistant catechist at Ruwe, and Isaya Goro, a church elder, agreed to accompany Mango to Uriya, the forest at the western end of Ruwe, where the Holy Spirit had knocked Mango and his companions down on their return from Alego in 1916. From that place, the pastor was able to continue home safely.

In the early 1930s, it appears that in addition to tension between Luyia and Luo Anglicans because of the land controversy, a rift appeared within the Ugenya Luo community itself. The Mudhiero incident was but one manifestation of this rift. On one side were those Kager who allied themselves with Mango and the anti-Wanga agitators; on the other side were those Luos who sided with Archdeacon Owen and the government. The actions of Archdeacon Owen only further exacerbated this split. Bethwell Ogot views Owen as an active supporter of the British administration's policy of divide and rule—a policy at work in the government's fostering of Wanga subimperialism in western Kenya. Ogot accuses the archdeacon of "exploiting clanism" in Buholo by applying the same policy in the church:

> Owen now persuaded the other pastors who were not members of the Kager clan to form separate groups—the Mudhiero and Got Osimbo groups. The first group comprised Mudhiero, Lolwe, Luanda and Sidindi Churches and it was led by Isaya Musiga (later Canon Isaya Musiga). The second group, the Got Osimbo group—led by Mariko Oduor and Gideon Bodo, comprising Got Osimbo, Ulwan and Magoya, also broke away at the instigation of Owen. The churches which remained loyal to Mango were Madungu, Nyamuoso, Mahondo, Umola, Ruwe, Msejere, Ihonje, Masawa, Murumba and Lithele. (1971, 101–102)

Some historians give a more nuanced reading of Owen's complicity with the colonialists' hegemonic programs in Luoland (Whisson 1962, 17; Strayer 1973, 26; 1978, 86–88; Lonsdale 1970, 607). However, it is safe to say that regardless of Mango's ethnic roots, Owen would have rejected the deacon on a number of counts and would have sought to undermine the latter's influence amid Owen's flock.

Ruwe Roho elders explain that, after the incident at Mudhiero, Mango no longer undertook preaching safaris but prayed with those willing to gather in his compound at Musanda. For the rest of 1933, he remained mostly at home. Although he never stopped trying to communicate the word of God, he was not as effective as he might have been, had he been free to travel. Fortunately, there were others ready to proselytize in his place. Antipa Ngutu, Daniel Musigo, and Isaya Mola were all evangelists (*jopuonj*) who had led the Musanda Luo congregation while Mango was in Gem Ulumbi and now assumed the pastor's safari responsibilities.

The Ruwe elders recount that another young, enthusiastic member of the Musanda Luo church began preaching the gospel in neighboring communities. This young man was Silvano Nyamogo. Although Nyamogo was not a trained catechist, one day he became possessed of the Holy Spirit and received instructions in a vision to spread the word. Ruwe oral tradition is consistent with the

information District Officer Hislop uncovered in his investigations into the Musanda tragedy:

> Silvano has informed me that at the end of May 1933, following a long vigil
> of Prayer, both he and Lawi [Obonyo] had visions in which they were
> transported aloft. In his case he found himself in a large brightly shining
> house surrounded by white persons in white robes like Kanzus, and he heard
> a voice telling him to go on safari among the people to spread the gospel. He
> says he does not know the details of Lawi's vision, except that the latter also
> heard a voice giving him similar orders. Accordingly, both Silvano and Lawi
> became itinerant preachers. They had no authority to represent the C.M.S.
> to which they belonged: they were acting entirely on their own, and appar-
> ently at first only in a loose conju[n]ction, as they preached the same things.
> They do not appear ever to have travelled together.[73]

One of the places the Spirit instructed Silvano Nyamogo to visit was Ruwe. The
people at Ruwe were at this point apparently not aware of Lawi Obonyo's activities or of Nyamogo's affiliation with him. What oral tradition has retained is
that Nyamogo was the first man sent by the Holy Spirit to preach in Ruwe during
Mango's self-confinement in Musanda.

Ruwe Roho elders stated that a man named Dishon Obok Hayanga accompanied Silvano Nyamogo to Ruwe. Obok did not have the Spirit himself but was
a good Christian. When Nyamogo began preaching in Ruwe, many of the people
who had been followers of Ibrahim Osodo more than fifteen years earlier accepted Nyamogo's teachings. They affirmed that the Holy Spirit was with
Nyamogo and indeed in their midst once again: "He revived the roho issue"
(*Ochako ochiero wach roho*). The Christians at Ruwe did not want to draw attention to themselves by spreading news about the Spirit. As Inondi put it, "We kept
quiet about it, but the news entered into us" (*Wabende wakawe waling' kode, to
odonjo nwa*).

In Ruwe, people were not fully aware of what had happened between their
pastor, Mango, and other leaders in the C.M.S. church. All Inondi knew was
that teachers such as Daniel Musigo—who lacked the Holy Spirit—came from
neighboring congregations to preach at Ruwe. Musiko warned that supporters of
Mango and other Holy Spirit preachers would not be tolerated within the C.M.S.
church.[74] Inondi and her group at Ruwe felt abandoned and prayed to God for
guidance. The Joroho (People of the Spirit), as they were beginning to be called,
were seen by others to have deviated from Anglican Christianity and were no
longer welcome at Musanda Luo or at the C.M.S. church in Ruwe itself.

Anna Inondi then received a message from the Spirit indicating that Mango's
followers would not lose their church. The message came to Inondi in a dream.
She heard a bell ringing, followed by a loud voice that said: "The church is yours
[pl.], nobody will take it from you" (*Kanisa en maru, ng'ato kan omau*). Inondi
reported the dream to evangelist Barnaba Walwoho, asking him whether the

dream could be true, now that Mango's followers had been expelled from the Anglican churches and forced to worship privately in their homes. Barnaba affirmed that her dream did indeed contain God's message. Inondi trusted Barnaba's statement, for he was a man of great spiritual power. He had been the one who, under Daniel Otang'a, prayed for people when the Spirit grabbed hold of them. Only he could stop the terrible disturbances caused by the Spirit—stones flying, earthquakes, noises, and people being knocked down. Barnaba was very young at the time, and it was a marvel to many that such a young man could pray with such efficacy.

Two days later, the voice returned to Inondi as she slept. She heard a high-pitched bell followed by these words:

> Pay attention! A helper is going to be born in either the Kager or the Joboro clan. He is the one who will relieve you from the work of slaves.
>
> (*Chik iti! Ibiro nyuolo jakony e dhood kager kata dhood joboro. En ema obiro golou e tich wasumbni.*)[75]

The following morning, she recalled her dream and pondered. Her people had been terribly neglected. The Kager were not welcome in the area. The most difficult tasks were being relegated to Luo women, who were constantly being insulted by Wanga wives. How was it, she wondered to herself, that her dream promised relief, yet she could see no sign of it anywhere? Again, Inondi consulted Barnaba. Barnaba responded that a helper had already been born, that he was in fact fully grown. "What is left," Barnaba declared, "is simply for him to begin his work" (*tich ema odong'ne*). Inondi remarked that Barnaba had the power to see clearly, and it was not surprising that he would be the one to have discerned the existance of *jakony*, "the helper."

After receiving this reassurance from Barnaba, Mango's supporters took courage. They trusted that someday they would be relieved of their burdens and continued to gather regularly in Anna Inondi's house to pray. The Roho group in Ruwe at this time included Anna Inondi, Abisage Muriro, Leah Were, Nora Nyadero, Perez Atieno, Barnaba Walwoho, Isaya Goro, and Musa Ochieng. Some of the people gradually began to forget the message about *jakony*, but Anna kept the faith. All this occurred during *bonyo-osodo*,[76] the time of locusts.

Conclusion: Land, Politics, and the Spirit

In this chapter, I have taken the basic outline of Mango's life story up to 1933, as related to me by Ruwe Roho church elders. For them, this story is as much about the workings of the Holy Spirit as it is about the person of Mango. The former is an anterior and ever present actor, from its original 1912 manifestations in Ruwe, to its possession of Ibrahim Osodo, and to its anointing of Mango and its self-disclosure to others through visions and miracles. Roho oral history thus centers on a series of key events or episodes through which the plan of the Holy Spirit gradually unfolds: the Spirit's early possession of Osodo and his group expressed God's interest in the Luo inhabitants of Ugenya; the Alego vision and the Uriya forest episode established Mango's divine calling; the miraculous St. Steven's prayer constituted dramatic proof of Mango's spiritual stature; and the visions and support that Mango's followers received during his exile demonstrated the Spirit's commitment to the Roho community.

Into this narrative, I have integrated information gleaned from archival documentation and from B. A. Ogot's 1971 biographical essay. The resulting composite picture of the Roho founder is definitely more politicized than the characterization most members would offer. I do not mean to suggest that my informants were unaware of Mango's involvement in a long-standing land dispute. On the contrary, they were all too aware of this fact. Most elderly residents of Ugenya were in one way or another affected by the intertribal bitterness fueled by the lost lands controversy. The volatile quality of that period—and the hand Europeans had in creating the situation—is well remembered. That the Roho narrative does not highlight the land dispute reflects a particular socioreligious orientation that outside sources do not share. First, in the interests of harmony and in deference to the government's rhetoric of *Harambee, Nyayo,* and *Umoja,*[77] common folk did not—as of 1991— generally discuss ethnic wars from their past or animosities of the present very openly. This cautious reticence may be waning in the new national climate of multipartyism. Nevertheless, an inclination on the part of Roho members to downplay interethnic tension remains consistent with their firm belief in the universality of their religious message and their stated desire to evangelize peacefully among all peoples and races of the world. Second, although church elders do not explicitly comment on Mango's involvement in the Wanga-Kager territorial dispute unless asked, the content of the Roho narrative clearly addresses the issue of land ownership through its insistence on the efficacy of Mango's religious activities in Musanda.

To appreciate this particular symbolic content, one needs to know something of the significance of land in Luo religion and culture. In the nineteenth and early twentieth centuries, a fundamental feature of Luo society was the distinction between landowners (*weg lowo* or *jopiny,* lit., masters of the soil or people of the land) and land clients (*jodak* or *jobedo,* lit., those who stay). Frequently mislabeled "tenants" in English, *jodak* did not actually pay rent but were granted usufruct rights by their hosts in return for loyal support in battle, assistance in building and maintenance projects, and a continued attitude of respect (Wilson 1961, 56–57; Shipton 1984b, 126). Clients were commonly affines or maternal kin of their hosts, but clans eager to expand their numbers and influence would periodically take in squatters from neighboring ethnic groups, as in Kanyamkago, where Luo patrons accepted Luyia clients (Shipton 1988, 107). Neither lengthy occupancy—a client's stay could last an entire lifetime—nor faithful service entitled a client or his descendants to assume the role and rights of a landowner. Yet, it is well documented that, in practice, immigrant families frequently managed to establish themselves permanently in the territories of their patrons, either through assimilating into autochthonous lineages or through gaining supporters from outside and gradually usurping their hosts' rights, thus relegating the latter to the status of *jodak*. The fear of many patrons that they would one day be squeezed off their land, should their clients become too numerous, was therefore well founded. (Shipton 1988, 107–108; 1984b, 126; Wilson 1961, 56; Ocholla-Ayayo 1976, 126–128).

Certain Luyia subtribes, such as the Logoli and Wanga, also took in nonclan clients or strangers known as *abamenya/avamenywa*.[78] It appears that many of the restrictions placed on clients in Luoland applied to *abamenya* as well.[79] Like *jodak*, *abamenya* were expected to show respect and to publicize their patrons' virtues at beer fests. The prohibition against land clients' building permanent houses and inviting other tenants onto the land without permission similarly applied. In the 1930s, the Wanga considered many of the Luo Kager living in Wanga to be squatters. The Luo, by contrast, saw themselves as having legitimately acquired their holdings there and elsewhere in North Kavirondo through conquest prior to the Hobley wars. When Alfayo Odongo Mango began erecting houses in his Musanda compound for his Christian colleagues and welcomed parties of guests from Alego and elsewhere for extended periods, he was thus behaving as the landowner he considered himself to be. Yet, in the eyes of the Wanga community, he was brazenly violating a basic principle of clientship. Even after the Wanga Council of Elders succeeded in forcing Mango to acknowledge his tenant status, he continued to hold religious retreats, a move that, as we shall see in the next chapter, partly provoked the attack of January 1934.

That Mango habitually invoked God amid a growing circle of followers and offered special revelations as proof of his divine commission could only have outraged his neighbors further. In both Luo and Luyia culture, it was traditionally the male household head or a respected lineage elder who was responsible for addressing God and the ancestors on behalf of the community. Land clients and other dependents were ritually inferior, performing only marginal roles at sacrificial rites and ceremonies (Southall 1970, 37; Shipton 1984b, 126; Ocholla-Ayayo 1976, 128; Wagner [1949] 1970, 283–285). When Mango and his followers offered prayers in Musanda and furthermore performed miracles as proof of God's favor through the Holy Spirit, they were symbolically asserting both their social standing in the community and their claim on the land.

The emergence of the Roho movement, the lost lands controversy, and the Musanda massacre occurred when the Luo were developing a deeper emotional and ideological attachment to their land. Over the preceding four to five hundred years, the originally pastoral Luo had slowly become a predominantly agricultural people. Yet, this gradual process of sedentarization accelerated dramatically in the late nineteenth and early twentieth centuries. Increased population pressure in western Kenya, coupled with the colonial policies of land registration, freezing of tribal boundaries and the formalization of customary law, curbed the fluidity and flexibility of indigenous land acquisition systems and bound families more rigidly to particular territories. One result was an intensified identification with one's *piny* (territory) (Cohen and Atieno Odhiambo 1989, 31–33) as homelands took on increased symbolic and economic significance:

> Only a few generations ago, it appears, the Luo held no special esteem for the land per se, but tended to treat it in a matter-of-fact and utilitarian way (see Evans-Pritchard 1965, 224; Whisson 1962, 2; Ogot 1967, 38–39). People did not strongly identify themselves with particular pieces of land; they did not stay close to their ancestors' graves or conduct their rituals in fixed spots. Today, ancestral graves are the most important fixed points in a Luo's life, and the land associated with them is regarded with considerable reverence. (Shipton 1984b, 124)

Soon after Mango's death, Roho adherents began honoring Musanda as hallowed ground. They established rites that reinforced the sanctity of Musanda and constructed permanent graves for Roho pioneers in the vicinity. These efforts occurred in the 1930s and 1940s as the Luo in general were constructing and negotiating their collective identities within a rapidly changing world (Cohen and Atieno Odhiambo 1989, 31–40).

We can conclude that, although Roho elders may not specifically mention the lost lands controversy when chronicling Mango's life, their oral accounts, coupled with the church's commemorative rituals, do speak to the issue of Mango's relationship to the land. In recognizing Mango's special connection with God and the latter's endorsement of Mango's Musanda enclave, they accord him the status of a traditional *wuon lowo*, who would have been the one responsible for approaching God and the ancestors in order to ensure the well-being of his family.

Mango himself clearly believed his landholdings in Wanga to be permanent and expressed this conviction both directly (in court) and indirectly (through his religious activities). Acknowledging this fact, however, is not to interpret the Roho movement as a clever strategic component of Mango's campaign to have his land rights recognized. It is more accurate to say that Mango's efforts to claim his land were part of a larger desire to assert his community's autonomy—from missionary control, as well as from colonial interference. Finally, in our analysis of Mango's motives, we do not wish to exclude the possibility that an individual's priorities can change. In the next chapter, I suggest that, after returning from exile in April 1933, Mango turned away from involvement with the UKA and the Kager-Wanga dispute and concentrated more on church matters. Even Captain Hislop, who investigated the Roho case, came to the conclusion that "the land question had ceased to dominate his (Odongo's) thoughts."[80] Mango's retreat from property politics, my informants admit, was no doubt partly due to fear of punishment; exile had subdued him. At the same time, his association with Lawi and their open proclamation of empowerment through the Holy Spirit was by no means free of danger. In fact, the temptation to renounce the Roho message in response to mounting opposition must have been great, for local people reported that many Roho believers did abandon Mango to return to the missionaries' fold. According to the testimony of Roho elders, Mango and Lawi knew—or at least strongly suspected—that they would be killed, but, instead of abandoning course, they took steps to ensure the survival of their dispensation after they were gone. When studied closely, Mango's claim to a uniquely African Christian witness and his desire to establish a church free of European control cannot, therefore, be passed off as an opportunistic project. Even if one were to maintain that Mango was as much a political agitator as a religious leader prior to his exile, one cannot overlook the marked shift in his orientation during the nine months prior to his death. Whatever connection the Roho movement may have originally had with the lost lands controversy, in the final analysis, it was the members' conviction in their calling as agents of the Spirit that enabled them to endure persecution and ultimately face death in Musanda.

2

Rejection and Crisis

The Roho Narrative: Ten Critical Months (April 1933–January 1934)

Lawi the Helper

Lawi Obonyo is a central figure in Roho oral history. Church elders maintain that there was a long-standing and close relationship between Mango and Lawi and that the older man launched his nephew's preaching career. Following his conditional return to Musanda in April 1933, Mango was forced to keep a low profile due to government surveillance. At this point, Roho members believe, God sent them a helper (*jakony*) in the person of Lawi—an energetic individual who was able to move about with more freedom, while Mango's proselytizing was sharply curtailed.[1] The Roho narrative underscores Lawi's success as miracle worker, particularly in Alego, where he is claimed to have resurrected many dead people. Anna Inondi's account, which continues in this chapter, is the most detailed, but other versions make reference to this miracle and to Lawi's resulting confrontation with the missionaries. Archdeacon Owen's written records also document Lawi's involvement in large open-air meetings in Alego, although Owen's interpretation of events is, of course, irreconcilable with the Roho perspective. As before, in this chapter I present Inondi's narrative (elaborated by other church members) and then consider it in light of the colonial and missionary documentation.

Let us then return to the latter half of 1933 and the small circle of Joroho forced to worship privately at Inondi's home in Ruwe. The group was quietly awaiting the *jakony*, whose arrival had been promised in Inondi's dream vision. Many local Anglicans were straying from the Christian path—smoking, drinking, and reverting to witchcraft. When Inondi heard rumors about a fiery preacher named Lawi Obonyo who was bringing new life to churches throughout the district, she was heartened. Soon Lawi came to preach in Ruwe, and Inondi sent her husband, Isaya Goro, together with Barnaba Walwoho, to discover whether this young man could be the person referred to in her dream. Isaya and Barnaba returned, affirming that Lawi was indeed the *jakony*. Upon receiving the news, Inondi said to the two men, "Now let us pray that we not forget [God's promise to us]" (*Koro walam ma miwa ok wil*).

Lawi Obonyo was a carpenter who resided in Musanda with Mango, his uncle. Mango had urged Lawi to heed a dream in which he had been instructed "Spread the Word of God!" (*Land wach mar Nyasaye!*) Lawi, therefore, embarked on a career of preaching the gospel. Prior to receiving his divine call, Lawi had a reputation for selfish behavior. Inondi notes that Lawi often recalled how, prior to his conversion, his wife would cook *kuon*[2] and chicken, and the two of them would shut themselves in their home and eat it alone, a profoundly asocial act in a Luo community. After Lawi received the Spirit, however, everyone saw a marked change in the carpenter's character. He showed compassion for others and indicated that those children named after him should act in generous ways to compensate for his previous self-centeredness.

One day, not long after Baranaba and Isaya had gone to hear Lawi preach, Lawi himself suddenly appeared at Anna Inondi's house for he had heard that someone among them had been struck down by the Holy Spirit. Inondi's husband, Isaya Goro, prepared to escort Lawi next door to Daudi Arinda's home where Nora Nyadero, one of Arinda's wives, was indeed afflicted. As they were leaving, Lawi revealed that Isaya's land would one day become the site of an important church. "People from everywhere will come to pray here," he said, pointing to a field where, years later, the first Ruwe Holy Ghost church building was constructed. This was the first of Lawi's prophesies concerning the Ruwe Roho community. Some—such as this one—have already been fulfilled; other prophesies, the Joroho believe, will still come to pass.

Upon entering Arinda's home, Lawi found Nora Nyadero making grunting sounds like somebody possessed by demons. As soon as he began praying for her, the noises subsided, but he continued to pray well into the evening. Inondi explains that several days earlier Nora had approached her, inquiring what she should do "in order to see the Spirit" (*eka dine Roho*), for Nyadero had been feeling jealousy (*nyiego*)[3] toward her cowife. Her friend instructed, "If you pray and devote your heart, you will see the Spirit" (*Kilamo kendo iketo chunyi to inene Roho*).

Lawi agreed to spend the night in Arinda's home and first prayed over the blanket provided by his hosts. This practice of sanctifying new or borrowed items through prayer is still observed by some Roho members. The following morning, Lawi prayed for each individual in the home and then told the adults to wait until they heard a bell (*olang'*)[4] toll in Musanda, whereupon they should make their way to Mango's compound.

After curing Nora Nyadero, Lawi traveled southwest to Alego Hono, where an enthusiastic crowd had assembled to hear him preach. Amid the crowd were two white missionaries who were suspicious of the Roho movement. One was a schoolteacher named Miss Moller (Inondi remembers her as "Musmula").[5] The other (whose name Inondi has forgotten) was the pastor at Ng'iya at the time.[6] Lawi preached for a while and then began praying with such vigor that nearly everyone became filled with the Holy Spirit such that, according to Inondi, "all collapsed and died" (*ogore piny te motho*). In Luo, *otho* (he or she is dead) can be used to describe both a person who is comatose and someone who has actually died.[7] Traditionally, a recent death is taken as an ambiguous state, with the possibility for life to return to the body present up to the time of burial (Roscoe 1915, 288). Ruwe Pastor Daniel Were offered an explanation of the Alego miracle that builds on this indigenous understanding of the overlap between unconsciousness and death: "[A person's] soul[8] is carried up [to heaven] while the person lies absolutely silent, like a dead person" (*Ose podho to oling' thi, oter chunye malo, koro oling aling'a thi ochal ng'ama otho*). Another common response of people struck by the Holy Spirit is writhing, hyperventilating, and unintelligible grunts and shrieks—behavior traditionally exhibited by individuals possessed by spirits for the first time. In the case of possession by Roho, it is through prayer that the individual overcome with intense spiritual power regains self-control and can then effectively tap into the Spirit for productive purposes. On behalf of those who had collapsed, Lawi thus asked God first to receive their souls and teach them about heaven and then to restore them, at which time the afflicted individuals returned to their normal state. Moller, the schoolteacher, then confronted Lawi and demanded to see his permit authorizing travel and holding public prayer sessions. Lawi replied that he did not need a piece of paper giving him permission for the Lord had authorized him. Moreover, he retorted, "You who came from your homeland, who gave you a permit?" (*In ma nene ia thuru cha to ng'ano ma nene omiyi barua?*) Moller promptly reported to "Bwana" Leech that a witch doctor had come into the area, casting spells over people.[9] Roho elders recall that the missionaries wanted to detain Lawi, but they were unable to establish adequate grounds for arrest, so he was left alone for the time being.

A subsequent incident attests to the members' faith in Lawi's miraculous powers. While Lawi was preaching at Alego Hono, his son died back home. By the time Lawi received the news and returned to Musanda, the child had already been buried. In his grief, Lawi demanded a hoe, intending to dig up the grave and bring his son back to life (*ochiero*). However, Mango, who was present, urged Lawi to leave the grave alone, saying that the boy had gone to his Father. At first Lawi persisted, but then Mango convinced him to wait at least until morning. When morning arrived, Lawi was willing to forget his plan, and he and Mango prayed for the child's soul. Lawi then prepared for another journey, this time to Alego Usingo.

Many miracles occurred during the large open-air prayer meeting Lawi held under a cluster of eucalyptus trees in Alego Usingo. Inondi says that Lawi had been praying for some time when suddenly they all heard an angel of the Lord singing the following song:

> See, the angels have come down to earth singing this way. The world is now peaceful and people are happy, the Lord has visited people. The world is quiet as they listen to the song from heaven.
>
> (*Ne malaika olor e piny to ne giwer kama. Piny koro okwe ji betgi mor, Nyasaye olimo ji. To piny oling' ko winjo wer moa e polo cha.*)

Lawi exposed many sinners on that day. Wizards who kept leopards converted and came forward. People wearing *tigo* and *ris* (charms)[10] repented; as Lawi prayed, the strings of beads snapped and fell to the ground of their own accord. Other individuals stricken with disease or possessed by evil spirits presented themselves to be cured by Lawi.

Soon afterward, Lawi received a message from the angels that there was a sick girl at Alego Nyajuok. So he headed to Nyajuok, where he found Patricia Amis. Amis had been ill for two years, suffering from *chira*,[11] an incurable disease resulting from a broken taboo. Lawi saw her sins clearly and asked her to confess. Amis did so, whereupon he prayed for her and instantly cured her, enabling her to stand up and walk. This healing of Patricia Amis appears in other versions of the Roho narrative, such as the brief history of the movement written by Harrison M. Kojunju (n.d.), a young male member of the Ruwe Holy Ghost congregation in Manyatta estate in Kisumu. His account states that Lawi was in Alego Kango-nga, Bar Osimbo (not Alego Nyajuok) when he encountered Patricia "Hamsi," a "crippled woman . . . [who had] . . . never walked on her legs though she was old." Lawi "prayed for her and she walked. This was an example of Jesus's healings," Kojunju remarks. According to his version, Lawi also cured a two-month-old baby who had refused to suckle and resurrected a child who had been in the grave for two days. Moreover, while Lawi was delivering a sermon under a tree, "all sorts of birds" assembled above him to assist the crowd in singing. Both accounts indicate that a number of those who had witnessed these miracles were inspired to return with Lawi to Musanda. Inondi sets the figure at thirty and lists Stephen Orodi, Sila Chwir, Amelea Abudha, and Patricia Amis among the converts. Kojunju's record indicates that Mica Odima, Mica Olel, Peter Ngutu, and Persila Ocholla were also in the party.

Government and missionary authorities were aware of Lawi's activities in Alego in late 1933. They were not clear as to when Lawi actually moved into Mango's homestead but were under the impression that the two men did not join forces until Lawi "the prophet" had already built a significant following of his own. Archdeacon Owen and the Reverend Leech believed that it was Mango who fell completely under the sway of "the Lawi Obonyo movement."[12]

The earliest written documentation of Lawi's activities that I came across was a lengthy letter describing a nighttime prayer meeting held by Lawi in Alego

Usingo on October 23, 1933, which Archdeacon Owen, Moller, and Canon Pleydell attended (cited above). The scene as Owen describes it is amazingly consistent with what one would observe at a Roho worship service today, suggesting that basic expressive forms within the religion have not changed much in sixty years. The archdeacon opens his letter with a secondhand account of Lawi's activities, which also shares much in common with the story as preserved in the oral tradition of the Ruwe Holy Ghost Church. Members' reports of miraculous cures, demands by colonial and/or missionary officials that Lawi carry authorization papers, and, most important, claims that Lawi, in Christlike fashion, had raised people from the dead, appear in both bodies of material:

> I found Pleydell very full of a movement, supposedly religious, with which he had been dealing all morning. It appears that an old Maseno School boy, now about 22 or so (it is difficult to tell their ages) had entered Pleydell's district without seeking any recognition from Pleydell and had been holding "Holy Ghost" revival and evangelistic meetings which had been characterised by the most extravagant forms of hysteria and emotionalism. A body of about 100 from the place where this fellow, by name Lawi, was holding services, had been to Pleydell that morning, Monday 23rd, accompanied by Lawi and the local teacher, called Robert. Lawi made the most extravagant claims that he, like our Saviour, could raise the dead, heal the sick, cause the dumb to speak, the blind to see, and had with him a poor fellow suffering from elephantiasis of the leg, whom he claimed to be able to heal. At Lawi's meeting, people, pagan and baptized, dropped down in swoons in dozens, confessed their sins on coming to; had mass St. Vitus's Dance, and spent hours and hours praying, in fact morning service the previous Sunday, Oct. 22nd lasted from 9 A.M. till 6 P.M. and then went on through the night till dawn. These meetings sometimes took place under a tree, sometimes in a school and sometimes in a dwelling. Pleydell was very disturbed about the whole business, and endeavoured to reason with the more responsible people, like the local teacher, and persuade them that this all night praying and hysteria was not of God. The only impression he thinks he left was that he "was outside the movement" and had not yet received the baptism of the Holy Spirit. Something like this was pretty fully hinted at.[13]

What Owen and his colleagues observed when they made their surprise appearance at the prayer meeting horrified them. The "hysterical" dancing, the "tumult" of rhythmic hymns, and comatose "lads with their heads in the laps of a couple of hefty wenches" struck their puritanical sensibilities as lurid and out of control. When Lawi prepared to resurrect the two young men, Owen challenged him outright:

> Up to this time I had been feeling my way cautiously as to what I should do. It was an excited gathering and a wrong word from me might let loose forces of disorder, which I should have difficulty controlling. Besides I had to think

of Miss Moller's presence. However, when Lawi boldly asserted that the huddled lads were the "SIGN", the "SIGN", I felt I had my clue. I asked him very distinctly did he assert in the face of the gathering that the lads were dead, and that he would raise them. He emphatically repeated his assertion. I asserted that they were not dead and that he was deceiving the people.[14]

Owen then proceeded to shake and pinch the two youths on the floor; they did not respond. He tried to prove to the crowd that the young men were alive by making a display of taking their pulses, but people were apparently unconvinced:

> I now felt that I had prepared the people for a stronger denunciation of the prophet so I boldly accused him in the plainest language of being a "Deceiver". I rubbed this in for a few moments, and then thought it was about time to make an effort to get the gathering to disperse. My prestige was such that I thought Lawi would find it difficult to openly rebel against a determined effort on my part. So I said that I wanted the gathering to disperse.[15]

After an argument with Lawi and resistance from the assembly, the archdeacon did manage to bring the worship session to a close. However, he completely failed to rouse the two unconscious youths and finally handed them over to the district officer, who was camped a few miles away, where they eventually came back to their senses.[16]

Archdeacon Owen staked his reputation on being the champion of the native against burdensome colonial laws, yet the Lawi affair is one of a number of cases demonstrating that Owen and his colleagues worked in league with the administration to suppress indigenous initiatives of which they disapproved. The archdeacon supported Canon Pleydell's request that the district officer enforce colonial boundaries and have Lawi sent back to North Kavirondo:

> When interviewing the A.D.C.[17] in the middle of the night, Pleydell pointed out that Lawi belonged to North Kavirondo and was operating in Central Kavirondo, and asked if it would be possible to deport Lawi under the Native Authority Ordinance back to North Kavirondo. This the A.D.C. said he thought could be done. Pleydell had written him his request first thing on the following morning, and when we again visited the camp, Lawi had just been brought in.[18]

Once Lawi had been returned to Musanda, Owen saw to it (through the vehicle of the District Church Council) that Lawi "was put under the charge" of Mango.[19] The Church Council sat in Maseno on November 15, 1933, and called Lawi, Mango, Silvano Nyamogo, and "one Yohana" to be brought before them. According to Owen's detailed description of the proceedings, it is clear that Lawi was expressing considerable defiance toward church authorities:

[Lawi] fixed on my eyes a most intense concentrated gaze, which he maintained for well over half-an-hour. In this respect his behavior was most
abnormal; and attracted the attention of the whole Council. I have reluctantly come to the opinion that he was definitely trying on me that power of
the eye, whether hypnotic or not, which experience had shown him he
could exercise over many of those who attended his meetings and fell down
in "hysterical fits."[20]

Moreover, Lawi's responses to the council's queries reflects a firm conviction in
the integrity of his own mission:

Questioned with the utmost particularity, [Lawi] would not budge from the
position that while he must accept my evidence that the two lads I saw, who,
he had said, were dead, had good pulses and were, in fact, not dead, yet with
regard to others whom I had not seen (some two score or more) they were
really and absolutely dead. "Chunygi ochot" they had given up the ghost was
his claim. He ended by declaring that time would show whether or not the
movement was of God.[21]

Lawi was here referring to the large revival held on Sunday, October 22, in Alego
Usingo, the memory of which, as indicated previously, has been well preserved
in Roho oral tradition. Interestingly enough, the remark "time will tell" is still
used today by members of Roho churches in response to those who question the
authenticity of their dispensation.

According to the C.M.S. record of the council meeting, Mango denied backing Lawi's actions or even being privy to them. Therefore, after condemning "the
hysterical character of Lawi's meetings," the council ordered Mango "to restrain
Lawi's unauthorized activities, and generally be responsible for his good behav-
iour."[22] Captain Hislop later observed, however, that this order proved wholly
ineffective, as Lawi and Silvano Nyamogo promptly resumed their preaching
tours in Alego.[23]

Mango's and Lawi's Followers Gather at Musanda

The Ruwe Roho elders explain that before Lawi Obonyo went to Alego Nyajuok
(to cure Patricia Amis), he had spread the message that his and Mango's followers
should gather at Musanda on December 1, 1933. This call was still evidently in
effect despite the District Church Council's November 15 ruling. Anna Inondi
remembers that Lawi returned to Musanda from Alego on November 30. The
following day, many of the Holy Spirit group assembled in the house that Mango
had constructed in his compound for the purpose of daily worship. The practice
was to summon believers with a bell rung at six in the morning and six in the
evening. On December 1, Lawi, Mango, and their followers prayed together
from eight in the morning until four in the afternoon, after which time most of

the gathering dispersed. Others such as Barnaba Walwoho and Abisage Muriro from Ruwe remained behind with Mango and Lawi, as well as the group of approximately thirty followers from Alego who had moved into Mango's compound in Musanda. Indeed, this version of events is corroborated by Captain Hislop's report, which states that in December "followers began leaving their homes in order to reside for a period at Musanda where they would be taught by Lawi. Iwinda boma became a 'resort' of people from Alego principally and also from Ugenya, Buholo and Wanga."[24]

Inondi recalls that on the evening of December 1, after people had concluded their session in Mango's chapel, it was proposed that those who remained should move to Lawi's house to continue their prayer. Mango asked if he were invited: "May I also go and pray with you?" (*Abende dadhiye kodu mondo alam?*) Lawi responded, "How can we stop you from going to pray? Just come and let's pray" (*To kendo wan dong' wasindi lamo nadi? Bi abiya wadhi walem*). Mango thus entered Lawi's house. Rael Oloyo, Mango's wife, was with them, as was Kiloyi Odimo, Lawi's wife.

When asked about the possibility of rivalry between Mango and Lawi, Roho members repeatedly assert that there was none. Lawi "the Helper" simply stepped in to take on a more active role as Mango's movements were increasingly curtailed by the Europeans. Some go so far as to say that the Holy Spirit was transmitted through Mango to Lawi, empowering the latter to perform the miracles for which he became famous. Yet the brief exchange between the two men cited previously does suggest that the authorities' perceptions that there was friction between Mango and Lawi may not have been entirely unfounded.

According to Inondi, the Christians spent twelve days in December praying in Lawi's home. Supporters and other members of the Roho movement brought them food. For example, one day Isaya Goro (Inondi's husband) arrived in Musanda with two cocks and some grain for them. During this twelve-day period, several people received the Holy Spirit and were sent out as disciples or messengers (*joote*) to spread the word in their home areas. The first *joote* were Nora Nyadero from Ruwe and Sila Chwir and Stephan Orodi, both from Alego.

Jaote (sing.) Nora Nyadero proved to be quite successful in Ruwe, and people gathered to listen to her preach. After her return to Musanda a week later, the Christians with whom she had worshiped remained together for two more days, praying in the home of Isaya Goro. Then, the entire group proceeded from Isaya's home in Ruwe to Musanda, where they joined the rest of Mango's followers for a month of retreat. Iwinda, Mango's village at Musanda, was thus unmistakably becoming a major locus of the Roho movement in North and Central Nyanza. Despite church council orders, Mango quietly condoned Lawi's proselytizing, and the former's home emerged as a base for Holy Spirit converts.

Archdeacon Owen's records indicate that in December Mango openly flouted mission authority for the first time. On November 29, Owen received a letter from Pastor G. S. Okoth in Alego, asking whether his colleague, the Reverend

Alfayo Odongo Mango, might be permitted to present his candidates for confirmation together with Okoth's candidates in Hono, Alego, rather than at Butere, the seat of Mango's home pastorate. Alego, as we have seen, is Luo territory; Butere is in Bantu country. Owen was determined not to let Mango "make a cat's-paw" of the church:

> I regarded [Okoth's request] as an attempt to assert through the Church that which the civil authorities had decided [the Kager in Musanda] were not entitled to assert, i.e., that they should be independent of the authority in whose area they resided. That authority in our Church matters was the missionary in charge at Butere, Mr. Leech. I therefore, returned an answer that the request could not be granted, and that the Rev. A. Odongo [Mango] was to present his candidates at Butere. Alufayo thereupon saw Mr. Leech at Butere who examined his candidates, and Alufayo arranged to bring them to Butere on the 6th.[25]

However, when the bishop arrived in Butere on December 6 to conduct the confirmation ceremony, Mango and his candidates did not appear. Again, on December 20, Mango "absented himself" without explanation from the District Church Council meeting at Maseno. In Owen's eyes, Mango thus repudiated "his canonical vow of obedience to the Bishop and authorities of the Anglican Church."[26]

Another occasion on which Mango openly ignored the mission authorities was the Musanda church service of December 17. This particular service has been kept alive in the collective memory of Roho members as an important "sign" (*rang'i*) of the Holy Spirit among them.[27] On that Sunday, some members of the Anglican church on the hill, known colloquially as Musanda Luo, wished to have their children baptized. Inondi explained that Mango was the only one present who was authorized to baptize and that he was wearing the appropriate cassock (*kanzu*). However, because of his notoriety and the consequent abuse that his supporters had been receiving, he decided to move into the background. Mango therefore removed his cassock and placed it on Lawi, symbolically authorizing the latter to offer the sacrament of baptism. As Lawi began to baptize the children, there was an uproar within the church. People protested that Lawi, who had no pastoral training and had not been appointed by the archdeacon, had no legitimate right to baptize. Furious, many members of the congregation stormed out. Even some of Mango's previous supporters objected to this act, abruptly dissociated themselves from the movement, and returned to their own homes after the service rather than to Iwinda with the rest of the Joroho. Undaunted, Lawi continued to baptize those children who were brought forward, among them Jeremiah Ogutu, Damar Atieno, Zadock Omondi, and Persila Adongo.

In the middle of Lawi's prayer for the children, a violent earthquake rocked the stone church until it almost collapsed. The Lord "had seen the sinful an-

noyance of the people" (*nene koro oneno rach mar kecho mar dhano*), explained
Inondi. "The people in heaven came and shook the building so that people
would recognize the power of the Lord" (*Nene jopolo obiro go moyiengo ayienga
ot mondo ging'e teko mar Nyasaye man kanyo*). The story of this violent storm is
known by many Roho Christians and takes different forms. Elijah J. O. Ayodo, a
former member of the Musanda Holy Ghost Church who recently established his
own Roho denomination, mentions the storm in one of his pamphlets but
combines it with the legend of Mango's head touching the sky (discussed in
chapter 1):

> When Alfayo stood praying, Owen noted him standing on earth with his
> head reaching heaven; a windy rain removed the roof of the church and
> replaced it after the rain stopped. The people in the Church became wet
> some of them deserted the Church looking for shelter, but Alfayo and his few
> f[o]llowers remained dry in the Church. (Ayodo 1990, 1)

Eyewitness Ibrahim Owuor Mango, Mango's son, recalled that the earthquake
was accompanied by gusts of wind and torrential rain. Ibrahim was a Maseno
schoolboy at the time, at home for the Christmas holidays. The Roho group had
received a divine message in advance, foretelling the occurrence of a miracle
during that Sunday's church service, and Ibrahim and his friends had eagerly
attended, determined not to miss anything. Ibrahim remembers that, as rain
pounded the roof, his father stood up in front of the congregation. First, he
prayed for the storm to end and then instructed everyone to come and stand
before Lawi. Lawi peered into the eyes of the people, pulling down the lower
eyelids of each person with his finger in order to determine who had the Holy
Spirit and who did not. He told those individuals with the Spirit to step to the
right, those without to move to the left. Lawi spared no one.[28] Even the evangelists were subjected to the test, and not everyone passed! Of course, this incident
further infuriated people.

A letter written by Archdeacon Owen in February 1934 contains a thirdhand
account of this very same service. Owen interprets the transfer of robes as indicative of Lawi's having usurped Mango's authority rather than as an intentional
conferral of responsibility by the deacon:

> It was at this [December 17th] service that [a Luo master at Butere Normal
> School] and many others were scandalized, by seeing when the officiating
> persons entered the church that Lawi was robed in Alufayo's full robes,
> Alufayo being without any. Lawi now usurped the position of leadership,
> telling Alufayo that he must take second place to him, Lawi. At this service it
> was announced that Holy Communion would be celebrated on Christmas
> Day. Alufayo was a deacon, not a priest, but Lawi had announced in Octo-
> ber that if we did not recognize his "laying on of hands" he would institute
> his own rites of Holy Communion.[29]

The remainder of Owen's brief account contains two features that are also central
to the Roho version, the storm being perceived as a sign from God, and the
separation "of the sheep from the goats":

> A violent storm of rain and wind descended which beat through the open
> windows & drove the congregation to huddle in various parts of the building
> where its effect was least felt. Alufayo and Lawi began excited prayers to God
> to avert the storm and bring peace, but the storm went on. The Luo teacher,
> with others, left the building for shelter in another nearby, till the storm
> passed, when they returned only to find themselves the subject of that por-
> tion of the sermon, the preacher announcing that it had been revealed that
> the storm had been sent to separate the sheep from the goats, those who had
> left the building temporarily being the goats and in utter darkness. [30]

It would appear that the December 17 service precipitated a struggle between
the Roho faction and their opponents over the use of Musanda Luo. As Anna
Inondi put it, "That's the day the division occurred" (*Odiochiengno ema pogruok
obietie*). [31] According to her, those members who had been angered by Mango's
and Lawi's actions accused them of "having been corrupted" (*ose kethore*) and
went the following day to report to the district commissioner and the missionary
authorities. They complained that their church was being monopolized by the
Joroho. On January 6, the matter was brought before the Wanga Tribunal, which
ruled that "the use of the buildings must remain with those loyal to the original
organization (the C.M.S.) and that the separatists must worship elsewhere." [32]
Inondi recalls that officials arrived at Musanda Luo with *askeche* (tribal retainers), [33] intent on chasing Mango's followers out of the building. "The church
belongs to the missionaries," Mango's group was told. "If you are opposed, you
will have to pray at home." Many felt this decision to be unfair; not only had
Mango built that stone church with his own hands, but also he was the one
largely responsible for introducing Christianity to Musanda in the first place.

The Month of January 1934

The Roho group concluded that it would be risky to continue attending Sunday
services at Musanda Luo, but they did visit their church on the hill on weekday
evenings when no one else was there. They would leave Mango's compound at
dusk and run to Musanda Luo hill—a kilometer away—in order to reach the
church and return home before sunset, a fact mentioned in the district officer's
report as well. [34]

During these evening prayer sessions in the church, Inondi recalls, individuals emerged within the Roho group who could predict future events. They
were called *jokorwach* (prophets, or foretellers). [35] Among them were Amelea
Abudha, Abednego Otin, and Anna Lang'o. All were from Alego. Other leaders

within the Roho group began coming forward to assume new roles. As Officer Hislop later rightly observed, "there were indications of the small section organising itself."[36]

On January 6, the day of the Wanga Tribunal, and again on January 14, the Reverend Leech and Archdeacon Owen made an attempt to see and "reason with" Mango, but he shut himself in his house and refused to receive the missionaries. Owen remarks, "The atmosphere of awe which [Mango] had created in the minds of his followers was extraordinary. He had adopted a policy of withdrawing himself from view, and remained secluded, invisible in his house from whence he issued his instructions."[37] Mango's wife later told Owen that her husband had refused to see them because he had been observing forty days of silence, "following the example of our Saviour who fasted for forty days in the wilderness."[38]

It is clear, however, that Mango was not observing silence with his followers, according to both administrative records and the oral tradition. Hislop's report contains detailed information about the activities of the Musanda Roho community from January 1 through the fatal fire of January 21, and it is evident that Mango and Lawi were in fact preaching, communicating visions, and establishing an organizational structure that would outlive them. As I proceed to describe this important period in the life of the Roho church, Anna Inondi's version of events again serves as the basic narrative, with the written sources to revise and augment her story.

During the month of January, Inondi explained, the followers of Lawi and Mango remained closed within the latter's home in Musanda. Due to the hostility of the local people (particularly the Wanga), the Joroho were not free to come and go. It was unsafe for them even to venture into Mango's outlying fields to collect cassava and other vegetables. Thus, they had to rely on donations brought secretly by supporters. The congregation often went hungry, but their faith was strong and they remained happy.

Both written and oral sources show that Mango's followers were sometimes beaten by other villagers. Inondi explained that women might travel to Musanda on their own just to join Mango's community. Yet, their husbands would frequently track them down and drag them home, beating them all the way. The women never failed to return, however, for, in the words of Ibrahim Owuor Mango, "their thoughts were focused only on Heaven."

Most of the Joroho had already been confirmed in the Anglican church. At some point in early January, they received a second confirmation (*nwang'o lwedo*)[39] from Mango, this time "in the Spirit" (*mar Roho*). The people gathered in the chapel within Mango's homestead and knelt before him. There were Anna Inondi, Barnaba Walwoho, Isaya Goro, Abisage Muriro, Leah Were, Julia Omol, and Musa Muga from Ruwe and many others from distant places. Placing his hands gently on the head of each one in turn, Mango said:

Christ, when you come, you've said you will give us the Holy Spirit; you've also promised to give us help and a clean heart/soul. You have come to give us work, this is indeed the work that we are doing. Strengthen the hearts of your people so that they are strong and follow your way.

(*Kristo kibiro iwacho ni mondo imiwa Roho Maler, kendo iwacho ni mondo imiwa kony gi chuny maler. Ibiro ni mondo imiwa tich, to mani e tich ma watiyo. Jiwo chuny jogi obed motegno oluw wang' yori.*)

After the blessing, the candidates each received communion in the form of a piece of wheat bread and a drink of orange juice.

As public opposition increased, the Joroho feared that they might be blocked from going to Musanda Luo in the evening. Therefore, one morning they rose at about four, just after the cock crowed. They made it peacefully to the church on the hill, completed their prayers, and had just started back down the hill when they heard people calling one another to bring machetes and clubs in order to attack Mango's party. Most of the shouts were in Kiluyia, indicating that the Wanga had joined forces with the Anglicans against the followers of Mango and Lawi.

A large angry crowd descended on the small unarmed group of Christians. Roho elders claim that the attackers beat Barnaba Walwoho until he died; Johana Omwayo, Barnaba Ogano, and a youth from Ulwan were injured. The women were spared; some of the younger ones fled, while others carried Walwoho's body back to Mango's home. Everyone prayed for Barnaba, particularly Lawi:

Lord, you hear how we are beseeching you, this is not a death we had expected. How can our friend die at the hands of an evil person? If you consent, let him arise and live.

(*Nyasaye, iwingo kaka koro wakwayi, mani ok en tho ma nende wang'eyo. Osiepwa ni tho nadi e lwet ng'ama rach. Kiyie ochung' obed mangima.*)

As Lawi was uttering these words, Barnaba suddenly jumped to his feet and cried: "Put your hearts in the Holy Spirit! Don't be afraid, just continue with prayer" (*Un keturu chunyu kuom Roho Maler! Kik uluor, dhi uru mana nyime kod lamo*).[40] Tradition has it that a drunkard named Elijah Siguru Ohola had arrived on the scene, beer straw in hand, to view the body of the man killed in battle. When he discovered that Barnaba had been brought back to life, he was so astonished that he broke his straw in half and converted on the spot. From that day forward, Siguru never again touched alcohol and became an active participant in the Roho movement.

After the attack on the hill, the Joroho stopped going to Musanda Luo altogether. They remained in Mango's homestead, worshiping there. Occasionally, Mango sent representatives to try to persuade members of other Anglican congregations to join the worship at Musanda.[41] These messengers would form a small band, singing the following song as they marched from village to village:

Chung'i Jakristo, ne jasiki cha, bedi ka jachir mar Yesu.
(Stand up Christian, look at that enemy of yours, be like a brave person of Jesus.)

Kik uluor Saitan, kata tekone, gen Yesu Kristo ni wach Nyasaye.
(Don't be afraid of Satan, or his power, trust in Jesus Christ because of the word of God.)

Aye nindo bedo ka jakedo, chung'i ikedi, wana lo Saitan.
(Wake up and be like a warrior, stand firm and fight, we will overcome Satan.)

Kik waluori, Yesu en jatelo oseloyo lweny gi tekone.
(Let's not be afraid, Jesus is the leader, he has won the war with his power.)

Kaw uru okumba yie gi ogut konyruok kendo ligangla mar muya.
(Take the shield of acceptance and the helmet of assistance, also take the sword of air.)

Kik uwe lamo, mani e tekoni, Yesu okonyo askeche ne.
(Don't neglect to pray, for this is your power, Jesus helps his soldiers.)

When glimpsing these small bands approaching, strangers sometimes mistook the Joroho's determination for aggression and would run and hide in their granaries.[42] In other instances, the Roho messengers were ridiculed. For example, on his way to beckon people in Mahondo, Isaya Goro met a man named Thoma Ooko who was a catechist at the Madungu Anglican church. Ooko denounced Isaya's leader saying, "Too much prayer has made him [Mango] mad!" (*Lamo mang'eny omiye neko!*) Ooko remarked that the archdeacon was about to visit Got Osimbo. What, then, could possibly tempt one to join the followers of a madman from Musanda when one could hear the archdeacon preach nearby? Thoma Ooko was a sick man, however, and died before ever making it to Got Osimbo. Inondi's implication that he had made the wrong choice is clear!

Isaya Goro, who returned to Musanda with only one convert, reported that rumors were circulating to the effect that Mango was insane. Mango then turned to his close kin (*jo anyuola ne machiegni kanyo*) for support but was unsuccessful. He sent a group of women out to try to persuade their own clan members to come pray with the Joroho, but, wherever the women went, people heard their marching song and fled.

During the first few weeks of January 1934, amid a growing atmosphere of isolation and ostracism, Mango made a series of predictions about the future state of the country. He proclaimed that roads would one day be built in the area and that alongside these roads houses roofed with *mabati* (corrugated iron sheeting) would appear, which would serve as shops. He also predicted that a time would come when the money people used would not be stamped with a picture of King George, but would bear the head of an African. Power would no longer rest with Europeans but with African people. Inondi maintains that Mango's vision of the future entailed a unified Africa with one king to rule over the entire continent. The general secretary of the Ruwe Holy Ghost Church, Zadock Ochoma, suggests, however, that Mango envisioned many African nations: "The Apostle Mango prophesized the end of colonial rule in Africa . . . saying that a time [would] come when all those oppressed and being enslaved would become masters of their respective countries" (Ochoma 1991, 2, spelling corrected). Ochoma also claims that Mango urged people to "fully utilize their land," to "be clean," and to send their children to school—an assertion that Mango's son's testimony contradicts. As an educated man himself who works at the Information and Broadcasting Office in Kisumu, Ochoma's claim that Mango saw ignorance as "one of the worst enemies of mankind" may be a reinterpretation of the spirit of Mango's message within contemporary assumptions about empowerment and progress. Ochoma's articulation of Mango's words and intentions must be considered carefully, for it represents the view of a growing segment of more recent Roho converts.

Records suggest that the colonial officials were suspicious of Mango's movement but that neither they nor the missionaries were actually aware that Mango was making such "political" prophesies until they conducted investigations following his death. On February 1, 1934, Archdeacon Owen wrote:

> Early in December, Alufayo began to exhibit marked symptoms of religious hallucination, telling his eldest son that God was so close to him that he could handle Him and feel Him, and relating weird "visions" and dreams, one of which was that his son would see him no more and that God was going to take him to "*od panga*" [a *mabati*-roofed house] in heaven. Of this the son informed me after the tragedy. Another, which he preached about, was that there was going to be six days darkness on the earth, and after it none of the ungodly would be found alive, only those of the sect.[43]

I did not hear Roho members mention the particular prophesies which Owen lists, but such predictions are consistent with the increasingly millennial character of the Roho group in December 1933 and January 1934.

According to the Roho narrative, Mango's final days were marked by several miracles that attest to his divine selection. One occurred just before dawn on January 16, when Anna Inondi and the other women adherents were rising to attend prayers at the small church within Mango's compound. (It was common for believers to pray at dawn in the early days of the movement.) Mango, Lawi, and several other male leaders were also awakening in Mango's house, where they had spent the night together. Lawi came to the women's house to borrow some kerosene to light a lamp, for it was still dark and the leaders were having difficulty putting on their clerical robes. The kerosene was all used up, however, so Lawi returned to the men while the women began to make their way to the church. Someone then rang the church bell, and Lawi was heard to remark, "Oh, my Lord, what shall we do? People have entered [the prayer house], how can we manage [without any light]?" (*Ay Nyasacha, tin watimore nadi, ma ji to ose donjo, tin wabed nadi?*) Suddenly the women saw that Mango's house was filled with an abnormally bright light, surpassing the light cast by a lamp. It lit up the entire house and even flowed out over the gap between the wall and the roof (*yiend ambewa*). The women were astounded: "Oh! What is glittering so brilliantly inside that house?" (*Eh! To gima kakini mana e ot kakini ni en gima nadi?*) Lawi, too, confessed his astonishment:

Oh people, the light came to us, we didn't have a lamp and I was just marveling [at it]. We used it to dress as if it were a lighted lamp, we didn't have kerosene.

(*Yawa, ler obiro nwa, manende waonge taya, bu bende awuoro awuora, bu koro wa rwakore mana kod taya mar ler no. Nende waonge mafuta.*)[44]

The Joroho had planned to raise their own flag and appoint a "king" on the morning of January 16, and they took the miraculous light as a sign that the Holy Spirit approved of their plan. Some months earlier, the Spirit of God had appeared to Odongo Mango, asking him whether he would prefer to rule the world or to rule in the kingdom of God. Mango responded that he would choose heaven. The Lord told him that he had made a good choice[45] but cautioned him not to neglect the world, for, after Mango was gone, the world would suffer. "Before you die, establish an example (*ranyisi*) of a king," God instructed him.

Mango and Lawi looked for volunteers to set an example of kingship. They approached many men, but all refused. They wanted Daniel Ongeche from the chief's camp at Ambira to stand as king. He was a Kager and widely feared, but Ongeche refused to join Mango's followers. So they searched for another candidate and settled on Elijah Oloo, one of the three men deported with Mango in April 1932 and member of the Kamlwang' clan.[46] Elijah Oloo agreed, saying that because he was capable, he would offer himself (*oyie ochiwore owuon ni adwa, anyalo*).

On the morning of January 16, more than two hundred fifty Joroho lined up with clubs and sticks in Mango's compound. Upon Lawi's order, they marched single file past Elijah who stood completely still before them. As they passed, each person hit him twice. The understanding was that, if Elijah proved able to withstand the beating, then Africa would one day definitely get its king.[47] However, if Elijah had run, Daniel Were explained to me, "we would have known that the power of the blacks would not win out" (*wang'eye ni loch mar jorateng'ni, ok wanyal yudo loch*). Elijah stood fearlessly, withstanding blow after blow. No blood was shed, but he finally fainted from the beating. He was wrapped in a

white cloth as though dead and carried to Mango's house, where several participants prayed for him. The prayers returned him to consciousness (*oduoko chunye
kendo*), and he soon recovered, emerging from the house to stand before a
fascinated crowd that included many newcomers, who had arrived to witness the
unusual event.

The Joroho then held a celebration (*nyasi*). Elder Johana Omina was present
and described the scene as follows: People formed a large circle in the center of
Mango's compound. Elijah Oloo stood at the center of the circle, still cloaked in
the white sheet his colleagues had wrapped around him after his collapse. Someone then erected a short flagpole next to Mango's house and raised a small flag.
People watched, stood "at attention," shouldered their sticks like rifles,[48] and
honored the flag. There was some confusion among the elders I interviewed as to
the color of this original flag. Inondi, for example, recalled that it was red,
whereas Johana Omina claimed it was a tricolor flag, made from blue, red, and
white cloth.[49] Regardless of the color, all my informants agreed that raising the
flag was symbolic of the fact that, just as other peoples had their own rulers, one
day blacks "would also have power" (*bende biro bedo kod loch*). While standing at
attention, the crowd sang:

> *Chung' uru Jokristo, luor uru bendera,*
> (Stand up, Christians, show respect to the flag,)
>
> *Ka uyikore un duto lando wach Nyasaye.*
> (If you all prepare to spread the word of God.)
>
> *Kuonde ma udhiye we uru Osana,*
> (Wherever you go, sing "Hosana,")
>
> *Yesu ema oloyo malo cha!*
> (Jesus is the victor up there [in heaven]!)

Mango's wife, Rael Oloyo, then brought Elijah Oloo a cup of water to drink and
placed upon his head a "headdress of power" (*kondo mar loch*). Oloo sat on a
traditional Luo stool (*kom nyaluo*) with a woman named Persila Obel representing his queen crowned beside him.[50] Once both were seated, a taller red flag was
erected just outside the compound gate.

The crowning of the king is remembered by Roho members as an event of
great significance. Every year on January 16, Roho pilgrims commemorate the
occasion by raising flags in Ibrahim Mango's compound and by paying homage to
Elijah's grave, whose headstone reads "Kingi Elijah Oloo" on one side and its
translation in Dhoroho[51] on the other. However, it is not easy to ascertain in
what way the founding Roho community considered its king to be important or
what role he was expected to fill. On the one hand, elders recounting the oral
history of the church referred to Oloo's coronation as a "symbolic ceremony"
(*nyasi mar rang'isi*), suggesting that the Joroho acknowledged that this coronation

conferred no actual political power on him. The overall impression I received was that this ceremony was important in the sense that it offered a vivid foretaste of national independence, a promise of what was to come.

On the other hand, the title of king seems to have carried definite responsibilities along with it, such as assisting Mango and Lawi in appointing leaders for the Roho community. In fact, historian B. A. Ogot sees 'King' Elijah Oloo not as a figurehead but as the official whose function was to "deal with all external matters." Ogot, like the district officer who investigated the Musanda massacre, views the flag ceremony as evidence that the Roho sect was organizing itself politically. Ogot explains that Mango and his followers were essentially in "a state of siege" at Iwinda and, in response, began organizing themselves on "a quasi-military basis":

> Mango, assisted by Lawi Obonyo . . . became the spiritual head of the community. Like Christ, he chose "twelve disciples" from amongst his faithful followers. Elijah Oloo was appointed 'King' to deal with all external matters, and he was given a red flag as a symbol of his authority. . . . A flag pole was erected in the centre of the village from which a red flag flew, and around which the Jo-Roho sang their moving and highly original hymns. It was also around this flag pole that open air prayer meetings were held. Lawi Obonyo undertook to train soldiers and Silvana Nyamogo became Captain of the garrison. A women's wing was also formed led by Dorisilla Nyayonga, Norah Opondo and Turfosa Aloo. The pass-word was 'One Religion.' (Ogot 1971, 105)

The elders I spoke with made no mention of twelve disciples or a special pass-word, but they did state that on January 18, two days after the coronation, Mango, Lawi, and *Kingi* Elijah designed an administration (*gichano kaka ji tiyo* [they planned how people would work]) to ensure the smooth running of the Roho group. Mango felt that his death was imminent, and he wanted to make arrangements so that his community would remain intact after he was gone.

Mango, in consultation with his cadre of close male followers, decided that Lawi Obonyo would be the archbishop and Barnaba Walwoho would be the bishop. They selected Silvano Nyamogo and Isaya Goro to be the church catechists. The former had been educated by missionaries, and the latter obtained a basic education in the army; both were thus deemed fit to serve as teachers. Josiah Obala, who taught at the teacher training college in Kericho, was placed in charge of secular education. Mango himself did not have a post, for he was above even the archbishop. Mango is variously described as "their leader" (*jatendgi*), "the head of the church" (*otelo ni kanisa*), and "the head of everything" (*jatend weche duto*). Pastor Daniel Were stated that, when Mango explained the administration to Barnaba Walwoho, he invoked the image of a house with an upper story (*orofa*): "Now we will leave; you will hear our footsteps on the upper floor" (*Koro in ema wabiro weyi, niwinj woche tiendwa ei orofa*). Mango and Lawi, residing on top (heaven), would convey messages to Barnaba, who would, in turn, relay the orders to the rest of the congregation. When people had problems, they were to present them to Barnaba, who would, in turn, communicate them to Mango and Lawi. Lawi and Mango would approach God if necessary; thus, the status of the two founders as intercessors was established.

Once the new administration was in place, Mango preached to his disciples (*jopuonjre*) with a number of important instructions about how they should carry on. (1) They were advised to remember that the colonial government still had power over them. Mango told his listeners to mark the date when their hut taxes were due and to take them to the proper authorities in advance so that officials would not badger them. Control of Africa by Africans would come in the future, but, in the meantime, people should be patient and cooperate. (2) However, Mango also indicated that, as soon as they learned of any movement or effort to unite blacks, the Joroho should join in wholeheartedly. (3) He counseled respect for brothers and sisters who had not joined the Roho community and urged his followers not to view others as "standing on the wrong side" (*gichung marach*), for they were all one. (4) Disciples should heed the Holy Spirit only. Mango warned his disciples against listening to former colleagues at Musanda Luo who had sided with the missionaries, for they would never amount to anything. He then invoked a parable about a magician named Omolo Wangoya who gave advice but was ridiculed by his own people. As a result, their enemies prevailed throughout the land, and everyone suffered. Mango warned that the same fate would befall the Joroho if they ignored his advice. (5) Finally, Mango urged his followers not to stop praying. "If you see people confused and in a flurry, pray so that they calm down" (*Ka uneno ka ji tungini, to ulam mondo giwe tungini*). He also stressed the importance of praying for widows, orphans, and the sick.

Mango's sermons during his final days expanded on these main themes of prayer, patience, guidance by the Holy Spirit, and respect for existing authority. His teachings thus advocated strategic quiescence until such time as a revolt against oppression became feasible. There was no doubt that such a time would come, however, and he urged his faithful to remain happy, secure in the promise that one day Africans would control their own destinies.

War, Fire, and Death in Musanda

Captain Hislop reported that during the month of January 1934, the Joroho engaged in three activities that got them into trouble with the government: first, the removal of school equipment from Musanda Luo; second, attempts to force individuals loyal to the C.M.S. to join the Roho group and send their children to Lawi's school in Mango's compound; and, third, raids on nearby *bomas* to obtain food for the many mouths at Iwinda. Owen had written in his correspondence with government officials and with other missionaries that Mango's followers used threats to pressure people to join them and predicted terrible fates for those who refused to convert. Yet, the Roho elders I spoke with insisted that they never tried to coerce others into accepting the Holy Spirit. Admittedly, people used to run away whenever bands of Roho representatives approached, but this was not the fault of the latter. One elder told me, "We find that the power we have makes others scared; they don't even want to come near us" (*Wanuang'o ka pawa ma wankodo jogi koro luor aluora, koro ok gidwar kata biro kodwa machiegni*).

It may well be that attempts by Roho members to approach frightened, reluctant individuals were taken as a provocation. This is probably what occurred at the home of Isaya Goro's cousin Lazaro Gombe in Muroro, where, according to Inondi's testimony, Mango had sent a number of Joroho to proselytize. When the Roho party arrived at Gombe's homestead, the residents ran inside one of the houses and locked the door. The Joroho stood outside making appeals:

> Just come and hear what is being said with your own ears. If you reject [the Roho message], at least you will have heard it [yourselves] and can then leave the matter to us.
>
> (*Uwinjye awinja gik ma iwacho kod itu. Kata udag to uwinjo, chieng' du uwe nwa bura.*)

Suddenly, a spear burst through the papyrus-reed door from within and struck Daniel Ondego, a man from Alego, in the calf. A second spear followed, hitting Isaya Goro in the chest. Isaya's cousin Lazaro Gombe was then heard to exclaim, "I have speared you with my spear called 'Nyaldiema.'[52] Let me see if you can heal yourself!" (*Achuowi gi tong' Nyaldiema, aneye ka ikwoye ware!*) Defeated, the Roho party carried their two wounded members back to Musanda, where Lawi prayed for them. Isaya remained there to convalesce; Daniel Ondego went back to his home in Alego.

Unfortunately, we do not have a firsthand account of the other side of the story. Archdeacon Owen's version presents Gombe's family as victims and lacks any reference to injuries sustained by the Roho party:

> [On the night of Saturday, January 20][53] Lawi's fold entered five huts of Christians faithful to us (one of whom was Lazaro Gombe) who had refused to join him, took about a score of fowls and other property, damaged the huts and remained till morning endeavoring to force them to join them.

Owen then explains that Gombe was rushed to Kakamega with a slightly wounded arm, while the girls living in the "raided kraal, fled the place."[54] Captain Hislop, who had consulted with Owen and was no doubt influenced by his testimony, referred to the unfortunate event as a "vindictive raid" visited on "a loyal C.M.S. follower (Lazaro Gombe)."[55] The district officer goes on to describe another raid that took place two days later, Sunday, January 21:

An Iwinda party went to the boma of Oloo Ogola, a pagan Kager, and commandeered a large bull, which was taken to Iwinda and there slaughtered. The owner made no resistance as he was afraid. There were also other acts of violence initiated by the Jo-Roho against other Kager.

Inondi's narrative, however, presents the bull incident as an unfortunate misunderstanding. Because Mango's home was a busy missionary center, where everyone was occupied with praying or receiving visitors, there was no one available to herd Odongo's cattle on a daily basis. Mango had therefore farmed his animals out to neighbors. By January 21, Mango's followers were very hungry, as they had been confined for several weeks, surviving exclusively on the fruit available in Mango's compound. Seeing their hunger, Mango offered them one of his bulls that was being cared for by an uncle whom Inondi called Omogo (she confessed that she was not certain of his name). Mango sent a lady named Julia Omol to fetch the bull. However, many of the local people were not aware of the arrangements Mango had made concerning his livestock, and they later accused the Joroho of stealing the bull. It is likely that the person known to Inondi as Omogo was Oloo Ogola, for the local community, as well as Roho tradition, record only one famous bull incident.[56]

When the bull was just about to be slaughtered, Elijah Oloo offered the gathering some grain from his farm across the river so that they could cook *kuon* (the staple dish) to eat with the meat. Inondi recalls that only the women *askeche* (soldiers) were sent. According to his testimony recorded later, however, Oloo sent both "men and girls" to collect the grain.[57] Earlier that morning, Lawi had received a message that local people were preparing to kill any Jaroho who dared to venture toward Musanda Luo church. Given the tense climate, Oloo's party armed itself with sticks and clubs and, singing their song, proceeded toward the river.

The Wanga, however, knowing that eventually some of the worshipers would have to leave in search of food, had been watching Mango's compound. They had collected various weapons—shields (*okumbini/kuodi*) and spears (*tonge*)—for attacking Mango and his associates. Shortly after the women *askeche* had started down the path toward the river, the horn (*tung'*) of the Wanga sounded, and a large group of armed men advanced toward Mango's home. Someone from Iwinda called to the women for help, "Hey! You people who are leaving, there's war over here!" (*Eeeeeh! Un ma udhi no, lweny nitie!*) At once, the *askeche* turned around and rushed back toward Mango's compound.

As they entered the Iwinda *boma*, one young *askari* was speared in the thigh. She had only married recently; when her young husband, a man named Obwaka from Alego, saw that she was injured, he cried out, "Oh! My new wife is being killed here!" (*Ayaye! Chiega ma nyocha eka anyuomo, inego mana ni ka!*) He rushed to try to help her, but he, too, was struck in the wrist by a spear. When the leader of the women, Dorsila Kinyou, saw her fellow Joroho wounded, she commanded her companions to begin fighting. "Now we were warriors!" (*Koro wan jolweny!*), exclaimed Inondi.

The women warriors converged on one of the ringleaders of the enemy, a man named Muhwana of the Wanga clan, and beat him until he died. The second ringleader, Abwodha of the Buholo clan, met the same fate. Both men had been drinking home-brewed whiskey that day, and drunkenness may have caused them to rush recklessly into battle. Jeremiah Ogutu, who was a boy of about ten at the time, recalls that Muhwana and Abwodha entered Mango's *boma* down by the fruit trees where the children (according to Ogutu's estimate, more than two hundred fifty in all) were eating oranges under the guardianship of Isaka Obayo. Obayo, a kind, elderly, blind man, served as the children's teacher during the weeks of retreat. He was the first to notice Muhwana and Abwodha, which amazed the Wanga, who wondered how a blind man had spotted them. Obayo wrestled with Muhwana and reportedly wrenched the spear from his enemy's hands, breaking it in two. Hislop reports that Obayo "was speared and then burned to death" during the second clash, but no one is sure exactly when this occurred.

As the fighting continued, two Roho men, Mica Olel from Alego and Silvano Nyamogo, sustained head injuries. The women *askeche* eventually managed to drive the attackers out of Mango's home. They succeeded in pushing the enemy up to the road that marked the outer perimeter of Mango's fields. Anna Inondi then cautioned her fellow *askeche* that if they pursued the Wanga beyond the end of Mango's property, they might be accused of provoking the attack.

The women withdrew toward Mango's compound. Yet, as they did so, the Wanga followed them. Dorsila's warriors turned again and pushed the enemy back to the boundary, only to be pursued once more on their return to Mango's home. This running back and forth continued for some time. The Joroho could hear their attackers exclaiming, *Abahasi butswa!* in Kiluyia, "Just women!" The enemy simply could not understand how they were being defeated by mere women. The Roho women ridiculed them further, pointing out that even though they lacked real weapons, the women were nevertheless able to prevail.

Finally, Ibrahim Obworo, an elderly male Roho adherent who had been fighting alongside the female soldiers, grew tired from all the running. "It was as if his energy was all used up" (*Chal ka gima nene tekone orumu*), Inondi explained. He fell behind, and the Wanga captured him. They hit him with sticks until he collapsed. Anna Inondi saw him drop and recalled that Mango had told his followers not to stand by and watch one of their group being beaten to death. So she interfered and hit one of the attackers with her stick. She was, in turn, struck hard on the head and fell to one knee, but she somehow scrambled away.

Some of the enemy hurled their clubs at her, but she escaped, managing to strike another Wanga man in the process. "It was a miracle!" (*Gicha ne hono!*), Inondi remarked to me, laughing.

This diversion gave the Joroho enough time to rescue Ibrahim Obworo. A group of adults ran to him, followed by some youths. As the adults reached the unconscious man, a Wanga warrior tossed his spear toward them, but the weapon arched high over their heads. It came down on the line of youths in the rear, struck Musa Muga in the torso, and sliced through his ribcage. Surprisingly, Musa did not die instantly. He lived for two more days and sang Christian songs all the while. He finally passed away en route to Kakamega hospital.

The battle continued until six o'clock in the evening. The Wanga were furious. "How can women defeat us! We must kill them," they exclaimed. The fighting eventually seemed to diminish, as the enemy began to carry their casualties home. What the Joroho did not realize is that a fresh contingent of Wanga reinforcements was about to arrive on the scene.

The 1990 oral account I have just presented is amazingly consistent with the report filed by Captain Hislop fifty-six years earlier. Hislop interviewed many people on both sides and, despite frustration with the number of "contradictory statements" he received, felt satisfied that, after careful consideration of all the evidence, he had arrived at an overall picture of events that was accurate.[58]

In consonance with my informants' version, Hislop's account explains that Elijah Oloo, "a prominent secular member of the Iwinda community," sent people to his *boma* to collect supplies. As the party moved down the road it passed the "double Wanga *boma*" of "Mukhwana" and "Ambotha," who were indeed drunk. In sum, Hislop blames these two drunken Wanga (Mukhwana being the leader) for provoking a fight by appearing on the path "armed with spear and shield" and intent on reviling the Kager and blocking the Joroho from continuing down the road. He labeled this action "a gesture of mere obstreperousness and racial dislike."[59] Hislop was aware that Musa Muga (or Musa Paulo)[60] was "speared in the stomach" and that Joshua Obwaka from Alego was "speared in the arm." In keeping with Anna Inondi's testimony, Hislop states that after Muhwana and Abwodha were "felled to the ground" by the Iwinda group, it was "principally the women" who "went in and beat the two Wanga with their sticks so unmercifully that they were both killed." Hislop concludes his description of this incident by stating that the Wanga managed to drive the Joroho back: his account does not contain information on the fight that took place back inside Mango's *boma* at the time. However, he noted that the attackers set afire four of the houses in the western end of Mango's *boma*—something that was quite plausible, though not mentioned by my informants.

Inondi and Hislop both refer to the Wanga's return to Iwinda around eight o'clock Sunday evening as "the second clash" (*lweny mar ariyo*). According to several Roho elders, when the Wanga reinforcements appeared around the edge of Mango's compound, they took the Joroho by surprise:

We had just said, 'Phew! Now we can relax.' But when we looked up, we saw a whole crowd with spears and arrows.

(*Koro wawacho ni eh! koro wa yuweye. To ka warongo ni, to waneno oganda ma oting're, man kod tonge, kata kod kuodi.*)

Hislop estimates that the returning Wanga numbered several hundred.[61] Inondi explains that she and Turfosa Aloo[62] started out to meet the enemy, but they were completely surrounded. A spear suddenly sailed through the air and struck Aloo. Inondi turned to find that her colleagues were no longer behind her; all had fled back in fear, so Inondi, too, turned and ran back into one of the houses.

Aloo was carried from the field and taken to Lawi, who prayed for her. She almost died. Then Lawi saw her heavenly boat (*yie*) in a vision coming to take her to the Lord, but Lawi begged God, "Let not my sister precede me. I must enter that boat first" (*Kik nyamin kwong tel na. Akwongo donjo e yie no*). Aloo remained alive, singing hymns. She did not pass away until the following morning, after Lawi had been killed.

While warriors were attacking Turfosa Aloo and other *askeche*, the rest of the Wanga crowd set fire to most of the roofs in the compound. Mango was inside his house with a large number of children, whom leaders had hidden there. This point is corroborated by Hislop's report: "At first it appears the children were collected in Antipa's house . . . then transferred to the house of Alufayo himself through some vague idea it might be spared." Among the children were Anna Inondi's sons, Meshak Ogola (who was still nursing at the time) and Benjamin Oduor. When the house began to burn, some of the clever ones managed to escape through a window. The Wanga warriors had forced both the front and back doors ajar and were clustered there, waiting to kill anyone who should try to escape.

Mango, however, did not attempt to escape. He stood erect in the center of the house, holding a Bible in his right hand high above his head. Another Bible was tucked under his left arm. Followers heard him exclaim, "Jesus, Son of God, the sky is cracking, the hills are tumbling down!" (*Yesu wuod Nyasaye, polo barore, gode mukore!*), and then Mango began to sing this song:

Ero kamano, Yesu, ero kamano, Yesu.
(Thank you, Jesus, thank you, Jesus.)

Jawar ji duto, wod Nyasaye,
(Savior of all people, son of God,)

Ihero ji, ihero ji duto.
(You love people, you love all people.)

Ipuonjo gi wach mari, nyaka giyie.
(You teach them your word, until they accept it.)

Isetho nwa musalaba.
(You have died for us on the cross.)[63]

As he sang, the small children stood riveted, watching and listening to him, unaware of what was happening.

At that moment, Anna Inondi spied her sons through the back door of Mango's burning house. Throwing down her stick—which she refers to as her "gun" (*bunde*)—she gathered courage and ran past the Wanga into the house. Once inside, she quickly realized that, if she remained there, she would burn to ashes with her children, and no one would be able to identify their corpses. Better to be speared to death escaping, she decided, for at least her relatives would be able to recognize her body and those of her sons. So Inondi grabbed both boys and slipped out past the enemies while hidden from them by a cloud of smoke. Miraculously, she and her sons were unharmed.[64]

Mango, whose robes were now on fire, yelled for those who were still in the house to run out. Some, like Leah Were and Nora Nyadero, managed to escape at the last minute with their children. Elijah Oloo fled the burning house just as two sides of the roof caved in.[65] According to the testimony of Mango's son, Ibrahim Ouwor Mango, Mango's wife, Rael Oloyo, at first refused to abandon her husband,[66] but Mango ordered her to jump quickly out of the door and promised to be right behind her, for he did not want her to die. Oloyo leapt out, but her husband did not follow. At that moment, one of the enemy, a Kawango named Wang'enga, threw a spear into the burning house and hit Mango. This claim is again corroborated by the eyewitness reports Hislop collected: "It is asserted, and I believe it is probably true that Alufayo was speared in the chest when he went to the door to push Rahel out. She ducked and a spear passed above her and took Alufayo."[67] The entire compound was in flames. Every house was ablaze except for Antipa Ngutu's kitchen. The fighting had now lapsed, as people gathered around Mango's house, gaping and marveling at this man who stood wounded and unflinching, burning to death.[68]

Many Joroho fled downstream. After escaping from the fire, Inondi and her children took to their heels, along with another woman named Grace Oracho. Suddenly, Inondi panicked and became confused: "It was as if I were shot in the head" (*To ne awad kata rashingwa*). She found herself loudly repeating the phrase, "Jesus, your friend is being burned! Jesus, your friend is being burned!" (*Yesu, osiepni wang'! Yesu, osiepni wang'!*) Then, she heard Mango's voice loud and clear, "Goodbye!" (*Oritu!*) Inondi looked back toward the house and saw something "which was red and rounded like the sun" (*ka wang' chieng' makwar, ka ong'inore*) rise through the roof, "heading straight into the sky" (*ka ochimo polo tir*), where it disappeared. Anna Inondi turned to Grace Oracho, "Ah! The elephant has now gone" (*Ah! Koro liech ose dhi*), she said. They decided to keep themselves and their children hidden, so they spent the rest of the night together in the bush.

Other church members I spoke with about the founder's death also mentioned that his soul could be seen rising into the sky. They describe it as "the red ball" or a sphere that was "very big like the sun." Pastor Daniel Were (not an eyewitness) said people saw something "rounded like the 'power heart' of the lion" (*gimoro nene ong'inore ka ohet simba cha*) going up to heaven. In the past, Luos used to say that a very red sunset meant that an important man was about to die. The souls of prominent figures were believed to rise directly up into the sky (Hobley 1903, 35). It is likely that Mango's followers experienced and represented Mango's fiery death through this indigenous eschatological framework, which, as we shall see in chapter 4, was compounded by an added layer of significances stemming from indigenous spirit possession.

Excluding information on Mango's prophesies, what he sang and said while dying, and his soul's ascension, the elders' testimony about the second clash is, once more, consistent with what Hislop uncovered in his investigation. On the issue of Lawi Obonyo's murder, however, there is considerable discrepancy, first, among reports given by various members within the Roho community itself and, second, between those accounts and the facts as Hislop presents them.

Roho tradition holds that, while the battle was raging, Lawi remained at the edge of Mango's compound to pray over the wounded. In the middle of the night, after the commotion had died down, Lawi went to hide for a while in a small banana grove (or, alternatively, in a stream). According to Inondi, when Lawi was sure the way was clear, he moved to a vacant hut (a kitchen, or *jikon*) in Silvano Nyamogo's home, adjacent to Mango's. During the battle, most of Mango's neighbors had taken their cattle and fled, so no one was left in Nyamogo's home. Owen suggests that the kraal in which Lawi was killed—which "had been vacated some few days previously"—indeed abutted Mango's homestead. Yet, Hislop states that the hut in which Lawi hid was actually inside Mango's *boma*. In any event, Lawi wrapped himself in a mat and kept still.

When the Wanga returned at dawn on Monday morning, January 22, it is unclear whether they simply wanted to loot whatever was left behind (as Inondi and Ibrahim Mango maintain), whether they were looking for survivors to ensure "by daylight that the job was complete" (as Hislop concludes), or whether they realized that they had not killed Lawi and were hunting specifically for him (as Owen claims). Eventually, one Wanga warrior entered the small hut where Lawi was hiding and happened to touch the mat. He saw it move. There are different versions of what happened next. Inondi and other members of the Ruwe Holy Ghost Church claim that the Wanga man called to his colleagues that someone was alive in the hut. When they discovered it was Lawi, they prepared to kill him, but the preacher asked to be by himself for a few moments to pray. They went outside and left him alone. In the words of Zadock Ochoma:

> After a few minutes he (Lawi) burst out in full force like a warrior. . . . He knelt down in the open and called them to spear him and according to those who witnessed the event, two spears passed on either side. They heard him . . . asking God what was wrong, for the time had reached for him to leave; then, the spear thrown by a left-handed[69] man struck him on the

chest. He pulled the spear, held it, aimed to throw it back but heard a voice calling him not to revenge. He then held it across his chest and collapsed and died in that position, with the spear lying across his chest. (Ochoma 1991, 1; spelling and punctuation altered)

Inondi concludes that the warriors then cut out Lawi's tongue and left the corpse on the ground for the colonial authorities to collect. [70]

Ibrahim Mango refutes this version and argues that it is highly unlikely that warriors who had been fighting all night, on finding an enemy leader, would not try to kill Lawi instantly. According to him, when the Wanga saw the mat move, they thought to burn down the house but hesitated, wondering whether they ought to find out who—or what—was inside first. At that moment, Lawi leaped out aggressively. The Wanga chased him back into the house and set it ablaze. Lawi burst out once more but this time ran directly into an oncoming spear and died. Hislop's version is close to this one. He surmised that Lawi had locked the door from the inside and refused to come out. Thus, "the roof was fired, and he was driven to leave by a window. Once outside, he was speared and killed and his body left lying on the spot marked C."[71] The distinguishing feature of the Ruwe tradition, then, is the glorification of Lawi. The Ruwe Holy Ghost Church clearly establishes a parallel between Lawi and the nonvindictive martyred Christ. The claim that Lawi died in the shape of a cross is now a widely accepted part of the Ruwe historical canon.

At about seven in the morning, Anna Inondi and others hiding in the bush heard people calling them to come back because the white men had arrived. Most Joroho were frightened, however, and went to their homes instead. Inondi's companion, Grace Oracho, for instance, did not want to return "to a place where people were dying." However, Inondi was not afraid. When she arrived at Mango's compound, she found several Europeans there. The Reverend Leech, the missionary in charge of Butere diocese, received news of the incident before dawn. He immediately rushed off to Kakamega to inform the district commissioner:

On the receipt of Mr. Leech's information, every available Police Constable and Tribal Policeman was packed into a lorry, and sent off to the scene, the Provincial Commissioner and the District Commissioner following and Asst. Inspector, Mr. Grant of the Police, following later. The expedition reached the scene of the trouble about 11.30 A.M., when it was obvious all was over.[72]

It seems that Leech then proceeded to Maseno, where, according to Ruwe elders, he informed Archdeacon Owen. Ibrahim Mango reports that Owen contacted him at Maseno Boys School, where he was a student at the time, and drove him from Butere to Iwinda, together with a carpentry teacher named James Adala. When they arrived, the district commissioner was already on the scene with policemen and prison officers to restore order. Canon Pleydell from Ng'iya—known locally as "Bwana Orengo" after the fly whisk he often carried—was also present. They all walked over the compound to inspect the damage. According to Hislop's report, the Wanga had torched a total of thirteen houses in Mango's homestead, plus three houses in Elijah Oloo's *boma*. Smoke was still rising from the remnants; Mango's house was completely destroyed.

Ibrahim Mango could see the body of his father clearly. Odongo Mango's corpse was recognizable from the waist up—his head, face, and cassock were intact. His legs, however, were completely burnt. According to the Roho elders, Pleydell (Mango's former teacher) considered Mango a good person and was chagrined to see what had taken place. As Anna Inondi put it, he was crying, "A good soul has left us!" (*Chuny maler oweyowa!*) Leech also seemed sad. Inondi recalls that Archdeacon Owen, by contrast, mockingly addressed the corpse, "Stand up and go to Ambira!" (*Chung malo idhi Ambira!*)[73] Owen then heaped more wood on the fire in hopes of reducing the entire body to ashes, but Mango's torso wouldn't burn. The archdeacon ordered Antipa Ngutu to collect sticks to contribute to the fire, but Ngutu refused. Finally Leech produced a gunnysack and put Mango's remains inside.

Three children had been trapped in the house with Mango and had burned to death: Joel Owino (Lawi's son),[74] Zadok Aol (son of a man named Enoka, who had also remained in the house with Mango until the last minute), and Persila Adongo, a girl under 10 years of age, whose body was nothing but ashes. The district commissioner had his guards dig a big grave for the remains of the children and the bodies of the two adults killed in the fight: Turfosa Aloo (a married woman and lead warrior) and the old, blind man, Isaka Obayo. Lawi's body was also placed in the grave. Leech performed the burial service. The authorities did not allow Mango's remains to be buried in Iwinda for very definite reasons. Hislop explains that they hoped "to avoid possible political complications in the future, in view of the strained relation on the land question between the Wanga and the Kager; Iwinda was Alufayo's *boma*, and his grave within it, or close to it, would have provided a rallying point for the Kager."[75]

A message had been sent to a Dr. Briscoe from South Maragoli to summon him to the scene. The doctor arrived at about six that evening and worked throughout the night to administer first aid to the injured, "who had gradually drifted back from their hiding places in the vicinity." Hislop guessed that about forty Joroho had sustained injuries during the battle. The most seriously wounded individuals were transported in a truck to the Native Civil Hospital at Kakamega. Among them were a girl of about fifteen named Salome Omondi, who had been very badly burned, and Musa Muga, the youth hit by a spear during the Wanga attack. Muga died on the way to the hospital; Omondi passed away the following morning.

When Roho members praise their nine founding martyrs, then, they are referring to their leaders, Alfayo Odongo Mango and Lawi Obonyo; two adults,

Turfosa Aloo and Isaka Obayo; two teenagers, Musa Muga and Salome Omondi; and three children, Joel Owino, Zadock Aol, and Persila Adongo.

Conclusion: Challenging the Schism Model

Most historians who have written about the establishment of the Roho denomination view Mango and his followers as having made a conscious decision to leave the Anglican church (Ogot 1971, 103; Perrin Jassy 1973, 80; Nundu 1982, 25–26; Odinga 1967, 69).[76] The way in which these scholars have pinpointed Mango's final "break" with the mission church is not borne out by the testimonies I collected. Bethwell Ogot, for example, places a lot of stock in the memo written to the district commissioner by Archdeacon Owen, stating that when, in December 1933, Mango disobeyed Owen's orders twice, the latter had "repudiated the authority" of the bishop as well, thereby having "broken away" from the Anglican church.[77] "The bulk of the congregation at Musanda dissociate themselves from Alufayo in his break with the Anglican Church," Owen added.[78] Ogot accepts Owen's claim that such disobedience was tantamount to secession, even if Ogot is clearly sympathetic with Mango's supposed motives:

> It should by now be evident that the decision of Mango to leave the Anglican Church to found his own Church was based partly on the realization that the Anglican Church led by Owen was not sympathetic to the aspirations of his people in South Wanga and partly on the belief that the Church was "dead" and needed spiritual renewal. (Ogot 1971, 103)

There is no evidence to suggest, however, that Mango ever made a declaration of secession himself. On the contrary, it was *Owen* who announced that Mango had seceded and who subsequently urged people to leave Mango's congregations. It is true that in prophesying the eventual demise of colonialism, Mango and his followers had to be aware that they were treading on thin ice with respect to the status of the C.M.S. missionaries, who, in western Kenya, often aligned themselves with the colonialists. Yet, Anna Inondi, for one, maintains that she and the circle of Christians who acknowledged the spiritual abilities of Lawi and Mango never considered themselves involved in a schismatic or rebel movement. After all, they did not even know the name of the Anglican Bishop in Kampala, so how could they oppose him? They had been labeled "Joroho" (or, alternatively, "Antikristo") by others; Mango's supporters simply referred to themselves as *jogo mose yudo Roho Maler* (those who have received the Holy Spirit),[79] and Inondi claims that they did not choose to renounce their Anglicanism. It is true that, as we have seen, in late December 1933–early January 1934, Mango and his followers appointed their own officers and installed their own rites of baptism and communion. Yet, they did so only after being barred from attending services at Musanda Luo. Although they may have had trouble with Owen and the leaders of Butere pastorate, Mango's followers suggest that they did not confuse particular church officials with Anglicanism itself, evidenced by the fact that even after the massacre, the Joroho for several months continued to consider themselves Anglicans.

It would appear that marking the point at which the Roho movement ceased to be a charismatic revival within Anglicanism and became a separate body has been more of a preoccupation for scholars and outsiders than it ever was for the adherents themselves. According to believers living in Ruwe, the Holy Spirit first appeared to them in the person of Ibrahim Osodo in 1912. When the young evangelist Silvano Nyamogo visited Ruwe nearly twenty years later, he expressed himself in an ecstatic form already familiar to many people and welcomed by some. When the relationship between Mango and the Holy Spirit was made known to this group in Ruwe, they simply viewed their ostracized pastor as part of the continuum of gradually developing charismatic Christianity in the locality.

The interpretation of Ogot is in keeping with a convention established in the 1950s and 1960s by Western observers, who termed congregations such as the Joroho "schismatic" movements or "breakaway" churches, for they were seen to have "broken" from mainline Christian denominations.[80] As a conceptualization of the historical process of independence, the model of schism employed by the first chroniclers of African churches in Kenya can be summarized as follows: An ambitious, mission-schooled deacon or catechist quarrels with his European superior and leaves the church, taking some portion of the congregation with him. He then founds his own denomination, which is often better adapted to the needs of local people. This new church in turn spawns more breakaways (Whisson 1964; Barrett 1968; Barrett et al. 1973; Welbourn and Ogot 1966).

The notion of schism is not a neutral, descriptive idea, however. Like heresy, schism is a normative, theological term that derives meaning from the context of authority and power of those who use it to refer to others whom they reject for their own reasons. The early students of Kenyan Christian independence were all missionaries or mission-schooled scholars who, building on Sundkler's now classic works on South African Zionism, viewed schism as a sign of weakness, a failure on the part of mission churches to understand and accommodate African ways of being.[81] Scholars recognized that independent churches provided Kenyans with a "place to feel at home" (Welbourn and Ogot 1966), a sense of belonging that was absent in mission churches. Their perception was coupled, however, with a thinly veiled frustration with the creators of these new religious homes for promoting division within the Christian community. Founders of African churches were often depicted as opportunistic or self-interested. Hence the widely held view—still prevalent today—that African churches are established for primarily political reasons. Many agreed (and still agree) with John S. Mbiti, who condemned the "excessive denominationalism" of Christianity in

Kenya, maintaining that church fission was "often created and sustained by the self-interests of church leaders" (1973, 145).

In the 1970s, some scholars started using the more positive label *independent*—in place of the terms *schismatic* and *breakaway*—to refer to these churches. People still frequently distinguish between "those groups that have broken off from established churches or Islamic congregations" (separatist) and bodies "which have been started under the initiative of African leaders outside the immediate context of missions or historic religions" (indigenous) (Jules-Rosette 1987, 82–85). Overall, however, there has been a growing attempt to define African-born churches with respect to themselves only and not in comparison to or as derivative from mission churches.

Although the schism model in a normative sense is no longer in vogue, as a historical, processual concept it is still largely taken for granted. Yet, I would maintain that the model of schism is poorly adapted to the emergence of Christian independence in Kenya between 1910 and 1940. When mission Christianity was introduced in western Kenya, it did not permeate the countryside as a monolithic, institutional entity from which smaller, localized deviations branched. Rather, I would argue that people initially regarded mission Christianity in Kenya as a number of distinct cults alongside other local movements. [82]

The Mission Station and the Christian *Dala*

When missionaries arrived in East Africa, they established mission stations that operated as insulated, strictly run colonies that revolved around the figure of the founding missionary. Thomas O. Beidelman has likened the original Church Missionary Society stations in Tanzania to sects as Weber would define them, for they were "immune to and militant against the outside world" (1982, 21). People identified the individual missionary with the message he brought. Elderly members of the Ugenya Luo community recall that they first came to know Anglicanism and Catholicism by the names of the Europeans who introduced the respective faiths into their area. The Reverend J. J. Willis, who established the first C.M.S. mission in Maseno in 1906, was nicknamed "Ogore" ("Good Morning") after his frequent use of the common Luo greeting. The mission station Willis built came to be known as "Kogore," literally, "the place of Ogore." Early converts referred to Anglicanism as *dini Kogore* (the religion practiced at Kogore), stressing that they were followers of the rules of that particular homestead. Similarly, Dutch Father (Père) Bouma, who in 1904 was one of the first Catholic priests to settle in Kisumu, was known as "Opere" and his mission station was dubbed "Kopere."[83] Even today, an elderly person on the way to the local Anglican—now the C.P.K. (Church of the Province of Kenya)—church might remark, "I am going to Kogore."

As early as 1910, Christian converts in western Kenya began to turn their own homes into mission stations. We recall that, in 1916, Willis remarked on the

large number of small Christian congregations in Nilotic Kavirondo (now
Nyanza) under the "self-imposed charge" of an African convert who may have
had no contact with a European mission for years (Welbourn and Ogot 1966,
24). About the expansion of Anglicanism in Luo country, Michael Whisson
wrote:

> The faith was to be spread and maintained by lay readers scattered over the
> district, part of whose work appears to have been to establish Christian
> homes to which all those who were prepared to accept the new faith were
> invited to live in a Christian environment. Various features of the traditional
> home were to be omitted from the home and the people living there left their
> cattle in their original places of residence, a church in some cases filling the
> place where the cattle *boma* had been, and polygamy was not allowed. These
> homes for whose establishment there were very strong arguments both in
> terms of hygiene and in spiritual purity for their members, express the
> approach of the early converts far more than the teaching that they received,
> most of which is completely forgotten. They were beacons in a heathen
> night, and their members were ever encouraged by their leaders to bring in
> those from the outside. (1962, 16)

By the time Mango opened up his home to those who would heed his message,
he was following the paradigm of the Christian *dala* (home), which had become
an integral part of Anglicanism in Nyanza and indeed throughout much of East
Africa.[84] The Christians who resided in his homestead observed a strict prayer
schedule, fasted, were instructed in Scripture, eschewed all forms of witchcraft,
and obeyed their leaders. In his testimony before the district officer and Wanga
elders immediately following the Musanda massacre, Elijah Oloo simply identified Iwinda Musanda as "a Christian village inhabited by members of the Kager
tribe who belonged to the C.M.S."[85] There was nothing unusual about the
arrangement. Whisson's passage even corroborates Ibrahim Mango's claim that
removing one's cattle from a missionary home—such as Iwinda—was common
practice during the colonial period.

That Alfayo Odongo Mango's followers revered him, moved into his compound, and accepted his teachings about Roho should not therefore be taken as a
sign of manipulation and self-aggrandizement on the part of Mango and Lawi.
One can hardly view such reverence as exceptional in an environment in which
one's religious identity was so profoundly tied to the person heading the mission
station—be he a European or an African. Taken in context, we can now see why
Mango's followers did not find their obedience to Mango and Lawi excessive or in
conflict with their Anglican faith.

From the point of view of the Luo populace, Anglican missionaries had no
claim upon an established religious or ethical norm. Moreover, there was no
such thing as standardized institutional Christianity in western Kenya in the
1920s and 1930s. Christianity during this period consisted of a multiplicity of

European mission stations and indigenous Christian *dalas* headed by strong-willed and often charismatic individuals. Converts accepted the teachings of one of these individuals and the puritan lifestyle promoted in a particular village, but as accounts presented in Chapter 3 suggest, there was a great deal of interchange between such Christian bases. Such a context forces us to reconsider any discussion of schisms or breakaway sects that posits the existence of a dominant established body from which innovative (or rebellious) segments split off.

Spirit Possession, Revival, and Nomiya Luo

Although the institution of the Christian *dala* was common enough, Mango and Lawi's emphasis on the agency of the Holy Spirit and the ecstatic fervor of their followers' worship was less common but not unique. In the latter half of the nineteenth century, a number of indigenous possession movements arose in Uganda, Tanzania, and Kenya. These millenarian and frequently militant movements bore a striking resemblance to one another, despite having originated in different ethnic contexts. Some of these movements intensified during the First World War; new ones appeared during this period as well. More research needs to be done into the nature of the links between these cults, but, given the migration of Luos into Tanzania and the travel of C.M.S. delegates from western Kenya to Mengo in Uganda, channels for mutual influence clearly existed.[86]

One such movement was the Nyabingi cult of southwestern Uganda whose adepts—predominantly women during the nineteenth century—manifested "a stylized trembling movement, ventriloquism and the ability to hold a 'dialogue' with the spirit in an esoteric language and falsetto" (Hopkins 1970, 259). Much like Lawi, the Nyabingi priestesses (known as *bagirwa*) had powerful stares; when they looked at someone, that person would tremble. In the late 1800s, the *bagirwa* of Mpororo raided other communities and killed the leaders of invading groups. During the 1920s, men also became Nyabingi mediums, and the cult in Kigezi "became the organizational focus for open and widespread anti-European resistance" (Hopkins 1970, 314).

In 1914, another militant cult known as Mumboism spread through southern Nyanza. Audrey Wipper (1977) asserts that the movement originated in the possession experience of Onyango Dunde, a Luo man from Alego who proclaimed the imminent demise of the *wazungu* (Europeans), a message that found an enthusiastic audience in Gusii country, where colonial repression had been particularly brutal. Mumbo is an enormous snake spirit, who according to Luo tradition dwells in Lake Victoria. Henry Owuor Anyumba explains that Luo cults associated with lake spirits (*juok nam*) suddenly escalated around the turn of the century, as did possession of Luos by the ghosts of Nandi warriors (*lang'o*), whom they vanquished in a series of bloody raids at that time (1974, 8).[87] Scholars have pointed out that East African spirit possession cults are frequently stimulated by interethnic contact and strife (Allen 1991, 383; Johnson 1980, 177–364). When misfortune strikes, such as war, pestilence, drought, or disease—all of which occurred in the late 1800s and early 1900s on a wide scale—it is frequently attributed to alien spirits that are perceived to be more lethal than local ones.

Kinjikitile Ngwale, the leader of the 1905 Maji Maji uprising in Tanzania, was a devotee of the god Hongo, who was also believed to take on the form of a snake (Gwassa 1972, 207). The prophet and his followers maintained that the power of their patron deity would turn German bullets to water, just as the Nyabingi cult leader in Kiga declared in 1928 that his soldiers were impervious to European guns (Hopkins 1970, 315). Belief in the power of possessing spirits is profound and persistant in East Africa. As recently as 1987, hundreds of followers of the Acholi medium Alice Lakwena marched to their death unarmed and singing hymns, certain that the weapons of Museveni's army could not harm them. Alice Lakwena's possessing spirit was not one of the many *tipu* or *jok* (ancestral shades or spirits) traditionally recognized by the Acholi; instead, she was possessed by the Holy Spirit of the Bible.

In Acholi country where acceptance of Catholicism is the norm, Lakwena's claim to be a prophet of the Holy Spirit served "to resolve the ambiguities of possession and assert the moral probity" of her activities. As Tim Allen has pointed out, although the syncretism of Lakwena's movement was in some respects deliberate, it developed in a milieu in which the association between *jok* possession and Catholicism was long established and where Acholi metaphysical notions were already well blended with Christian cosmology (1991, 392–395). Throughout much of East Africa, the phenomenon of possession by the Holy Spirit or baptism in the Spirit is today taken for granted—a testimony to the combined impact of the East African Revival of the 1930s and 1940s, the growth of ecstatic African Independent churches, and the popularity of Pentecostal missions to Africa.

In Mango's day, however, Christian symbolism, much less religious forms and beliefs associated with charismatic Christian revival, were hardly pervasive. As we have seen, Ruwe Roho members are firm in their conviction that Holy Spirit possession first appeared in their area in about 1912. Moreover, Pleydell recalled that Mango had been involved in some kind of revival movement in 1916. However, scholars generally assert that evangelical revival did not permeate Nyanza until after World War II. They link the birth of revival in Nyanza with the spread of the well-known East African Revival, a movement that originated in the Anglican church in Rwanda around 1930, swept through Uganda during that decade, and then took root in western Kenya in the 1940s (Welbourn and Ogot 1966, 28–44; Hopkins 1970, 323; Perrin Jassy 1973, 80; Whisson 1962, 26; Mambo 1973, 111).

There was, in fact, an earlier, less famous revival initiated in Uganda by a C.M.S. missionary named George Pilkington. While on holiday in the Sesse Islands[88] in 1893, Pilkington read a book by a Sri Lankan evangelist that prompted an experience of intense spiritual awakening. Pilkington returned to

Mengo and said that he had "received by faith the baptism of the Holy Ghost, and [that] manifestations of his power had followed" (Baskerville quoted in Pirouet 1978, 25). Together with his fellow missionaries, Pilkington immediately organized a number of large prayer meetings and invited African Christians to receive the Spirit, sparking a reinvigoration of the church and a renewed interest in Bible reading (Stock 1899, 451–452; Pirouet 1978, 25). Not much is known about this 1893 revival except that it prompted Ganda Christians to volunteer to go out to other regions as catechists, an initiative "strongly encouraged by the missionaries, and seen as a proof of the genuineness of the converts' new spiritual experience" (Pirouet 1978, 26). Pirouet maintains that the impetus of the 1893 revival (as well as that of a subsequent revival in Uganda 1906) did not last long. Yet it may well be that beliefs and practices fostered by Pilkington's revival, such as emphasis on personal experience of the Holy Spirit, the second baptism, and public confession of sin, were conveyed to Kenyans either by Ganda catechists (e.g., those who first accompanied Willis and Owen to Nyanza) or by Kenyan Christians who traveled to Mengo and back (Ochieng 1971, 75). It remains to be seen whether the practice of glossolalia as "the tongues of the Pentecost" also filtered into Nyanza as part of an indigenized Christianity from Uganda around the turn of the century, whether it was a local reinterpretation the Luo practice of *dhum* associated with *juogi* possession, or whether—as seems likely—it was a combination of both.

Another important manifestation of Holy Spirit religion flowered in the late 1920s among the Abaluyia. When American Quaker missionary Arthur Chilson initiated the 1927 Kaimosi revival, the African leadership within the Friends mission considered the religious fervor he unleashed to be dangerous. They banned ecstatic worship and the American Friends Board of Missions did not send Chilson back to Africa after his furlough in 1928 (Rasmussen 1995, 62). Some of Chilson's supporters, led by Daniel Mundia and Jakobo Buluku, refused to renounce their charismatic faith, which, like that of the Joroho, stressed public confession, spiritual rebirth, and speaking in tongues. The presence of Holy Spirit possession in Ruwe at least as early as 1912 makes it unlikely that the Reverend Chilson was the first to introduce it among the Luyia people. The extent of cultural and social exchange between Bantu and Luo groups would, instead, suggest that Roho religion had slowly been developing throughout western Kenya and that early Luyia and Luo proponents mutually influenced each other. There were definite links between Buluku's following and Mango's, as is brought to light in the next chapter. To this day, each Roho community considers itself the original recipient of the Spirit and claims to have transmitted it to their neighbors.

According to most historians of independent Christianity, Mango's Roho church was the second indigenous Luo denomination, preceded only by the Nomiya Luo church. *Nomiya* means "It was given to me." The *it* can refer to the founder's revelation (Barrett 1968, 10) or to the Holy Spirit (Burgman 1990, 288).

Haggai Nundu (1982) claims that church was known locally as *dini Kowalo* and that Owalo, the founder, was indeed the first man in Nyanza to receive the Holy Spirit.[89] Others read the name *Nomiya Luo* to mean that the new denomination was specially given to the Luos by God (Whisson 1962, 24; Ochieng 1973, 59).

The vision experience of founder Johana Owalo around 1907[90] contains grounds for all these interpretations. In his vision, Owalo was transported aloft by the angel Gabriel through a series of heavens:

> [Owalo] asked where the Pope was, and was told that nobody there knew anyone of that name. They only knew those whose names were written in the book which was kept there. He was shown into the presence of God who wore a white robe and sat on a throne. From his mouth came the Holy Spirit like a cloud of smoke. On his right side sat Jesus. Johana knelt before Jesus but Jesus rebuked him and said that God alone was worthy to be worshipped. Jesus told him that they were equal as both were the messengers of God, and that Johana should return to preach the gospel to all the Luo people. This experience taught him that the Anglican church was wrong to worship "three gods," and forced him to leave it. (Whisson 1964, 154)

Owalo's vision reflects his experience with a variety of religious traditions. Biographical accounts differ, but it is known that Owalo was baptized a Roman Catholic at Ojolla, Nyanza, converted to Islam while working in Mombasa on the Swahili coast for a Unitarian, and at some point became a catechist with the C.M.S. His mystical journey through a multilayered heaven is similar to an account given by St. John in the Book of Revelation, but it is also highly reminiscent of the popular Swahili epic *Utenzi wa Miraji*[91] (The ascent), which details Muhammad's guided tour through the levels of heaven and his encounter with important souls of deceased prophets and patriarchs along the way (Knappert 1967, 202). Jesus' order that Owalo not bow before him similarly evokes the well-known Islamic legend of Iblis, the fallen angel who refused to bow to Adam but would worship God only (Awn 1983). Islam's emphasis on the oneness of divinity would have reinforced whatever Owalo might have learned from his Unitarian employer about the nature of God, leading Johana to reject the Catholic and Anglican triune God.

There is some continuity between the beliefs and practices of the Nomiya Luo church and those of the Roho churches. For instance, Lawi's and Silvano Nyamogo's conversion experiences, as recorded by Hislop in 1934, recapitulate Owalo's heavenly ascent.[92] Mango, like Owalo, believed Jesus had been the prophet for the whites, but that he lacked the Holy Spirit now given to blacks. However, unlike Owalo, Mango did not insist that his male followers be circumcised (the Luo do not practice circumcision) nor did he allow men up to four wives, as Owalo did, after the Muslim custom. Instead, Mango and the Joroho always advocated monogamy, as did their Luyia counterparts in the Friends revival movement. An ecstatic style of worship, coupled with the use of Anglican liturgy, is common to both denominations, but it is difficult to determine how much of this similarity developed later, during the East African revival. In short, although we do not have enough evidence to draw a direct line between Nomiya Luo and Mango's Roho movement, one should note that many of the Roho adherents, if not Mango and Lawi themselves, would have been exposed to Owalo's Luo church.

We have considered a number of new religious forms entering Nyanza from across its borders between 1900 and 1930. These forms—the mission station, the militant possession cult, and the Holy Spirit revival—clearly had a shaping influence on the Roho religion emerging under the guidance of Lawi Obonyo and Alfayo Odongo Mango. In addition, we have reviewed several kinds of Luo religious phenomena and one early Luo eclectic movement that may have contributed to the developing Roho faith in Luoland as well as in Luyia country. Finally, we ought to examine briefly the nationalistic stirrings in central Kenya during this period that were transforming a traditional Gikuyu secret society into a vibrant anticolonial cult.

The new movement that arose among the Gikuyu in the 1920s was given the Swahili name *Watu wa Mungu* (People of God), although its leaders retained the Gikuyu label *arathi* (prophets). Like the Nyanza Roho movements, the *arathi*—also dubbed *akurinu* (roaring prophets)—sought possession by the Holy Ghost, a state evidenced by trembling and animal-like cries. Rawcliffe's description of their sessions is, again, very familiar:

> During these gatherings the *arathi* worked themselves up to a state of hystero-epileptoid frenzy accompanied by violent trembling as the Holy Ghost "took possession" of their bodies. At the same time they gave utterance to a wild "roaring like young lions," a piece of symbolism based on the fifth chapter of Isaiah. It is probable that the name of the secret Mau Mau cult, which was soon to emerge, originated from the onomatopoeic imitation of this "roaring like lions." (Rawcliffe 1954, 30)

Through the Spirit, the *Watu wa Mungu* believed themselves to engage in direct communication with God, who enabled them to foresee events (Kenyatta 1965, 264). Like the Joroho, they prayed that the colonists would vacate the land, "leaving the country to its rightful owners" (Kinyanjui 1963, 125). They opposed the missions' denunciation of polygyny and clitoridectomy and rejected Western money, amenities, and clothing. Devout *arathi* gave up their belongings, and traveled widely to heal the sick and establish their own schools.

We know that, while Mango was attending St. Emmanuel's Divinity School in Mombasa, he had Gikuyu classmates and learned of the struggles in central Kenya. He surely knew something of the *Watu wa Mungu*. Ogot states that, in February 1929, Mango met one of the cult's leading—if secret—members, Freedom Fighter and future President of Kenya Jomo Kenyatta (1971, 99). Again, it is impossible to assert with certainty that *arathi* religion or Kenyatta's nationalistic thought had any impact on Mango, but it seems highly probable that the concerns—both spiritual and political—of other Kenyans suffering the yoke of colonialism did have some effect on the Luo deacon. The Joroho's crowning of an African king did not arise out of purely local resentment against Wanga-British domination but suggests a broader vision. The founding members of the Roho church were not cut off from the larger society or ignorant of the ferment in other regions of the country. A number of the Roho movements' original adherents, such as Elijah Oloo and Isaya Goro, had served in the army in Tanzania, and many others traveled to different regions of the colony in search of employment. The stereotypical image of rural Africa as consisting of isolated villages formed within rigid, closed ethnic systems has long been exploded, yet studies of indigenous religious movements generally lack this basic insight. One is left to follow thinly documented links of interconnection between what are normally presented as balkanized, tribally circumscribed religious realities.

All these continuities taken together raise doubt about the usefulness of the schism model for understanding religious change in western Kenya during this period. The notion of schism does not accurately represent the historical process whereby independent churches came into being, nor does it capture the way such movements were experienced by Kenyan Christians. As Burgman states with reference to the Nomiya Luo church, John [Johana] Owalo "stayed long enough with the [Anglicans] to earn for his followers the name of being breakaways from the Anglican community," yet his movement in fact grew out of a blend of Catholicism, Unitarianism, Islam, and local Luo belief (1990, 288). The same observation applies to Roho religion. Rather than invoking a metaphor of abrupt, clear-cut rifts and splits in a unified institutional setting, it is more appropriate to conceive of Christianity in Nyanza from 1900 through the 1940s as very fluid, with few firm links to institutional hierarchies of any kind, missionary or otherwise. Discussions with elders from a variety of churches indicate that, at this time, groups of Christians, many of them white-robed, gathered in homes to pray and sent missionaries into other regions to spread the gospel. Some continued to worship on Sundays in mission churches; others drifted away or were chased out of established denominations. There appears to have been a great deal of interchange between these groups. As we shall see in the next chapter, leaders of what later became distinct, even rival institutions, initially prayed together, baptized each other, and recognized many of the same African prophets.

3

Roho Expansion and Church Formation

The Roho Narrative: Visions and Missions (1934–1960)

Aftermath of the Musanda Massacre

Anna Inondi and her children returned to Mango's home early on Monday, January 22, 1934, after spending the night in the bush. She found that several government officers had already arrived and that a large grave for the Roho victims was being dug. Wanga elders had assembled under a tree. One of them, a Muslim man named Fadmullah Obadha who saw Inondi arrive, exclaimed, "This woman is stupid! How can she bring children back to a spot where people have been dying?" Obadha was related to Inondi's husband through marriage and felt protective of her children. He took them away to the safety of his home.

After the burial was over, a European official called the assembly to order. Inondi referred to this European as "the D.C." [district commissioner] but it is likely that he was actually the district officer of South Wanga, Captain F. D. Hislop, who was in charge of the Musanda disturbance investigation. Isaya Goro and Elijah Oloo were among the few Roho men who returned to Mango's compound after the fire. Everyone present was called on to give his or her version of what had occurred.[1] Inondi recollects that the Wanga leveled several charges against Mango and his followers. First, they alleged that Mango had been organizing the Kager to take Wanga land. Second, they claimed that Mango was morally corrupt and had married his own daughter[2] in a large ceremony. (Many outsiders mistook the January 16 coronation ceremony for a wedding.) Third, they accused Mango's followers of provoking the attack by stealing Omogo's bull. (Julia Omol, the one who had been sent to fetch the bull, later testified that the animal was, in fact, Mango's.) Finally, Wanga elders alleged that Isaya Goro and Elijah Oloo had killed Muhwana and Abwodha and thereby sparked the conflict. Both Isaya and Elijah had served in the armed forces during the First World War, and the Wanga argued that only trained soldiers could have done the killing.

78

Administrative guards took Isaya and Elijah to await the investigating officers at Silvano Nyamogo's home. After questioning the two men, the presiding official called in Susan Munyala and Martha Ogut. These two women had helped watch over the children gathered in Mango's home during the month of January. Because Munyala and Ogut had been preoccupied with child care, they were unable to provide details about the chain of events leading to the battle. Inondi explained that each person was interrogated privately and did not know what his or her colleagues were saying. Then Inondi herself was called on to testify. She was taken into a room with rifle-bearing guards stationed in each corner, but she was not afraid. When asked whether Elijah and Isaya were the ones who had killed Abwodha and Muhwana, she replied, "No. We women, we women are the ones who killed them" (*Da, wan mon, wan mon ema wanego gi*).

The presiding official apparently did not believe her. He had his translator repeat the question three times; each time, Anna gave the same response. The translator himself finally insisted, "How can you say that women killed them when it is only Isaya Goro and Elijah Oloo who know how to fight?" Inondi exploded, stamping her foot:

What! Do you want to control me, eh? You want to force me [to lie]! I am a mature adult and I tell you that we [women] are the ones who killed them!

(*Choke! Udwa chika, choke! Udwa chika! An ng'ama ng'ongo aloso n'u kaka wan ema waneko!*)

Anna was determined that Elijah and Isaya should not be tortured or killed for crimes they did not commit.

Did those people [Elijah and Isaya] destroy anybody's belongings? They were just worshiping the Lord.

(*To jogo ne oketho gir ng'ato? Ne gilamo mana Nyasaye.*)

She told her questioners that, rather than punishing innocent people, it would be better that they kill her, for she had been involved.

The European investigator (probably Officer Hislop) was sitting silently, shaking his head. His translator declared, "This woman is mad! The same madness that caused Mango to remain inside a burning house has seized her also." The official told his assistant to release Inondi and leave her alone.

A young girl named Elizabeth Adhiambo was also questioned by officials. Adhiambo, a follower of Mango's from Sira Buholo, witnessed the entire battle. She led the authorities to the exact spot where Abwodha and Muhwana were slain. By confirming that the two Wanga men were killed inside Mango's gate, Roho elders maintain that Adhiambo proved beyond doubt that the Joroho had acted in self-defense. Elizabeth Adhiambo thus fulfilled a prophesy Lawi made before he died, that "the person who would finalize the judgment of the Joroho would be a young girl" (*ng'at ma notiek bura no bed mihiya manyako*).

There are no minutes preserved from this initial investigation held on January 22 or 23, but District Officer Hislop's lengthy report of February 9 summarizes his findings. Hislop's results indeed vindicated the Joroho by proving they did not instigate the bloody confrontation, but his report states that Muhwana and Abwodha died on the road midway between their gate and the entrance to Mango's compound, not inside Iwinda, as Roho elders maintain:

> That the Wanga were anxious to cover up the real cause of violence breaking out is shown by four statements made by the 2 wives of Mukhawana and 2 wives of Ambotha to the Police Inspector. These statements are all identical and accuse the Jo-Roho, headed by Elijah Oloo of marching into the Wanga bomas and murdering the 2 men out-of-hand. The place w[h]ere these men were actually killed was identified beyond doubt by bloodstains and the sacrifice of a hen; it is outside their bomas half way between them and the westernmost houses of Iwinda, and this place is in itself significant.[3]

After several futile attempts to identify the particular Wanga warriors responsible for the deaths of Mango and his associates, officials concluded that collective punishment was the only viable option. Acting on Captain Hislop's recommendations, District Commissioner Anderson wrote the provincial commisioner that "no charge of Murder or manslaughter could ever be brought against any individual or individuals with any chance of success. . . . Action must be directed against the Wanga, or certain sections of them, as a community."[4]

Anderson held four Wanga *mlango*s (clans) responsible for the Musanda disturbance. Under the Collective Punishment Ordinance, the clans led by headmen Ngamia, Natshisakha, Musakulu, and Shuundu, respectively, were charged with making "common cause against the members of the Kager tribe residing at Iwinda (Musanda)," burning fourteen houses, and causing the deaths of six Kager individuals.

Wanga elders had an opportunity to answer these charges in a *baraza* held by Hislop on February 26, 1934. The district officer nevertheless found the Wanga guilty and ruled that Ngamia's *mlango* (deemed primarily responsible) should assume 50 percent of the liability, and members of the other three clans should together assume the remaining 50 percent.[5] Anderson determined that the Kager victims' kin should receive compensation of 6,400 shillings (3,000 for property loss and 3,400 for loss of life). He recommended that the provincial commissioner levy a fine of 10 shillings on every adult male in Ngamia's *mlango* and a fine of 5 shillings on household heads in the remaining three clans in order to meet the stipulated amount.[6] Colonial Governor Byrne ultimately imposed a fine of 8,125 shillings, of which 6,000 was for the relatives of the Roho victims,[7] the remainder going to the North Kavirondo Local Native Council.[8]

Both oral history and colonial documents record that relatives of the Roho victims refused to accept any blood money. Anderson suggests that the Kager considered the 8,000-shilling fine ridiculous and insufficient punishment for the Wanga.[9] Anna Inondi, however, claims that Isaya Goro and Barnaba Walwaho—speaking for the families of the deceased—refused compensation on religious and moral grounds. Mango and Lawi died in the name of God, and the Joroho considered it sinful to capitalize on their leaders' suffering. Therefore, they left all the money to the government. For more than six years, the administration tried unsuccessfully to pressure the Kager to accept compensation for the Musanda massacre. The matter was finally brought to a close in 1940, when the district commissioner called thirteen Kager representatives, including Rael Oloyo (Mango's widow), Silvano Nyamogo, Isaya Goro, Antipa Ngutu, and Andrea Odera, to sign a document to formally "renounce all claims" to any compensation for the deaths of their kin in the Musanda riot and to state that they agreed to "the money being credited to the Government."[10]

Let us return, however, to January 22, 1934. Once the district officer completed his preliminary investigation at Musanda, Inondi states that he took her husband, Isaya Goro, as well as Elijah Oloo, Rael Oloyo, and Kiloyi Odimo (Lawi's widow), to Kakamega. They were detained there for a month while tempers in Musanda cooled. At first, a district warden locked the four Joroho inside a single room or house (*ot*). Roho tradition holds that the doorlock jammed, preventing the detainees from receiving food for an entire day. A locksmith was finally sent for but failed to open the lock. The warden had no choice but to break down the door. After that, the door could no longer be shut properly, so the Roho members were free to roam the detention camp grounds for the remainder of their stay. This event has been interpreted by the Roho community as a miracle from God and proof of the party's innocence.

Ibrahim Owuor Mango, Mango's son, states that his mother had not been detained long when she and Elijah Oloo were picked up by the Reverend A. J. Leech and driven to a cemetary in Kakamega. The district commissioner joined them to witness the burial of Alfayo Odongo Mango, whose body had not been placed in the group grave at Musanda but carried to the District Headquarters by Archdeacon Owen. Oloyo and Elijah did not actually see the corpse, but authorities told them that the bundle being lowered into the ground was Mango's body; they supposed that it was. The administration did not want Mango buried at Iwinda for fear that his grave would be used by the Kager in their effort to assert land ownership. Bethwell Ogot indicates that the Abaluyia were not content even to leave Mango's body in Kakamega but wanted it removed from the region:

> Later there was fear by the Abaluyia of the then North Nyanza that the Luo might one day use the grave of Mango as a basis for claiming the land from Musanda to Kakamega. The Local Native Councillors of Kakamega sup-

ported by the government secretly exhumed the body of Mango and transferred it to Namirembe Cathedral in Uganda where it today lies buried.[11]

None of the Joroho, not even Mango's son, indicated to me that he or she had
any knowledge of the transfer of the body to Kampala. Most believed Mango's
grave to be somewhere in Kakamega; others were mystified as to what had become of their founder's remains.

Mango's Followers Move to Ruwe

District and provincial records contain little mention of the Roho sect between
April 1934, when the Musanda victims' relatives first refused to accept blood
money, and November 22, 1940, when they finally signed the written statement.
The oral history that follows is therefore largely undocumented.

As senior Roho members recall, during the month that Mango's four close
associates were in detention, no one was allowed to enter the Iwinda *boma*,
which the government kept under tight security. Elders claim that the district
commissioner later gave Barnaba Walwoho—a leading Roho teacher from
Ruwe—permission to rebuild the houses destroyed in the fire. The Wanga community strongly opposed this prospect; they were convinced that a renovated
Roho center at Iwinda would lead to more conflict. The Musanda Kager were
equally outraged at the idea of Barnaba taking over Mango's land. Even though
Barnaba was a Kager himself, his established clansmen in Musanda resented the
recent influx of new Kager immigrants and blamed them for causing the death of
Mango in the first place. They reportedly threatened to kill Barnaba if he should
decide to act on the district commissioner's permission:

> Our brother [Mango] has been killed. But Barnaba remains here—to do
> what? We will kill him too! . . . Ruwe people came from their places, they
> gathered here with people from Alego, causing our brother to be killed.
> Therefore they will also be killed.
>
> (*Oneg wuodgi. Koro Barnaba to dong', otimo ang'o ka? Obende wan-
> ege! . . . JoRuwe oa kwondegi, gichokore kani gi JoAlego gimiyo oneg
> wuodwa. Gibende koro oneg gi.*)

This piece of oral datum challenges the perception of most colonial authorities
that trouble was essentially interethnic. Captain Hislop, an unusually perceptive
official, had understood that clashes, in fact, occurred between the Joroho and
other local Kager, as well as between the Joroho and the Wanga. Indeed, the
intra-Kager conflict was significant enough, Hislop felt, to be called a "Kager
Civil War."[12] In his opinion, this strife arose for exclusively religious reasons[13] —
"a division of opinion" between the Joroho and those Kager remaining loyal to
the C.M.S. Roho oral tradition, however, reminds us that an element of re-

gionalism was also at play. The Musanda Kager clearly did not want outsiders weakening their already tenuous status as *jodak* (land clients or squatters) in Wanga country.

In the face of such hostility, Daudi Arinda, a brother of Isaya Goro in Ruwe, urged Barnaba Walwoho to return there, offering to donate some of his own land as a site for the new Roho community. Elders note that, by offering land, Arinda was fulfilling a prophesy made by Lawi. Several months earlier, when he had visited Arinda to heal the latter's wife, Lawi had pointed to the spot where, he said, an important church would one day stand.

There is no official record of the district commissioner's discussion with Barnaba Walwoho, but the former does note controversy over Mango's *boma*. In a "précis of recent events" dated September 21, 1935, Anderson states that Mango's land was taken over by the Local Native Council and turned into a seed bulking farm "to prevent either Kager or Wanga claiming it."[14] The administration eventually granted a small tract of the property to Mango's widow so that she could feed herself and her children, but the rest remains in the hands of the government as a tree nursery to this day.

After the massacre, many adherents abandoned the movement, but a few individuals such as Leah Were, Norah Nyadero, Jared Ayuth, and Daudi Arinda persevered in the faith. Before the new church was built, Mango's remaining followers met in the house of Isaya Goro and Anna Inondi. While Goro was still in detention, his wife tried to hold the discouraged group (*joma okichore*) together. They worshiped in whispers and sang softly so as not to draw attention to themselves. They prayed five times daily, rising at dawn to pray before going to their fields. At nine o'clock, they would return from their gardens to pray together, dispersing afterward to their respective duties. At noon, they would congregate again for prayer before their afternoon work. They prayed again at four o'clock and after dinner at nine. This prayer regimen suggests the influence of Islam on the Roho practice.[15] To this day, Roho members—particularly women—often prostrate themselves when praying, although the five daily prayers are no longer mandatory.

Inondi explained that this program of frequent but brief prayers was an innovation by the survivors of the fire. During the December–January retreat in Iwinda, Mango and his followers had not worked on their farms, so they were able to pray for much longer intervals.[16] Their daily routine in Musanda had also included marching in drill formation every morning. Now, the survivors did not dare march or sing for fear of arousing suspicion. Instead, they grieved and prayed quietly "like orphans" (*kaka nyithi kiye*). They addressed God, "Now we people who remain, are we the bad ones? . . . Have you abandoned us, or what?" (*Koro wan joma odong' gi, koro wan ema waricho? . . . Iweyo wa, koso nadi?*) Just as Jesus' disciples lamented after their leader's death and received an answer to their prayers, one senior *laktar* (healer) explained to me, so too were the Joroho hoping for a message from God.

About a month later, after the four detainees returned home, the Roho adherents in Ruwe did receive a sign from God, reassuring them that they were not forgotten. The message came as a song, revealed to a woman member named Abisage Muriro:

Un jochan kik uwe lamo ma ne ruoth ose weyo nu.
(You poor people, don't stop saying the prayer that the Lord has left for you.)

Kik uol, kata nene chon bende ne ok giyie.
(Don't grow tired, for even long ago, they did not accept [i.e., Jesus' disciples were not heeded either].)

Ka nene obiro ne wahulo yie ma loko chuny.
(Once he [Roho] had come, we said the creed that changes the heart.)

Wa wer uru jakonywa oseko loyo tho,
(Let's sing that our helper [Roho] has overcome death,)

Wan bende wadwaro luwe gi teko nyaka chieng' imiyowa.
(We, too, want to follow him with the everlasting power you've given us.)

Wan waparo ruodha ber wapaki adiera gi mormimiyowa.
(Our good king, we wish to truly praise you with the happiness you give us.)

Remo olwoko wa wabe di mapoth; jahera mar Nyasaye owarowa girembe.
([Your] blood washes us and we become smooth; the love of God saves us with his blood.)

E tinde dak upara ka ne an gi sand?
(Now why didn't you think of me when I was suffering?)

Un gi wuoro rembe lwoko duto richowa.
(You have a father, his blood washes away the sins of all of us.)

To paruru jakedo oseko loyo tho;
(Just think, the warrior has overcome death;)

Kawuru ligangla mar Nyasaye.
(Take the sword of God.)

Although Inondi's group tried to be unobtrusive, many Ruwe inhabitants did not welcome Mango's followers. Local people (*jo gweng' ka*) hid around the boundary of Isaya Goro's home and attempted to spy. Some even wanted to attack the compound but were uneasy about initiating unprovoked violence without a pretext. One day, a Luyia woman from Kirindo Nyagwela appeared at Anna's door to say she had overheard people plotting to attack Goro's home that very night. The woman was a relative of Inondi's through marriage. When she had heard of the plan, she took pity on her in-law and ran to inform her. "If you sleep here tonight, you will all be finished" (*Ka ugalo unindo e dala ka tinende, to tin notiek u*), she warned. So, everyone in Goro's home secretly moved to Daudi

Arinda's, and that evening Barnaba Walwoho, Isaya Goro, Johana Omina, and Musa Ochieng began the long trek to the district headquarters in Kakamega to report the plot.[17] The following day, they told the district commissioner that local people were intent on killing them "just as Mango and Lawi had been killed."

The district commissioner assured the delegation that they were free to worship as they chose and that he would send someone to investigate the death threats. He nevertheless advised them to fence their compound well, deal politely with their neighbors, and welcome converts from other clans. Finally, the commissioner cited a Luo proverb, *Bondo opodho e nyimi* (A gum tree has fallen in front of you), emphasizing that Alfayo's life had been a boon that they must not waste.[18] The district commissioner's response gave the Ruwe Roho representatives reassurance, and they returned to their homes with new confidence.

One repercussion of the Musanda affair was that colonial authorities realized that the Kager would never receive a fair hearing in the Wanga *baraza* "as [then] constituted."[19] In May or June of 1934, they therefore divided Wanga Location into two parts, separated by the Nzoia River. Mumia's half-brother, Chief Murunga, was transferred from Malakisi to serve as headman of the new South Wanga sublocation (which included Musanda and Ruwe). The authorities hoped that this headman, who was required to live in the location, would be more sympathetic and diplomatic in his dealings with the various clans under his jurisdiction.[20] The Kager had hoped for a headman from their own ethnic group,[21] but had to settle for a more representative *baraza*.

Inondi saw a direct link between the Roho delegation's visit to the district commissioner and the appointment of a number of Luos to local administrative posts in South Wanga. Shortly after this visit, the first Luo, a man named Ndonj, was selected by the district commissioner to serve as subchief in Ruwe. Inondi states that, in addition, the district commissioner appointed a man named Ongoma (a Luo) and another named Ngolo Ngolo (a Wanga) to help administer the area.

Inondi recalls a confrontation she had with these two officers. Shortly after their appointment, the hut tax came due. Joel Ayiro, a relative of Isaya Goro, was late with his payment. Ongoma and Ngolo Ngolo arrested him in his village and marched him along a path near Goro's home. Inondi and Abisage Muriro saw the officials beating Ayiro and followed the men. Inondi grabbed Ongoma around the neck and threw him against a fence. "What is this woman doing to me!" (*To dhako ni timre nadi koda!*), he cried, as his colleague struck her on the thigh with his whip. Inondi then turned on Ngolo Ngolo, at which point Abisage joined in, demanding to know why they had apprehended Ayiro, but the agents shoved the two women aside and proceeded on their way to the camp of Paramount Chief Mumia.

In Mumias they discovered that someone had already spread the word that Ngolo Ngolo had been fighting with women, although Ongoma had also been involved. Roho elders maintain that, when news of the incident reached the district commissioner, he sacked Ngolo Ngolo and ordered that no Wanga would again be authorized to collect taxes among the Joroho. Mango had always instructed his followers to pay their taxes before the deadline, so Isaya Goro began collecting the taxes of the entire Roho community early and taking them to Kakamega himself. This arrangement continued until the hut tax was eventually lifted.

Visions from the Holy Spirit

Roho elders explain that, despite sporadic confrontations with members of the surrounding community, the second half of 1934 was fairly peaceful for Mango's disciples in Ruwe, who were left to worship in their own fashion. In response to their vigorous prayer and loud singing, miracles began to occur.

For example, one night Mango appeared to Anna Inondi while she was sleeping.[22] He was walking his bicycle into her compound, and, as he leaned his bicycle against the wall of the house, he sang:

> *Jaduong' mar muya ema oduogo.*
> (The elder of the air/spirit is the one who has come back.)

Mango then entered Isaya Goro's house—where the Joroho customarily gathered—and proceeded to destroy the interior wall that divided the sitting room from the sleeping quarters. He carried out the debris in a flat basket (*odher*). Inondi interpreted the visitation to mean that she and her husband should vacate that house and reserve it strictly for prayer "because the angels don't want to enter where people sleep" (*nikech malaika ok dwa biro kama ji ninde*). No one doubted the significance of the dream, so Inondi and Isaya began sleeping in their kitchen.[23] Although the separating wall was never torn down, the Joroho continued to use the house as a place of prayer. Even when the congregation finally built the new church, they continued to use Isaya's house for ritual purposes, such as baptism.

According to Roho tradition, two mornings after Inondi's vision, the Holy Spirit visited the Joroho just as they concluded their nine o'clock prayers. Patricia Amis, a Roho member from Alego once healed by Lawi, was waiting for a song (*orito wer*) from the Holy Spirit. When the Spirit came, it nonetheless took her by surprise. She collapsed, and her body began to shake. The Spirit entered her heart and conveyed the following lyrics:

> *Chieng ose rieny e piny, Yesu biro waro joge.* (repeat)
> (The sun has shone on earth, Jesus is coming to save his people.)
>
> *Ng'ama okelo wichkuot, Yesu ose weyo chutho.* (repeat)
> (He/she who brings disgrace, has been completely abandoned by Jesus.)
>
> *Bondo ose lwar e piny, tinde gimor e polo.* (repeat)
> (A *bondo* has fallen on earth, nowadays heaven rejoices.)

Shortly thereafter, another song of spiritual victory was revealed to Abisage Muriro. It celebrates the bravery of the women *askeche* in the Musanda fracas:

Wan nyi kedo, wan nyi mach; (repeat)
(We are women of war, we are women of fire;)

Wan nyi loyo, wan nyi tong; (repeat)
(We are women of victory, we are women of the spear;)

Wanamor, wanamor, wanamor ei polo. (repeat)
(We will be happy, we will be happy, we will be happy in heaven.)

Langi Lawi, wanamor, wanamor ei polo. (repeat)
(Followers of Lawi, we will be happy, we will be happy in heaven.)

Joka-Odongo, wanamor . . . etc.
(People of Odongo, we will be happy . . . etc.)

Langi Yesu, wanamor . . . etc.
(Followers of Jesus, we will be happy . . . etc.)

Isaya Goro also soon received a song. He was "struck down by the Holy Spirit" (*roho ogoye piny*) and remained in bed for an entire week, singing:

Wuoguru woko ka uwer!
(Go outside whenever you sing!)

Israel jawarwa idho gode kalo nam.
(Israel our savior climbs mountains, passing the lake.)

When Isaya recovered, he explained that he had received divine orders to spread the word of God. It had been revealed to him that Mango was called "Israel" in heaven, so Isaya began praising Mango with the now common invocation *Jawar* [Savior] *Israel*. The injunction to declare the message of Mango the Savior is conveyed in Isaya's initiatory hymn. As we shall see, hymns were an important part of Roho proselytization.

In addition to a new sense of mission, the kinds of revelations that Roho collective memory has preserved from this period reflect a developing group identity. For a month or two after the Musanda massacre, the Joroho continued to conceive of themselves as Anglicans. However, by about the middle of 1934, their perception of their faith as a unique (and truer) form of Christianity was becoming apparent. Barnaba Walwoho had a revelation in which he was shown the letter S and a cross, symbols highlighting the connection between Christ and the Roho founders. The S stood for the word *Israel* because S is its dominant sound. The symbol associates Mango with Christ through the common epithet they share. The cross similarly establishes a symbolic connection between Lawi and the crucified Christ, at least for members of the Ruwe Holy Ghost Church.

The latter asserts that when Lawi was struck by the Wanga spear on the morning of December 22, he pulled the weapon out of his body and died lying on his back with arms outstretched, holding the spear horizontally across his chest, mirroring Christ's death on the cross. [24] The Holy Spirit told Barnaba that the Joroho should mark (*gowu*) themselves accordingly. Tradition has it that Barnaba did not know how to interpret this command and asked the angels, "Are we to brand ourselves like cattle, or how should we do it?" (*Du gowa kaka dhok kose di tim nade?*) The angels answered that the Joroho were to sew the marks on their clothes and showed Barnaba the image of three types of gowns: a long, white[25] kanzu-style robe, which is the standard prayer garb for Roho men; a slightly more elaborate gown for officials; and a simple, triangular, loose-fitting gown for women, known as a *dwara*, which was to be worn with a black belt. (Later, women designed gowns with waistbands, pleats, and darts, but the original dress was simple.) Not being a tailor himself, Barnaba could only draw the three styles in the sand. Eventually, someone bought a sewing machine, and, from that time on, Mango's followers wore white uniforms with the emblem (*namba*) S followed by a cross stitched in red on front.

In late 1934, yet another development in Roho religion contributed to the group's growing sense of collective identity and divine selection: Paulo Rang'eng'a's presentation of a unique, secret language. Dhoroho (language of the Spirit), is, in fact, an encoding of Dholuo, and it is still used today by members of the Ruwe Holy Ghost Church in their liturgy (see "Note on the Roho Liturgical Language" in the appendix to this volume).

Developments such as personal experiences of the Holy Spirit, new hymns, and special forms of dress and speech appear to have bolstered the confidence and resolve of the Joroho. District records indicate that in November 1934, Chief Murunga placed new restrictions on Roho proselytization in South Wanga, suggesting that their local outreach was increasingly effective, particularly among women. The chief had no objection to the Kager practicing Roho religion "by themselves" but determined that "the attendance at meetings of the JeRoho Sect of Wanga women was likely to lead to a breach of the peace and was therefore forbidden." Responsibility for adhering to the chief's orders "rested on both the women themselves and the Instructors of the Religion."[26] In part, these restrictions on local ministry may have prompted the Joroho to begin a vigorous missionary campaign in other regions.

Missionary Journeys

By the end of 1934, the movement had entered a new phase. The Roho community initiated a process of missionary expansion that continues until this day but was most aggressive from 1935 through the mid-1950s. During these years, women were given the greatest freedom in assuming positions of authority and leadership. Also during this period, a rift gradually appeared between Mango's followers living in Musanda and those living in Ruwe. It appears that the former community successfully proselytized and established ties with other charismatic communities in Maragoli and Kitosh, whereas the latter concentrated its efforts in Luo regions to the west and south.

Roho adherents first preached the gospel in their natal villages and among their in-laws. Missionaries organized preaching safaris to their relatives' homes where they could be assured of food and shelter, if not a sympathetic audience. The visits that Roho elders chose to recount to me were those they considered important—involving the "bigger places" (*kuonde madongo*)—where dramatic cures or miracles occurred, events they always took as proof of divine endorsement.

The five journeys I describe next were conducted by the Ruwe Roho community between 1934 and 1940. The accounts trace a network of ties that formed the basis of what is today the denomination of the Ruwe Holy Ghost Church of East Africa. This oral material reveals the use of hymns in proselytizing and bears witness to the active role of women in propagating the faith. It also expresses the significance of healing both as an actual factor in the process of conversion in Nyanza and as the ultimate stamp of legitimacy in the official oral account of the acts of the church founders.

UYOMA

One day, some time after receiving his call to mission, Isaya Goro had a second visionary experience. The Holy Spirit instructed him to travel with Elijah Oloo to Uyoma to the home of a man named Matthayo Opiyo. Neither Isaya nor Elijah had ever heard of Matthayo Opiyo, but, accompanied by several Roho women, including Mariam Abonyo, they set out for Uyoma. There they asked directions to Opiyo's home; they found it, and Opiyo welcomed them. As the missionaries entered the compound, the Holy Spirit struck Mariam Abonyo with a song *Ne War Mach* (Behold the Salvific Fire), which she promptly sang for her hosts (see pages 149–150 for the lyrics).

Abonyo's lyrical hymn remains a favorite in today's Roho churches, although most members do not know its origin. It conveys the fundamental tenet of Roho Christian theology: Mango's suffering in the Musanda fire as the ultimate salvific event for believers. The final stanza of the second verse reflects a social reality— the movement's predominantly female membership—and acknowledges that Mango was ridiculed for this reason.

Opiyo and his family were impressed by Abonyo's singing and by the party's preaching. It was not long before Matthayo, his two wives, and their children converted and made preparations to return to Ruwe with Isaya and Elijah.

Meanwhile, the Joroho who had remained behind in Ruwe received a message from the Holy Spirit and the angels[27] that new members would be arriving and that they must go out to greet them with a song. What the hosts were to sing was revealed to Abisage Muriro: *Wapako hera mar Nyasaye, koriwo joga e pinje duto* (We praise the love of God, for it unites people from all lands) (see pages 154–155 for the full lyrics). The Ruwe congregation waited at Simenya—a market several miles from Ruwe—for their visitors to appear. They greeted the Uyoma folk with Abisage's song which stressed the unity of Mangos' followers everywhere, and were delighted when their visitors responded with a surprise of their own—Mariam Abonyo's inspirational hymn. Everyone then proceeded to Ruwe together.

Matthayo Opiyo was dubious about the phenomenon of speaking in tongues. He observed people falling to the ground and speaking gibberish but did not believe their claim of being possessed by the Holy Spirit. One day, as if to teach him a lesson, the Holy Spirit suddenly took hold of Matthayo—*ngan'o roho odonjo ni mang'eny* (lit., the spirit entered that person too much)—as he was returning from the bathhouse. Matthayo placed his water pot over his head and began behaving like a madman, crawling in the dirt and speaking in tongues (*dhum*). People prayed for him until he calmed down. He then declared, "I was saying that it couldn't happen to me . . . (but) when I finished bathing, the people of heaven took me and dipped me in water!" (*Awacho ga ni gino ok di tima, an . . . ka asetieko luok, jopolo ae okawa bu oling'a e pi!*) Soon afterward, Mattahyo and his family returned to Uyoma, but one of his sons remained in Goro's home for a long time, learning Dhoroho as well as basic reading and writing skills.

Roho churches began to spring up throughout Nyanza. Baranba Walwoho, Isaya Goro, Esta Songa, Leah Were, Nereya Auma, and others spent weeks walking from place to place proselytizing—*piny mangima nene wawothe!* (We walked through many places!). Isaya preached while Baranba baptized converts. Isaya also exposed and healed many witchdoctors. He broke their pots (in which they kept evil spirits), burned their implements, and prayed for them. People such as Matthayo, who had gone to Ruwe and experienced the Holy Spirit, returned to their home areas and started new congregations. The elders described these safaris as follows.

ALEGO NYAJUOK

One of the earliest safaris made by the Ruwe Joroho was a trip to Alego Nyajuok. Isaya Goro, Persica Adere, Esta Songa, and Anania Okelo decided to "do God's works" (*wadhi tiyo tij Nyasaye*) and travel to the home of Mica Olel, a follower of Mango who had been slightly injured in the Musanda fire. When the party arrived at Olel's home in Bar Osimbo, they learned that many of his family were sick, including the child of his brother, Eliazaro Odida. Isaya healed them all through prayer. The missionaries then returned to Ruwe.

Isaya led a second Roho contingent to Bar Osimbo, but this time they went to the home of Ruben Okech. Okech was the father of Patricia Amis, a girl whom Lawi had healed. Their mission was a sad one. Okech's young son had been staying in Isaya's home, learning to read, when he had taken ill and died. Thus, the delegation went to inform Okech that the boy had been buried at Ruwe. When the party arrived, a village elder conveyed the false report to the chief that the Roho people had taken nine children to Ruwe and all of them had died. The chief, a man named Amoth Owira, listened to this lie and promptly arrested Isaya and all the others.

Once at the chief's camp, Isaya defended himself. He explained that the Joroho did not kill children:

> We have not killed a single person. . . . Only one child has died (due to illness), and we are bringing the news to the father."
>
> (*Wan ok wanego ng'ato, kata ng'ato achiel. . . . Mihia achiel ema otho kende, to wabiro kelo wuon mihia.*)

Impressed by Isaya's presence, Owira said, "You, man-from-Ugenya, [I can see that you] cannot tell a lie" (*JaUgenya dak rias*).

As they left Amoth Owira's camp, they had to pass through a crowd of curious villagers who had gathered to get a good look at the strangers. In the confusion of the arrest, Esta Songa had forgotten to put on her Roho uniform and emblem, and a male bystander now asked Isaya if he could have the young lady who was not wearing a *namba* (emblem). The crowd laughed, but Isaya said, "She has remained with us since the fire; I can't give her to you!"

The party returned to Ruben Okech's home and prayed all night long. The following day, many people converted, which pleased the Joroho, who, after having been arrested, were eager to demonstrate their good intentions. Okech and his wife then accompanied their visitors back to Ruwe, for they wished to see their son's grave. Later, the couple constructed a church in Bar Osimbo. Okech was a carpenter who periodically returned to Ruwe to build benches and blackboards for Walwoho's church.

YIMBO

The third important safari that Roho elders recounted was a journey to Yimbo in 1935. Isaya Goro, accompanied by Esta Songa, traveled to the home of Roslida Ajanja in Usenge, Yimbo. Roslida had joined the movement before the death of Mango, despite her husband's opposition. Isaya and Esta led prayers for a full day and night, whereupon Roslida's husband was converted and called ten more people to come listen to the preachers. Among them was a sick person who begged Isaya to heal her, which he did.

Isaya and Songa then moved on to Goye to the home of Nora Anyango, also a follower of Mango's. Anyango brought them a powerful female witchdoctor (owner of deadly spirits [*wuon juogi ma rabede*]) named Otira. Otira had eight pots in which she kept evil spirits, known as *sepe*, and eight calabash rattles. When Isaya smashed her gourds and pots,[28] Otira began to roar. She was later baptized and given the name Mariam. Roslida Ajanja, Norah Anyango, and

Mariam Otira were hardworking, strong women. It was they who built the Roho church at Yimbo and "converted the entire area" (*mon go ema oloko pinyo*).

Concluding their stay in Yimbo, the missionaries returned to Ruwe to obtain more "medicine" (*yath*). Their practice after every journey was to go straight to the prayer house, where Barnaba Walwoho prayed for them. Renewed and filled with the power of the Holy Spirit, they dispersed to their respective homes.

NYAKACH AND SOUTH NYANZA

The Joroho's fourth significant journey, which occurred sometime between 1935 and 1940, began with a visit to Barak Otiende in Owalo, Nyakach. Many people went along: Esta Songa, Anania Okelo, Persica Adere, Turfosa Malowa, Grace Akungu, Mica Olel, and Laban Warinda. Persica Adere, a *laktar* (healer), perceived the sins of individuals, and Isaya prayed for them. Esta cooked and blessed the food. Everyone contributed in some way.

Otiende was a friend of Isaya Goro, although not a Roho convert. News had reached Isaya that no baby born in Otiende's home managed to live beyond infancy, so Isaya organized a Roho party to pray for Otiende's wives. Their efforts were successful; soon afterward, two of Otiende's wives conceived and delivered healthy babies who survived.

The missionaries then moved on to the home of Barnaba Tindo, also in Owalo, where they had heard that a malicious demon had killed every last one of Tindo's children and had even entered his cattle.[29] The entire party fought against the demon through prayer. Word reached them later that they had indeed overcome the demon and that Otiende's home now prospered.

Next the Joroho went to the home of Zephania Obewa in Nyakach Agoro. Obewa had, at one time, been a follower of Mango, but he had left the Roho movement to become a teacher in his original denomination, the African Inland Mission (A.I.M.). When Isaya and his colleagues arrived, they found Obewa locked in his house, supposedly deep in prayer. One of Obewa's live-in A.I.M. students had just died of smallpox, and Obewa refused to come out and bury the young man for fear of contracting the disease. Isaya naturally insisted that the man be buried, so the Roho group performed the task. Rather than being grateful, Obewa complained to the chief that Isaya had come to the area with the intention of taking over Obewa's ecclesiastical duties. A village elder rebuked him, saying, "Zephania, if this is the man who converted you, how can you now complain that he has come to [interfere with] your domain?" (*Zephainia, ka ng'atni ema oloki to koro sani iramo ni obiro e pinyi?*) A small *baraza* was held about the issue; Isaya was vindicated, and he and his colleagues went on their way.

From Nyakach, the Roho missionaries traveled on foot to South Nyanza. They crossed over the Miriu river to Kendu Bay (Karachuonyo) and stopped in the home of a man named Dishon Gunde. Several people in Gunde's large home were possessed by spirits (*sepe* and other *juogi*), and others suffered from various common physical ailments. While the Joroho were working to heal the afflicted individuals, a number of well-versed, local preachers from the Seventh Day Adventist Church (S.D.A.) came to Gunde's home to challenge the visitors to a preaching competition. The debate became heated, with the S.D.A. representatives accusing the Joroho of being "people who just walk around aimlessly" (*jowuoth awotha nono*).[30] Finally, Isaya, who had been inside another room, came out and began to preach. Through prayer and his straightforward exegisis of Scripture, he calmed the two parties.

The Joroho then moved on to Kamagambo, where they paid a visit to the local chief, a man named Ondiek. One of Ondiek's wives was barren and was constantly being ridiculed by her cowives as a result. Isaya was therefore asked to pray for the childless wife; some years later, he received news that the woman had given birth to two children.

The missionaries' next stop was the home of a disabled man named Barnaba Sije, whose wife had just died. Sije, an Anglican, had been told in a dream that a group of the Lord's people (*Jonyasaye*) and a group of musicians would congregate in his home. Indeed, the day that the Joroho arrived, his deceased wife's relatives came for the funeral, playing their instruments. After all the visitors had feasted on chicken, Sije called some of his C.M.S. friends to challenge the Joroho to a preaching competition. The Anglicans accused Isaya of "ruining the country" (*ketho piny*), but Isaya just responded calmly with passages from the Bible.

The Holy Spirit next guided the group to the *boma* of Petro Nguju in Kitere (still in Kamagambo). Petro had difficulty in marriage. He married one wife after the other, but each left him as quickly as her predecessor. The Joroho prayed for Petro's household and baptized his current wife and daughter. As usual, neighbors came to listen, and a number converted.

The missionaries then began their long trek to Ngodhe, at which point they planned to turn back toward Ugenya. On the way, they stopped in at the residence of Daniel Dida in Kanyamua. Dida, a native of Ruwe who had migrated to South Nyanza some years earlier, was happy to receive visitors from home. When his guests arose the next morning, to their surprise they found four rhinos standing just outside Dida's gate. Some elephants soon appeared as well, moving very slowly. Isaya Goro prayed that the wild animals would pass by without incident, which they did. By that time, however, it was again dark, so the Joroho spent a second night with Dida, leaving early the next day.

The journey to Ngodhe took the travelers through a gorge flanked by two hills. Esta Songa and Anania Okelo had dropped behind; Isaya and the others were up ahead, out of sight. Suddenly, Esta and Anania heard a pair of animals roaring to each other across the gorge. Then a lion crossed the path just in front of them. The two Joroho froze, terrified, as the lion stopped to look directly at them. God protected them, however, and the beast continued on its way.

The party made its way to the home of Naftal Riwa in Ngodhe, where they worked hard to heal and convert people in the area. One woman whom they healed there had been sick for two full years. Soon they began to prepare for their homeward journey. The missionaries had been gone approximately eight months. They left home when people were weeding their main grain crop (*doyo mar chwir*) in April or May, and now people had already harvested their smaller year-end crops (*ose ridho opon*). From Ngodhe, they went to Mirunda, where they took a rowboat across the lake to Naya in Uyoma, from there proceeding directly home.

MIRUNDA AND KADEM, SOUTH NYANZA

The fifth missionary journey that elders recounted in detail also took place sometime between 1935 and 1940. Isaya Goro again decided to head into South Nyanza but organized a smaller party this time: Persica Adere, Anania Okelo, Esta Songa, and himself. They traveled via Alego and Yimbo and stayed along the way with friends and Roho communities. In Uyoma, they stopped at Matthayo Opiyo's home for a few days and then continued across the lake to Mirunda, South Nyanza, by boat. In Mirunda, the Holy Spirit led them to the home of a man named Daudi Opanga, an S.D.A. catechist and the head of a local congregation. When the Joroho succeeded in converting him, his entire "school" followed suit. Thus Mango's church gained a new congregation over-night.

Isaya and his associates traveled on to Kadem, one of the most remote regions in South Nyanza. The Spirit directed them to the *boma* of Paulo Bwayi, a practitioner of traditional religion, like many of the inhabitants of that area. After converting Bwayi's entire family, the Joroho removed a lot of traditional Luo religious paraphernalia and chased out evil spirits. They then entered the home of a Msukuma named Osoro. Osoro practiced traditional religion also, and his family greeted the missionaries with a customary song of welcome.[31] The visitors stayed with Osoro a while until they converted him and many associates. They baptized him as Jeremiah and returned to Ruwe via Lake Victoria.

These five safaris provide an illustration of the way Roho adherents responded to the call to spread the faith. The elders I interviewed purposely focused on their most impressive journeys. However, they did mention less successful trips, such as two journeys made by Roho missionaries to Rusinga Island in 1936 and 1941, during which they failed to gain a single convert.

They adopted a pattern of interspersing visits to the homes of already estab-lished contacts with excursions that "followed the spirit" into strange villages. This pattern was—and still is—common to many charismatic groups in western Kenya. Even today members of charismatic churches speak of receiving divine messages to visit certain places.[32]

The custom of preaching competitions, in which representatives of local denominations would debate outsiders, appears to have been well established by the late 1930s, as suggested by the Roho members' experience in South Nyanza and interviews I have conducted with members of other independent churches. Clearly, these debates were not merely about theology. The visitors had to justify their reasons for operating in regions outside their own. Without authorization from colonial authorities, such travels could get people into trouble, as Ruwe Roho missionaries experienced in Alego Nyajuok and Nyakach Agoro.

Roho elders with whom I spoke were under the impression that cultivating ties with local administrators helped them gain legitimacy throughout the country-side. After Kenya gained independence in 1963, this strategy may have been effective, but in the 1930s and 1940s it often backfired. For example, the Joroho claim to have been on good terms with Chief Gideon Magak, an old army buddy of Isaya Goro,[33] who was in charge of Mumbo (near Oyugis). Roho elders also recall going to pay a visit to Chief Paulo Mboya in about 1935 and encountering no resistence. However, district and provincial records indicate that both these chiefs were reporting back to their colonial superiors about the group's activities. In April 1941, for example, Chief Paulo Mboya informed Provincial Commissioner S. H. Fazan of Nyanza (formerly Kavirondo) that the Roho sect "was strongly anti-Government and anti-white . . . [and] that the followers believed and taught that the Holy Spirit had removed its blessing from the British."[34] Prompted by his conversation with Mboya, the provincial commissioner launched an investigation into the strength of the movement in each of the three administrative districts—north, central, and south. Repeatedly, chiefs such as Mboya, Magak, and Murunga expressed their dislike of the Joroho, but authorities were at a loss as to how to take action against them.

Once apprehension about the potentially subversive nature of the "unpleasant Holy Roller sect" spread among government administrators, things again became more difficult for the Joroho. In 1940 in North Kavirondo, the Local Native Council refused their application for a church site "on the ground that they had no properly constituted governing body".[35] In May 1941, the district officer suddenly "discovered" that Isaya Goro, Baranaba Walwoho, and his brother had been making collections to finance church projects (e.g., cementing the grave of Elijah Oloo; baptisms; hosting visitors) without a license. After Mango's death, Colonel Anderson (then district commissioner for North Kavirondo) had given the Joroho permission to make collections, and they had been conducting their own affairs peacefully ever since. Now, however, government officials began to place obstacles in their way.[36]

Authorities were most concerned about possible interregional, intertribal connections between charismatic movements. As long as the Roho cult was strictly a Kager religion, as it was perceived throughout the 1930s, it posed little threat. When Roho communities began springing up in Kitosh, Kakamega, and Kisii, however, the government became alarmed. Officials began to look for connections between the Joroho and the Kikuyu-based African Independent Pentecostal Church. They also looked for ties with certain charismatic groups, such as Jakobo

Buluku's Holy Spirit followers in Luyia country, that may have come under the influence of the "socialistic" Friends mission in Kaimosi.

There were, in fact, connections between Jakobo Buluku's Holy Spirit sect in Bukoyni and the Roho churches in Ugenya. Teams from the Musanda Roho community, in particular, paid visits to Buluku's congregation, and Buluku reportedly participated in a few early Musanda-organized proselytizing efforts. Silvano Nyamogo, a leading follower of Mango's in Musanda, married one of Buluku's sisters, further strengthening bonds between Bukoyoni and Musanda. Today Buluku's disciples form the Holy Spirit Church of East Africa, a denomination distinct from both the Ruwe Holy Ghost Church of East Africa and the Musanda Holy Ghost Church of East Africa. The latter two take Alfayo Odongo Mango to be their savior, whereas Holy Spirit Church members venerate their martyr-founder, Buluku, who died in 1938 as a result of injuries sustained in a violent confrontation between Holy Spirit adherents and noncharismatic African Friends (Anderson 1971,17–18).

Today, members stress the distinctiveness of their particular churches. Each denomination claims to be the original possessor of the Holy Spirit, which was then transmitted to the founders of other charismatic movements throughout Nyanza. A number of elders in a variety of independent churches have claimed that "in the early days," however, anyone who wore a cross stitched onto a white gown, was part of *Dini ya Roho* (Religion of the Spirit); there were few rigid boundaries between local charismatic groups. This far-reaching indigenized revival evolved into a multitude of separate denominations, partly as a result of an intrinsic development and partly due to colonial "regularization," which confined indigenous organizations to particular districts or tribal territories.

Division within the Church

In 1941, Mango's followers in Ruwe and Musanda parted ways. It is difficult to determine whether the provincial commissioner's campaign of subtle opposition against the Roho movement, initiated the year before, facilitated the split. A letter sent by Chief Murunga to the district commissioner of North Kavirondo simply states that, in November 1941, the Joroho living in Musanda came before the chief's *baraza* and requested the right to "have their own Bishop." They no longer wished to recognize the authority of Barnaba Walwoho but chose to govern themselves separately under a man named Andrea Okoyo.[37] Murunga and the elders refused to grant their request on the grounds that the district commissioner, who had previously recognized Walwoho as the head of the Roho community, would have to rule on the case.

There is no written record of the district commissioner's decision, but Ruwe elders recall that he reprimanded both factions for being unable to settle petty differences. Warning each group to stick to its region and not to interfere with the other, he then proceeded to approve the split. He also agreed with the Ruwe Joroho that the Musanda sect must use a different emblem, so Andrea's party dropped the S, and kept the cross and soon became known as the Roho Msalaba (Spirit Cross) Church.

Ruwe Roho members explain that leadership disputes actually arose prior to Mango's death. They naturally claim that their elders, Barnaba Walwoho and Isaya Goro, gained Mango's approval, whereas Musanda leaders Silvano Nyamogo and the aging Andrea Odera Okoyo did not. Whether or not Mango anointed the former pair before his death, it seems that the colonial authorities— wary of more strife in Musanda—were all too happy to see the movement establish its base in Ruwe.

The quarrel, nevertheless, was not deep enough to prevent the two groups from attempting to unify for the purposes of registration. Ruwe Senior Teacher Meshak Ogola reports that, in the late 1950s, local leaders encouraged small Spirit churches to band together in forming recognized organizations. The Ruwe Joroho (Barnaba's party) and the Roho Msalaba (Andrea's party) joined another Luo charismatic group known as *Duond Warruok* (Voice of Salvation) to form the Holy Ghost Society. In 1956, Oginga Odinga became the society's advocate and helped them draw up a constitution—a prerequisite to registration with the state. According to the society's constitution, all three churches were united under a single central office; however, each of the three member churches was free to draft its own bylaws and manage its own affairs.

In 1957, the three churches were registered collectively as the Holy Ghost Church of Kenya. (The government did not accept names in African languages.) The organization remained intact until 1960, when animosities between Ruwe Roho and Roho Msalaba surfaced again, and the two churches decided to part company for good. The Ruwe party registered itself as the Ruwe Holy Ghost Church, and Andrea's group changed their name from Roho Msalaba to the Musanda Holy Ghost Church. In 1990 and 1991, there was again talk among some leaders of reuniting the two denominations, but, to date, most members seem content to maintain good ties and to congregate in the savior's home on the anniversary of his death.

Conclusion: The Institutionalization of Roho Religion and Women's Changing Roles

For more than six decades, the rapid growth of independent churches and other religious movements in sub-Saharan Africa has caught the attention of scholars from a variety of disciplines. Between 1968 and 1985, the number of African independent churches and indigenous movements grew from three thousand to more than seven thousand and today claims more than thirty-two million adherents, or 15 percent of the Christian population of Africa (Barrett 1968, 6–7; 1982, 782). The actual number of Africans involved in various kinds of indigenous Christianity may be much higher still, for the figures published in large surveys frequently exclude small, local Christian groups that stand distinct from established religious denominations but are not officially listed or recognized by their respective governments.

In scholarly literature, these prolific and varied religious communities are commonly subsumed under the term "new religious movements" (NRMs). The conceptualization of these phenomena as "new" is problematic and reflects the impact of Eurocentric taxonomies on the study of African religions. Outsiders have often perceived African religious movements to be derivative of European Christian "penetration," without a history of their own prior to contact with the West. In reality, many of the so-called NRMs have immediate precolonial precursors, whose roots, in turn, may reach even further into the past, had we the means to discover them. Not only is the designation *new* obfuscating, in that it belies many movements' earlier roots, but also it is too broad. Benetta Jules-Rosette points out that the religious groups generally discussed in the literature on new religious movements in Africa are those that have emerged since the early 1930s (1987, 82). The term, then, can refer to a prophetic movement such as the Lumpa church, which formed during the height of the colonial period in Northern Rhodesia, as well as to a spiritual science movement emerging in Calabar in the 1980s (Hackett 1989, 200–203). Hannah W. Kinoti has suggested that continuing to use the word *new* to refer to Kenyan independent churches founded more than a generation ago, is misleading. She argues, for example, that denominations such as the African Israel Church Nineveh and the Legio Maria— founded in the 1940s and 1960s, respectively—"have a history" and now form part of the landscape of established, stable Christianity in Kenya.[38]

Although scholars such as Igor Kopytoff (1980), Tim Allen (1991), Iris Berger (1976; 1981) and Wyatt MacGaffey (1983) have raised the issue of change within African movements, the diachronic dimension of Independent Christianity in Africa has not, I would argue, received sufficient attention. The institutionalization of indigenous Christianity has not roused nearly the kind of interest that sociologists and historians have devoted to the routinization of charismatic movements in Europe and the United States (Johnson 1992; Lindholm 1990; Palmer and Bird 1992; Wright 1992; Wallis 1982a, 1982b). This section attempts to analyze one feature of historical change within the Ruwe Holy Ghost Church— the transformation of women's roles with the increasing institutionalization of Roho religion. I demonstrate that the exclusively ceremonial character of present-day female Roho leadership is the result of a historical process that involved both Western and indigenous patterns of routinization of charismatic religion. This process had a certain intrinsic momentum, yet it was nonetheless contingent upon a number of specifically Kenyan factors, to be enumerated here.

Women's Present Roles

The Roho church, like numerous other African indigenous churches, has a predominantly female membership. Reliable statistics on women's participation in independent Christianity are unavailable, but many researchers have commented that women comprised a majority of the adherents of the churches they studied (Jules-Rosette 1979, 127; Barrett 1968, 148; Sundkler 1976, 79). According to my findings, a consistent 70 percent of the people attending any Roho church-sponsored event were women. Despite their numerical dominance, women rarely occupy top positions in local, regional, or national church administrative hierarchies. Instead, like their counterparts in many independent (and mission-based) churches throughout Africa, Roho women command what Benetta Jules-Rosette has termed "ceremonial leadership," a leadership entailing the use of mystical talents such as healing and mediumship during specified and limited occasions authorized by men (Jules-Rosette 1979, 127).[39]

The major female role in contemporary Roho religion is the elderly healer, or *laktar*, a name probably derived from *daktari*, the Swahili word for "doctor." *Laktache* (pl.) are generally postmenopausal; in some congregations, it is required that they be widows, for widows are considered better able to dedicate themselves exclusively to the church. As a group of elderly *laktache* in the Masumbi congregation explained:

> Our (husbands) died and we don't want any more. Now we want to work for God. Now Jesus, God is our husband.
>
> (*Wan magwa ne ose tho ok wadwar. Koro wadwa tiyo ni Nyasaye. Wan koro Nyasaye, Yesu koro e chworwa*).

Laktache are generally organized in a loose hierarchy, with the senior *laktar* (*laktar maduong*) either the eldest among them or the one who has belonged to the church the longest. Each *laktar* has a different role to fulfill, although she frequently assists other *laktache* in their respective duties. One *laktar*, for example, is in charge of washing the bodies of the deceased and preparing them for burial. Another's specialty is healing children. Yet another is responsible for fetching the water to be used in ritual cleansing, and her colleague is assigned the task of transforming it into holy water. This holy or "hot" water (*pi maliet*) is the special medicine of the *laktache*. Water is collected in a clean pan and made "hot" through a prayer that exorcises evil spirits.[40] In their role as healers, some *laktache* open up their homes, creating a ward for sick people who come for treatment and remain to convalesce. These home wards are similar to the "therapeutic households" Cohen and Atieno Odhiambo (1989) describe in their study of Siaya, except that, unlike other female practitioners who offer long-term specialized care, the *laktache* do not charge payment for their services. They are simply doing "God's work" (*tich Nyasaye*).

Roho *laktache* function as midwives. After delivering a baby, a *laktar* performs a ritual cleansing. According to the Luo custom, a newborn should remain in the house for a brief period before being seen by others. Traditionally, baby boys were kept inside for four days, girls for three. Many *laktache* encourage a more extended seclusion. In a Holy Spirit congregation in Masumbi, near Ng'iya, baby boys were kept inside for as long as thrity-three days, girls for sixty-six days. If the mother of the baby agrees, the *laktar* initiates the seclusion through a simple rite of holding the child while reciting a prayer for protection. During this period, the parents must refrain from sexual relations and no one except the parents, immediate siblings, and *laktache* may see or touch the child. As the baby may not be taken out to a hospital, the well-being of the child is in the hands of the Holy Spirit and God, mediated through the person of the *laktar*. When the period of seclusion is over, it is the *laktar* who carries the infant out of the house and introduces him or her to the community in a ceremony called *golo nyathi* (taking out the child).[41]

Laktache are both healers and guardians. They are responsible for the spiritual protection of church members, not only during physical ordeals such as illness and childbirth but also during spiritually dangerous times such as infancy, death, or occasions when the soul of a person in trance leaves her or his body. Yet, they generally conduct these indispensable services behind the scenes or on the fringes of public worship sessions. They heal the sick at home and absolve people of their sins quietly outside the church. This overarching—yet, nonetheless, backstage— role as guardian was quintessentially expressed during the 1991 commemoration of Mango's death, when two senior *laktache* holding large wooden crosses were stationed on either side of the Ruwe church chancel, silently reciting prayers of protection as the bishop led the service.

Of course, the vast majority of Roho women are not *laktache*. Most female members are young or middle-aged mothers who occupy no post. Collectively, these women make their presence felt through hymn singing. Singing is an extremely important part of Roho religious expression. Well-executed songs are taken as gifts of God and likened to the music one will encounter in the afterlife.[42] Hymns are understood as a link with the heavenly realm. Some women recount experiences of waking up in the middle of the night singing a song they have never heard before, which they claim has been revealed (*nyise*) to them in a dream by an angel or an ancestor.

The Joroho distinguish between two types of hymns, or *wende* (sing., *wer*): *wende mag Nyasaye* (songs of God) and *wende mag Roho* (songs of the Spirit). The former are standard Christian praise songs common to many Kenyan Protestant churches.[43] They are often rather solemn and tend to be sung a cappella in harmony. *Wende mag Roho*, however, utilize original, fast-paced melodies that lend themselves to dancing and drumming. These songs are initiated by a cantor (*jakwano*) who sings a one-line solo that is then answered by the congregation or chorus (*jo-olo*) (see the songs in Chapter 4 and in the appendix to this volume).

During these long, repetitive songs, which gradually increase in tempo, people are most likely to become possessed by the Holy Spirit. In some congregations, it is in the midst of a *wer mar Roho* that individuals—generally women—begin to prophesy, grabbing another member by the arm in order to deliver revelations and prescriptions into his or her ear. This style of prophesy is personal, communicated by the seer to the individual privately. In other churches, immediately following such a hymn, individuals who have received messages during their ecstacy, present their revelations to the entire congregation. In either instance, women's agency is crucial to this central aspect of Roho religiosity.

Through their singing, women exert a great deal of influence over the shape and character of people's collective worship experience. They create the atmosphere conducive to trancing and are the primary bearers of prophesies and heavenly messages for the gathering. During the course of a sermon or testimony, anyone in the congregation can jump up and interject a song when so moved, but women exercise this freedom far more often than men. Frequently, a woman commences a song whose lyrics punctuate the point a preacher is making. At other times, she initiates a song when she decides that the pastor has talked long enough. In either case, the speaker is obliged to wait until the song is over.

Many male leaders appear uncomfortable with the relative autonomy and assertiveness that women singers exhibit. During a large sabbath service at Ruwe, I once heard a pastor admonish the women in his congregation for repeatedly interrupting the preachers. He announced that the women were not to sing until whoever happened to be speaking concluded his statement. The pastor's instructions met with mixed success. In another service held in a small Roho parish in Siaya district, the presiding pastor railed at the all-female choir for not standing when he and the other male officiants entered the sanctuary. Obviously disgruntled, the women obliged him. Such attempts on the part of male leaders to set the parameters of women's ritual practice or to rein in women's self-expression are by no means peculiar to the Roho church. In her study of the Apostles of John Maranke in central Africa, Jules-Rosette concludes:

> The concept of Christian equality, with the expectation that men and women enter heaven side by side, is basic to Bapostolo doctrine. However, the expression of equality in political leadership is denied women. Whenever men are present at ritual events, Bapostolo women show them particular respect and express their control through interaction rather than formal leadership. Women are reprimanded when their participation transgresses the boundaries of song, healing, and mediumship. (1979, 30)

In addition to their ceremonial roles, women leaders in independent churches are expected to perform frequent domestic tasks, such as sweeping church floors, preparing food for visitors, and generally serving men. Sheila Walker's comment that in the Ivorian Harrist church "women play the same domestic roles that they fill in other areas of life" (1979, 92) also applies to the Joroho. Just as women in Luo society are responsible for cleaning and straightening items in the house, so are Roho women the ones who arrange the altar and decorate the sanctuary with greens. Some Roho women have ritualized these tasks; they may chase demons out of the church before sweeping, for example, or they may recite a blessing over the altar centerpiece. There are numerous mundane chores that are not ritualized, however, which women are simply expected to perform because they do so in everyday life. When a party or delegation travels from one congregation to visit another, for instance, women carry the men's vestments (as well as their own) and whatever supplies are needed for the journey. Male pastors and officials are free to send women members to do errands, bring water, take messages to people in other homes, and so on. More and more, the activities of Roho members conform to the gender roles of the local Luo environment, roles that entail a general attitude of obedience on the part of women.

Women's Past Roles

Information I collected in the field, supported by studies on the emergence of other African indigenous movements, suggests that at one time women exercised more direct authority over congregations than they do today, now that their movements have become routinized. I use the word *suggest* because only within the last fifteen to twenty years have scholars paid attention to the character of women's involvement in African independent churches. When we try to adopt a diachronic perspective that takes into account the changes in women's roles since the inception of precolonial, colonial, or early postcolonial religious movements, we are faced with a glaring paucity of material. One compelling piece of evidence in our favor, however, is the simple fact that most sects founded by African women—that have managed to survive—are today controlled by men. The Lumpa revival movement, founded by the young Bemba prophetess Alice Lenshina in 1953, is a case in point. As the movement evolved into an independent church, it became increasingly politicized, and Lenshina reluctantly allowed her authority to be usurped by her politically minded male deacons (Hinfelaar 1991, 100; Roberts 1970, 541). The Deima (Holy Water) Church, founded in the 1940s in the Ivory Coast by Marie Lalou, is another case in point. After her death in 1951, Lalou was succeeded by a series of prophetesses who carried on her healing ministry. Women have continued to retain their therapeutic roles within the Deima church, but men now occupy the official posts, direct worship services, and control the administration (Walker 1979, 95–96). Many other now-institutionalized movements appear to have followed the same evolutionary pattern: Mai (Mother) Chaza's church in Zimbabwe (founded 1952); Christina Abiodoun's Cherubim and Seraphim Society in Nigeria (founded in 1925);[44] and Grace Tani's Church of the Twelve Apostles (founded around 1915) are a few examples (Jules-Rosette 1979, 84; Barrett 1968, 148; Breidenbach 1979, 104).

The recognized founder of the Luo-based Roho church, as we have seen, was a man. However, women were central to the inception, development, and spread of Roho religion. Contrary to published histories that posit the roots of Roho religion in the activities of Odongo Mango and Lawi Obonyo in the 1930s, my major informant, Anna Inondi, traces the beginnings of Holy Spirit religion in her area to Ibrahim Osodo's movement in 1912. That year, she claims, marks the Spirit's first appearance in Ruwe sublocation and the emergence of the original Roho movement. This early charismatic religion was sustained by young women throughout the First World War. When the young Anglican catechist Alfayo Odongo Mango had his first possession experience in 1916, some of these same Ruwe women affirmed the authenticity of his experience. When Mango reappeared on the scene in 1933 and openly embraced Roho religion,[45] he found a ready core of supporters among clusters of charismatic Christians, such as those in Anna Inondi's circle. When Holy Spirit believers were denounced by the Church Missionary Society authorities in 1933, the majority of the approximately one hundred people who withdrew with Mango into his Iwinda homestead were women and children. Again, during the period of hardship immediately after the Musanda fire, it was largely women who sustained the movement.

Unlike missionary and colonial reports, which, as we have seen, characterized Roho women as ignorant, hysterical, "lusty wenches,"[46] Roho oral tradition portrays the founding women as strong-willed and defiant. Elderly women members maintain that the one thing that originally attracted them to Roho religion was that they had the freedom to preach, something forbidden them in mission churches at the time.[47] For many, this freedom of self-expression in worship was worth much suffering. Women endured beatings from their menfolk and sacrificed their reputations in order to attend Roho meetings.

Roho practice keeps alive the memory of the important part women played in the founding of the church in a number of ways. One powerful method is hymn singing. The lyrics of the song "We Are Women of War," for example, celebrate the courage of the *askeche* in the Musanda battle and present the deaths of those women and girls killed by spears and flames as an ultimate victory. The hymn "Behold the Salvific Fire" reminds people that Mango's early followers were predominantly women and that he was taunted as a result. Mention of Turfosa Aloo, the only married female Roho martyr, comes up frequently in elders' testimonies and visions. Her name has also become incorporated into the standard Roho greeting, *Mirembe Jo-k'Odongo, Jo-k'Aloo, Jo-kaLawi!* (Greetings, people of Odongo, people of Aloo, people of Lawi!) Another important vehicle for conveying the history of women's contribution to the founding of the church occurs during the annual *Sikukuu mar Rapar* (Celebration of Remembrance).

Every January, Roho pilgrims from all over Kenya travel to Ruwe and Musanda to commemorate the martyrdom of their founders. Festivities include a reenactment of the fire staged by women elders. "It is a good thing," I was told by one male onlooker. "This way we will never forget that it is women who started this religion."

About a year after the massacre, as described, a new phase in the church's history began. The Joroho, who had moved their headquarters to the home of Anna Inondi and her husband, Isaya Goro, in Ruwe, sent out their first missionaries. Thus began a process of expansion that continues until this day but was most aggressive from 1935 through the mid-1950s. During this phase, women were given the greatest freedom in assuming positions of authority and leadership. In the 1930s and 1940s, Roho women undertook long, arduous missionary journeys, often with men and sometimes alone. They traveled mostly east into Luyia country, west into Alego and Yimbo, southwest around (and across) Lake Victoria, and into Tanzania. At times, they were imprisoned for their activities. Senior Roho women take great pride in recounting these adventures. They speak with relish of the unusual terrain they traversed, their confrontations with wild beasts, and the miracles they witnessed and performed through the Spirit. Such trips, which could last as long as seven or eight months, gave Roho women missionaries a breadth of experience and exposure not readily available to young Luo women at that time.

During this phase of expansion, some independent-minded Roho women engaged in a practice that ran counter to dominant Luo cultural norms. Women such as Esta Songa, Phoebe Apondi Ger, Mariam Adhiambo, Grace Oracho, and Leah Nyalwal Omondi, all from Ugenya, took vows among themselves to postpone marriage in order to work for God. Such a decision was highly unusual in the Luo context, and the women brought ridicule and criticism on themselves and their families (Ominde [1952] 1977, 40–41). Esta Songa, who at the time of the massacre was in her early twenties, chose to work as a Roho missionary for ten years before agreeing to get married:

> People really laughed at me. But I said that I must do as I had promised. . . . My sister said, "Your breasts are beginning to sag," [indeed] they were sagging. The Spirit had found me when I was young and I could have married earlier. But if [the Spirit] gets you, then you must do what it arranges.
>
> (*Ne onyiera ndi. To awacho ni kaka asingra cha nyaka atim. . . . Nyira owacho thuno igo pas, an ema ne ogo pas. To Roho onuang'a ka nene da adhi tedo chon. To ka Roho onuyang'i to nyaka itim gima ochan.*)

Songa explains that, when she did eventually marry, she still would not abandon her calling as a missionary. Only now that she is in her eighties has she ceased to travel and proselytize. "I stopped," she added contentedly, "when I had seen [lit., completed] the world" (*Awuok ka wase tieko piny*).

A small percentage of the Roho women in Songa's generation never married, choosing to devote their entire lives exclusively to the church. Most of these individuals have already died and are remembered by their congregations as intrepid women of great piety. *Laktar* Persica Adere from Alego is one such example. Forgoing marriage, Adere walked in the Spirit (*wuotho gi Roho*) until her death in 1988. The entire denomination honored her memory in 1991 with a drive to raise money to erect a cross on her grave. Other Roho women established Christian communes where single, divorced, or widowed female converts were welcome to reside. One such individual was Sarah Agot of Mirunda in South Nyanza, a powerful Roho prophetess who in the 1940s converted her home into a ward for sick people and Roho enthusiasts. Turfosa Okoko and Saline Ndiwa from Asembo as well as Dorca Omolo and Judith Ogola from Uyoma are some of the women who went to Sarah to be treated for illnesses. After being cured through the Holy Spirit, these women acquired spiritual vocations themselves as *laktache* and *joote* (seers). They remained permanently in Mirunda, along with approximately fifteen other women. Agot granted all of them space to build houses and small plots of land, which they farmed collectively.

Roho women were responsible for founding and nurturing the growth of many local Roho congregations that are today headed by men. One such pioneer was Nereya Owuor of the Masumbi parish in Siaya. While still single, Owuor had become an adherent of the Nomiya Luo movement in Gem in the 1930s. After her marriage in Masumbi, she introduced Holy Spirit religion to that area in the late 1940s. She led her small church there for thirty years, earning herself the nickname *Jakinda* (one who perseveres, the zealous one). Other women who founded and ministered to Roho congregations are Roslida Ajanja, Norah Anyama, and Mariam Otira, all of Yimbo. Ajanja had joined the Roho movement before Mango's death; the other two converted in late 1934. Together, the three women established the thriving Yimbo branch of the Ruwe Holy Ghost Church.

Information on the different ritual functions that Roho women performed between 1935 and 1960 differs from region to region. Yet, it is certain that a wider variety of posts and choices were open to Roho women than is the case today. For one thing, assignment of religious roles to different gender spheres was not yet fixed. As was the case in the East African Anglican revival of the 1940s, charismatic fervor tended to open up participation and ignore established gender and gerontocratic restrictions, at least initially (Robins 1979). Thus, in the first decade after Mango's death, both women and men were ordained as teachers or catechists (*jopuonj*), healers (*laktache*), and pastors (*pate*). In many Roho churches throughout Nyanza, the wife of a pastor (*padri*) shared his title and status. She had her own *padri* gown and could perform baptisms, burials, and even ordinations in her husband's absence. It was not uncommon for a pastor's wife to assume full responsibility for her husband's parish after his death. Two of the women mentioned previously, Anna Inondi of Ruwe and Sarah Agot of Mirunda, were wives of pastors. In both cases, the women had embraced Roho religion before marrying and went on to became important figures in their husbands' parishes. As widows, Inondi and Agot truly came into their own as authority figures in the church. In part, their prominence can be explained by the fact that, after their husbands' deaths, both women were able to exercise their official prerogatives more freely. They were now solely responsible for all the baptisms and ordinations of church officers within their pastorates. As time passed, they came to be respected as senior clergy within the denomination as a whole, having served longer than many of their male colleagues. Thus, it was Inondi who was called on to preside at the funeral of the first Ruwe bishop and to ordain the second one. Agot, similarly, not only delivered the ritual blessing at the installation of Roho bishops in her area but also had a great deal of say in their selection.

The increase in the stature of these two women over time involved, as well, a combination of their individual attributes with the community's general assumptions about age and gender. As Inondi and Agot became grandmothers, their renown as healers increased, a fact consistent with Luo assumptions about the mystical powers of old women. The spiritual and therapeutic leadership exhibited by these women—and by others like them—cannot be divorced from their strength of character or their personal charisma. Inondi, with whom I spent many hours, was a woman of deep faith and honesty, prodigious memory, and keen insight. Although she was ill and frail, she continued to receive Roho visitors who came from all over the country to express their gratitude for past kindnesses. Sarah Agot, who died in 1986, was reportedly a person of remarkable presence as well. In fact, some of her followers today consider her a divine figure, sent by God.[48]

The religious career of Anna Inondi spanned seventy years; Sarah Agot's lasted fifty. Their biographies mirror the evolution of women's leadership within a church that has matured with them. Both women joined the Roho movement in its early stages, when it was largely a movement of youth. Inondi became a female warrior, a role the church today remembers and celebrates for its courage, but which is no longer a viable option for young women. As pastors alongside their husbands, Inondi and Agot traveled and proselytized at a time when women were founding new branches throughout Nyanza and northeastern Tanzania. Today, no woman can become a pastor; that role, together with the posts of teacher, lay reader, and bishop, is reserved exclusively for men. Nor are young women encouraged to conduct missionary journeys on their own. The option of leading a single life devoted to the Spirit is no longer recommended for Roho women. Unmarried women are certainly welcome to participate in Roho worship but cannot qualify for the post of *laktar* or, as far as I can establish, become *joote.* Instead, the value of marriage and domestic obedience is frequently expounded in sermons, conveyed through drama, and reinforced in ritual requirements.[49]

In their later years, Inondi and Agot embodied the current Roho ideal of feminine spirituality. As elderly widowed healers, they ran successful therapeutic households. For many, the miraculous cures performed by these women constitute their crowning achievements. It is as superlative *laktache*, rather than as warriors or pastors, that Joroho now remember these pioneering women. Dominant gender constructs have thus obfuscated the record of Inondi and Agot's earlier contributions in the collective memory of the Roho community.

Complementary Processes of Routinization

Throughout the church's most dramatic period of growth, inspired Roho women spearheaded religious innovation and exercised charismatic authority in a variety of roles. The early 1960s, however, marked the beginning of a new phase of Roho history, as women's opportunities for leadership were systematically reduced.[50] The range of leadership options open to Roho women was increasingly curtailed until it came to be restricted to a narrow, senior age group. I contend that this change has come about as a result of two mutually reinforcing processes of routinization. A male-dominated colonial institutional model has combined with Luo patriarchy in the process of Roho church formation to limit women's influence to well-monitored ceremonial settings.

To help illuminate the changes that have taken place in the character of Roho leadership, I turn to Max Weber. For Weber, true charismatic authority is, by its very nature, transitory. Because its character is "specifically foreign to every-day routine structures," charismatic authority "cannot remain stable but becomes either traditionalized or rationalized, or a combination of both" (Parsons [1947] 1964, 363–364; Wallis 1982b, 35–36; Johnson 1992, S7). Processes of traditionalization or rationalization are by no means automatic but are the result of choices made by a movement's members.[51] Both ideal and material interests can motivate charismatic leaders and followers to make their mutually beneficial relationship permanent. Weber stresses that the founder's administrative staff generally stand to gain the most from stabilizing the movement and that they frequently attempt to direct the process in such a way that their status acquires everyday legitimacy. In the case of the Roho movement, it was, indeed, individuals from among Mango's inner circle who assumed leadership posts after his death. In early January 1934, Mango reportedly received a vision in which God told him of his impending death and instructed him to make provisions for his flock. According to Mango's son, Ibrahim Owuor, Mango originally proposed that his eldest daughter, Salome Ndiany, should succeed him. However, Mango's associates made it clear that people would not accept the authority of a woman. Mango did not persist. The six officers finally appointed to lead the Roho community were all men. The individuals Mango chose to fill the posts of archbishop and bishop were selected for their loyalty and closeness to the founder, as well as on the basis of their spiritual powers. The position of king was filled by an ex-army sergeant, and two literate preachers were appointed to serve as catechists. A convert from Kericho teacher-training college was placed in charge of secular education.

WESTERN INSTITUTIONAL MODELS

We do not know all the deliberations that took place prior to the selection of these first officials. Even before Mango's death, however, a partial rationalization of leadership roles had begun. Literacy, education, and professional experience in colonial institutions such as the armed forces were already emerging as criteria for official leadership. It has been well documented that in Africa institutionalization along these lines discriminates against women, who have lacked equal access to formal education (Robertson and Berger 1986; Hay and Stichter 1984; Obbo 1980; Sudarkasa 1986). In her discussion of the widespread shift from age to gender as the controlling factor in people's access to resources in Africa, Claire Robertson cites lack of schooling for women as a primary cause:

> One major cause of this change has been the restriction of female access to the most significant new resource, formal education. Formal, western-type education was crucial in the process of removing authority from older people by giving young men, in particular, the power of independent earnings and mastery of new technology. . . . In modern Africa formal education is the basic requirement for jobs entailing high prestige, power, and authority. But women's access to higher education has systematically been restricted by colonial prejudice, cultural norms, and the consequent lack of facilities. (1987, 103)

Although much has been written about the detrimental economic impact of Western educational and developmental strategies on African women's economic and social status, less has been said about the ramifications of these changes on women's religious activities. In the Roho church, although Mango introduced the norm of an educated male hierarchy before his death, in practice, as we have seen, women continued to exercise a great deal of leadership on the local level for years afterward, assuming many of the same responsibilities and ritual functions as men. Why, then, did this more or less egalitarian state of affairs change in the 1960s? Iris Berger's discussion of the Nyabingi and Emandwa cults in Rwanda and Uganda offers some clues. Berger observes that, during the precolonial period, the cults were led by female priestesses. In the late nineteenth century, however, the cults became venues for organizing resistance to European domination, and men usurped the leadership.

> Thus, as in the Unyamwezi lineage cults, women seemed to gain some positions only at times when they possessed relatively low value. This raises

the question . . . of whether women participated more actively in the initial stages of spirit cults when possession might have been more spontaneous and less regulated than in later stages. (Berger 1976, 179–180)

Rationalization of charismatic authority may appear to take on an inexorable life of its own, but, in fact, it is always managed by living agents whose actions are influenced by a particular set of historical circumstances. I suggest that a number of changes in the social, political, and economic climate of Kenya in the 1960s combined to make positions of leadership in the Roho churches in rural Nyanza suddenly attractive to, in particular, literate men. Although interest in religious office should not be categorically explained away as political or social aspiration in disguise, involvement in religious activities and institutions for nonreligious reasons is an ever-present reality that increases in certain periods and decreases in others. In the late 1950s and early 1960s, leadership posts in independent churches offered more possibilities for self-advancement than before, and a number of factors worked to privilege men in capitalizing on those opportunities.

First and foremost, there was the impact of the Societies Ordinance passed by the colonial government in 1957.[52] This ordinance, which required local bodies of all kinds to register with the state, distinctly shaped the institutionalization of Roho religion in favor of male authority. In an attempt to monitor popular movements in the countryside after the devastating experience of the Mau Mau, the administration encouraged community leaders to assist local groups in drafting constitutions and bylaws. As a result of governmental envoys going into rural constituencies, many Christian groups selected bishops and archbishops for the first time, chose names for their churches, and came to conceive of themselves as distinct from other groups of Christians with whom they had been worshiping. The registration requirement had the effect of both ossifying and fragmenting popular Christianity in western Kenya. The government agents who facilitated this process naturally looked to the legal documents of male-run mission churches and existing male-dominated public agencies to provide the blueprint for structuring independent church hierarchies.

Moreover, by the mid-1960s, a primary school education was no longer enough to qualify a person for employment in the urban sector or in government agencies throughout the provinces. Christian men with some schooling who failed to find employment and were forced to return to the village apparently found an attractive outlet for their skills in reading and teaching Scripture in independent churches, where there were no seminary requirements for clergy. In the Ruwe Holy Ghost Church, it was the responsibility of *jopuonj* (teachers) to transmit the fundamentals of Roho religion to new converts. Adherents from other regions sent their children to stay for extended periods at Ruwe, where the young people assisted their host families in farmwork and domestic chores in return for instruction in the Bible, Dhoroho (the sacred language), and rudimentary reading and writing skills. Throughout Nyanza, teachers and pastors constructed chapels or small churches, which doubled as schools. [53]

Successful preachers—particularly those with wives who would tend to the sick—were able to create an informal system of patronage. Their homes became centers where charismatic Christians could receive healing and literacy in exchange for labor and loyalty. Having more hands at home freed Roho leaders to undertake missionary journeys and to build bonds with other Roho congregations, thereby strengthening the church and expanding their own networks of contacts at the same time. [54]

A third factor that helped attract literate men to leadership roles within Kenyan indigenous churches at this time was *Uhuru* (national independence) in 1963. This event suddenly gave African religious and cultural forms a legitimacy they had previously lacked. Missionary bodies such as the C.M.S., which worked with the colonial government to suppress the Roho movement, now turned a more tolerant face to their African brothers and sisters in Christ. Vatican II, with its theological claim that God was present among indigenous cultures throughout the world, also had a profound impact on both Catholic and Protestant missionary projects. Schools such as St. Paul's United Theological College in Limuru now welcomed clergy from independent churches to participate in courses alongside ministers from mission-based churches. A number of other Christian organizations made attempts to draw independent church personnel into ecumenical programs, although these efforts met with mixed success due to lack of funding within the indigenous churches (Beetham 1973, 151–153). The 1960s thus brought educated independent church leaders new opportunities for involvement, advancement, and recognition within wider Kenyan society.

The final factor that contributed to certain Luo men seeking to secure Roho posts for themselves in the 1960s was political. A number of male Roho leaders I encountered during my fieldwork indicated they had joined the church during the first blush of *Uhuru*, when the anticolonial roots of black churches were being reclaimed and celebrated. Some young men, harboring hopes for the creation and ascendancy of a Luo-dominated party in Kenya politics, looked to the Luo independent churches as possible arenas for mobilizing popular support. Some were attracted to the Roho church in the immediate preindependence and early postindependence period, when Luo statesman Oginga Odinga had become temporarily involved in the movement. In fact, it was Odinga who drafted the first constitution for the Roho church in 1957. [55] It was soon clear that the hopes of political activists were misplaced and that the vast majority of Roho adherents were primarily concerned with healing and evangelization. Today, the overt attitude of Roho members is apolitical. The constitution of the Ruwe Holy Ghost Church expressly states that the church "shall have no connection with any political organisation," and will encourage the maintenance of the "Law and Order of the Republic." One constantly hears this position proclaimed in Roho sermons and reiterated in private testimony. Roho churches go to great lengths to make their projects known to local government officials in order to remove any suspicion as to the "true nature" of their activities.

INDIGENOUS INSTITUTIONAL MODELS

The Western-style institutionalization of Roho religion was reinforced by a complementary process of indigenous routinization embedded in Luo patriarchal norms. This parallel process is captured in Weber's idea of "traditionalization." Traditional authority, according to Weber, is "bound to precedents handed down from the past" (Parsons 1964, 361). While the Roho church was forced to establish itself according to the legal requirements of a developing nation-state, its leaders were building legitimacy in rural Nyanza, where the vast majority of the Roho congregations are located.

At this point, a brief overview of rural Luo society and traditional gender roles is necessary. Luo society is patrilineal, exogamous, virilocal, and organized into territorial segmentary lineages. Within this system, people acquire land primarily through patrilineal inheritance. Under Luo customary law, women do not have independent rights in land but are assigned plots by their husbands. Women have no jural autonomy and no independent legal rights over their children (Muigai 1989, 115; Hay 1982, 113; Pala Okeyo 1980; Potash 1978, 381; Shipton 1984a, 616; Glickman 1974; Evans-Pritchard 1949). Betty Potash convincingly argues that, despite informal methods of getting what they want, most women, given the structure of Luo society, are subordinate to men:

> Luo men . . . have considerable formal control over the behavior of their wives. While women have means of evading such control and regularly do so, if a wife wishes to keep her children and to maintain a good reputation, she must maintain her marriage. To this extent she must conform, at least superficially, to her husband's requirements, and must avoid antagonizing her mate to the point of separation. (Potash 1978, 384)

There are Luo women who "opt out" of the system, such as widows who refuse to remarry and women who live on their own in the cities. As with the Roho women who eschewed marriage during the 1930s and 1940s, however, these individuals have "ceased to operate by Luo norms" and are definitely exceptional (Potash 1978, 384).

In Luo society, a woman's primary role, then, is as a mother and a laborer. Girls are instructed in the importance of obedience to one's husband, responsible mothering, and diligent work both in the home and in the garden. Women gain respect in the community largely through bearing many children (particularly sons) and raising them well (Ominde 1952, 34–36). Luo culture values age and the wisdom it is seen to bring. In the past, male elders formed territorial councils (*buch piny*) in which they made decisions affecting the clan. Women were generally excluded from these important councils, but Odinga Oginga recalls that certain older wealthy women were able to participate and even occasionally functioned as chairs (1967,10).

In addition, people sought the wise words of grandmothers with respect to domestic conflicts and the education of children. The *pim*, an important figure in Luo society in the past, was an aging widow who came from another locale to raise the children of a particular household or neighborhood (Hauge 1974, 13; Onyango-Ogutu and Roscoe 1974, 24; Cohen 1985, 191). The *pim* lived together with her charges in the nursery (*siwindhe*), and there "much of the critical social intelligence of the Luo world" was passed on to new generations (Cohen and Odhiambo 1989, 92).

We now turn to the role of women in Luo indigenous religion. Luo religion, like any other religious system, has many facets and involves individuals on a variety of levels with varying degrees of intensity. In the past, people of both sexes performed rituals that reinforced the existing social order and participated in spirit-possession cults that, to some extent, challenged it. Men tended to dominate in the arena of lineage-strengthening rites and in making frequent offerings to the ancestors (*kwere*) in small shrines located within each homestead. Women, too, participated in some of this lineage-based religion, such as the naming of infants after ancestors and the installation of a married son in his new home, a rite that could not be performed without his mother's presence (Potash 1978, 390).[56]

However, it is in the realm of Luo ecstatic religion, involving direct contact with spiritual forces, that women have predominated (Wipper 1977, 52). Although Nyasaye is today worshiped by the Luo as a Christian high God, his power has not eclipsed the strength of the ancestors and anomalous spirits in popular belief. Spirits are known generally as *juogi* (sing., *juok/jok*) and may be called *jochiende* (sing., *jachien*) or *tipo* if they become malicious. Apart from the ghosts of distinct ancestors, *juogi* are generally believed to exist in clusters. Each cluster or family of *juogi* has its own name and characteristics. Thus there are the spirits that cause smallpox (*juok nundu*), the spirits of the enormous snake divinity Mumbo (*juok Mumbo*), the spirits of Lake Victoria (*juok nam*), and so on.[57] *Juogi* can affect individuals in a variety of ways, but a common manner is through entering (*donjo*) or possessing an individual and causing her or him to run wild. Relatives then take the victim to a possession expert (*jajuogi*) who can discern which *juogi* are causing the trouble. People say that the victim often instinctively rushes to the home of an expert who has been possessed by the same spirits and now functions as their medium (Owuor Anyumba 1971, 11–12).

One of the most prevalent Luo cults during the first half of this century was Lang'o, a cult whose devotees were and still are primarily women. Henry Owuor Anyumba traces the Lang'o cult to a series of bloody battles between the Luo and the Lang'o (the Nandi or Kipsigis) around 1900: the Lang'o warriors were reportedly "excessively wild, yelling, jumping, and throwing their swords up in the air. The longing for war possessed them . . . so that their bodies trembled violently" ([1954] 1971, 4–5). Owuor Anyumba, who collected his data around

1953 in Seme, suggests that the horror and bloodshed of these Lang'o night raids may have precipitated the widespread phenomenon of possession of Luos by the ghosts of slain Nandi warriors. [58]

The influence of possession cults such as Lang'o on Roho religious forms is impossible to miss. There are clear continuities between the mannerisms of individuals possessed by Lang'o spirits and individuals in a Roho ecstatic state: violent trembling, glossolalia (*dhum*), hyperventilation, and stylized, jerky movements. The domestic arrangements of Lang'o and other *juogi* experts has also had an impact on the development of Roho institutions. Consider the similarity between Owuor Anyumba's following description of a *jalang'o*'s homestead and prophetess Sarah Agot's therapeutic Christian commune in Mirunda:

> At the home of the expert a possessed person will find other people also suffering from lango. Usually they live together as people of that home. Those whose conditions have improved may take part in all domestic activities. None of them is allowed to go to any distant place until the expert has taken him or her there. I visited an expert who had four women "patients." All of the four women worked together as sisters. They respected the expert and called her mother. All of them conversed together as any ordinary group of women. The four women accompanied the expert to work in the field. They also did all the domestic work. They cleaned the house, fetched water from the stream, ground the millet, and cooked the food. . . . The position of the "patient" may vary according to different experts, but I think this is the general plan. In case of male "patients" they are expected to assist in all the male duties in that home. He may go to dig in the fields, or to milk, or to help erecting new huts. (Owuor Anyumba [1954] 1971, 15)[59]

One feature of Lang'o belief that may partially account for the attraction of women to the cult was the tradition of Awiti *nyar Lang'o* (Awiti, the daughter of the Lang'o). Legend has it that at the time of the raids there was a young Lang'o woman of unsurpassed beauty and bravery. She accompanied her kinsmen to war and had made a vow not to marry until she had "brought home cattle captured by herself from the enemies." Owuor Anyumba's informants told him that whenever Awiti killed someone, she "took out her breast and pointed it at the corpse saying, 'Don't you suppose that your murderer is a man as yourself, I am a mere woman!'" ([1954] 1971, 4). Again, we see that the Roho women *askeche*—who marched around the Nyanza countryside, singing militant hymns, postponing marriage, and defending their leaders in battle—drew on popular cultic models.

The process of indigenous routinization has transformed Roho religion from a movement that originally had the contours of an antiestablishment possession cult,[60] into an orderly, male-run religious system that reinforces the status quo in rural Luoland. Luo female mediumship has been "tamed" and integrated into the dominant religion, in which men perform the sacraments and make appeals to divine forces on behalf of the community. One might argue, however, that the central experiential aspects of women's participation in Lang'o and early Roho possession have remained essentially unchanged. Indeed, it is true that healing, visions, speaking in tongues, ecstatic release, and spiritual reinvigoration, which were all aspects of previous cults, still have pride of place in contemporary Roho worship. Nevertheless, the variety of contexts in which Roho women are free to direct the ritual process has been gradually reduced.

Today the apex of female authority within most Roho churches is the elderly *laktar*, a person who combines the role of the spirit medium (*jajuogi*) with the role of the wise old *pim*. The collapsing of two previously distinct feminine roles into one serves to drastically cut the number of women eligible for formal leadership. Whereas spirit mediums could be females of any age or social standing, the *laktar* must be postmenopausal, like the bygone *pim* (Whisson 1962, 19). The ideal of feminine spiritual power has thus been restricted to the model of the wise old grandmother, the upholder and healer of society.

Such a routinization of female possession is entirely in keeping with Luo patriarchal norms that require unmarried young women to be controlled and socialized into proper wifely obedience. Traditionally, women were believed to be socialized through the various components of the extended marriage rite. Through a series of rituals (*meko, diero, lupo, duoko, powo, riso*) that take place over a number of months, the unsettled young bride is gradually subdued into staying permanently with her husband (Evans-Pritchard 1950, 136). The socialization of a woman and her *juogi* through marriage finds definite expression in the rites associated with the launching of a new fishing boat. In E. S. Atieno Odhiambo's description of a launching ceremony (*nyasi*) held in Uyoma Katweng'a, he explains that the community treats the vessel as a bride whose *juogi* must be "tamed, adopted, socialized" before the boat can be put to daily use. As it is about to be launched, the new boat assumes the name of one of the owner's married daughters (*migogo*). At this point, people believe that the woman's *juogi* seizes the boat, rendering it "wild" and dangerous. Her *juogi* must be pacified through *riso*, the culminating rite of the Luo marriage ceremony. After being "handed over" to "the groom" and made "lakeworthy," the boat is welcomed back into its natal homestead as a married woman in a festive celebration known as *ruako or dwoko* (Atieno Odhiambo 1970, 14–21; Cohen and Atieno Odhiambo 1989, 99–103). Symbolism of this kind suggests that Luo society acknowledges an inherent spiritual power in women and in her natal family's *juogi*. Society seeks to harness and "socialize" that energy through marriage for the benefit of the clan.

Dominant Luo and Christian male emphases on wifely obedience in marriage have clearly fused in contemporary Roho ideology. Roho members are fond of citing the fact that God created Eve out of Adam's rib to be his helpmate (and not the other way around) as proof of women's divinely ordained domestic role. God's command to "be fruitful and multiply" corroborates the woman's role as procreator, as well as the Luos' love of large families. Male preachers cite age-old biblical justifications for excluding women from the ministry, such as Paul's First Epistle to Timothy (2:12) which states that women must be submissive and silent and should have no authority over men in the church.

Are Roho women bothered by their exclusion from top administrative posts? Do they even perceive themselves to be excluded, or is this an imposed issue, of importance only to Western feminists and researchers? A number of scholars have suggested that the question of authority and hierarchy in African religions is more a concern for outsiders than for women participants themselves, for whom spiritual renewal is the focus (Fernandez 1978, 218; Schwartz 1989, 71–72). Much of the testimony I received from a cross-section of Roho women, indeed, supports this view. Women indicated that they consider their participation in singing, trancing, praising God, and, most important, healing to be what Roho Christianity is all about. When asked what they valued most about their involvement in Roho religion, women repeatedly stressed their own health—"Now we don't get sick" *(Dendwa koro ok tuo)*—and a sense of peacefulness or "feeling free." Many spoke happily of the visions they had received while "in the power" *(e teko)* of the Spirit: "You see the angels and the light extremely clearly" *(Ineno malaika ineno ler kabisa)*. *Laktache* presented themselves as fulfilled and proud of their ability to do God's work *(tich Nyasaye)* in curing other people's illnesses.

Not once did a woman member express any desire to become a pastor or a teacher. When asked about the lack of women in administrative posts, women gave responses consistent with the dominant cultural ideology:

> A woman's power is secondary [lit., behind], she cannot be a pastor, a leader in front of men; therefore men are given the leading posts.
>
> *(Dhako en teko ni chien, ok onyal bedo padri, jatelo e nyim chwo; koro chwo ema imiyo telo maduong'.)*

With respect to decision making in the church, one woman member said:

> The leading pastors are the ones who talk. The leaders ahead of us are the ones who discuss, then we say yes, we agree with them.
>
> *(Pate madongo ema wuoyo. Jotelo madongo ema kwongo wuoyo, koro eka wabe watime yaa, wayie go.)*

Nancy Schwartz's interviews with members of the Legio Maria, another independent, Luo-based church, similarly suggest that women saw their exclusion from the priesthood since the 1960s as a natural consequence of the church's growth and regularization. Like some Roho women, Legio members explained that in the early days women had to serve as clergy because there were not enough men to fill the posts: One woman told her, *Kigoyo ligala igoye marach to idwaro lose maber* (When you are erecting a new home, you build it in a rough and ready way; then you want to fix it up nicely). The assumption on the part of many was that the Legio administration would naturally, with time, model itself more closely after the Roman Catholic hierarchy (Schwartz 1989, 65).

In addition, a couple of my informants explained that women who menstruate (*dhi e boke*) are unclean and unfit for religious office. Postmenopausal women, they explained, were clean (*ler*) and that is why they could serve as *laktache*.

Professor Hannah Kinoti has suggested that the tendency of women leaders in Kenyan independent churches to "slip" into the background was the result of cultural conditioning: "Women like to encourage their men to be strong and take control. They also are very aware of the pattern in the mainline churches. They don't need to be told to take a backward step."[61] In other words, outsiders should not be surprised that women have absorbed the "male-dominated ideology concerning appropriate female behavior" that is part and parcel of their cultural context (Robertson 1987, 112). Then again, Kinoti notes a "two-way" orientation in women in independent churches: They are at once "very charismatic and very retiring" or, as Schwartz would put it, able "to show deference to men without detracting from their own 'strong character'" (1989, 71). In their "public transcripts," to apply James Scott's useful category, the majority of the women I interviewed did not challenge current gender roles within the church. (1985, 296). In a formal interview setting, women spoke into my tape recorder as representatives of their church. Many clearly sought my approval and harbored hopes that I (and my sponsors) might be an eventual source of financial support. They were bound to respond in ways consistent with their male superiors; it would not be prudent to betray any tensions or problems to the visitor. The advice Roho women publicly gave one another always promoted the ideal of nonconfrontational, peaceful coexistence with one's cowives and deference to one's husband. Yet, there were also times when they clearly experienced frustration at having to obey male officials whom they considered unimpressive, inexperienced, or spiritually inferior.

On several occasions, I observed women members quietly expressing annoyance among themselves at being ordered about by male officers. Senior female members were more likely to express disapproval in these instances than junior women, for elderly women are more autonomous and are culturally granted greater latitude in self-expression. I once overheard a *laktar* complaining to a friend that a new young catechist put too many demands on her. During an interview, a senior *laktar* broke the normal code of etiquette and openly rebuked a male church elder for talking authoritatively about events that had occurred when he was "a mere child who knew nothing!" This same woman spoke out boldly against rulers who could not take criticism and did not know when to step down.[62]

Two skits performed during the 1991 *Sikukuu mar Rapar* (Celebration of Remembrance) convey the tension between opposing ideals of female resistance and female compliance in Roho tradition. The first skit was a reenactment of the 1934 war (*kedo*) between the celebrated women *askeche* (soldiers) and the Wanga army. Despite the somber theme, the audience roared and applauded to see the women killing the enemy warriors. Immediately afterward, a skit about a couple carried a contrasting message. Arimbe, the husband, was a bully (played by a woman in trousers). Nyardusi, the wife, was "saved" (*mowar*). As the skit opened, she sat quietly cooking, fulfilling the traditional wifely role. Arimbe thundered in and began to beat Nyardusi, but the properly behaved junior wife did not at first retaliate. Finally, she could endure it no longer and struck back, knocking her aggressor to the ground. Arimbe's mother then appeared and chastized her daughter-in-law: "How can a saved woman hit someone?" That single blow, delivered in self-defense, had corrupted Nyardusi; she promptly abandoned her faith and became a trouble-making drunkard like her husband.

The lesson of this skit was obvious: truly pious women suffer abuse rather than engage in violence. Yet, the historical model of female piety presented in the previous skit was that of strong, brave women who used weapons and fought back. It is true that the situations depicted in these two skits are very different. In the context of the war, women were not fighting their husbands or kinsmen but striking back at men from another ethnic or religious group. Their brave struggle against the Wanga thus would not, theoretically, serve as a model for their interaction with males from within their own group. Nevertheless, I suggest that Roho women did, at times, draw inspiration from the *askari* model to stand up to their own men—be they fathers or husbands. The testimonies and life stories presented in chapter 5 suggest that women looked to the models of the Roho female soldiers and martyrs in explaining their decisions to postpone marriage or to join the church, despite opposition from home. In reality, it would seem that the model of the female soldier is fast becoming a myth. The army of fearless *askeche* may be interpreted by future generations in symbolic terms but is not put forward as a viable role for modern Roho women.

In this section, I have discussed the gradual transformation of women's leadership roles in Luo Roho religion over the last sixty years. The Roho Christian movement that crystallized under activist Alfayo Odongo Mango in the early 1930s synthesized a number of different local and regional religious strands, including spirit possession and female mediums. This synthesis partly accounts for the resilience of women's assertive leadership during the subsequent period of Roho missionary expansion, despite Mango's endorsement of exclusively male officers prior to his death. From 1934 through the mid-1950s, women continued to draw on and reinvigorate these older forms of female spiritual adepthood in their own various Roho ministries. During that period, converts had few restraints placed on them by loosely organized, informal denominations whose centers in Musanda and Ruwe constituted important pilgrimage sites but did not function as real administrative headquarters. Throughout Nyanza, women, as well as men, were free to serve as pastors, teachers, healers, and seers. Strong Roho converts of both sexes established congregations in their villages and embarked on proselytizing campaigns.

By the 1960s this fairly open situation changed. Roho missionary expansion slowed as an influx of European, American, and independent churches in the region created competition for converts. In the wake of the Mau Mau uprising, the government pressured local leaders to monitor grassroots social and religious groups. The ratification of the Societies Ordinance in 1957 precipitated the regularization of independent church organization according to male-dominated institutional and ecclesiastical patterns that worked to exclude women from formal leadership. The accelerated rationalization of popular charismatic Christianity in western Kenya according to Western sexist norms was further reinforced by an increase in the number of literate Luo men seeking posts within independent churches for personal, political, and economic reasons.

This Western-style institutionalization of Roho religion was strengthened by a parallel process of indigenous routinization, according to established Luo gender norms. I view this second process as a "taming" of women's ecstatic practices, in which indigenous models of female mediumship have been further domesticated. Much as the institution of marriage socializes women and integrates them into the patrilineage, so does the model of the tradition-preserving *pim* inherent in the figure of the *laktar* subsume the ideal of the female *jajuogi*. The victory of Luo patriarchal and gerontocratic norms means that the vast majority of Roho women members are not eligible to exercise formal leadership within the church, should they wish to do so.

THE GREAT PREACHER—JAYALO MADWONG.

THE REVEREND ALFAYO ODONGO MANGO KA KONYA.
FOUNDER OF A RELIGION "ROHO" AND MUSANDA LUO SCHOOL.

Reverend Alfayo Odongo Mango; portrait courtesy of Ibrahim Owuor Mango.

Soso (Mama) Anna Inondi, daughter of Odhialo. Inondi was an elder *laktar* (healer) of the Ruwe Holy Ghost Church and a revered *Mama Kanisa* (Mother of the Church). She is pictured in 1990, two years before her death.

Elders of the Ruwe Holy Ghost Church of East Africa at the Ruwe headquarters. Back row (*left to right*): Mesak Ogola, Jerusa Omolo, Jeremiah Ogutu. Front row (*left to right*): Johana Omina, Esta Songa, Phoebe Apondi Ger, Damar Atieno.

Silvano Nyamogo, one-time Roho evangelist and colleague of famous Roho prophet, Lawi Obonyo; he is pictured here with his wife, Rebecca Esendi.

Ibrahim Owuor Mango, bishop of the Musanda Holy Ghost Church of East Africa, with his wife, Hilda Anyango Mango.

Ibrahim Owuor Mango, standing next to a tree planted on the spot where his father was killed.

Now called St. Paul's (Church of the Province of Kenya), this brick church was built by Alfayo Odongo Mango in the 1920s. It replaced an older mud-and-dung church that Mango had erected on the same spot around 1912. It was referred to by Joroho as "the church on the hill" or "Musanda Luo."

During the 1991 *Sikukuu mar Rapar* (Celebration of Remembrance) held at Ruwe, Roho members reenact the founding story of the 1934 *kedo* and the *mach* (the battle and the fire). A man playing the role of Mango marches with the women *askeche* (soldiers).

The annual *Sikukuu* offers Roho pilgrims opportunities for fellowship and relaxation.

Elijah Oloo's tomb in Nyamila, Musanda front (*top*) and back (*bottom*). His name and title in Dhoroho, "Chefe Urewo Irii" (meaning "*Kingi Elijah Oloo*") is inscribed on the back. "Died 1939" is inscribed on the front.

The headstone on the grave of the first bishop of the Ruwe Holy Ghost Church, Barnaba Walwoho. Note the spear and club depicted on the base of the cross, indicating Walwoho's participation in the 1934 battle.

The headstone on the tomb of Soso ("Mama" in Dhoroho) Abisage Muriro, active Roho leader and wife of the first Ruwe bishop, Barnaba Walwoho.

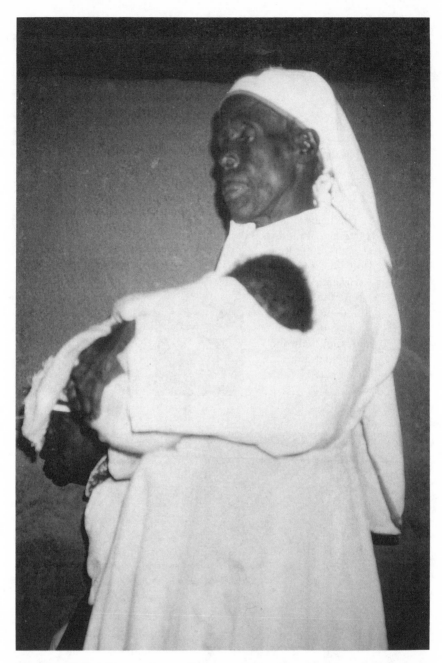

Masumbi *Laktar* Nereya Owuor, known as Jakina (the one who perseveres),
participating in the naming ceremony called *golo nyathi* (taking out the child)
for a newborn who has been secluded.

A procession of Masumbi *laktache* participating in *golo nyathi*.

A typical rural Roho church in Siaya District.

Pastor Elisha Eliakim Ndong'a of Sinaga and Teacher Morris Akeich ascending Got Rowalo in Seme for a day of fasting and prayer.

For Joroho in rural Nyanza, doing God's work entails hours traveling along footpaths. Here pictured is Pastor Joel Muuda Okwany preceded by *laktar* Joan Akello of Masumbi.

Roho women pay their respects at the tomb of founding Roho missionary Isaya Goro of Ruwe. Note the spears painted on Goro's grave indicating his involvement in the 1934 struggle.

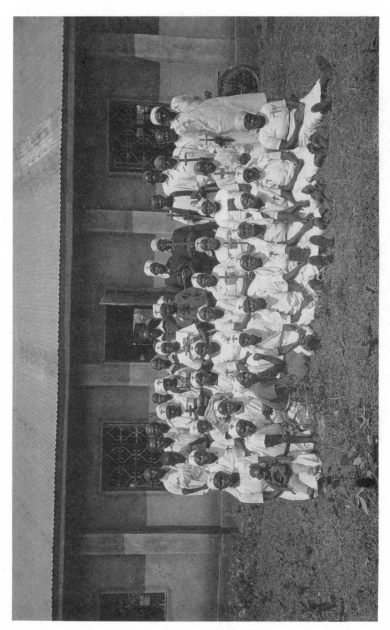

Members of the Ruwe Holy Ghost Church seated in front of the large sanctuary at their denominational headquarters. Known as "the church with twelve doors," the Ruwe church was built according to specifications prophesied by Lawi Obonyo in 1933.

A woman overcome by the Holy Spirit during a worship service in the Masumbi Roho congregation recently incorporated into the Holy Spirit Church of East Africa which is headquartered in Bukoyoni, Maragoli. She is supported and restrained by the arms of an experienced *laktar*.

4

Sacrifice and Redemption:
The Roho Worldview

Mango's Sacrifice

In my initial interviews among Roho congregations in Nyanza in 1990, I attempted to cover a wide range of topics. No matter what sorts of questions I asked, however, members preferred to talk about Alfayo Odongo Mango and the Musanda fire of 1934. I might succeed in steering conversation away from church history for a time, but members always returned to the story of their founder's martyrdom. Had I been to Musanda and Ruwe? Had I seen the place where Mango died? Had I talked to the old people living around there? Did I know about the way Mango suffered, holding his Bible above his head, as he burned to death? Numerous members urged me to attend the *Sikukuu mar Rapar*, the Celebration of Remembrance held every year on the anniversary of Mango's death, at which time I could witness a reenactment of the massacre with my own eyes. "Then you will know how it all happened," I was told. It was soon clear to me that—irrespective of my own research plan—the Joroho expected me to record the complete story of this seminal event.

I set about my new task in a methodical, linear fashion. Once I had collected what I deemed to be sufficient information on "the fire" (*mach*) and events leading up to it, I tried to move on to aspects of subsequent Roho history. However, many people I approached for information on the years following Mango's death were less interested in my questions than in offering me their version of the fire. I eventually realized that for Roho adherents, the Musanda massacre is more than a moving moment in history. It is the perennial reference point, the pivotal event, in whose shadow the church's past, present, and future take shape. Allusions to the fire and "the battle" (*kedo/lweny*) permeate Roho hymns. Members invoke the names of Mango, Lawi, Turfosa Aloo, and other victims of the fire in greetings, prayers, and sermons. Elderly survivors of the

119

battle proudly wear club- or spear-shaped badges on their uniforms, and others never seem to tire of listening to their recollections of that fateful day. For believers, the Musanda event constitutes a central reality that permeates congregational worship on many levels.

The *mach* is considered by many—members and nonmembers alike—to be a compelling story of courage in the face of brutality and persecution. For example, Daniel Ogusu, who belongs to another Kenyan indigenous church, the African Israel Church Nineveh, was moved on hearing a Roho member recount the story of Mango's martyrdom. Ogusu spoke eloquently in praise of Mango's courage and self-sacrifice. Alfonse Otieno, a member of the Manyatta parish of the Ruwe Holy Ghost Church, also spoke with great pride about Mango and the nine Musanda martyrs: "This is an *African* church. Nine people died for us!" He then challenged me, "I don't think that in the States you have anyone who died for religion, other than Christ."[1] The centrality of this story in Roho piety, however, lies not so much in its emotional or moral appeal—although this is important— but in its theological and ritual implications.

The Roho Savior

Joroho believe that on January 21, 1934, Mango gave his life for the sake of Africans. His self-sacrificial death opened heaven to blacks and ushered in the reign of the Holy Spirit in Africa.[2] Roho members invoke Mango as "our Savior" (*Jawarwa*). They envision him stationed at the gate of heaven, acting as intercessor with God on behalf of his faith community. Historian B. A. Ogot has observed that Mango's martyrdom is "the cornerstone of [the Joroho's] inspiration if not their ultimate theology" and that Mango seems "to be at par with Christ" (1971, 109). I would agree with Ogot that Odongo Mango is definitely a figure of at least equal importance to Christ in Roho theology.[3] When asked, members readily acknowledge Christ's status as an important person (*Yesu e ng'at maduong'*), and they habitually assert Christ's divinity through the formal Anglican components retained in Roho liturgy. Yet, Christ is an ambiguous figure, for he is also associated with white missionaries and colonizers, the very people who rejected Mango's message and stole Africans' land. Moreover, there is a sense in which Mango, the final (*mogik*) redeemer, has, through the power of the Holy Spirit, established a new era superseding that of Christ.[4] As Margaret Uba from South Nyanza put it:

> The whites who came first [the missionaries], they brought only the word of God. Christ was all they brought. They didn't bring us the Holy Spirit.
>
> (*Wasunge ma ne obiro mokwongo, mano to wach Nyasaye kende ema ne gikelo. Kristo no kende ema ne gikelo. To gin ok gikelo n'wa roho.*)

Roho doctrine is not codified, and there is no official theology within the church. In some congregations, members regularly recite the Apostles' Creed (known as *Ayie* in Dholuo, or *Njonzari Osheu* in Dhoroho), but this creed has never been augmented to incorporate convictions about Mango, Lawi, or the Holy Spirit's self-disclosure in Nyanza. Nevertheless, the basic tenets concerning Mango's sacrificial death in the fire, his relationship to the Holy Spirit, and the Roho community's place within Christian salvation history are more or less consistently conveyed through hymns, prayers, and sermons.

For example, preachers sometimes invoke the metaphor of "the three horses" when commenting on the uniqueness and superiority of the Roho dispensation. In this allegorical image, they depict the Christian trinity sequentially, associating each divinity with an increasingly advanced or more powerful stage (*okang'*). Daniel Otang'a of Yiro, a longtime member of the Ruwe Holy Ghost Church, gave the clearest exegesis of this "horse trinity." He explained that there has been a succession of horses occupying the throne in heaven. The first was a white horse (*ambuor ma rachar*) who was God the Father. God the Father was the God of the Europeans; when he had the throne, Europeans controlled the world. However, he was then superseded by the brown horse (*ambuor ma silwal*), God the Son, who was the lord of the Asians. The brown horse reigned for only a short time—Otang'a alluded to the influx of Indian laborers and merchants to Kisumu and Kakamega in the 1920s—before the rise of the black horse. The black horse (*ambuor ma rateng'*) is the Holy Spirit and lord of the Africans. Odongo Mango's reception of the Holy Spirit marked the ascendancy of the black horse to the heavenly throne and the dawning of the final age on earth—an era in which Africans carry the Christian banner and are the keepers of the spiritual power.

This allegory most likely has roots in the vision of the Hebrew prophet Zechariah (1:8), recorded in the Old Testament. Roho preachers offered slightly different versions, but all maintained that the story was found in the Bible, although no one I spoke with could cite the particular chapter or verse. The presence of the word *ambuor* in each Roho version suggests that this scriptural text was integrated into local oral tradition early on. *Ambuor* actually means "eland," but it was used by the first missionary translators to denote horse, there being no word for that nonindigenous animal in the Luo language.[5] (Nowadays, people are familiar with horses, and recent Luo editions of the Bible use the Swahili term *faras* instead.) Roho members have adjusted Scripture to meet their conception of Christian history as a series of periods dominated by specific races, as evidenced by the fact that in the original passage from Zechariah, the third type of horse is not black but red (*ma rabuor*).

Another image that Roho members commonly use to convey the outstripping of older brands of Christianity by Roho religion is that of the retired or resting (*yuweyo*) Christ. God and Jesus are depicted as seated quietly on their thrones in heaven—aging figureheads who have "left the work for the Holy Spirit" (*oweyo ni roho tich*). One woman from South Nyanza likened the Holy Spirit to a last-born boy (*chogo*). This image suggests the tenderness a mother has for her cherished youngest son, the one who will remain in the family compound and care for his parents in their old age. The metaphor also expresses a perception of the Holy Spirit as vital and youthful. Another informant whom I pressed to explain the Mango–Holy Spirit relationship also stressed the agency of the latter. She likened the Holy Spirit to a telephone line through which Mango and Lawi send their voices to their followers on earth.

The theological content of these images and metaphors is fairly straightforward. There are other Roho themes, however, that appear less fixed and more malleable, at least from the point of view of the outsider. For example, Roho oration gives varied application to the Christian notion of the counselor or helper (_jakony_) who Jesus promised would be sent to his followers after his death (John 15:26). Members sometimes label Lawi _Jakony_, for he served as Mango's active counterpart when the former was in exile or seclusion. Alternatively, they sometimes see Mango himself as _Jakony_, sent by Jesus or God specifically to the Africans. Yet, members also identify the Holy Spirit as _Jakony_ sent by Mango to comfort and empower his survivors. In this final instance, Joroho perceive themselves to be currently working with Mango's helper to spread faith and healing throughout Africa and to the rest of the world.

The founding story of the Roho church is not unique. Many African independent churches established in the first half of this century were started by messianic prophets who, like Mango, called for an end to colonialism, spoke out against missionary control, and suffered persecution as a result. Among the most famous are Simon Kimbangu, who founded the large Kimbanguist church in Zaire; Isaiah Shembe, the messiah of the Nazareth church in South Africa; and Josiah Oshitelu, who established the Aladura churches, which have spread throughout West Africa. Like Christians the world over, members of African independent churches have interpreted the gospel in terms of their particular sociohistorical circumstances. They have embraced the biblical notion of messiah or savior and applied it to their own charismatic leaders who protested European domination. Scripture is fulfilled for them by their own saviors, figures who are not generally seen to negate Christ but to extend—and, in the case of the Joroho, to improve on—Jesus' legacy (Omoyajowo 1982; MacGaffey 1983; Turner 1967; Peel 1968; Welbourn and Ogot 1966; Barrett 1968; Wipper 1977; Jules-Rosette 1975; Sundkler 1961, 1976).

The standard scholarly approach to such movements has been to view them as examples of indigenization or Africanization of Christianity. On a general level, this interpretation is acceptable. We can, indeed, view Roho beliefs about Mango's death as an indigenization of the Christian paradigm of Jesus' martyrdom. For the concept of indigenization to be truly useful, however, we must bear in mind two points. First, the process of indigenization is always a two-way affair. When people adapt imported beliefs to local thought patterns, not only is the received material altered but also the "traditional" worldview is simultaneously reconsidered and transformed, as certain component features are given increased or decreased emphasis. As Christina Toren has pointed out in her discussion of the indigenization of Christianity in the Fiji islands:

> In the act of constructing the present, people may also be constructing a past with which it is continuous and in whose terms it is explicable. The question is whether this process necessarily does violence to either the present or the past. Here I argue that it need not, for what constitutes a living tradition may reveal an extra dimension to the past—one whose validity is not a matter of "what happened" but of how it may be understood. (Toren 1988, 696)

Toren goes on to demonstrate how the images evoked by Fijians' appropriation of Leonardo da Vinci's *The Last Supper* "at once bespeak the continuity of Fijian tradition and transform it" (696). We can identify the same dialectic at work in the Joroho's perception of the activity of the Holy Spirit in Ugenya. As a result of exposure to (and acceptance of) missionary teachings about the pervasive nature of the Holy Spirit, early Roho adherents interpreted what would otherwise have been seen as unrelated episodes of *juogi* possession in their area as manifestations of a single divine force. In turn, this reinterpretation gave new shape and immediacy to those scriptural passages in which Christ exorcises demons by the power of the Holy Spirit, causing Roho religion to develop emphases that diverged from formal Anglicanism and its rejection of ecstacy and present-day miracles.

Second, even though indigenization is admittedly a two-way process, the indigenous forms have more determinant power. Adaptation or acculturation is rarely a self-conscious creative act. Unlike the making of an object of art, people generally do not "create" new, believable worldviews for themselves. Rather, people make sense of new ideas through their dominant categories of understanding and integrate new institutions or forms of expression in ways that are consistent—aesthetically, morally, or spiritually—with their deeply held convictions and experiences. In other words, the end of Roho theology was not the creation of a Luo-Anglican synthesis. The end of Roho religion was—and is—spiritual wholeness, personal and communal well-being, and truth. The religion evolved the way it did as people strove to bring their daily lives into congruence with their perceived sense of ultimate reality. For this reason, indigenization should not be seen as effectively different from the reinterpretation or recontextualization of religious dogma in any place or at any time in history. Pursuing this line of argument, I suggest that as the central story of Mango's martyrdom evolved in Roho piety it was shaped less by Western Christian notions of martyrdom and more by notions about sacrifice in Luo culture. Tracing the continuity between members' representations of Mango's self-sacrifice and the Luo conception of ritual sacrifice (*liswa* or *misango*) enables us, as Toren would say, to see how "a living tradition may reveal an extra dimension to the past."

Luo Ritual Sacrifice

Unfortunately, information on traditional Luo sacrifice is patchy. The earliest written reports of sacrificial rites among the Kenya Luo appear in works by East Africa Protectorate administrators such as C. W. Hobley (1902, 1903) and G. A. S. Northcote (1907). These men collected ethnographic information about the peoples under their jurisdiction, including the Nilotic Kavirondo, as the British then called the Kenya Luo. Within their descriptions of Luo warfare, life cycle rituals, "ancestor worship," "superstitions," and so on, Hobley and North-cote mention rites involving animal slaughter but do not present these rites in any detail and offer only cursory remarks on their significance.[6]

Early missionary surveys of Luo customs (Stam 1910; Roscoe 1915; Hartmann 1928; Owen 1933) provide fuller descriptions of sacrificial practices, but, again, no attempt is made to analyze the rites carefully. Like their administrative counterparts, missionaries of this period perceived ritual sacrifice among the Luo to be tied to "demonology" and "superstition" and thus took little interest in its mechanics. True religion for the Europeans entailed belief in a high God. Okot p'Bitek has shown how the first Christian missionaries to eastern Uganda, in their failure to find a ready translation for the word *God* in the Acholi language, claimed that the Acholi were instinctively nontheistic (1971, 41–51). This stereotype about the Central Luo, promulgated in the late nineteenth century, was quickly extended to the Kenya Luo by the Europeans working in Kavirondo. That foreigners found no traces of temples or altars dedicated to an omnipotent creator deity further reinforced their presupposition that the Luo people had "little religion" (Roscoe 1915, 291).[7]

In the 1950s, the writings of anthropologist E. E. Evans-Pritchard placed both belief in spirits and rites of sacrifice squarely within the realm of 'real religion.' He described sacrifice as "the most typical and expressive act of Nuer religion," arguing that Nuer spirits "may be regarded as hypostases, representations, or refractions of God . . . so we can say that a sacrifice to any one of them is a sacrifice also to God" ([1956] 1977, 200). In a careful application of Hubert and Mauss's basic model, Evans-Pritchard presented sacrifice as the central mechanism for mediating between the living community and the divine. These classic studies of the mechanics and meaning of sacrifice have had some impact on scholars' interpretations of Luo sacrifice.[8]

Yet, very few students of the Luo have attempted to analyze the nature of traditional sacrifice, and the comments of those who have are all too brief. Even after publication of Evans-Pritchard's systematic exploration of sacrifice among the Nuer, most students of Luo culture have continued to provide information on sacrifice as an aside. They mention sacrifice in passing, within the context of discussion of other topics such as possession cults (Whisson 1962, 21; Owuor Anyumba 1954/1971, 24; Wipper 1977, 50), traditional religious and philosophical beliefs (Sytek 1972, 173; Ocholla-Ayayo 1976, 170, 179; Hauge 1974, 51–53,

79–83), and general information on Luo culture (Onyango-Ogutu and Roscoe 1974, 9–41).

An overview of the data available in both the older and more recent sources suggests that *liswa* rites followed at least three and perhaps all four of the basic phases that Evans-Pritchard identified in sacrificial ritual among the Nuer: presentation, consecration, invocation, and immolation. With regard to the Luo, the questionable element is the act of presentation—what the Nuer refer to as *pwot*—which entails tethering the victim and placing the animal before God ([1956]1977, 208). Most published accounts of Luo sacrifice do not mention the act of tethering in particular, but it is obvious that someone captured and constrained the sacrificial animal in some fashion before slaughter. Whether the tying of the victim had the symbolic significance of a "presentation," however, cannot really be ascertained.

The act of consecration of the victim is achieved among the Nuer through *buk*, rubbing ashes over the animal's body. Evans-Pritchard has shown that this act of smearing ashes not only sanctifies the soon-to-be offering but also establishes an identification between the sacrificer (the person on whose behalf the sacrifice is being performed) and the animal victim (261–262). Smearing (*wiro*) and ashes (*buru*) appeared in traditional Luo sacrificial rites and likewise conveyed a symbolic connection between the patient or sacrificer and the animal victim, but this identification could be established after, as well as before, the immolation. For example, in a booklet prepared by Ojolla Secondary School students in 1983, one student cites the following method for expelling an angry spirit, taken from the testimony of an old man from Kisumo Karateng:

> The diviner collects four piles of dry grass. The patient ("nyamreche") is then ordered to light fire to each. The diviner pours a specially prepared ash on top to extinguish the flames and the patient is supposed to stamp on each pile until the fire is completely out. The diviner next takes a black hen and cuts off its head. The beak of the dead hen is opened and some of the ash poured in. Carrying the head, the diviner encircles the patient four times. Finally, the head is buried and the hen's body is taken home where it is roasted for the patient. He will eat it with cold ugali and the spirits will no longer haunt him. (1983, 14)

In this instance, the ashes that the patient stamped with his foot were then poured into the beak of the slaughtered victim. Sometimes the identification between sacrificer and animal victim was achieved through tying the latter's entrails around the former's neck (Roscoe 1915, 287; Owuor Anyumba [1954] 1971, 25) or by smearing the creature's innards on the chest of the individual for whom the sacrifice was being performed. In a short article, "Ghostly Vengeance among the Luo of Kenya," Evans-Pritchard describes Luo sacrificial ritual as reflecting the four structural components he had found in the Nuer rites (although in a slightly different order):

Luo who fall sick get a diviner (ajuoga) to discover the cause, and if he says that the sickness is due to a particular ghost on account of some grievance they hasten to compensate (colo) the ghost for the wrong they have done him by sacrificing an animal or fowl at his grave. It is customary to sacrifice a quail or fowl for a sick woman and a sheep or goat for a sick man. When a beast is sacrificed it is first tethered while whoever is conducting the ceremony makes an invocation (lamo) over it. If the sacrifice is acceptable to the ghost the animal urinates. They then rub its back (wiro) with the moist earth where it has urinated, and afterwards sacrifice it. The meat is eaten by the sick man's kin and a strip is tied round his wrist. (1950, 86)

Many descriptions of traditional Luo sacrifice focus on the invocations to God or the spirits. This is not surprising for, as both Evans-Pritchard and Lienhardt in his study of Dinka religion indicate, the invocation, or *lam*, is the heart of the sacrifice. The Luo cognate of *lam* is *lamo*, which means "prayer" in the general sense. The standard liturgical phrase *Walam* (Let us pray) signals the commencement of collective prayer in Christian churches throughout Luoland, and the statement *Wa dhi lamo* means simply "We are going to worship." The term *lamo* today thus covers all sorts of supplications, confessions, and praises given to Nyasaye. One of William Sytek's informants, L. Ochieng, suggested that in the past, however, *lamo* was always accompanied by sacrifice:

God could receive a rooster from you which you roasted in his name to ask for help. You would say, "God, eat this so that you may help me." You hold Liswa (sacrifice) in your own homestead, never in the field. You prayed when the animal was being slaughtered. The white man has discarded that kind of praying. . . . It is only these days that they pray without Liswa. (Sytek 1972, 161)

Just as prayers today vary, given the context, invocations accompanying sacrificial rites in the old days differed, depending on the circumstances giving rise to the ceremony. An old man from Kapisul, South Nyanza, gave Hans-Egil Hauge the following example of the prayer that one would have uttered during a sacrifice to a troublesome deceased grandfather spirit:

Oh my good grandfather, what are you intending to do in your home? As you know, everyone's wish is that his family (or clan) be prosperous and happy. Whenever you come here, may you identify yourself clearly. Will you please frankly tell us what you require of us. As you are our great grandfather, you can drive away bad luck and bring good luck to us. Take this sacrifice together with your friends (the dead ancestors) so that you leave us in peace. Leave us together with good fortune.

(*Oh kwara maber, to kendo itimori nade edalani, a dhano, yuago mana kare. Kiduogo edalanika toyangri mana maber. Gimidwaro to mondo iwacho awacha. Luyia maricho riemb to luyia mabecho idonjogodo. Kau gini icham gi yawu mondo ilos kari maber. Wewa gi luiyini mabecho.*) (English translation by Hauge 1974, 115)

In response to Sytek's question about what Luo people did "when they needed something from the sun," informant L. Odongo gave an example of a simpler invocation:

Communication with the sun was accomplished in the same manner the white man communicated with his God. We staged a Liswa and prayed. Liswa was held in the home of the person in whose name the occasion was to take place. We said to the sun, "Now that you are going down, let this happen, and when you rise tomorrow we'll be expecting the best from you." (Sytek 1972, 173)

Luo *lamo*, like *lam* in Nuer or Dinka sacrifice, could be perfunctory or lengthy, but it was always the pivot of the entire ritual (Lienhardt 1961, 236).

According to Evans-Pritchard's scheme, the fourth phase of the sacrificial rite is the immolation, the slaughter of the victim. The Nuer officiant would kill the victim (generally an ox) with a single thrust of the spear, or (if a goat or sheep) he would slit its throat. Among the Luo, the latter was apparently the most common method for slaughtering a sacrificial victim, but chickens were occasionally beaten to death (Hartmann 1928, 270). In piacular rites, Evans-Pritchard maintains, the animal's life was offered to the deity in place of the life of the sacrificer, the intent being to satisfy the troublesome ghost with a substituted life. Gods were not thought actually to "eat" (*cam*) the meat, Evans-Pritchard insisted, but simply to "take" (*kan*) the life ([1956] 1977, 212–223).

Accounts of Luo sacrifice are not detailed enough to enable us to speak conclusively about how Luos viewed the act of immolation. However, invocations such as the one delivered by the elder from Kapisul (cited previously) indicate that Luos believed their offerings to be consumed by the spirits, in some sense. The imperative *Kau gini icham kod yawu mondo ilos kari maber* (Take this thing and eat it with your people so that you make your place comfortable) can be taken literally or figuratively, for the word *cham* (eat) has a wide range of meaning. However interpreted, the statement clearly conveys a desire to satisfy and to please the ancestor spirit. In return, the sacrificer expects the spirit to oblige him by leaving his family in peace.

Mango as the Paradigmatic Sacrificial Victim

For members of the Roho church, Mango's death in the Musanda fire constitutes what Victor Turner has called a root paradigm, a central myth or story that informs members' existential lives (Turner 1974, 64). We have seen how Mango's martyrdom, as preserved in Roho theology and worship life, gives a new cast to the theme of Christ's self-sacrifice. When we examine the collective memory of Mango's martyrdom more carefully, we find that Roho members' representation of his death also reveals the four-phase structure characteristic of traditional Nilotic sacrifices.

During the fracas of January 21, 1934, Mango was trapped in his hut, deep in prayer. Believers explain that he was prescient of his fate and resigned to it. In other words, we can view this period of quiet and withdrawal as a kind of self-dedication, Mango's placing of himself before God.

At some point Mango donned his clerical robes, an act I suggest is congruent with consecration. In the Roho context, as in other Kenyan independent churches, dress is not simply expressive of status but actually sanctifies and empowers the wearer. The faithful believe that the emblem (S †) on their gowns "chases away Satan and diseases." The red cross on the hat or headscarf opens a pathway for the Spirit to enter the body through the head. Joroho consider proper liturgical garb to be crucial for performing the tasks God has assigned. Baptism performed by someone without proper uniform, for instance, is illegitimate and ineffectual. Thus Daniel Otang'a, a catechist, referred to his teacher's gown as his "working tool," enabling him to fulfill his calling.

The *lamo* that Mango uttered just prior to his death was in keeping with the kinds of invocations elders spoke during the third phase of traditional sacrificial rites. Holding a Bible in his right hand above his head—much as the Nuer grasp their spears while invoking God—Mango reportedly cried: "Jesus, Son of God, the sky is cracking, the hills are tumbling down!" This declamatory speech expressed the Joroho's desperate situation. Mango then addressed his God directly in a hymn: "Thank you Jesus, thank you Jesus, Savior of all people, son of God. / You love people, you love all people. / You teach them your word until they accept it. / You have died for us on the cross." The final reference to Christ's ransom both foreshadows the self-sacrifice Mango was about to make and underscores the connection between the victim and the people he represents.

Some Roho members are aware that a Wanga warrior threw a spear into Mango's burning hut and wounded Mango in the chest. Yet, most maintain that what really killed their founder was the fire, which he endured with awe-inspiring courage. The way in which Roho oral tradition characterizes Mango's death reflects both the centrality of the sacrificial fire in traditional Luo religion and the indigenous conceptualizations of the afterlife. An origin legend obtained from Chief Gori Kogalo of Kanyamwa around the turn of the century describes the land of the dead as "a beautiful country" in the heavens "where the people were all bright like fire" (Hobley 1903, 331). It was commonly believed that upon death, people's souls (*chuny*) rose up into the sky. At night they would "light their fires and cook their food, just as they did on earth," creating the sweep of stars across the night sky (Onyango-Ogutu and Roscoe 1974, 16; Hobley 1902, 35).[9] The sacrificial and eschatological frameworks through which Mango's followers experienced and, in turn, represented Mango's fiery death were compounded by an added layer of significance stemming from spirit-possession cults. According to Roscoe's 1915 findings, a possessed individual who fell into the fire during an ecstatic fit was not helped but was allowed to burn to death, for it was "said that the ghost [had] claimed him and would resent any interference" (1915, 286). Testimony from Roho believers indeed makes clear that they believe Mango's soul was immediately taken by God or the Holy Spirit. Inondi recalls that she heard Mango's voice calling "Goodbye!" When she turned to look back at the burning hut, she saw "something which was red and rounded like the sun" (*ka wang' chieng' makwar, ka ong'inore*) heading straight up into the sky. This image is consistent with the visions reported by people possessed by *juogi*, particularly within the Chieng' (sun) cult. Possessed individuals would see a "great terrifying light" coming from "a great disc-like organ (*pend wang' chieng'*) which seem[ed] to fill all the room, thus entrapping the victim" (Owuor Anyumba [1954] 1971, 10; 1974, 16).

It has been argued that the power of sacrificial slaughter lies partly in the "sacrilege," the disruption of the proper order that the murder of a person or animal surrogate entails. This disruption releases "an ambiguous force," "a kind of power of which others may avail themselves" (Beattie 1980, 34; Hubert and Mauss 1964, quoted in Beattie). In Roho cosmology, the event of Mango's death did disrupt the existing order ("the sky is cracking, the hills are tumbling down!"), and his death indeed resulted in the release of a powerful spiritual force—the Holy Spirit. Yet, the relationship between Mango's death and the coming of the Holy Spirit was not automatic. Instead, Joroho conceive of the relationship as an exchange, agreed on beforehand. The direct connection between Mango's death and the Spirit's coming to claim Africa is the result of a bargain, reflecting, I suggest, Luo indigenous attitudes toward sacrifice in which a living creature (or creatures) was offered to God or the spirits in return for something good. In Roho theology, this agreement between God and Mango has come to be embodied in the term *singruok* (covenant, agreement, promise). Members see Mango and the eight others killed during the *mach* as *joma no singore* (those who made the covenant). A Ruwe Holy Ghost church pastor succinctly explains:

> For God had told [Mango and his followers] "in order for the Holy Spirit to fill the land, you will have to die. If you run away from death, then the Holy Spirit will go to another country, but if you die, the Holy Spirit will remain in this country."

The belief that Mango and his followers died in return for the Holy Spirit's permanent residence with the Roho community in Africa is clearly an indigenization of the Jesus paradigm inherited from European missionaries. The *way* in which the Christian savior myth has been adapted so that it revolves around the concept of *singruok* also expresses a view of sacrifice as exchange that is widespread in Nilotic thought.[10]

I have ventured that the Roho church's root paradigm of the *mach* reflects both the basic structural form of the Luo *Liswa* and indigenous conceptions about the exchangelike character of sacrifice. We must now consider how the *mach*, in turn, becomes a vehicle for finding and making new meaning. The Roho community's reception of charismatic Christianity in terms of indigenous concepts and their reinterpretation of their own rites in the light of Christian Scripture led to their particular formulation of *singruok* as the motivating force behind Mango's martyrdom. Now Joroho employ the concept of *singruok* to give meaning to present choices and to reinterpret the past. For example, the ordeal test that Elijah Oloo underwent in order to prove himself worthy of being made king is now spoken of as *singruok*. The favorable outcome is not seen as mere proof of Oloo's fortitude but as indicative of his divine selection. Similarly, when today's Roho members recall the pact that a number of the founding women made with each other to eschew marriage in order to work for God, they now use the term *singruok* instead of the more common Luo word used in those days for such oath taking (*kuong'ruok*). In other words, contemporary Roho members reinterpret pioneers' actions so that they are consonant with Mango's paradigmatic sacrifice by using a theological concept that was not fully developed until after Mango's death. Joroho thus posit a moral continuity between the acts of their forebears and their own behavior. In modeling themselves according to the brave example of their founders, contemporary Roho adherents are also recasting that example according to their own deeply held religious convictions.

In order to enter into a *singruok* relationship with God or the Holy Spirit, people must be willing to suffer and exercise self-denial; in short, they must make personal sacrifices. When I once impatiently asked why it was always necessary to stay up all night while holding prayer sessions, I was told, "How can you expect God to answer your prayers when he sees that you are well-rested and at ease?" The hardships and exhaustion that Roho faithful endure in the process of doing God's work thus takes on new meaning—and new efficacy—in recapitulating Mango's ultimate self-offering and empowering their prayers. For example, Margaret Uba, a former Catholic, recalls that it was her unflagging "willingness to die like the people who had died in the [Musanda] fire" (*an be ajok ni koro atho kaka joka ne otho e mach*) that finally convinced her husband of the worth of the Roho faith.

The notion of suffering in return for blessings is present in other Luo charismatic communities, although, of course, the belief is elaborated somewhat differently than in those Roho churches who take Mango as *jawar* (savior). For example, Elisha Eliakim Ndong'a, pastor of a Sinaga church affiliated with the Bukoyoni-based Roho denomination, the Holy Spirit Church of East Africa (H.S.C.E.A.), also stressed the importance of personal hardship in increasing the efficacy of prayer. He, I, and Morris Akeich, a Roho catechist from Masumbi, had made the long, arduous hike to the top of Got Rowalo, a small, rocky mountain in Seme that is a pilgrimage site for local people of various religious persuasions. Ndong'a explained that, whenever he or members of his congregation journeyed to the mountain, they would fast, pray through the night, and await visions from the Spirit. The fatigue and hunger created by the long trek in the hot sun, the struggle to overcome fear of snakes and wild animals, and the cold, shelterless nights on the sheer rock face are seen as necessary prerequisites for making appeals to God that will be heard. Ndong'a explained that carrying food up Got Rowalo was not bad in itself exactly, but a pilgrim who ate during a vigil would not benefit from time spent there. God would not answer the prayers of "one who was satisfied," and a worshiper whose stomach was full would not be able to concentrate on God in the first place.

The belief that a supplicant must always give up something has roots, as we have seen, in fundamental indigenous ideas about sacrifice. These ideas are also integral to Luo traditional cosmology, which posits a gulf between God above and humanity below. The notion that one must deny one's natural desires in order to "connect" with God is expressed in a well-known Luo origin myth. The myth states that, in the beginning, the world was a happy place without death or suffering. One day, God ordered humanity to send up an offering of clean, fresh fat. The people erected a tall pole (or, alternatively, God let down a long rope) and chose Chameleon (*Ng'ongruok*) to carry their offering up to the sky. According to one version, Chameleon could not restrain himself from eating the best portion of the fat. In another version, he carelessly "soiled the fat with his clumsy feet." In both instances, God furiously rejected the defiled offering and punished humanity by introducing death into the world (Onyango-Ogutu and Roscoe 1974, 43–44; Hauge 1974, 36). Implicit in this story is the assumption that favorable communication with God requires ignoring one's hunger or going "unsatisfied." Offerings and prayers are only effective to the extent that they do not bear the marks of careless comportment or self-indulgence.

Other influences have no doubt fostered the flowering of this concept of self-denial in exchange for spiritual power that is at the heart of the Roho worldview. Whisson shows, for example, that the initiation rites of traditional religious practitioners demanded fasting, isolation, and journeys into the wilderness:

> The pattern of vision, fasting and returning with the power is a feature of many stories about the manner in which the jabilo—soothsayers, judges, magicians, doctors all combined in one person—gained his power. . . .
> The source of such power is not really known by the people. It may come from God—more likely it comes from the individual spirits which possess the magician, and which in turn are subject to his bidding. From the wilderness they brought it, by fasting and loneliness, and the power exudes from their every action. (1962, 14)

The teachings of Anglican and Seventh-Day Adventist missionaries about the value of self-denial and discipline as means to holiness enhanced these older paradigms concerning the optimum human-spirit relationship. Adherents of early Luo puritanical syncretisms such as *Dini k'Owalo* (Nomiya Luo) further reinforced this notion. For the followers of Alfayo Odongo Mango, these numerous layers of religiocultural meanings are interwoven in the crowning concept of God's *singruok* with Mango: the *mach* in exchange for the salvation and spiritual empowerment of his African church.

Musanda Our Home: Locative and Universal Vision

Every year in late January, Roho pilgrims converge on Ruwe and Musanda for the *Sikukuu mar Rapar* (Celebration of Remembrance). They come from all over the country to worship together and to celebrate the bravery of their martyrs in the 1934 *mach*. Most of all, they come to see Musanda, their savior's home, the place where monumental events occurred. Odongo Mango's homestead, Iwinda, no longer actually exists, for it was leveled in the fire. To this day, most of the land remains in the hands of the government as a tree nursery. Ibrahim Owuor Mango, bishop of the Musanda Holy Ghost Church and Mango's only surviving son, lives on the small piece of property that the South Wanga Local Native Council permitted his mother to retain after the massacre. Each year, on the anniversary of his father's death, members of Ibrahim Owuor Mango's denomination congregate in Musanda while members of the Ruwe Holy Ghost Church of East Africa simultaneously gather in their headquarters approximately three miles away. Relations between the two denominations are good. Therefore, on the night of January 16, the anniversary of *Kingi* Elijah Oloo's coronation, Ruwe members process to Nyamila in Musanda to honor Oloo's grave and to pay respects at Owuor Mango's home nearby.

Roho faithful cannot traverse the actual site of Mango's Christian compound or identify the unmarked grave containing the remains of some of their martyrs, which is now lost in a thicket of eucalyptus trees and scrub owned by the government. Yet, these constraints do not seem to diminish pilgrims' excitement at returning to the place of "things of the beginning." Visitors are still able to walk the roads trod by Mango and the "people who made the covenant" (*joma no singore*). One can still see the hills, the rivers, and the fields that he called home. The following hymn, which Roho members sang in a sabbath service at Ruwe during the 1991 *Sikukuu mar Rapar*, conveys the joy pilgrims feel at actually visiting their Jerusalem—the site of both their greatest tragedy and their ultimate salvation.

> JAKWANO: *Wang' oganda to ngiyo dalawa,*
> (CANTOR/SOLOIST: The eyes of the people are watching our home,)
>
> JO-OLO: *Dalawa mowar gi mach gi remo.*
> (CHORUS: Our home that was redeemed with fire and blood.)

JAKWANO: *Jomogalo, biuru ka nyuak,*
(CANTOR: Those who doubt, come here [to see it] and weep,)

JO-OLO: *Ma e en; onge modong.*
(CHORUS: This is it; no one survived/nothing remains.)

JAKWANO: *Wanamor kwang'iyo dalawa, Aleluya,*
(CANTOR: We rejoice when we see our home, Alleluia,)

JO-OLO: *Wanamor kwang'iyo dala maler.*
(CHORUS: We rejoice when we see our holy home.)

JAKWANO: *Ruoth chopo oganda pogore,*
(CANTOR: The Lord is about to arrive while the community is divided,)

JO-OLO: *Ka gipako Yesu Nazareth.*
(CHORUS: While they are praising Jesus of Nazareth.)

JAKWANO: *Kitimo hera to unene dala,*
(CANTOR: If you are loving you will see the home,)

JO-OLO: *Jerusalem imowar gi mach gi remo.*
(CHORUS: Jerusalem was redeemed with fire and blood.)

These lyrics make plain the centrality of Musanda in Roho piety. For the faithful, the eyes of the world are fixed on Mango's village and on the events that occurred within. Believers embrace Musanda as a place of unearthly power but also as a place of familiarity, love, and comfort. Phrases such as *Musanda dalawa* (Musanda our home) and *dala maler, dala mar hera* (holy home, home of love), which frequently pepper the hymns, prayers, and testimonies offered during this festival, carry a poignant multivocal resonance.

For a Luo person, the concept of *dala* (home) comprises many elements. Notions of *piny* (territory), *thur* (home ground), *jowa* (our people), *yawa* (our agnates), and *timbewa* (culture) all combine "into a fine seamless text" of meaning evoked by the word *dala* (Cohen and Atieno Odhiambo 1989, 9). When Joroho sing praises to "Musanda our home," they are thus not only glorifying the physical site of the historical origin of their faith but also lauding the founding actors. The possessive *our* asserts that the particular *timbe* (ways of doing things) mandated by Mango in his homestead are still the *timbe* of contemporary members.

The concept of *dala* derives additional meaning from its particular history in the context of Christianity in western Kenya. In chapter 2, we saw that, since at least 1910, some Christian converts in Nyanza organized their homes as mission stations "where all those who were prepared to accept the new faith were invited to live in a Christian environment" (Whisson 1962, 16). It was common for Christians to identify themselves with one catechist and to follow the brand of Christianity practiced in his *dala*. Adherents sang the hymns composed in that home and wore the costume of that particular religious commune (Ranger 1983,

225). Thus, when Roho members declare Musanda their *dala*, they are asserting themselves followers of the Christianity embodied in the teachings of Alfayo Odongo Mango.

As the holy center of the Joroho, Musanda bears some of the characteristics of Mircea Eliade's classic sacred center (Eliade 1957, 42–65; [1954] 1974, 12–92). For believers, the village is the spiritual, if not territorial, axis of their universe. When Mango died, his shining soul rose straight up through the center of the roof into heaven, creating a permanent link between heaven and the world. Mango's survivors in Ugenya believed that he and Lawi resided directly above them in heaven and pictured Mango and Lawi situated on the middle tier of a "three-story house." From there, Mango and Lawi acted as intercessors between Bishop Barnaba Walwoho, the living representative of the Ruwe Roho community "on the floor" below, and God, seated on the top floor. Roho members anywhere can—and do—receive visions from Mango and the Holy Spirit, but Musanda and Ruwe are seen as places of particular mystical potency, where visions and miracles happen more easily. Roho missionaries and healers from the 1930s through the 1950s always returned to Ruwe to receive more spiritual *yath* (medicine) or *muya* (spirit) when their resources were drained.

For Eliade, sacred centers and myths of origin go hand in hand. Indeed, the story of the *mach*, reenacted in Ruwe at the start of every year, in some respects functions as an origin myth for the Roho community. For instance, believers frequently give the nine Musanda martyrs the metaphorical status of ancestors. Members refer to them as the nine "tribes" or "nations" (*oganda ochiko*) and see them in some vague sense as the progenitors of the current Roho congregations.[11] Moreover, during the *Sikukuu mar Rapar*, bands of women's choirs arm themselves with wooden *bunde* (guns) and march around the Ruwe church grounds like Mango's *askeche*, singing *Wan nyithindo chakruok teko* (We are the children of the beginning of the power). For a moment, they participate in the envisioned religious fervor of the original Roho women. They become Mango's soldiers and lay claim to the bravery and miraculous achievements of their founders. The emphasis on recitation of the *mach* story, with its resonances of new beginnings, has the effect of strengthening people's identification of their collective roots with the specific space of Ruwe-Musanda.

Although one can legitimately argue that the village of Musanda—and, by extension, Ruwe—has gained some cosmogonic, primordial overtones in Roho piety, people are aware that it was the historical marking of this site that rendered it sacred. The special events that took place there—the manifestation of the Holy Spirit among the community gathered in Mango's *boma*, the covenant God made with Mango on that particular site, and the dramatic massacre—have made Musanda a sacred place. "This home is the home of the covenant and the word!" (*Dalani en ye kar singruok, kama ne wach nitie*) declared a pilgrim from Mombasa during a visit to Ruwe. Although many Joroho cannot state exactly when these events occurred, they know they are not part of a mythic, distant past but took place during the time of their parents or grandparents.

Musanda's sacredness, then, is primarily memorial. Historian of religion Jonathan Z. Smith has delineated this type of space in his discussion of the Australian Aranda, for whom each large rock and hill marks the spot where an ancestor perished in Dreamtime (1987, 11). The spatial orientation of the Luo is more congruent with this sort of "mental map" than with the architectural, temple-centered spaces of the Indic peoples, from whose cultures Eliade drew his paradigms. Portions of Nyanza are very rocky and rugged, sporting huge, oddly shaped boulders. The biggest and most unusual of these boulders are generally believed to be transformed animals or ancestral figures, whose memories are kept alive in legends. The huge rock in Kano that Luos believe to be the famous war hero Luanda Magere, the Stone of the Eldest Wife (*Kit Mikayi*) in Seme, and the Stone of the Diviner (*Kit Jajuok*) in the Kajulu hills are a few examples (Onyango-Ogutu and Roscoe 1974, 19; Hauge 1974, 34, 35, 38; Ocholla-Ayayo 1976, 177). The *juogi* of these rocks are sources of great power; hunters sharpen their spears on Lwanda Magere, for instance, and hope to imbibe some of the hero's prowess. Such rocks are often either hollow, such that a diviner may enter, or they contain springs or catchment ridges for rainwater, which is believed to have salubrious qualities (Onyango-Ogutu and Roscoe 1974, 19–20).

Luo independent church congregations impose new templates of meanings on the existing physical and symbolic landscape and often integrate older memorials into their own mythology. For instance, Roho members from Masumbi once told me that there is a lot of mud inside the two huge slabs of *Kit Mikayi*. An ordinary individual cannot extract water from that mud, they explained; only Roho pastors and seers have the power to do so. When a Roho pastor administers this water to a barren woman or to a woman who has gone for a long time without giving birth, they state, she conceives a child immediately.[12]

As the sacred center of the Roho community, Musanda-Ruwe reflects the basically anthropological or memorial character of Luo sacred places. However, the fact that Mango's martyrdom in Musanda is believed by Joroho to have universal relevance adds what Smith would term a utopian dimension to this largely locative orientation (1978, 101). The faithful travel to Musanda-Ruwe, a place charged with spiritual force, and then return to their respective corners of Kenya rejuvenated and empowered. Yet, their empowerment is less and less a question of carrying the particular *yath* of Ruwe into distant places and increasingly a question of strengthening their faith in the savior Mango who died for all Africans. There is thus a symbiotic relationship between, on the one hand, the center and the periphery and, on the other hand, between the believing community and the Spirit. Power and knowledge flow from the sacred center outward; far-flung members come to strengthen their faith in Ruwe, to learn the "real truth" from Mango's contemporaries, and to study Dhoroho. At the same time, the more widespread the Roho faith, the more the villages of Musanda and Ruwe are enriched by the diversity of converts returning to pay homage, an idea that is elaborated in sermons during the *Sikukuu mar Rapar*. Similarly, the stronger the Spirit within the hearts of individuals, the more powerful Roho is overall.

History as Myth and Myth as History

Most academic circles no longer accept the view that a myth is an age-old story passed down, unchanging, through generations. As Jonathan Z. Smith asserts, "regardless of whether we are studying myths from literate or non-literate cultures, we are dealing with historical processes of reinterpretation" (1990, 107 [emphasis deleted]). Yet, myths are important cultural forms that can shape (as well as reflect) the trajectory of history and thus have a certain historical resiliency. The Musanda myth is still very young, a mere sixty years old, yet it has already acquired a certain essential "fixedness," institutionalized within the Roho church. As a root paradigm, it has manifold resonances, mirrored in ritual and personal piety, particularly for Holy Spirit and Holy Ghost churches of Ugenya, where the proximity of Mango's *dala* and the clan ties to the founding pioneers have given Mango's story a certain grounded immediacy. For other Roho congregations such as Sarah Agot's parish in Mirunda, South Nyanza, the myth of Mango's martyrdom vies for primacy in members' hearts with accounts of local prophets' miracles. Large collective festivals, such as the *Sikukuu mar Rapar*, coupled with an increasingly centralized administration, will, I predict, bring the story of the *mach* gradually to the fore in outlying congregations that have joined the Ruwe and Musanda denominations.

The crux of the *mach* myth is the message of salvation and spiritual power through sacrifice. This essential kernel of religious truth has inspired thousands of Roho adherents and will, no doubt, continue to motivate future generations. It is the many subthemes within the Mango myth that introduce an element of indeterminacy, for all have the potential for future development and/or distortion. For example, as Mango's first followers began to apply the paradigm of Jesus' martyrdom to the Musanda event, the historical fact of Mango's murder in that particular colonial context, in turn, transformed the Christian myth. The latter thus became, among other things, a story about emancipation from white exploiters and missionary control. The particular Luo ethnic component of the Musanda event, by contrast, was insignificant or counterproductive to the goals of the Roho pioneers and, thus, never became part of the church's official canon. Such subthemes are revived or downplayed, depending on people's concerns in changing sociopolitical and religious circumstances.

In his seminal essay, "The Invention of Tradition in Colonial Africa" (1983), T. O. Ranger convincingly argues that African leaders appropriated and codified colonial neotraditions in ways that served their own interests. Drawing on Leroy

Vail's research on colonial Zambia, Ranger cites the creation of a Tumbuka "king" by a group of mission-educated Africans as a prime example of such activity. Appropriating the symbols of British neotraditional monarchy, Chilongozi Gondwe, who was appointed chief in 1907, began using the title "king," while local mission elites "were beginning to produce a myth history of the ancient Tumbuka empire" (1983, 242). Invention of "traditional" indigenous monarchies occurred in many places in East Africa during the colonial middle period (1920s–1930s) as native "paramounts" sought to "dramatize their internal authority with crowns and thrones, British style coronations and jubilees" (1983, 240). We have seen that the Joroho, during this period, also crowned *kingi* Elijah Oloo as the universal African king in a large ceremony. Until his death, Oloo retained the title of *Kingi*, or *Chefe*, as it appears in Dhoroho on his tombstone.

Within the immediate context of the colonial Wanga district, the crowning of a Luo king[13] was a symbolic act of defiance. It constituted a slap in the face of King George and a challenge to the regional ruler his government backed, Wanga Paramount Chief Mumia and his "royal" family. It gave eloquent expression to the Joroho's confidence in the moral authority of their cause while it appealed to collective Luo discontent. Their explicit rhetoric of pan-African kingship also cleverly attempted to play across ethnic divisions, appealing to the general frustration with European overlordship in western Kenya. Yet what may have originally been an effective way for Mango and his followers to rally grassroots support became, after the massacre, an enormous liability. The church's pioneers, therefore, did not cultivate or openly honor this monarchical-political aspect of their founding history, for it only cast suspicion on their endeavors.

The result is that the political dimension of the Roho past, which *Kingi* Oloo represents, is, in fact, surprisingly undeveloped in the group's collective memory. Members still commemorate Oloo's coronation on January 16, 1934, by laying greens on his grave at midnight every January 15 and singing praise songs until morning, but the event is clearly not part of their root metaphor. It does not form part of the backbone of their faith, unlike Mango's martyrdom in the *mach*. When today's Roho members recall the figure of *Kingi* Elijah Oloo, they remember him as a symbol of the pan-African unity that they still hope for.

Just as Roho leaders have let dwindle aspects of their tradition that proved detrimental to their cause, so, too, have they embroidered and distorted other aspects that can be used to legitimate their authority. Because men have gradually come to dominate all the official posts, they are the ones who currently supervise large ceremonies such as the *Sikukuu mar Rapar*, when the church's oral tradition is managed and disseminated. They thus control the information machinery of the denomination—at least, the official machine—and have fixed it so that it serves their interests. As Ranger points out, there is a definite ambiguity in much invented African tradition:

However much [invented African tradition] may have been used by the "progressive traditionalists" to inaugurate new ideas and institutions—like compulsory education under the Tumbuka paramountcy—codified tradition inevitably hardened in a way that advantaged the vested interests in possession at the time of its codification. Codified and reified custom was manipulated by such vested interests as a means of asserting or increasing control. (Ranger 1983, 254)

Ranger identifies four situations in which Africans during the colonial period typically manipulated "tradition" to justify their own dominance over other Africans: Elders invoked tradition to keep the younger Western-educated generation from usurping their authority, men appealed to tradition to maintain control over women as economic assets, chiefs used invented tradition to legitimate their power, and indigenous groups used the notion to keep migrants who settled among them in their place. These four situations are by no means restricted to the colonial period but have continued to play themselves out in a myriad of postcolonial contexts. A quick glance through letters to the editor in any Kenyan newspaper shows that men continue to appeal to African traditional values to discourage their women from working in urban areas, entering politics, or challenging their husbands. The celebrated S. M. Otieno case of 1987 likewise shows that clans continue to manipulate "custom" to resist state law and to deny widows any rights over their deceased husbands' remains or property (Stamp 1991).

Within the context of the Roho church today, we can observe similar vested interests influencing the process of codification of tradition. The sabbath service held during the 1991 *Sikukuu mar Rapar* offered clear evidence of the fact that the Mango myth is being codified in ways that marginalize women and young people, while at the same time it serves to integrate various geographical regions into a unified support base.

The five male pastors presiding over this particular worship service agreed on a program in which elderly representatives of each major region would be allowed to present their recollections about the *mach*. Residents from Ugenya were instructed to lead the remembrance about "Master Alfayo," residents of Alego were to speak about "Teacher Lawi," and female residents from Uyoma and Yimbo would speak about *"Laktar* Turfosa." Such a program involved shaping Roho history so that it conformed to the gendered, gerontocratic, administrative, and regional hierarchies of the current church.

Let us consider the series of invented hierarchies being codified in this orchestrated recitation of the founding myth. First, Alfayo is presented as the master (*jaduong*), at the pinnacle of the hierarchy. District reports from the 1930s suggest that Lawi may have, in fact, been the original force behind the Roho movement and that Mango joined later, but Roho oral history definitely presents Mango as the leader and Lawi as his *jakony* (helper). It is fitting, then, that Lawi is today associated with the post of teacher, a post subordinate to the office of pastor or leader of a congregation. In truth, Lawi was never a catechist but, instead, functioned as a seer or prophet (*jakorwach*) within the church. Turfosa Aloo was not, in fact, a *laktar* during her lifetime but a soldier (*askari*). (It is not clear that the position of *laktar* even existed prior to Mango's death; it seems to be a creation of the Roho church in the late 1930s and 1940s.) However, the orchestrators of the *Sikukuu mar Rapar* have adroitly recast the image of this foundress so that she is consistent with the only post open to women today, the lowest post in the congregational hierarchy.

A correlation of the administrative model with regional stratification is also evident in the pastors' reinvention of Roho history. Both Mango's and Lawi's patrilineage were of Alego origin, but Mango's family migrated to Ugenya before Lawi's. The association of the head of the church (the master) with Ugenya, the second in command (the teacher) with Alego, and the female *laktar* with Yimbo and Uyoma reinforces a subtle regional bias that legitimates Ruwe-Musanda as the church headquarters. In this mental diagram, the lakeside districts of Yimbo and Uyoma are peripheral, supportive, and female.

Finally, only elderly "eyewitnesses" were allowed to speak during this important annual remembrance. Yet, their reminiscences were managed and forced to serve the categories established by the controlling leaders. The stamp of elderly authority—both male and female—has thus been appropriated by the current generation of Roho leaders. We can see how this orchestrated reinterpretation of Roho oral history serves the vested interests of those who benefit from the gradual defeminization of Roho power and the institutionalization of the colonial-missionary code.[14]

Yet, myths, like rituals, are multifaceted. The official tradition may be the dominant version, but unofficial versions play themselves out within the context of smaller group gatherings, hymn sings, personal testimonies, and individual lives. The Roho message of empowerment has a revolutionary component, a potential for boldness, that cannot be fully routinized. We have to consider, for example, the recent founding of the Spirit Mother Church. This church comprises a small body of Roho worshipers who claim that Roho prophetess Sarah Agot is, in fact, the Holy Spirit incarnate. They venerate her as the true third member of the Holy Trinity, a figure who thus supplants Odongo Mango in significance. We must also consider the way in which individual Roho women still identify with Aloo the warrior, despite official attempts to render her memory more benign. In the final chapter, I consider these unofficial appeals to tradition.

A Service of Remembrance

What follows is a description of a sabbath service I attended in Ruwe during the 1991 *Sikukuu mar Rapar*. The expressed objective of "remembering correctly" was more of a focus on this occasion than during other services throughout the

year. Nevertheless, whenever members of the Ruwe Holy Ghost Church gather
to worship, they invoke their founders' names, sing hymns about the *mach*, and
bear witness to their belief in Mango, the African redeemer. The form, movement, and "feel" of this gathering is thus characteristic of Roho worship in
general. This section is meant to provide the reader with an appreciation for how
the themes of martyrdom, home, and history, previously discussed, are given
shape within the context of Roho congregational worship.

It was still relatively cool inside the large cinder block church when the senior
church teacher, Meshak Ogola, and I arrived for the sabbath service. Worship
had not yet formally begun, but more than a hundred people had assembled on
this Saturday morning, January 19, 1991, at the headquarters of the Ruwe Holy
Ghost Church. They were already singing hymns.[15] After removing our dusty
sandals and adding them to the pile of shoes and rubber thongs heaped at the
entrance, we made our way across the gritty cement floor to the center aisle,
marked by a slightly sunken, painted red line that runs the length of the sanctuary
and divides the rectangular room into two long segments. Although it is not
apparent at first glance, this central, eight-inch-wide red stripe is intersected
farther up by a perpendicular line extending the width of the sanctuary, about
twenty feet in front of the chancel. That morning, chairs and mats obscured this
horizontal axis of the enormous sunken cross, but members of the congregation
are well aware of the pattern underneath their feet; any individual who has sinned
and not confessed is technically not supposed to traverse the perpendicular line.
The upper portion of the sanctuary should remain undefiled.

People sat facing the altar; women, as always, were seated on the left, and men
on the right (as one faces the altar). Everyone bore the universal Roho emblem, a
red cross, sewn onto a white *kanzu*,[16] cap, or headscarf. A number of wooden
chairs on the women's side were reserved for female church elders and prominent
women guests. Several older women brought their own low stools or folding
chairs, but most sat on burlap sacks, legs outstretched and crossed at the ankles.
Many held babies in their laps; children sat quietly alongside. Someone had
borrowed long, thin desks with attached benches from a local primary school and
placed them in rows on the men's side of the church. Adult men, both young and
old, sat on these benches; those who had Bibles or liturgical booklets placed them
on the desks. Two rows of straight-backed chairs reserved for elders had been
placed in front of the desks; about half the seats were already occupied.

I paused at the aisle as some women I knew motioned for me to join them,
making space for me on their mats. I went to sit with them, but, as often
happened, a number of the male officials intervened, insisting that I use the small
table in the front on their side of the sanctuary for my tape recorder. They
positioned me so that I would be ready to photograph all the preachers from close
up. From my privileged spot, it was not easy to survey the congregation. I turned
and tried to count the number of people present. There were seven disjointed
rows of women, roughly thirteen women per row. The men did not sit as tightly
together; there were perhaps seven of them to a row and there were nine rows so

far. Approximately twenty-five to thirty children—both boys and girls—were present. It had been my experience throughout Nyanza Province that women constituted a consistent 70 percent of the adults attending any given local Roho event. The three-day annual *Sikukuu mar Rapar* drew representatives from Roho churches all over Kenya and northeastern Tanzania. Distant congregations that could afford to sponsor only one or two representatives tended to send a *padri* or another male official. It was therefore not surprising that the percentage of men in attendance this morning (40 percent) was slightly higher than usual.

Eventually, the officiating pastors emerged from the front office, where they had donned their robes. The congregation stood and sang as the five clergymen filed solemnly through the door on the right-hand side of the chancel. Each spread a small cloth on the floor in front of himself in preparation for prayer. They stood in a line facing us, keeping the altar table to their right so that they remained on the men's side of the sanctuary. A single row of chairs had been provided for them on the platform; from there, they would be able to see the men easily, but their view of the women's half of the room (as well as the women's view of them) was partially obstructed by a low-hanging decorative drape of banana leaves strung along the center aisle. The pastors made an impressive sight, their brand-new black cassocks and crisp white surplices in sharp contrast to the faded and torn gowns worn by the majority of the Joroho before them.[17]

The hymn with which the congregation greeted them was sung a cappella in unison in Dhoroho, the special language—in fact, an encoding of Dholuo—revealed by God to Mango's followers in 1935. Many people had difficulty with the lyrics. It was the elders who led the rest:

Cho bithe Sovend Cho Biri Pempi Shesimpu
Shortly before Heaven Will Be Sealed

Cho bithe sovend cho biri pempi shesimpu,
(Shortly before heaven will be sealed,)

Biri chandi so Shunga tumbiu itho itho.
(Jesus will build my house there in heaven.)

Ond otisipi ndundi biri biri,
(I long to see heaven,)

Vi ich njondongeche u bendsh socho socho.
(For we won't remain long on this earth.)

Njopempi thocheu u bendsh sojeund sojeund,
(We will live in a new world,)

Sinthi njonjumpe njump sosev, sosev, sosev,
(In which we will sing sweet, sweet songs,)

Cho njobochi Shunga te Jongoshu.
(When we praise Jesus and God.)

The Dhoroho lyrics are a word-for-word translation of the familiar Luo Christian hymn *Ka Podi Matin Ka Polo Biro Yimore*, (Just before Heaven will be Sealed), which heralds the end of the world and the joyful homecoming Christians can anticipate. The Roho version is sung to a different tune, however—a lovely, simpler melody. As the song drew to a close, the leading officiant, who had entered the sanctuary first and was now closest to the altar, announced the title of the next hymn: "*Jawarwa, Konyo Ji Yesu*, . . . *Wahero Pake*" (Our Savior Jesus Helps People). I had spent a number of Saturdays with the Ruwe congregation, and they had each time opened their sabbath service in the same manner. *Cho Bithé Sovend*, sung on one's knees, always accompanied the entrance of the clergy. The hymn that immediately followed might vary, but it was always in Dholuo and always sung kneeling.

As people paused after the completion of this second hymn, it became clear that a couple of members were already exhibiting signs of possession. One old woman hummed low and loud, rocking back and forth on her knees with her eyes shut. At the same instant, from the men's side of the room came a series of guttural exclamations, *Hep!* . . . *yip, yip!* The padri's command quieted them: *Nzari Mbethi* (Confession of Sins). The congregation, still kneeling, began to recite the prayer of confession in Dhoroho (Luo and English translations are provided in parentheses):

Nzari Mbethi
Confession of Sins

Njaindjo Sorithavi,[18]
(Wuonwa manyalo duto,)
(Our omnipotent father/lit., Who is capable of everything,)

   Chumi sochudhi fog, njong' poshi njonjushi njogshimpe
   (Kendo makech ngang', wasebayo waweyo wang'yori)
   (And never severe, we have strayed, we left the direction of your path)

      chompiyu simpauji.
      (karombe morouenyo.)
      (like lost sheep.)

Njong'u vesi onzejo teso dhajnjo njonjute bompichumu tiyi.
(Wase[19] *timo ahinya gima chunywa wawegi parokende gombo.)*
(We have truly done that which our own hearts alone desire.)

   Njonguchuki dhechnde sorump.
   (Waseketho chikni maler.)
   (We have broken your holy laws.)

   Njongunjushi tech sinjewimpu vesi chumi njongu vesi tech
   (Waseweyo gik mowijore[20] *timo kendo wase timo gik)*
   (We have left things that ought to be done and we have done things)

soch njewimpu vesi,
(mak wijore timo,)
(which ought not to be done,)

vi feso njoifu ti vi end ompaik.
(to ngima waonge go to in Aruoth.)
(for we have no health/life except you, O Lord.)

Echudhnjo; njond wi sompedhi so dhomimpu.
(Ikechwa; wan jo maricho ma chandore.)
(Have mercy on us; we are evil, troubled people.)

Ojong'oshu, e nju witi sonzari mepehite.
(Anyasaye, i we jogo mahulo richogi.)
(O God, forgive those people who confess their sins.)

Thinjich witi sorichimpu chais mpedhite
(Dowok jogo malokore kuom richogi)
(Repay those who have repented of their sins)

chocho ndeng'efi we thavi nde shunga chempengvi mpaidnjo.
(kaka nisingo ji duto ni yesu kiristo ruonwa.)
(as you promised everyone through Jesus Christ our Lord.)

Njaindnjo sochudhi fog esenjo ndechudh und simi njodhoch
(Wuonwa makecho ngang' imiwa nikech en[21] mondo wachak)
(Father who is never harsh, give to us in order that we begin)

vendumu raimp(i) end njonjaik chompu chumi njompevimpu.
(tinende luor(o) in wawuoth kare kendo waritore.)
(now to respect/fear you, we walk uprightly, we are awaited.)

Sognjind simi njoboch jefe sorump.
(Mang'won, mondo wapak nyingi maler.)
(Merciful [one], thus we praise your holy name.)

Osend
(Amin)
(Amen)

Upon the conclusion of the *Nzari*, the pastor immediately began to pray in rapid Luo, *Nyasaye mawuon ngima, roudh won esimbo, jadolo man kare, wagoyo ni erokamano odichieng' ma kawuono* (God, father of life, Lord of Glory, priest who is just, we thank you this day). Shrieks and moans drowned out his monotone as more people, swaying on their knees or on all fours, started to express the arrival of the Holy Spirit. Those not yet filled with the Spirit mumbled their own personal prayers. One could catch only snatches of the preacher's words above the mounting din, "Those who know what it entails, this is the third covenant[22] which you made with black people. . . . Therefore we, too, are doing his work in kindness and peace, in the flesh and the Holy Spirit."[23]

All responded, *Osend* (Amen).

The preacher then announced the Lord's Prayer in Dhoroho: *Rosi Somp Mpaik*. The congregation proceeded to follow his cue. People were generally more confident with this recitation than with the preceding Roho hymn or the confession, although some children and a few young adults remained silent. (Once again, I have divided and combined Luo words so they are consistent with the Roho spelling):

Rosi Somp Mpaik
Lamo Mar Ruoth
Lord's Prayer

Njaindnjo sonde ubiri,
(Wuonwa mani epolo,)
(Our father who is in heaven,)

　Jefe simi iputhe sorump,
　(Nyingi mondo obedi maler,)
　(Let your name be holy,)

　Bej mpaik some ipe.
　(Piny ruoth mari obi.)
　(Your kingdom come.)

Te sethnjompi simi tevesu ubej chocho ubiri.
(Gi midwaro mondo gitime epiny kaka epolo.)
(Let those things which you want, be done on earth as in heaven.)

Esenjo vendemu dheuyunjo somp vendumu.
(Imiwa tinende chiembewa mar tinende.)
(Give us this day our daily food.)

Enjunjo umpedhinjo,
(Iwewa erichowa,)
(Forgive us our sins,)

　chocho njond njonjuwi sovesindnjo sompodh.
　(kaka wan wawejo matimonwa marach.)
　(as we forgive those who have done evil to us.)

Cheche vumpinjo[24] *chais vus,*
(Kiki terowa kuom tem,)
(Do not carry us into sin,)

　Vi chijnjo empedhi.
　(To konywa ericho.)
　(But keep us from sin.)

Nde chudh bej mpaik, te vuchi nde chaise.
(Ni kech piny ruoth gi teko ni kuomi.)
(Because the kingdom and power are yours.)

Nzetende te nzetende.
(*higini gi higini.*)
(Forever and ever.)

Osend
(A*min*)
(Amen)

The pastor again launched into a very rapid prayer, whose words were difficult to catch as more members began speaking in tongues. One woman sang a hymn while others were gasping and grunting. The pastor again made reference to the covenant (*singruok*) between God and Alfayo Odongo:

God of above . . . [you were with] Alfayo as he traveled from home here in the South up to Mugoya and Yimbo in the East. . . . You called our father [i.e., Odongo] as you called the Jews. . . . Lord, pray with us, for we want to persevere. [Pray with] the priests, the teachers, especially the children of the church and the healers so that we meet you, Owner of Life. Lord, God you said that in the beginning there was the Word. Lord keep us during the Holy Sabbath, with the angels, through the Holy Spirit.

That last phrase, "through the Holy Spirit" (*kuom Roho Maler*), always signals the end of a prayer and is answered with *Osend*. Some individuals overcome with the Spirit continued to cry out after this point, but the majority quieted down once the collective *Osend* was spoken. After completing his prayer, the officiating pastor stood up, followed by the congregation. Upon his command, some women began to lead the congregation in a hymn in Dholuo, *Jolweny Mager* (Brave Warriors),[25] which proceeded in a slow, steady rhythm:

Jolweny Mager
Brave Warriors

Jolweny mayer mose loyo, unjoKristo, keduru matek.
(Brave warriors who have won, you Christians, fight hard.)

Ne wani e thim malich kama.
(We were in dangerous wilderness.)

Kawuono use neno nying' manyien maruoth osemiyowa.
(Today you have seen God's new name that he has given us.)

Jowuoth, jowuoth, ne ok gi yie ni mondi wuhuli Chuny Maler.
(Pilgrims, pilgrims, they did not permit us to tell about the Holy Spirit.)

Nyasaye owuon nowachonwa,
(God himself said to us,)

"Nyithinda, kiku parore; Aseko luoko richou."
("My children, don't be worried; I have said that I will wash your sins away.")

Jomalaika negiwer kama kagipako, "Wuon manie polo,"
(The angels sing like this when they praise [God], "Father who is in heaven,")

Kane gi omo ruodhi piny.
([they sang this] when they brought the Lord to earth.)

Kane gidhi negiwacho kama, "In wuon miloyo duto."
(When they went they spoke thus, "You are owner over all.")

Waseko, "Kelo Ruodhi piny."
(We said, "Bring the Lord to earth.")

Wuoro, wuowi gi Chuny Maler neno chiko obi duogo
(The Father, son and Holy Ghost; see, the law [which states] that they will return)

Kobiro yiero jomodhier.
(To select the poor.)

Jomani e piny ne okgi ng'eyo kaka Ruodhwa oseko duogo
(Those who were on the earth didn't even know that our Lord had said he would return)

Kobiro loso piny manyien.
(To make a new world.)

Nonwan'ga achiel nyarombone nenokawe kotere polo.
(He recovered one of his [lost] sheep and took it to heaven.)

Kanegineno negiyuak.
(When they saw, they wailed.)

Negichungo kumabori negi ngiye kano dhiyo—
(They stood far from there, they watched him going—)

Gigani no malieli mach.
(Those thousands are burning in hell.)

Ne ok obiro gi kido moro mana kitemo a go ipolo.
(He will not come in another form, only those of you who try will enter heaven.)

Maneno singore go chon.
(This was promised them a long time ago.)

Ne ok wang'eyo kamano: bi sikie echunywa koro
(We do not know how: come remain in our hearts so that)

Kigolo richowa duto.
(You remove all our sins.)

The "brave warriors" mentioned were the Roho members who fought in the battle that claimed the lives of their leaders in 1934. The pilgrims of the second stanza are the early Roho adherents and missionaries who, after Mango's death, were arrested and prevented from proselytizing. The hymn thus alludes to the particular experience of the Joroho but within the general understanding of Christians as soldiers for God, for the Roho community perceives its past as well as its future mission as part of the greater Christian reality; the parallels between Mango and Christ and between the Joroho and the early apostles are integral to the worldview articulated by the Roho churches.

As the hymn drew to a close, the pastors conversed among themselves, apportioning the morning's lessons. While people adjusted their mats and sat down, one stepped forward to announce the first reading: Luke 7: 1–10. He started to read the account of the Roman centurion who sent emissaries to Capernaum to beseech Jesus to heal the centurion's dying slave. After the opening verse, the pastor paused for a few seconds as a frenzied, middle-aged woman shouted in high-pitched, barking shrieks and gesticulated violently. Those near her casually moved aside to give her space. When she appeared to have calmed down, the preacher picked up where he had left off. The woman began to cry out again, although less loudly. This time, the pastor did not pause but read on over her noise.

Occasionally a few members of the congregation would join her, humming or moaning intermittently. Others simply swayed with their eyes shut. At times, the woman seemed to utter intelligible words or phrases, but the sequence made no sense: *Yiih, yiih . . . an bi koro ma! Abato. Yah, yah. . . . Boop . . . cho, cho.* Once she dropped her voice and cried out clearly, *Aleluya!* Finally, two senior *laktache*, their broad, colorful sashes indicating their rank, made their way over and attended to the possessed woman. Their experienced hands firmly clasped her waist and calmed her. By the time the pastor concluded with "This is the first lesson," all was still.

The head *padri* then announced the title of a Luo Anglican hymn, *Yesu Nobiro Pinywa Kae* (Jesus came down to this earth), which some women sitting toward the front instantly took up with enthusiasm. The hymn had a catchy tune that the congregation clearly enjoyed singing. Afterward, a third pastor announced that the second reading would be taken from Revelation 4, as the same woman resumed shouting but in a lower, less frantic voice. This time she was understandable: *Abiro, Abiro, Abiro . . . Aleluya . . . Abiro Baba* (I am coming, I am coming, I am coming . . . Alleluia . . . I am coming, Father!), she cried, clapping her hands above her head. The *padri* calmly read the Scripture passage, which recounted John's mystical journey to heaven and his encounter with four terrifying beasts seated at the base of God's throne. Just as the *padri* reached the verse containing the praise song repeated by the beasts day and night, a woman seated toward the back of the church began singing quietly to herself as if inspired by the passage.

The head *padri* then stood and announced a hymn in Dhoroho: *Peampa* (or *Biuru* in Dholuo) (Come). The Roho song is an exact translation of a popular Anglican Luo hymn, *Biuru Ire Yesu Jakony* (Come to Jesus the Savior). Once more, it was the older members who had mastered the sacred language that led the rest on the verses; everyone seemed confident with the chorus:

Peampa ema Shunga Wochij
Biuru ire Yesu Jakony
Come to Jesus the Savior

Peampa ema Shunga Wochij.
(Biuru ire Yesu Jakony.)
(Come to Jesus the Savior.)

Njodhndu sorump u sijenginjo shi.
(Wachne maler e monyisowa yo.)
(His holy word shows us the path.)

Shunga idhafi chimpi te cho,
(Yesu ochungo koro gi ka,)
(Jesus bore witness to these things,)

Chijodhi, Peampa.
(Kowacho, Biuru.)
(So that he could say, "Come.")

> CHORUS:
> *Njondosimb vi njojosim fog,*
> *(Wanamor to wanamor ngang')*
> (We rejoice and we are very happy,)
>
> *Ucho njondongeche te Shunga:*
> *(Eka wanasiki gi Yesu:)*
> And then we will remain with Jesus:)
>
> *Shunga wochij inzumbinjo,*
> *(Yesu Jakonywa oherowa,)*
> (Jesus our savior loves us,)
>
> *Chumi ndinjombinjo.*
> *(Kendo nowarowa.)*
> (Moreover he saves us.)

Shunga ndijodhi, Peampa cho,
(Yesu nowacho, Biuru ka,)
(Jesus said, Come here,)

And wi siwij savefi sobuch,
(Un jo mojony muting'o mapek,)
(You who are weary and heavily laden,)

Vi chech athuche, jendwamba njodh;
(*To kik udeki winjuru wach;*)
(But don't delay, listen to the word;)

We thavi ve tebe.
(*Ji duto to gibi.*)
(All people, come forth.)

(Chorus again.)

When the hymn was over, a fourth pastor delivered the third reading, which was taken from the seventh chapter of Paul's Epistle to the Hebrews (*Jo-Hibrania*), beginning with the fourth verse. The selection was about Melchizedek, an ancient legendary priest and king of Jerusalem prior to the Hebraic conquest, who, "resembling the son of God," continues to live forever. It is a long and complex passage, containing a discussion of Melchizedek's relationship to the Levitical priesthood and an analogy between Melchizedek and Jesus. The pastor did not offer any exigesis of the difficult text; members were left to interpret its significance on their own.

The head *padri* then stepped forward and announced the Roho hymn *Ne War Mach* (Behold the Salvific Fire). People bustled to their feet for this popular song:

Ne War Mach
Behold the Salvific Fire

Ne war mach ma oliel mi owaro piny duto.
(Behold the salvific fire, which burned and saved the whole world.)

Osiepe Yesu keduru!
(Friends of Jesus, fight!)

Timuru kukia; ngima nitie e polo.
(Do it if you don't care [about this life]; there is life in heaven.)

Rituru wa koth mochwe chunywa;
(Wait for the rain that cleanses our spirits;)

Israel warowa.
(Israel saves us.)

Ne bendera mawaro piny duto!
(Behold the flag that saves the whole world!)

Yesu yuak e piny.
(Jesus suffered in the world.)

Israel odhil e tho
(Israel endured death)

Kogeno waro nyithinde,
(So that he could save his children,)

Ka piny luonge Ruodhi mon.
(So that the world would call him the Lord of women.)

Madhuru wa remb Israel manyien!
(Drink the blood of the new Israel!)

Koriwo chungu uduto,
(So that all of you can stand united,)

Kuchamo duonde Ruoth Yesu.
(So that you receive [lit., eat] the voice of Lord Jesus.)

Israel odhil kochungo bendera
(Israel endured so that he could raise the flag)

Kane Ruodhe luonge.
(When the Lord called him.)

Yesu nowara ka piny odaga.
(Jesus saves me while the world refuses me.)

To an jaote mar Ruoth,
(But I am an apostle of the Lord,)

To un tinde genuru.
(And you, today, must trust.)

Aseko tweyo piny duto.
(I have said, bind the whole world.)

Ringuru ging'wech nikech Israel.
(Run quickly because of Israel.)

Beduru gi luor kuwinjo chik Ruoth.
(Fear the Lord's law when you hear it.)

Eka nudonji e polo
(And then you will enter heaven)

To unuyudi yueyo.
(And find rest.)

Ne War Mach is another one of the many Roho hymns that celebrates the founding story. The opening line refers to the fire that killed Mango and has become a symbol of supreme importance for the Roho community. As we have seen, the Joroho believe that through Mango's suffering and death in the fire, God redeemed the world, especially Africa. The analogy between the Roho founder and the martyred Christ implicit in this hymn is often openly articulated by Roho members. Israel, an epithet for Mango, came into use shortly after his death, when Isaya Goro, a leading Roho missionary, was overcome by the Holy

Spirit and kept repeating *Israel jawarwa* (Israel our savior). Lyrics such as *Israel warowa* (Israel saves us), found in this hymn, are thus common in Roho songs and suggest an identification not only with Christ's paradigm but also with that of the Old Testament patriarchs.

Bendera ("flag" in Kiswahili) is another important symbol for Roho Christians. The flag here referred to is the banner of the church that was first flown on January 16, 1934, at the coronation of Elijah Oloo, the "king" of the new community. Like all symbols, the flag stands for many things: victory, both temporal and spiritual; independence from colonial overlords; a divine mission. Members elaborated on all these themes over the course of the *Sikukuu mar Rapar*, particularly in sermons. While people sing *Ne War Mach* and other hymns that evoke images and incidents from the founding story throughout the year, they appeared to give them more attention during this weekend of remembrance.

Next, the head *padri* announced the Apostles' Creed in Dhoroho, *Njonzari Osheu*.[26]

Njonzari Osheu
Wahulo Ayie
Apostles' Creed

Osheu chais Jong'oshu njaindnjo sojori thavi
(*Ayie kuom Nyasaye wuonwa manyalo duto*)
(I believe in God our father of everything)

Sondi Phnjushi biri te bej.
(*Mano chwyeyo polo gi piny.*)
(Who created heaven and earth.)

Chumi chais Shunga Chempengui jaithuso sethumpi sompaidinjo
(*Kendo kuom Yesu Kiristo wuodema midero maruothowa*)
(Also in Jesus Christ, the only son of our father)

Chosend ndishoPh te mpinzi sorump.
(*Kamin noyach gi Roho Maler.*)
(Whose mother was pregnant with the Holy Spirit.)

Jochi sombeos usondijairu.
(*Nyako Mariam emanonyuole.*)
(The Virgin Mary gave birth to him.)

Ndindudi songompe[a] chai bindvei berovi nditampu.
(*Noneno masari(?) kuom Pontio Pilato nogure.*)
(He suffered as a result of Pontius Pilate (who) crucified him.)

a. I think there is a mistake here. The word should be *song'empo*, which would produce *masira* in Dholuo, or "suffering." The vowels may have been transposed over the years, or perhaps the informant made an error.

(Kendo notho min yikeno[b] lor kuom jomotho.)
(He died, then was buried and descended with the dead.)

Pheug somp othuch ndiPheump ndio chais wisiki.
(Chieng mar adek nochier noa kuom jomotho.)
(On the third day, he rose from the dead.)

Ndiedi u biri ucho ndiputhi chimp pov ovchimpoPh njePh Jongoshu
njaindnjo sojori thavi.
(Noidho e polo eka nobedo kor bat atekorach wich mar Nyasaye wuonwa
manyalo duto.)
(He ascended into heaven and then sat on the absolute right hand of God our
omnipotent father.)

Pheug ndio champi vi ndipe simi igothi pampo chais we sofeso chithe wi siki.
(Chieng, noa kuro to nobi mondo ong'ado bura kuom jo mangima kodi jo
motho.)
(At the end of time, he will come from there in order to judge the living and
the dead.)

Osheu chais mpinzi sorump,
(Ayie kuom roho maler,)
(I believe in the Holy Spirit,)

Chondeng'o sorump somp bej thavi,
(Kanisa maler mar piny duto,)
(The holy church of the whole world,)

Ror mpaich somp wi sorump,
(Lal ruok mar jo maler,)
(The fellowship of the saints, [lit., holy ones])

Njumpaich somp mpeiPhi,
(Weruok mar richo,)
(Forgiveness of sins,)

Chumi feso somp nzetende te nzetende.[c]
(Kendo ngima mar higini gi higini.)
(And life forever and ever.)

Osend
(Amin)
(Amen)

b. I have delineated these four words so that they are exact decipherings of the Roho
originals. However, the sentence would be clearer if the syllables in the Luo phrase were
grouped thus: *Kendo notho mi noyike nolor.* Note that the word *send* in the Roho original
should have an *i* affixed at the end, producing the requisite *o* in the Luo word *noyike.* This
omission is most likely an error.

c. This phrase simply has to be *Nzetende te nzetende* in Dhoroho, rendering *higini gi higini*
(forever and ever) in Dholuo. *Nzotende,* as was given to me, translates into *hagini gi hagini,*
which is nonsensical.

The congregation managed to recite only the first few phrases with confidence. Soon even the voices of most of the elders and priests trailed off. Everyone looked down at the floor, silent. Although not even half the creed had been completed, the head *padri* quickly rescued people from their embarrassment by announcing the *Rosi Somp Mpaik* (Lord's Prayer), which people said easily in Dhoroho on their knees. The pastor then extended a right hand over the heads of his kneeling congregation and launched into a loud, fast, stream-of-consciousness prayer, as is the custom. This type of prayer is delivered in a forceful, rapid-fire monotone, with only slight pauses between statements, evidence of the presence and strength of the Spirit. *Nyasaye maduong' wuon ngima kendo wuon adiera loch mon malo* (Great God, father of life, father of truth and glory of heaven), he began. Many people started to shake and moan. "We thank you, father of life, for protecting and carrying us to this day so that we can preach the true word. Jehovah, our God, we move with you spiritually (*wasudo kodi chunywa*), so pray for us." About a third of the congregation now displayed signs of possession. People swayed and shuddered. Some shook their heads from side to side violently, breathing heavily. Eyes shut, people spoke their personal prayers out loud. "These are the final days," continued the pastor. He prayed for a deceased Roho woman pioneer, "Look upon Rael[27] and bless her soul, remembering your promise to all apostles and prophets. Pray for our pastors and teachers. Put us in a worshipful attitude (*ketwa e lamo*), sustain us and hear our prayers in the Holy Spirit (*kuom Roho Maler*)."

All replied, *Osend*.

After a momentary pause, the pastor resumed, "Good listener, Jesus, son of God our sacrificial priest, continue to remember us according to your promise." Referring to the current era of the Spirit's residence among Africans, which Joroho believe superseded the reign of the Europeans and the Asians, he said, "These are the final days that you revealed to Alfayo and Lawi. We have reached the third stage (*okang' mar adek*). . . . Remember us, give us your words. . . . You are the quiet teacher that the world doesn't know." He went on at length invoking God and depicting the apocalypse, when Mango would open the heavenly gates for the faithful. He concluded with a prayer for worldwide unity, calling for blessings on people "from here and there, the countries of America and Uganda so that they become your people" (*mondo gibed jogi*).

After everybody had responded *Osend*, one of the other pastors stepped forward and announced a Luo hymn: *Wapako Hera mar Nyasaye* (We Praise the Love of God). This song celebrates God's special (and ultimate) dispensation to the Roho community. It praises "Israel," now seated on a throne in heaven, and speaks of awaiting his return in much the same vein as the preceding pastoral prayer:

Wapako Hera mar Nyasaye
We Praise the Love of God

Wapako hera mar Nyasaye,
(We praise the love of God,)

Koriwo joge e pinje duto.
(For it unites people from all lands.)

Kobiro wadende wapake,
(When he comes we will proudly praise him,)

Jowuodhi Israel mang'uon.
(The faithful followers of Israel.)

Koduogo wanamor, haleluya!
(When he returns we will rejoice, halleluia!)

Kiloyo piny wadendoi wapakoi.
(If you defeat the world, we will magnify and praise you.)

Wadwaro luwo bang'i Ruodhwa.
(We want to follow after you, Lord.)

Koyawonwa rangach polo.
(Open for us the gate to heaven.)

Musalape wating'o Ruodhwa.
(We carry his cross, our Lord.)

Wayawo kodo pinje duto.
(We will unfasten the ropes constricting the entire world.)

Wasingore mogik adier wapogore.
(We were given the last convenant; truly we are different.)

Wakawo Jehova gi wuowi.
(We receive God and the son.)

Kudwaro neno duong' polo,
(If you want to see the glory of heaven,)

Biuru wa wakulure wapako Ruoth.
(Come with us, we are heading out to go praise the Lord.)

Haleluya wadendo Ruodhwa.
(Halleluia, we glorify our Lord.)

Msalaba mari otweyo pinje.
(Your cross binds all lands.)

Chik achiel moloyo piny,
(One law over the whole earth,)

Mochweyo nam gi bel gi kal wawuoro ngang',
(Which created the lake and millet and sorghum, we are truly amazed,)

Gi gik moko duto mantie,
(And all the other things that exist,)

Jomose winjo duonde Ruodhwa.
(Those who have heard our Lord's voice.)

Makuru tiend Israel go kumba yie.
(Hold onto the feet of Israel, if you are willing.)

Haleluya Ruodh polo kwatieko watundo ipolo.
(Halleluia, Lord of heaven, when we are finished, we will arrive in heaven.)

Ichungoto ikwanowa imori ngang',
(You stand and count us, you are extremely happy,)

Ruodhiwa Israel maduong,
(Our great Lord Israel,)

Isingori mogik adier ikawo kom.
(You were given the final promise; you have assumed the throne.)

Wapedho othidhe ni wuowi.
(We spread palms; he is the son.)

Waruake to waweri ngang' waromone.
(We welcome him and really sing, we surround him.)

Imiyowa wachakogo piny manyien.
(We are given [the task] of starting the new world.)

Chech manyien noduogo e piny.
([At the time of] the new creation, he will return to earth.)

Ma Musa nene osingo chon oduokonwa.
(The convenant Musa made long ago is returned to us.)

Jomaparo yor Wuoro maler,
(People who remember the path marvel at holiness,)

Keduru kaka chich achiel mwakedogo.[28]
(Fight even the smallest doubt.)

Mani Were maduong' osingo kaka no chiko.
(This the great God, he promised and he decreed.)

Once the hymn was over, people sat back down while the pastors up front conferred with each other. The same pastor who had just selected the previous hymn began to pray: *Walam* (Let us pray). People knelt as he addressed God: *Nyasaye maduong', Jakwath maber, Wuon ngima kendo Wuon adiera* (Great

God, Good Shepherd, Father of life and truth). He expressed gratitude for the covenant (*singruok*) that God had made with his disciples. He then mentioned God's promise to send first a white horse, then a brown one, a black one, and finally a grey horse, all of which would die. This statement was a deviation from the nascent doctrine of the three horses that is commonly invoked in Roho sermons, as discussed earlier in this chapter. The pastor did not expound on his particular version of the horse story but went on to ask for blessings on all those present who had traveled long distances, from Central Province, Kakamega, and the south:

> *Imiwa chuny nogomar adier, nikech kawuono wa e rapar mar ndalono ma ne singruok obede e ndalono mar higa piero adek g'adek.*

> (Give us that spirit of truth, because today we are in remembrance of those days of the covenant [which was made] the year [nineteen] thirty-three.)

After concluding his prayer, he exchanged standardized greetings in Dhoroho with the congregation:

PASTOR: *Sang'onjo amba athavi.*   CONGREGATION: *Cher[29] sang'onjo*
     (*Musawa uru uduto.*)   (*Ee, musawa*)
     (Hello to all of you.)   (Yes, hello)

PASTOR: *Afeso?*   CONGREGATION: *Cher njofeso.*
     (*Ungima?*)   (*Ee wangima.*)
     (Are you well?)   (Yes, we are well.)

This interactive greeting signaled the fact that the formal, liturgical prayers, recitations, and Scripture readings were now over and that the lengthy portion of the service devoted to extemporaneous preaching was about to begin. People settled back to listen.

Jopolo, umor? (People of heaven, are you happy?) the pastor addressed the church.

Wamor! (We are happy!) the group shouted in unison.

"Thank you for this day, when we are in remembrance (*e rapar*). We are in what?" he asked.

"Remembrance," everyone called back.[30]

"Whatever we are going to learn this Sabbath day will concern the nine nations that were burnt in 1934 on the twentieth.[31] Halleluia!"

"Halleluia!" repeated the congregation. The pastor continued to speak clearly and deliberately about the significance of their coming together on this day to commemorate their covenant with Jesus. Except for a small child who began to cry, the entire congregation was still and attentive. He referred his listeners to the morning's lesson from the book of Hebrews: "We read in Hebrews that Abraham made a promise/covenant (*singruok*) with God just as Alfayo made a covenant with Jesus."

The preacher tested his audience, "Jesus spoke to Alfayo clearly, 'Alfayo, Alfayo, if you love me and keep my commandments, whatever you ask in my name, I will . . . do what?'"

"Grant you," said the congregation. A woman suddenly jumped up clapping and began to sing a lively tune: *Un kae duto nyithind Nyasaye* (All of you here are children of God). *Wabeduru gi chuny achiel kuom Ruoth* (We are of one spirit in God), came the response from the rest of the women as they also stood up, clapping and commencing a kind of shuffling dance step. As they repeated the first two lines of the hymn, the men joined in and the tempo quickened. The preacher up front was plainly irritated at having his train of thought interrupted and waited with lips pursed until the song was over:

Un Kae Duto
All of You Here

Un kae duto nyithind Nyasaye,
(All of you here are children of God,)

Wabeduru' gi chuny achiel Kuom Ruoth.
(We are of one spirit in God.)

Ruoth Yesu oseluonga ayiene,
(Lord Jesus called me and I complied,)

Ogola e jowa awe tich mudho.
(He has removed me from our people, I've abandoned the work of darkness.)

Odhi oora manyo rombene e thim koda lege,
(He will send me to seek and bring back his runaway sheep from the wilderness,)

Adhi amanygi ei otieno kata odiechieng'.
(I will look for them in the night and in the day.)

Ruoth Yesu osegwenyo jorieko,
(Lord Jesus has confounded the clever ones,)

Odhi olor ei mudho ei ogendini.
(He has descended into the darkness where the multitudes are.)

Obong'o, japolo, jakony jochan,
(Only son, heavenly one, helper of the poor,)

Yesu Ruodha japolo ochung' e dhorangach.
(Jesus my Lord, the heavenly one, he is standing at the gateway.)

Kuweyo mirima kod akwede,
(If you leave behind sorrow and rejection,)

Unudonj ei polo e od wuoro.
(You will enter into heaven in the home of the Father.)

To kumako mirima kod akwede,
(But if you stick to anger and rejection,)

To unudonj ei polo to ok ununene.
(You will enter into heaven, but you won't see him.)

Then, picking up exactly where he left off, the pastor continued, "Alfayo made a covenant with Jesus. . . . How many [people] were they?"

"Two," came the collective answer.

"They made a covenant concerning the soul, not the flesh, nor earthly riches. They did not make a covenant about things that are seen, but only about the soul, which is invisible." The pastor reiterated a number of his preceding points for emphasis and then went on to say that Mango's associates were well informed of the promise Jesus had made to their leader. They also understood that they would have to face death soon:

> That's why [the community] gathered for prayers on the twelfth day of the twelfth month. . . . They wanted to muster courage [*kwayo chir*] to face this day [i.e., January 20, the day of the fire]. For God had told them, "In order for the Holy Spirit to fill the land, you will have to die. If you run away from death, then the Holy Spirit will go to another country, but if you die, the Holy Spirit will remain in this country.

The pastor's next sentence was again drowned out by the voice of a woman who leaped up, singing the well-known Luo Anglican hymn *Yesu Oluongowa Mondo Watine* (Jesus Has Called Us to Work for Him):[32]

Yesu Oluongowa Mondo Watine
Jesus Has Called Us to Work for Him

Yesu oluongowa mondo watine,
(Jesus has called us to work for him,)

Waland injili e piny.
([and to] spread the Gospel in the world.)

Dhumbe gi ogendini onego giyudie
(Foreign tongues and tribes must receive it)

Ler mar Ruoth Nyasaye
(the holiness of the Lord God.)

> REFRAIN: *Injili mar hera, injili mar ng'wono,*
> (Gospel of love, gospel of mercy,)
>
> *Injili ni wach Nyasaye.*
> (The gospel is the word of God.)

Joote, jonabi noyalo injili
(The apostles, the prophets, they proclaimed the Gospel)

E pinje duto te.
(Throughout the whole wide world.)

Dhier gi kuyo, sand gi tuech,
(Poverty and disappointment, suffering and imprisonment,)

Masiche noyudogi.
(Troubles found them.)

Mudho mar pinyni ogeng'o injili
(The darkness of this earth obstructs the gospel)

To Roho otelonwa.
(But the Spirit leads us on.)

Pinje gi gode, thimbe gi nembe,
(Lands and mountains, forests and seas,)

Giyalo injili ni ji.
(They preach the Gospel to people.)

Yesu ochikowa dhiyo e pinje
(Jesus commands us to go throughout the lands)

Wapuonj ji wach Nyasaye.
(To teach the word of God.)

Jogo moseyie wakelo ni Ruodhwa,
(Those people who have let us bring them our Lord,)

Giyudi lokruok chuny
(Have had a change of heart.)

Koro koduogo mar omo nyithinde,
(So he has returned to fetch his children,)

Mosekotiyone,
(Whom he told to work for him,)

Osimbo mar ngima, oimbo mar locho,
(Crown of life, crown of victory[?],)

To Yesu rwakonwa.
(For Jesus welcomes us.)

The pastor stood still, looking frustrated, throughout the duration of the five verses. People clapped forcefully and tapped their feet. Some swung their bent arms back and forth as one does when jogging. Others trotted briefly into the aisle, then back, not yet really dancing, but anticipating the longer "spiritual" songs sure to come.[33]

As soon as the hymn was over, the same preacher resumed his instructional tone: *Wanie paro mar singruok mar Alfayo kod ruoth Yesu . . ."* (We are in the midst of remembering the covenant between Alfayo and Lord Jesus . . .). He went on to explain that Odongo was told that, if he remained obedient, whatever he requested in Jesus' name would be granted; Alfayo then asked for generations of believers from all walks of life (*koni gi koni*). Gesturing with a sweep of his arm to the people seated before him, the pastor declared that these were the very generations Mango had asked for. The preacher then referred to a prophesy made by one Joel foretelling that people would come from a mountain in the south where a certain man named Mindha, whose home was infamous for its pots, lived. (Pots [*agulni*] are reputedly used by witches to store harmful herbs or demons.) "Is this true or not true?" the preacher asked.

"It is true," affirmed the crowd.

He elaborated on the concept of pots: *Bas ma ema omiyo kawuono wabiro elo aguluni to agulu ma wabiro elono en chuny* (In the same vein, today we are going to open [*elo*] pots. But this pot which we are going to open up is the soul). He paused, then asked, "What is it?"

"The soul."

"It is the soul called the human soul (*chuny dhano*). . . . What is it called?"

"The human soul."

He explained how God's relationship with Mango bears on the status of the human soul in general. I include his words here in full for their implicit theological content and their expression of the centrality of the *Sikukuu mar Rapar* for the faithful:

> *Chuny dhano ema ne Nyasaye obiro dwaro, e momiyo ne onwango chuny Alfayo, ka odhi obedo kode machiegni, ne orwako kaka ochiegni, omiyo ka-wuono wanie rapar maduong' ahinya. Ka wan e rapar maduong' kama nyaka wanon gi chunywa ma iye ni to rapar ni ere kaka dirit, ere kaka obet. Omiyo jodongwa oringo matek, minewa oringo matek ka gichore ka gikawo nengo gi gach gi matek ahinya mondo gibi gine kama nene singruok obetie. Emonmiyo higa ka higa ka oloko Januar nyaka gibi gichopie ka.*

> (It is the human soul that God came for, therefore he received Alfayo's soul, when he [Alfayo] went, he sat right next to him [God], he [God] welcomed him very near. This is why we are conducting a huge commemoration today. We are conducting this large commemoration so that we consider in our inner hearts, where must it [the memory] stay? Where must it be? [I.e., how shall we keep the memory alive?] It [this occasion of remembrance] causes old women and men to travel from distant places in order to arrive; they meet the very great expense of transport by vehicle in order to come here and see the place where the covenant was made. Every year, when January arrives, they feel they must reach this place.)

A woman in the front row began another song. It was even more rapid than the last such that one could barely catch the lyrics over the enthusiastic clapping: *Ee jog Odongo tiyo!* (Oh the people of Odongo are working), sang the soloist.

Jaduong' ose loyo; ee jog Odongo tiyo; Jaduong' ose loyo (The elder [i.e., Odongo] has won; Oh, the people of Odongo are working; the elder has won), responded the congregation.

Responsive singing is popular in many independent churches throughout Kenya. Hymns of this nature, consisting of short statements and repetitive choruses, give the leader an opportunity to improvise without the kind of concentration necessary in preaching or delivering prayers. Such songs are often accompanied by drums, dancing, or both. They can continue for twenty minutes or longer, the tempo getting faster and faster and thus offering occasions for trancing.

As the singing began, the *padri* who had been preaching returned to his seat, indicating that he had finished his sermon. The pastor on his immediate left then rose, waiting his turn. Most members—laity and clergy alike—request that a prayer be said for them before they begin to preach. In this service, in which a number of pastors were slated to speak in sequence, each would pray for the subsequent preacher.

"Good God, Father of Israel, Revelation of Lawi and King Elijah," began the *padri* who had just finished his own remarks. Mention of these uniquely Roho praise names evoked an immediate outburst from a number of the gathering. "Oh Father, we come before your holy seat. We wish to beseech you through Alfayo Odongo, Lawi Obonyo, and King Elijah; Master, direct your eyes upon your people, Father." He asked for unity and a life in truth and concluded with a request for special blessings for the next preacher. The older, softer-spoken pastor, raising both hands in the gesture I have seen many Luos use when greeting a crowd, then addressed the group: *Mirembe,*[34] *joka-Odongo* (Hello/Peace, people of Odongo).

Mirembe, everyone answered in unison.

Mirembe joka-Lawi (Hello, people of Lawi).

Mirembe.

Mirembe, joka-Turfosa (Hello, people of Turfosa).[35]

Mirembe.

Umor kuom ng'a (With whom are you happy)? he inquired.

Wamor gi Yesu gi Roho Maler (We are happy with Jesus and the Holy Spirit).

The pastor's next sentence was eclipsed by an older man who leaped up and began clapping and singing, *Wang' oganda to ng'iyo dalawa!* (The eyes of the community/tribe are watching our home).

A few people provided the response: *Dalawa mowar gi mach gi remo* (Our home, which was redeemed with fire and blood). Yet, just as the congregation was beginning to participate fully, it was abruptly silenced by the preacher with the help of the head *padri*. At the same moment, another man near me was overcome and shouted so suddenly and loudly that I jumped: *Hey . . . hih, hih, hih, hih, hih, hih. Hih! . . . Hiih! . . . Hih! . . . Mm, mm, mm, hih, hih, mm . . . tsh, mm, mm . . . hih, tsh, tsh, mm.*

Mirembe duto, came the pastor's quiet but firm voice.

Haayihh! another member burst forth.

The congregation responded *Mirembe,* but there was a great deal of commotion in the church as a number of people became filled with the spirit and babies started to wail. The pastor projected above the din:

Jawer, ok amaki, an bende, ok a chung'ne ayalo. Adwa miyo ji thuolo kaka onego ong'iswa wach ang'owa?

(Singer, I do not mean to hold you back, nor have I stood to preach. I [simply] wish to give people a chance to speak the word of whom?).

Nyasaye (God), the congregation answered.

Koro, chik iti (So pay attention), the *padri* said kindly and began to outline the program for the remainder of the morning. He acknowledged that people had traveled from many different places to see the spot where the covenant had been made. "For whenever a person stands on his or her own property, he or she feels happy," he said, stressing the fact that Ruwe was the home of all Joroho. He assured them that anyone who wished to preach would be given an opportunity to do so. "Master Alfayo will open the meeting, then Teacher Lawi will speak, then Doctor (*Laktar*) Turfosa," he said, anchoring his program in the founding paradigm. "So the master will be given Ugenya, the teacher will be given Alego, and the doctor will be given Yimbo and Uyoma." In other words, representatives from Ugenya location[36] would speak first, followed by members from Alego, and finally from Yimbo and Uyoma. The pastor went on to make reference to a traditional Luo image, the cooking pot supported by three stones: *Ka kite adek ose teno kendo to koro gima ikonyruok go e bwo kite en ang'o?* (When three stones have supported the fireplace, what is it that is helping underneath the stones?)

Yien (firewood), people answered.

Yien. . . . En ang'o? (Firewood. . . . What is it?), he asked again for emphasis.

Yien! they repeated, raising their voices.

"Yes, [similarly] these three people [i.e., Alfayo, Lawi, and Turfosa] did not make the covenant by themselves, they were encouraged and backed (*kaso*) by others. . . . Therefore, you must all work until you realize their mission."

The intent of this analogy was to indicate that visitors from locations other than those previously mentioned should also feel free to address the assembly. The *padri* concluded his brief speech by giving the elderly man whose hymn was interrupted permission to begin again.

Wang' oganda to ng'iyo dalawa (The eyes of the community are watching our home), sang the man. *Dalawa mowar gi mach gi remo* (Our home which was redeemed with fire and blood), came the response.[37] People sang this song, which glorifies Odongo Mango's village, with zest and obvious pleasure. Everyone clapped and danced.

As the congregation was singing the last few verses, an elderly man with gnarled feet left his seat on one of the middle benches and, leaning on his cane, came slowly up the center aisle to stand at the base of the chancel. The pastors determined that he should mount the platform, which he did with effort. He turned to face the gathering, and the head pastor stood and asked for God's blessing upon the man from Ugenya:

> *Wuon adiera, soko ma ngo'ngo ma ji modho. . . . Wuon oganda, ne isingo Alfayo mi obedo siro ma ng'ong' ma oriwo ogendni; iwuoyo gi Lawi Obonyo mondo obi oten wach; aye kitundu mar adek ibiro gi nyako Turfosa kuom singruok, nyir ma oyudo kom. Baba lam, jaduong' ochung' mondo omos oganda gi. Jehova no chunywa ka imiyowa roho no ma in iwuon ema ing'eyo, ma odak apanda. Jotiji oringo ka gichando gidwaro modho soko no obe madier, kuom Roho Maler.*

> (Father of truth, expansive river from which people drink, you promised that Alfayo would be the everlasting buttress uniting the nations; you talked with Lawi Obonyo so that he would come and spread the word; and then in the third instance, you made a covenant with Turfosa so that women would be able to have posts. Father pray [for this] elder standing to greet this congregation. Jehovah strengthen us here, give us your Spirit, that which you alone know and which is hidden. Your servants hurry here, they are lacking and want to drink from the river which is truth, through the Holy Spirit.)

Osend, all responded.

Oyawore uru! (Good morning to all of you!), said the elder from Ruwe, raising both hands.

Oyawore, people smiled, happy to be being welcomed by someone from the locality.

Sangonjo amba u Safi (*Musawa uru e Mungu*/Hello in God), he said in Dhoroho.

Cher songonjo. (Yes, Hello.)

Afeso? (Are you well?)

Cher afeso (Yes, we're well), they completed the formal Roho greeting. The elder thanked the "children of God" for traveling to Ruwe. He spoke of the great happiness of this time of year, which marked the transmission of God's final commandments to their founder. He thanked the Lord for Odongo's bravery in enduring the torture of the flames and for Lawi's courage in facing the enemy's spear. *Omiyo, in ka ibiro ka ing'eyo ni ibiro e rapar mar Alfayo* (So when you come here, know that you have come in memory of Alfayo), he urged his audience. His statement was enthusiastically seconded by a woman, whose piercing soprano voice caught us all off-guard:

JAKWANO: *Alfayo Odongo lemo, jaduong ne okalo nam,*
(SOLOIST: Alfayo Odongo is praying, the master crossed over the lake,)

JO-OLO: *Lwe——ny*
(CHORUS: Wa——r)

JAKWANO: *Odongo lend——o.*
(SOLOIST: Odongo makes/made a clean sweep.)

JO-OLO: *Lweny ne ger e polo.*
(CHORUS: There was a fierce war in heaven.)

As far as I could discern, the song consisted of these brief lines repeated over and over. Presently, a young man from a visiting parish started shaking his reed rattler in accompaniment. Soon another visitor stood and, slinging the leather strap over his shoulder, hoisted a large flat drum onto his hip. The whole sanctuary throbbed as he beat the cowhide with his wooden mallet. He made his way slowly up the aisle while the women filed jauntily out of their seats to dance and clap around him.

It had grown hot inside the church. The air outside was still, and the sun, now directly overhead, beat down on the corrugated metal roofing with intensity. About ten minutes later, the song was over and the man from Ruwe continued his welcoming speech. He talked of the need for seriousness and dedication in religion and for conversion in one's life:

> *To ing'e gima okeli. . . . Kik kelni raw, bul ema okeli, nindo ema okeli, da. Ng'e gima okeli, to kendo ng'e gima omiyo ilokri ni roho.*
>
> (But know what brings you [to Ruwe]. . . . Do not come on your way to somewhere else, nor should the drum bring you, nor should you come here to sleep, no. Know what brings you and know that which changes you is the spirit.)

He spoke of his own lifelong commitment to the Roho faith:

> *An gini onwang'a ka atin, gir Alfayo ni, chakore higa piero adek g'ang'wen. . . . Onwang'a mana ka an ja higni, sijui, kok higni aboro to higni abiryo. . . . Onwang'a ka bende awotho mana duk . . . to in ka ibiro ka mokye kaka amoke ni. Ne higa piero adek g'ang'wen nyaka sani a pod an ka. Pod tienda moro ok ating'o bu adhi ago chonga piny e kanisa moro. Ang'eyo chandruok ma ne ji osandre Musanda, omiyo in ka ibiro ka to gima kata padri ok iwinj.*
>
> (This thing of Alfayo's got hold of me when I was still young, from the year [nineteen] thirty-four on. . . . It got me when I was, oh I don't know, not yet eight or seven. . . . It also got me while I was still walking naked. . . . So when you come here hold onto it, just as I have. Just imag-

ine, from the year [nineteen] thirty-four until now I am still here [i.e., with the Roho church]. I never wavered nor took my trumpet to go set foot upon the ground of another church. I know the suffering that people underwent at Musanda. So when you come here, even the pastors don't really understand.)

The old man went on to expound on the elusive nature of the Holy Spirit:

To koro in ka ise rwake, mi ise rwake e chunyi, make. To ka ise make to obiro bedo kodi maber. To ka imake ahucha to ok ibi nwang'e, obiro lonyore kuomi. En gima iluongo ni pamba olwaro chaf. Ing'e ni pamba ka imulo kod lweti hama ka ok aye ilogo to kanyo no chilo odongye. E kaka roho chal.

(Now that you have welcomed [the Holy Spirit], welcomed it into your heart, hold onto it. For if you clutch it firmly it will remain with you. But if you hold it loosely, you won't keep it, it will remove itself from you. You might call it cotton that has dropped into the dirt. You know that when you touch [dirty] cotton with your hand like this [he gestures], if you don't then wash your hands, the stain spreads. This is what the spirit is like [meaning, if you let the Spirit slip out of your life, it will be difficult to cleanse yourself again].)

Drawing his remarks to a close, he introduced himself as Joel Odiado. "I am the son of Odongo. Musa is my brother and Isaya is my father."[38] As soon as he mentioned the name of Mango, the woman who had been possessed early on began a stream of glossolalia in a loud voice: *Chih! . . . hih, hih. . . . Aleluya. . . . Kewnda, kwenda ma biro, e kwenda ba!* Odiado continued to speak over her, going on to state that all Roho disciples were his brothers. He concluded with a remark about the character of the Holy Spirit: *Omiyo en ka idhi nwang'e to ibedo mana gi kwe, ma kata gimoro ochwanyi, to aling'a thi.* (Therefore, when you receive it, you will be humble, such that even when something hurts you, you just keep quiet.)[39]

The next speaker was a middle-aged man from Alego who identified himself as Ismael Oduor from Alego Ko-odha. He indicated that he was but an infant in 1934 and so was not present in Musanda during the fateful fire. However, he was born to a prominent family of converts in Alego. His lengthy testimony was full of details about his father's conversion and prophesies he himself had heard. He made one interesting, brief allusion to a visit from "Jacob Muruku" (Jakobo Buluku), a Luyia man who later founded a major Holy Spirit sect in Maragoli. Oduor talked of having been a politician, trips to Uganda, and a period of backsliding from Roho norms, during which he attempted to learn to play the traditional Luo lute (*orutu*) and suffered from bouts of teeth gnashing.

Throughout the course of his long discourse, Oduor was interrupted four times by hymns.[40] One of the songs praised Kingi Elijah Oloo and prompted Oduor into a segue about what Oloo had done for him. Finally, the head *padri* interjected that the preacher's time was up. Oduor concluded the Elijah anecdote abruptly and asked for one of the pastors up front to pray before he returned to his seat.

The head pastor then stood and asked everyone to bear in mind the purpose of their gathering. They had come together to remember the acts of their founders (*joma no singore* [lit., those who had made the covenant]). The pastor realized that everybody "would like to talk about what happened to them at that time." In a clear criticism of Oduor, he told them all firmly, "I want someone to stand up here who knows the *truth* about the person he wishes to tell about" (*Adwaro ng'ama chung' ka ma ong'eyo* adiera *mar ng'ama odwa loso kuome no*). He reminded them that he had allotted discussion about Turfosa Aloo to people from Uyoma and Yimbo. He now wanted someone from that region who "knew the truth" about Turfosa to come forward, and he ordered that the witness be "a sister, not a brother." At this point, a woman jumped up and began singing, whereupon he silenced her, saying that hymns should be sung only when a speaker had concluded a statement, so as not to impede the remembrance process. He finished speaking shortly thereafter, and the woman was permitted to initiate her song. Everyone joined in with reed rattles and dancing.

An hour and a half had now passed since we entered the church. I believe my description here conveys the basic dynamics of Roho congregational worship. The commencement of Roho services is generally characterized by a flexible but nonetheless orderly progression through formal Anglican liturgy components: opening solemn hymns, confession, the Lord's Prayer, Scripture readings, and the creed. These components are interspersed among songs and glossolalia that become increasingly vigorous as worship proceeds. Laity come forward to preach the gospel only after the pastors have done so, and the words of elders are privileged over those of younger members. One notes an ebb and flow between the women's domain of spontaneous song and the ordering authority of male leaders, who attempt to structure and limit that spontaneity. However, the pastors are clearly able to rein in women's expressive worship only up to a point. Communal spiritual power, as cultivated within Roho collective worship, derives from a dynamic give-and-take between gendered forms of charismatic authority. In the Roho view, both forms are integral to the whole. While men may try to control women's voices, in fact, nobody really wants the kind of staid, "weak" worship found in mission-based churches. One main objective in Roho worship is the very infusion and overflow of the Spirit that manifests itself in women's outbursts. In other words, when male officials posture to restrain women's singing, they are, in part, only acting out their role, which entails directive leadership. I suggest that they would, in fact, be dismayed if their efforts to stifle women's ecstatic self-expression were actually successful.

My account of the remaining three and a half hours of the *rapar* sabbath service is a mere summary. I have chosen to skip over numerous hymns in favor of concentrating on personal testimonies I consider illustrative of Roho piety and orientation.

After the head *padri* concluded his reprimand and the hymn was drawing to a close, an elderly woman carrying a small wooden cross slowly approached the chancel and sought an opportunity to address the congregation. One of the officiating pastors prayed for her, asking for humility as the congregation was about to embark upon the recollection of Turfosa Aloo, one of "our nine people" (*jowa ochiko*), as he put it. He asked that God's spirit, together with the angels, be sent down from above to be with the woman and to bless her words.

The woman greeted her audience in the Dhoroho. Peppering her lively testimony with the salute *Mirembe, askeche!* (Hello, soldiers!), she proceeded to explain that she had been one of the many young people living in Odongo's compound during the month-long retreat in January 1934 and was therefore an eyewitness. She recalled some of the prophesies Odongo made concerning his imminent death. (Mango had predicted, for example, that fire would come from above—a prophesy that was fulfilled when his roof was set aflame by the Wanga.)

She spoke of her poverty and of her own personal faith in Mango's great sacrifice. *Ka ok iketo chunyi, to ok ibi neno* (If you don't have faith [lit., put your heart], you won't see [correctly]), she declared. She also comforted and encouraged her listeners:

Kata ka idwa dhi marach to oduoki e yo, kata ka idwa wuotho ariwa to oduoki e yo, kata ka tiendi kier to oduoki e yo.

(Even if you want to go wrong, you can/will be directed back to the path, even if you wish to wander astray, you can/will be placed back on track, even if your feet slip, you can/will be returned to the way.)

Messages delivered in church could save one's soul, she said likening the word of God to "water that comes from the earthen pot [such that], if we drink it, we will have humble hearts without anxiety, we will have humble hearts without restlessness (*pi ma wuok e aguluni gi ka wamodho gi, wabiro bedo gi chuny mokwe ma onge kibaji, wabiro bedo kod chuny mokwe ma ok chapni*). She concluded her brief remarks abruptly: *Mago oromou, kuom Roho Maler* (That is enough for you, through the Holy Spirit).

A number of people in the congregation called out, *Nyingi?* (What's your name?) She responded that she was called Turfosa Malowa and stated that she had been a *laktar* in Alfayo's home. At that time, they had all lived peacefully; the hardship came later. They tried to prepare, but they "had no idea how difficult things would become." She then told a pastor to pray for her.

People from Yimbo still had the floor. One of the *padris* seated to the far left was himself a visitor from Yimbo and rose to beseech elders from his parish to come forward. A particular Yimbo elder whom people had hoped to hear was now apparently hoarse from shouting with the Spirit, so the pastor was looking for other volunteers. A gentleman did finally move up to the chancel. Greeting everyone in Dhoroho, he claimed to be one who had "seen with his own eyes." He spoke about his own conversion and attributed it to the efficacious preaching and healing acts of Barnaba, the Ruwe church's first bishop. He appeared rather intense, speaking with conviction and force:

An kod midhiero mar roho ka wuod Luka wacho ni ng'ama tugo gi roho ng'ano rach. Ka imilori gi roho ni, roho rach. Kata ka iyenyo gi roho ni roho rach.

(I have a revelation [lit., mystery] from the Spirit that the son of Luka (Lawi Obonyo?) revealed as follows: Anyone who plays with the Spirit is evil. If you joke around with the Spirit, it is bad faith. Similarly if you abuse the Spirit, it's bad faith.)

The speaker then identified himself as John Odeny, son of Samson Onyango from Kagwa, but who had a home in Yimbo in Bondo division. Odeny explained how hearing the telling and retelling of the story of Mango's martyrdom moved him deeply. That Alfayo Odongo died so bravely amazed him. He then re-counted (his own version of) Mango's last words: "Jesus, meet me and my daugh-ters, sons and children; I'm coming to my heavenly home, but am being burnt on earth!" (*Yesu romna kod nyiwa kod yawuota gi nyithiwa; abiro e dala ma malo to owang' piny!*)

Throughout Roho services, members, particularly women, break into song when so moved. However, when one woman began a song after the conclusion of the brief prayer following Odeny's sermon, one of the officiating pastors inter-vened. He cut off her and her comrades with the rebuke, "If you are to sing, stand up and sing! When you are finished, what do you do?"

"Sit down," people responded.

Yawa! the head pastor was exasperated. "How many times must I repeat this!" He then went on to invite people from the south—meaning visitors from the other shore of Kavirondo Gulf (Nyakach, South Nyanza, and so on)—to come forward.

An aged man in the back row stood up, and the congregation was instructed to sing as he moved to the front. The gentleman began explaining that he was standing there as a result of the work of Joel and Daudi Opanga, sons of Oloo. He told the story of how these two early converts brought the faith into his home. After hearing many rumors about Musanda, "Paulo" (possibly Chief Paul Mboya of South Nyanza) sent Joel to discover what news was being revealed there. Joel returned and preached the good news of Roho in his area, prompting conversions among his kin.

The speaker made reference to his own personal reception of the Holy Spirit on September 29, 1979. He stated proudly that five months later he made the trip to Ugenya to participate in the *Rapar* ceremonies in January and to hear the story from actual eyewitnesses. He also told an amusing tale about a rat which I have condensed:

> There once was a rat who was fearful of cats so he went to a witch doctor (*ajuoga*) to be turned into one cat. As a cat, the creature was naturally afraid of dogs, so he asked to be changed into a dog. The rat continued to have himself changed into increasingly more powerful animals until he finally requested the witch doctor to transform him into a human being. At that point the witch doctor looked at the rat (by then a lion) and told him that nothing could be done for him because fear was permanently in the creature's heart (*luor osiko e chuny*). The witch doctor then promptly changed the animal back into a rat.

The preacher directed this story toward all recent Roho converts who had belonged to different denominations in the past. "It would be a pity," he said, "if you were to come here, pray with us, stay with us, only to have us send you back to drink alcohol the way you had been doing." The speaker concluded by giving his name: John Akuku, son of Petro Ogot from Komati.

The next person appointed to speak was a woman whom the head *padri* introduced as Mother Alango from Nyakach. Alango selected a passage from the second chapter of Galatians as the focus of her remarks. A man in the congregation stood to read the passage. It is the custom in Roho services for the preacher to interrupt the reader to exegete the text. The preacher then cues the reader to resume via the command *som* (read). Alango selected only a small portion of the epistle, which mentions Paul's journey with Barnabas and Titus to Jerusalem; she interpreted it to be teaching about peace and community. She quickly concluded her remarks by introducing herself as Miriam Odongo, from the home of old man (*Jaduong*) Dulmas Olang'o Ndolo in Nyakach Ndura.

The church's general secretary, Zadock Ochoma, who had traveled from Kisumu town to participate in the ceremonies, was the next speaker. He greeted the gathering as *Jo-k'Aloo* (people of Aloo) and welcomed visitors from all parts of the country. He spoke of the *Sikukuu mar rapar* as an important event during which people could have their misconceptions corrected and partial understanding augmented. Here one could learn the true facts about the history of the church and the meaning of Roho religion. He cautioned people to "be careful with life" (*tang' ni ngima*) and used the example of Turfosa Aloo, who made a vow to walk only with Jesus. Ochoma spoke for a long time, first preaching on Titus 3:9 and finally concluding with an outline of the schedule of upcoming events. A few more people came forward to speak: a woman from Kendu Bay, a man from West Alego, and Sylvan Nyamogo, who had been Odongo's immediate neighbor and a close associate of Lawi. Joseph Songa Opiyo, the subchief in Ruwe, also addressed the gathering. Although not a Roho member, he was respectfully invited to this special service as the local government representative.

Finally, the head *padri* closed the service. Like the general secretary, he had already seen the preliminary brief history I had compiled on the basis of my interviews with Anna Inondi and other elderly members at Ruwe. In his closing remarks, the pastor gave a sweeping sketch of the history of the Roho movement, citing, as Zadock Ochoma had done, details that I strongly suspect he had gleaned from my recently typed report. The impact that written histories will have on the codification of the Roho story remains to be seen. We can hypothesize that, just as leaders have sought to direct the development of an official oral canon that reinforces existing authority patterns, so, too, they are likely to be even more attentive to the management of a permanent written history.

Conclusion: Inspiration and Indigenization

Roho religion is a Luo indigenization of charismatic Christianity. In the emergence and development of the Roho worldview, indigenous beliefs about the nature of spiritual forces and methods for relating to them have exercised the determinant shaping influence. Nineteenth- and early-twentieth-century Luo conceptions of sacrifice, sacred spaces, and, in particular, spirit possession formed a set of deep paradigms onto which the story of Jesus, basic Christian claims, and Biblical symbols were grafted. This process not only rendered the grafted material dependent on a different source of nourishment but also prompted a new distillation or realignment of certain key elements in the base of the trunk. The Roho core paradigm of the *mach* that emerged entailed a heightened emphasis on perseverance and self-denial in exchange for spiritual power, an intensification of the memorial or historical component of sacred places, an elaboration of the symbolic significance of the *dala*, and a new nationalistic pride in the African dominion.

The metaphor of a grafted plant can take us only so far, however. Although the growth of a religious movement follows a certain inherent organic logic, it is the participants themselves, acting within a particular set of social and historical circumstances, who determine which features of the religion will be cultivated and which aspects will be discouraged. There have always been contradictions between religion as an autonomous phenomenon, arising from people's experience of divinity which resists easy ordering, and religion as a social framework, which implies strong forms of authority. Few Africanists have stressed the spiritual side of religious movement, but many have nevertheless appreciated the fresh vision and inspiration they offer. Most scholars have seen the basic intent behind religious movements and African independent churches to be the creation of new communities and structures of meaning that incorporate indigenous cultural values in the face of colonialism and "postcolonial dislocation" (Welbourn and Ogot 1966; Peel 1968; Fernandez 1978, 1982; Fabian 1971; Jules-Rosette 1975; Comaroff 1985; Barrett 1968; Perrin Jassy 1971).

Other scholars see religion as Bloch (1974) does, as "the ultimate form of traditional authority," and stress the way in which religious symbols and traditions have been manipulated and invented in legitimating exploitative relations in Africa (Fatton 1992; White 1987; Ranger 1986). The tension between rebellion and authority within religion is particularly apparent in a movement such as Roho, which grew out of a spirit possession cult that challenged everyday norms and hierarchies. Over time, as we have seen, the process of institutionalization has facilitated the distillation of forms of authority within the church that are consistent with dominant secular structures. Nevertheless, the somewhat fragmented "unofficial transcript" still retains the more egalitarian, radical contours of the youthful movement of female soldiers for the Spirit, some of which manifests itself in the give-and-take of worship services. I seek to explore this increasingly submerged face of Roho religion in the final chapter.

5

Quiet Wives and Questing Warriors: The Public and Hidden Transcripts of Roho Women

When one listens to Luo people recounting their interactions, one frequently hears the phrase *Naling' aling'a* (I just kept quiet). The statement usually connotes a veiled criticism of a situation in which the speaker was not at liberty to respond directly to an unfair action or comment delivered against her by someone else. When a person describes an event in which she "just kept quiet," she is actually communicating a great deal about the contours of the power relationship at issue. She is (1) suggesting that the perpetrator has abused whatever authority the perpetrator has over her, (2) making plain that she is angered, and (3) appealing to the listener's sense of fairness to concur with her, at least tacitly.

For example, I recently received a letter from a Luo friend who described how his uncle, with whom he had embarked on a small business venture, swindled him. My friend expressed no overt judgment and simply concluded his account with the statement "I just kept quiet." His outrage was pointedly clear, but he dared not openly criticize his classificatory father. In her account of early Roho history, Anna Inondi likewise utilized some variant of the statement *ne waling' aling'a* (We just kept quiet) or *ne waling' kode* (We kept quiet about it) to describe her community's response to various instances of repression from the Wanga or from colonial authorities. She thus made it clear that the Joroho felt unjustly persecuted but that they did not express this resentment openly.

In Luo culture, quiet obedience is the appropriate response of a subordinate to a superior. Children are socialized to remain silent when rebuked by their elders; women are told not to protest when disciplined by their husbands; employees do not contradict their bosses. But, when the phrase "I/[or we] just kept quiet" is uttered in discourse between peers of equal status, the words themselves serve as a kind of signal, a coded expression of resistance to domination. Moreover, the

172

statement can often be slightly ominous, for it suggests that the speaker may secretly be garnering the strength to strike later. Once, when I called on a close friend in Siaya, I found her extremely upset, for she had just been beaten by her husband. After recounting the insults and unfounded accusations he had hurled at her—things that hurt her as much as the actual slaps—she stated that she had "just kept quiet." Then, she told me confidentially that, if she were to leave her husband at that particular moment, people would rebuke her for abandoning him in the midst of economic hard times. She therefore resolved to wait until a day when things were going well for him. She told me in a low and steady voice that, when that day came, she would, without warning, leave his house forever.

James Scott has argued that it is within relatively safe contexts such as personal friendship that subordinate people can voice their anger, "beyond direct observation by powerholders" (1990, 4). The remarks my friend made to me that day in her kitchen were consistent with the private testimonies of oppressed and exploited individuals in many periods and places. For example, Scott discusses Aggy, a black cook in the antebellum South, whose words were recorded in the memoirs of governess Mary Livermore. After "the master" beat her daughter, the enraged cook waited until the man left the kitchen, then turned to her friend, Livermore, and delivered a scorching condemnation of whites, heralding the apocalypse when whites would suffer all the atrocities they visited on others. Aggy's vision constituted, in Scott's terminology, a hidden transcript, cultivated in the "offstage culture of slave quarters and slave religion," which contradicted the public transcript of obedience that slaves generally maintained in front of their masters (1990, 6–7). These hidden transcripts of oppressed peoples reflect the hardship of material exploitation but tend to center on attacks on human dignity:

> Slavery, serfdom, the caste system, colonialism, and racism routinely generate the practices and rituals of denigration, insult, and assaults on the body that seem to occupy such a large part of the hidden transcripts of their victims. Such forms of oppression . . . deny subordinates the ordinary luxury of negative reciprocity: trading a slap for a slap, an insult for an insult. Even in the case of the contemporary working class it appears that slights to one's dignity and close control of one's work figure as prominently in accounts of exploitation as do narrower concerns of work and compensation. (1990, xii)

Aggy's vision of blacks' eventual triumph over whites indeed turns the tables with respect to the denigration her people suffered. In similar fashion, my friend's comments reflected her anger and hurt resulting from the indignity of not being free to defend herself against insults and false accusations.

In its initial inspiration, Roho religion shares many characteristics with American slave religion and messianic movements among subjugated and colonized peoples in many places. In its vision of a black-run church, a black

sovereign, and, most important, an age in which Africans would have a mo-
nopoly on spiritual power, this popular religion clearly spoke to the indignities
Nyanza peoples suffered under colonialism. It also responded to missionaries'
denigration of indigenous beliefs and rituals by presenting an ideology and theology in which things were turned upside down.[1] The prescriptions that Mango
gave his community reflect the contradictions of subordinate peoples torn between, on the one hand, the necessity of cooperating with state authorities and,
on the other hand, daring to hope and plan for a day when their oppressors will be
overthrown. Before his death, Mango urged his followers to "remember that the
colonial government still had power over them" and that they should therefore
pay their taxes promptly. However, he simultaneously instructed the Joroho to
remain vigilant so that as soon as they caught wind of a movement to unite blacks
against the whites (i.e., an effort that had a chance of succeeding) they could join
in wholeheartedly. Thus, advice to "just keep quiet" and "remain calm" went
hand in hand with a promise and hope that one day their hidden transcript would
explode triumphantly into the public domain.

Roho religion, then, was shaped by the oppression its founders suffered, but
the Roho movement was not *caused* by the angst and anger of the oppressed. The
church is not simply a reaction to colonialism and its attending missions but
grows out of the strength of older beliefs and ritual forms that, when forced
underground, contributed to the content of new hidden transcripts. An important
constitutive element of Roho religion, is, as we have seen, *lang'o* beliefs and
practice, traditionally the preserve of women. It is largely due to women's initiative in *lang'o* and other *juogi* cults that early Roho women had the courage to take
up swords, march around the countryside, leave marriages, and establish all-
female communes. As Roho religion evolved during the colonial period, it spoke
not only to the Luos' collective suffering at the hands of the British and their
Wanga collaborators but also to women's oppression within Luo patriarchy.
Like the overall Roho ethos, which is contradictory—urging obedience on one
hand and rebellion on the other—so, too, are the teachings directed toward
Roho women. The women's official transcript—the values they espouse in
public discourse with men—is in many ways antithetical to their hidden transcript, which one glimpses in their songs and in their discourse with one another.

Conversion: Gendered Perspectives

In considering the extent to which Roho women's piety partakes of the church's
dominant images of gender and the extent to which women's self-representations
resist those norms, it is appropriate to start with conversion accounts. What draws
men and women to Roho religion in the first place? Are the sexes attracted to the

Holy Ghost church for the same reasons? Once members, do they experience Roho religiosity differently? The testimonies that follow provide some insight into these basic questions.

The word for "conversion" in Dholuo is *lokruok*, derived from the reflexive verb *lokore*, to change oneself or one's direction, attitude, or opinion.[2] The Luo term is not specific to religious conversion and does not necessarily convey the dramatic shift in belief that conversion connotes in English (Suchman 1992, S15). In Kenya, it is not uncommon for one to belong to a number of different denominations over the course of one's lifetime. Each successive move into a new church is referred to as *lokruok*[3] and is consecrated through receiving baptism (or laying on of hands) from the clergy of the denomination one is entering. An individual thus may be baptized many times.

Many studies of African independent churches have emphasized the central role that faith healing plays in the conversion process. A number have documented the fact that healing is among the most frequent reasons people cite for joining a new church (Jules-Rosette 1975, 70; Peel 1968, 211–215; Sundkler 1961, 233–237; Turner 1967, 2: 90; Hackett 1989, 352). My discussions with Joroho—and members of other charismatic Kenyan churches—support this view. A majority of the Roho members I met explained that when their illnesses—or those of loved ones—were not effectively addressed within their previous denominations (most commonly Nomiya Luo, Catholic, Anglican, or Seventh-Day Adventist), they turned to the Roho church for help. After being healed by a Roho representative or prayer party, the patient, grateful and convinced of the authenticity of the Joroho's superior spiritual power, joined the church. We have already seen the important role that healing ministries played in the success of early Roho missionary campaigns (see chapter 3). Nereya Owuor, the head *laktar* at the Masumbi branch of the Holy Spirit Church of East Africa, explains conversion as the natural result of effective faith healing:

> Take these people here, if one of them falls sick, he/she calls me to come pray for him/her. After I have healed him/her, we pray together, then I sew the emblem (of membership on a piece of clothing) for him/her, and the person joins us.

> (*Kama gin kani giduto, ka ma tuo ogoyo giluonga to adhi alemo ne, to ka ase kwoye to wa lemo kode to any atuang'o ne namba to aye odonjo e ma.*)

When members speak of being healed, they can refer to the amelioration of a broad range of physical, psychological, and social afflictions or abnormalities. Among them are an inability to conceive (*mamigumba*) and/or deliver healthy children, smallpox (*nundu*), stomach pains (*ich mwor*), emaciation (*dhero*), crippled legs (*puth*), madness (*neko*), and poverty (*dhier*). Frequently, members attributed these afflictions to the agency of spirits of various kinds and claimed that the Joroho were able to conquer (*loyo*) these negative influences through the power of the Holy Spirit. Being healthy (*mangima*) or disease-free (*machweni*) is considered the foundation of every other good. Once, when I pressed a group of predominantly older female members to enumerate benefits of Roho life that were *not* related to personal health, they laughed. "But what else is there?" one of them protested. Together, they went on to explain that helping people and carrying out all the responsibilities associated with doing God's work is possible only when one is in good health.

I found that the central role that recovery from illness plays in the conversion process was a common theme with Roho members of both sexes, all ages, and all ranks. However, I noted a difference between the stories of men and those of women when it came to the way they enumerated the changes in their lives after their conversion to Roho religion. Even if these changes fall under the general rubric of mental and emotional health, there were, nonetheless, differences in what might be called the secondary characteristics of well-being for men and for women. Men tended to stress the ability to see the truth more clearly and to live more disciplined lives. They also identified dramatic reversals in their lifestyles after joining the Roho church. Women, while sometimes mentioning these features, generally emphasized "feeling free." They spoke of feeling free from fear of witchcraft, from anxiety over spouses' deaths, and from the loneliness of widowhood. They also stressed the peacefulness that permeated their interpersonal relationships after they "entered Roho."

I shall relate first two men's conversion accounts and then two women's accounts. Jeremiah Otang'a, an elderly Ruwe catechist who often uses his Dhoroho title *Wopnjiw Thondeur* (*Japwonj*[4] [Teacher] Daniel) in formal introductions, likes to recount his dramatic conversion experience of 1935:

> I was first an Anglican. By the year 1916 I was reciting [lit., reading] the Bible from memory. When the Archdeacon [Owen] arrived, we were already adept at reciting Biblical passages from memory. . . . Later, I returned to traditional ways, courting and flirting with girls, a custom known as "*maranda*."[5] I had that traditional harp, a *nyatiti*, and I used to play it; in our home here, everyone played it. . . . Then I left and went to work in Kitale, Mount Elgon.
>
> Then one night, as I lay in an exhausted sleep, God brought me a message [lit., a voice], telling me to abandon the kind of harp music I was playing and to make music that would reach heaven. [That message came to me] when I was in the habit of smoking hemp in a *poko*.[6] I was with a certain friend named Phesa Ogido,[7] with whom I used to smoke. So I suggested to Pheso, "Let's take [the *poko*] and place it before God. If God sees that it is bad, we will abandon it, but if he sees that it is good to worship him and to smoke [at the same time], we shall smoke." So we took the hemp and the *poko* and placed it in the center of the house, before God. God removed me from it and I quit [the habit] forever.

The [Musanda] fire occurred while I was in Elgon. I didn't know that it had taken place and no Holy Ghost member ever came to preach about the Spirit to me. I found salvation by myself.

(*Ne an ja Anglican. Mwaka mar apar gauchiel onuang'o ka asomo muma gi wiya mokalo. Ka Achdikon obiro to wasomo Muma gi wiwa kabisa. . . . Bange, ne aye adok e tim piny ma ne chon, iluongo ni maranda, chodo sero nyir, iluongo ni maranda. Koro ne abedo ne an gi thum mar nyatiti, mar kienyeji,*[8] *ne agoyo ga, dala wa ne ji ogo te. . . . Koro ne awok adhi tich Kitale, Elgon.*

Bang'e nene Nyasaye okelo na duol go otieno ka an e nyosruok gotieno ne we thumi ma igoyo ga ni, i igo thum maka igoyo to chopo e polo. Bang'e koro ne onuang'o ka amadho ga kata poko mar njaga. Ne wan kod osiepna moro ma iluongo ni Pesa Ogido ema ne wamadhe ga kodo. To ne koro a penjo Phesa no nu . . . wakawe wakete e nyim Nyasaye, ka Nyasaye oneno ni orach mondo waweye, to ka onene ni ober dwa lame ga to wamadhe, mondo wamadhe. Ne wa kawo wakete e dier ot, njaga kod poko e nyim Nyasaye. Nyasaye ne ogola bu ne aweyo chuth.

Mach ne oliel ka an Elgon kanyo, ne ok ang'e ni mach oliel kendo ja roho moro ne ok owotho ma obiro yalo na kata wach roho. Da, anuang'o mana warruok kenda.)

Otang'a goes on to explain that, shortly after his conversion experience, he had a series of puzzling dreams while still in Kitale. First, two acquaintances from his native locale, Barnaba Walwoho (the first bishop of the Ruwe Holy Ghost Church) and Mariam Abonyo (a leading woman member) appeared to him saying that from now on, he was "one of theirs" (*in ng'atwa*). Shortly thereafter, Alfayo Odongo Mango himself came "carrying a *dindo* spear[9] and draped in skins from head to toe" (*kod tong' dindo, to kod ka orwake, pien ma otudo bu ogik nyaka piny*). In a final dream, Saint Peter transported Otang'a to the top of Mount Elgon. Otang'a had been planning to climb Mount Elgon with his friend Pheso, although many had discouraged them, saying "even whites" had not managed to reach the peak. Otang'a's vision now set him atop this peak, from where he could survey the vast countryside spreading below. Saint Peter said that one day Otang'a would see all the places he longed to see, as well as lands he had not even heard of. Soon after these puzzling dreams, Daniel Otang'a returned home on leave. He stopped in at a neighbor's house during a rainstorm and discovered that Mariam Abonyo—the woman in his dream—and two other Roho women happened to be visiting his neighbor. He told them he had heard about a new denomination (*dini*) in the area and that he wished to learn more about it. The women took him to Isaya Goro's church compound in Ruwe. Otang'a said to himself, "If they are worshiping God, I will [immediately] know it; if they are worshiping something else altogether, I will also know it" (*Ka gilamo Nyasaye ang'nawinj, to ka gilamo gimo nono ang' nawinj*). As soon as Otang'a entered the gateway, Nora Nyadero greeted him and led him to a corner, where she told him to kneel and confess his sins. She then recited the Lord's Prayer over him, and he knew at once that they worshiped the same God he did. Within a week, Otang'a joined the Roho church and had his long, wild hair[10] shaved, a symbol of his new state.

When Daniel Otang'a talks about this *lokruok*, he contrasts his former decadent lifestyle with his postconversion successes. He cites his travels as a soldier in the colonial army and his later effectiveness as a Roho evangelist who threatened the well-known founder of the Catholic mission at Nyabondo, Father Leo, by "taking away" his parishioners. It is interesting that Otang'a draws a distinction between his initial conversion, which he experienced "on his own" in Kitale, and his later discovery of the Roho church. He depicts the church as the community in which he acted out his own divine destiny, rather than as a body that dictated his spiritual or professional life.

Let us now turn to the testimony of Johana Mariko Omina, a man who joined the Roho movement before Mango's death. Omina was born in Ruwe around 1913. He spent his childhood as an Anglican. In 1924, Omina witnessed an outbreak of Holy Spirit religion—people falling down and speaking in tongues— and was bewildered by it. During this flowering of ecstatic Christianity, Omina had a strange vision, which he considers the beginning of his involvement with Roho:

> I saw it when I was looking after cattle, [at the time] I still covered myself with skins, I was a child. . . . I saw a person dressed like a Mswahili, with long hair and a bushy beard and he was driving a sheep. He said, "I am Moses." Being still young, I [ran away from] there crying, I wailed and even left the cattle over there across the stream, I cried all the way home.
>
> (*A nene ka adhi kwath, pod ang'uolara ang'uola, an nyathi. . . . Ne a neno ng'ato, ma orwako, orwakre ka muswahili, ma wiye oyugno to tike oyugno, to osembo rombo. To owacho ni an e Musa. Pod atin, nene aa kuro ka aywak, ago nduru bu aweyo dhok kuchande, loka kuma ne antie bu ago nduru nyaka e dala.*)

He goes on to recall that after his brief encounter with the biblical Moses, Omina suffered shaking fits for some time. His family concluded that he was being tormented by a demon (*jachien*),[11] but Omina attributed his experiences to the Holy Spirit's activity in the location. The event that caused Omina to convert to formal Roho religion, however, came several years later when he was a young man.

Omina explains that one day his brother sent him on an errand to buy a few cigarettes. Omina tucked the cigarettes in his pocket. Arriving home, he found that his father had organized a prayer session and that Lawi Obonyo was presiding. Immediately after Omina had entered the house, Lawi burst out, "Someone here has cigarettes!" He pointed to Omina. The latter was amazed: "I wondered, I placed the cigarettes in my pocket, but how has this person seen them?" (*To an ni eh, to ndawa nende ayie ei ofuko, to ng'at ni ong'e nadi?*) "That's what converted/ changed me" (*Gima okelo loka ero*), Omina declared. Impressed by Lawi's ability to perceive the truth, he heeded Lawi's call to join worshipers in Musanda on January 1, 1934. Despite the tragic outcome of that retreat, Omina remained with the Roho movement. He became one of the church's first catechists, as well as a *laktar*. He emphasized the latter occupation: "Praying for the sick is the most important [task I performed], so if you have to list something, write 'doctor'" (*Lemo ni ng'at matuo ema duong'ie ahinya ema ka aye indiko to indiko ni, kaka* "doctor" *mar lemo*).

In 1940, Johana Omina left Ruwe to serve in the army and returned two years later. In the 1950s, he did a brief stint as a cook for settlers in Nairobi. Otherwise, he spent much of his adult life proselytizing and teaching in Roho churches in Ugenya.

Both Daniel Otang'a and Johana Omina link their involvement in the Roho movement to earlier experiences of the Spirit. This fact supports the contention that grassroots forms of ecstatic Christianity had a cultural impact, at least in eastern Luoland, well before the establishment of most Kenyan independent churches. Their visions of encounters with patriarchs or ancestor-like figures (Mango dressed in skins) are characteristic of traditional lineage-based religion; Otang'a's vision of being transported aloft is common in possession cult initiation. For both Otang'a and Omina, however, these phenomena signaled a break with the past. That they were visited by personages from the Bible connoted a call to Christianity (Judaism was not present in western Kenya) and implied a rejection of "traditional ways" (*tim piny*). The abandonment of tobacco, hemp, and alcohol is the most common index of conversion in men's stories. Women occasionally mention letting go of these habits, but beer drinking and, to a lesser extent, smoking were central features of the traditional Luo male social world,[12] and giving them up was a more serious affair for men than for women.

Finally, there is the element of truth (*adier*), which, again, is important to both male and female members but is given more emphasis in men's testimonies. Omina was so struck by Lawi's uncanny ability to see through appearances that he converted on the spot. In characterizing the difference between Anglicanism and Roho religion, Bishop Ibrahim Mango similarly emphasized truthfulness and the ability to perceive the truth as part of the very essence of Roho religion:

I myself see no difference between Anglican and Roho except that Roho is stronger. Anglican is weak. What I mean is this: in Holy Ghost prayer, . . . you say all your sins and you ask to be forgiven and you try to be so honest with God, not cheating. But in the Anglican [church] even if I am a thief, I just sit [in church] with those people and when I leave, I start stealing again. If I am a drunkard, [it is] only when I go to church that I stop drinking. But immediately [after] I leave, I go for a drink. So there [in Anglicanism] you pray, but you are free to do anything. . . . But with Roho, if I go and drink, even if I didn't tell anybody, when people are praying, somebody who does not even know me will just say "so-and-so, I see you with a glass in your hand, what is this glass?" Even if I steal this tape-recorder of yours, Roho will [address] me through another person, "I see something in your house [that does not belong to you]. What is all this?" With Roho you can see things and moreover, God is speaking to people. He tells people what is happening, which is not the case in all other religions.

Meshak Ogola, who listened to Ibrahim Mango's comments, interjected that one can become a saved person (*jamowar*) in any denomination. The experience of being saved—or born again—is the same anywhere, he argued. What is different is that denominations like the Anglican and Catholic churches do not recognize spiritual power or do not know how to cultivate it. Mango agreed that, within the context of other churches, one's spiritual fervor "automatically disappears." It is difficult to maintain the sense of being saved in such environments. "But if a saved person joins us, this Roho will keep him on his toes! If he wants to 'deteriorate,' somebody will catch him."

Themes of honesty, openness, and keeping members on the right path are foregrounded in men's conversion stories and in their estimation of the value of Roho religion.[13] These features are important to women also but, as we shall see, are couched within the context of good interpersonal relationships. Let us now consider the perspectives of several women on conversion and the Roho faith.

Margaret Uba is a middle-aged Roho member from South Nyanza. She describes herself as a leader of women (*jatend mon*) in her congregation. Her duty is to care for women and to instruct them. She travels to large meetings and festivals, such as the *Sikukuu mar Rapar*, and then returns with a report of what took place and transmits information from headquarters. Uba converted to the Roho religion from Catholicism, a religious community whose "behavior" (*timne*) did not impress her:

When the Holy Spirit found me I was a Catholic. . . . My husband and I were wed in the Catholic church, but we didn't have any peace. We constantly quarreled for no reason. . . . We were drinking beer, because in the Catholic church we were not prohibited from doing so; we were left free to drink. After drinking until we were drunk, we would fight, and there was no peace in our house.

(*An to ne roho onuang'a ka an jaKatolik. . . . Ka ne wan e Katolik, ne wakwano arus gi chwora, to ne waongo gi kwe. Ne wasiko wadhawo adhawa maonge tiende. . . . Wamadho kong'o to wanuang'o ni Katolik ne ok otamo wa madho kong'o; koro ne oyawo nua ni madh uru kong'o. Koro ka wase madho kong'o to wamadho wamer to wagore, koro waonge gi kwe e odwa.*)

Margaret's domestic troubles continued for some time. Then, in 1960, she had occasion to hear Ruwe Roho missionary Isaya Goro on one of his preaching safaris in South Nyanza. After listening, she converted and joined a local group of Roho adherents. However, her husband's people noisily protested, saying "the religion this woman is bringing is no good" (*din ma dhako okelo no din marach*)! They urged him to rip off the cross she had appliqued onto her dress, which he tried to do:

> My husband started to tear off my emblem of membership, [saying] "I don't accept that religion, it shall not be worshiped here!" I was also angry and refused, "I'm not going back to the Catholic church which I left. I refuse! The Roho church is where I'll worship until I die."
>
> (*Jaoda ochako okawo namba ma oyiecho, ni koro din ni adage, koro din ni ok ilimie! An be aichra akwere, ni an bende ok achak adog e din mar Katolik ma ne aaye cha. Adagi. Roho ema alamo nyaka athoye.*)

Margaret's husband then told her that she would have to look for a new husband if she would not abandon Roho. She bluntly told him that she would do neither, whereupon he threatened: "Then you shall die" (*to itho*).

"I accept death" (*ne ayie ne tho ni ee*), she answered. Margaret's husband sent her away, but, as they had six children to care for, when she returned the following day, he did not stop her. For the next two years, Uba's husband continued to oppose her religious practice. Gradually, however, as he watched the way his wife prayed and persevered, and as he observed the positive effects of faith healing on his children, he came to accept the validity of her faith:

> Later when he saw that I had refused, and that I was willing to die like the people who had died in the [Musanda] fire, and that I would not leave this religion, he converted. For he saw the goodness and peace this religion brings.
>
> (*Koro bange ka ose neno ka adagi, an be ajok ni koro atho kaka joka ne otho e mach, an din ni ok awe, koro eka bange koro eka olokre, koro oneno ka dind no ber okelo kwe.*)

Margaret stated that their move into the Roho denomination brought harmony and security at home and introduced a degree of flexibility into her life. She is now free to travel around the country on church business, and her husband does not get suspicious. "Then when I return," she stated, "we just love each other" (*Koro ka wadok, wan mana gi hera, waherore ahera*).

Margaret Uba's account of her conversion contains some of the same themes as those of the men discussed previously. Rejection of intoxicating substances and denunciation of the lax lifestyles "permitted" in mainline Christianity are familiar motifs. Yet, Margaret's entire drama unfolds within the dynamics of her marriage. The tendency to delineate the significance of religious affiliation in terms of its impact on the marital home is more characteristic of women's testimonies than of men's. This fact should not surprise us. The vast majority of the women who make up the Roho membership live their lives amid their husbands' kin, occupying a position that can at times be very difficult. Luo men exercise "considerable formal control" over their wives, and women must strive "to avoid antagonizing" their mates to the point of divorce, or else they stand to lose everything—children, land, belongings (Potash 1978):

> The women of western Kenya—the Luo, Luyia, and Gusii, in particular—seem to have strikingly limited access to all forms of property, in comparison with many other areas of Africa. These limits generally operate to require that a woman remain in a viable marriage in order to enjoy access to agricultural land, livestock, children. They place the greatest burden for maintaining marriages on the women's shoulders, and make it difficult for rural women to survive outside marriage. (Hay 1982, 112)[14]

When a man works in town and his wife manages the family garden on her own, the little profit she might glean from surplus crops or from her own handicrafts (e.g., clay pots, reed mats, decorated calabashes, sisal strings) is negligible, given Kenya's severe economic crisis. Thus, women and children are increasingly dependent on their husbands' and fathers' wages for clothing, school fees, and medicine, not to mention supplementary foodstuffs during drought or low-yield years. In a recent *Washington Post* series on Third World village women, a number of rural Luo women describe their lives as "beyond their control." Given rising prices, land scarcity, and lower crop yields, rural families—many of which are polygamous—are increasingly desperate: "Men can't stay happy, because the women want them to feed them and they can't get enough. . . . They produce more children, and they can't get enough food so some children become thieves," said Benta Ukoni of Rariw, one of the women interviewed by *Post* reporters.[15] Studies by scholars such as Margaret Jean Hay, Achola Pala Okeyo, and Sharon Stichter reveal that Luo women's marked economic dependence on men began during the colonial period and has worsened (Hay 1976, 1982; Stichter 1975–1976; Pala Okeyo 1980). The stressful reality of striving to maintain one's dignity—let alone to feed one's children—while caught in a position of subordination, dependency, and growing hardship would naturally be reflected in women's religious stories.

Inspired by the model of the Musanda martyrs, Margaret Uba took the brave step of standing up to her husband, although she and he both knew she was risking everything. Whether or not he could have literally killed her himself, his threat ("Then you will die") was ominous enough, given the grim social and economic ramifications of divorce for women in rural Luoland. Yet, Uba remained intransigent. The underlying motivation behind her conversion to a

Christian ecstatic movement thus could not have been solely instrumental—that is, a means to garnering support in a "sex-war" in which she had no acceptable means of redress—as I. M. Lewis's theory of deprivation contends (1966, 314-315). When Uba made her choice, it was not at all clear that she wasn't asking for overwhelming disapproval from everyone who mattered in her life. Indeed, she endured opposition—rather than support—from her husband's kin for at least two years, a daily strain that could only have placed additional stress on her marriage.

However, it is clear that participation in Roho religion empowered Margaret in a number of ways. As a Jaroho, she has been able, at least from time to time, to reject the self-effacing posture that dominant cultural ideology prescribes for women. Through the healers in the church, Uba has had access to new therapeutic resources for her children. Her husband's fortuitous subsequent conversion, moreover, resulted in increased freedom for her. These kinds of gains can be measured within the objective constructs of Luo society, but other benefits and important transformations cannot. The peacefulness that Uba and other women converts speak of, for example, is not simply the product of smoother personal relations. It is also the result of their gradual personal spiritual development, grounded in a new worldview and faith.

Let us now consider the story of Nereya Auma, a *laktar* in the Ruwe Holy Ghost Church. Nereya is the daughter of Roho pioneers Anna Inondi and Isaya Goro. Unlike most adult Joroho, who have made a conscious choice to leave other denominations in order to join the Holy Ghost church, Nereya was raised in the church. Her account is of particular interest, for it traces the changes and growth of an individual who came of age within Roho religion and whose parents were staunch proponents of the faith. Born in 1928 in Ruwe, Auma was baptized as Ludya in the Anglican church. When Mango, the deacon of their congregation, was denounced by Archdeacon Owen, Auma's parents continued to pray with Mango and Lawi and to affirm their brand of ecstatic Christianity—an affirmation that involved Inondi and Goro in the Musanda massacre and remained central throughout the rest of their lives.

When asked how she came to be a *laktar*, Nereya Auma began by recounting her earliest religious experience. As a small child of about five, Auma suffered from foot sores. Her mother bathed her feet in a stream, soaked them in herbal medicine, and bandaged them. Inondi then took Auma to Musanda to be prayed for by Lawi. During their visit, Auma heard Lawi claim "that he had run and walked on top of water" (*ni aye aringo bu awotho, aringo e wi pi*) when hurrying to cross a river on his way back to Musanda after a preaching safari in Alego. Auma didn't believe him—"I doubted in my heart" (*achok gi chunya*):

I said, "How can this large man walk on top of water? Even a piece of paper, which can float for a while, eventually dissolves and sinks." Then I kept quiet.

*(To awach ni ng'at ma rabet ne du woth e wi pi? Ma kata kalatas fuya afuya
to ka ochopo kamoro, notuonore mo nodog piny, bas adok aling'.)*

On the way back home, Auma's feet were giving her such pain that her mother
had to carry her much of the distance:

> When we arrived at the stream [called Okwero] my mother carried me and
> she walked on top of water just as that man [Lawi] had walked; that is the
> Spirit's miracle I saw. That's why they now call me healer, which means that
> we are those who pray for bad things to go away.

> *(To tundo e aora, minwa ni koro oting'a to owotho e we pi kaka ne ng'acho
> owotho, e hono ma nenen a neno kuom roho. Koro omiyo sani giluonga ni
> laktar, tiende ni wan jolemo moko ma konyo lamo mar gimoro marach.)*

Auma says that, like Thomas in the Bible, she had doubted Lawi's claim and was
later proven wrong. Three other people who were walking with them, Leah
Were, Jerusa Omolo, and a girl named Mariam Obonyo, also witnessed the
event and exclaimed in amazement as Inondi traveled over the surface of the
chest-high stream without wetting a leg. The experience rather frightened little
Auma (*Kaka ineno gini otimore hama, an be aneno to aluor*).

As the party reached home and entered Inondi's house, it encountered the
sound of angels singing on the roof:

> *Ng'at ma geno Nyasaye achiel*
> (A person who trusts in one God)

> *En odonji, ei polo gi mor;*
> (Will enter heaven with happiness;)

> *Eno bedi ei polo kucha.*
> (And will remain there in heaven.)

> *Kata ibet ka ionge wadu,*
> (Even if you have no companions,)

> *Kik ipari ni Nyasaye onge.*
> (Don't think that God isn't there.)

> *En e buti, ok oweyoi.*
> (He is near you and has not left you.)

Auma explains that they knew the singers were angels by the nature of their
voices:

> That was the voice of angels, we cannot say that it was the voice of the Holy
> Spirit, we say that it was the angels because they sing in a high-pitched
> voice. I was young, . . . I was trying to cover my ears, and I looked at the

roof and then at those people and said [to myself] "Am I the only one hearing this thing? I'll just go to the bedroom. There I can block my ears." But the song continued to be sung by the people and by [the angels].

(*Mano duond malaika, mane ne koro ok wawach ni en duond roho, ne wawacho ni en malaika nikech ower gi duol matin. An koro atin . . . atimo ga itha nii ni adin, to arango tado to arango jogi, to awacho ni a "an ema awinjo ga gini kenda kose? Aring adog e gul. To adhi adin kuro itha." To wendno jogi wero to gibe giwero.*)

The statement "That's why they now call me healer" that Auma made after recounting the water episode posits a connection between this early epiphany and her vocation as a *laktar*. However, in response to my probing, Auma seemed to say that this childhood encounter with spiritual power was reinforced gradually and that, as a result of her perseverance and piety, God, over time, provided her with the gift of healing:

This work [of being a *laktar*], it came to me later, unexpectedly. It is not [the childhood experience] which made me [a *laktar*], it is just determination and prayer that caused God to increase my power to [heal others] bit by bit.

(*Kaka tij no obe, apoye ka ahonore na bang'e, ok ni mano ema omiyo, en mana ni koro kinda kod lamo emomiyo Nyasaye medo n'a teko mondo a tem go matin tin.*)

As the daughter of Roho evangelists, Auma saw many people healed through faith. She grew up in a home that functioned as a mission station, where the sick could come to recuperate and where converts were always welcome. She recounts having lapsed once when, as a teenager, she sneaked away to have her front lower teeth extracted. According to Luo custom, when a person reached puberty, his or her front lower teeth were extracted, a rite that marked the end of childhood.[16] Roho churches in Nyanza, like mainline Christian missions, prohibited this practice. As Auma's mother states, "Why should that which God has created be removed?" ([*To*] *gima Nyasaye ose chweyo, ang'o momiyo ka igolo gi?*) Auma's grandmother was of a different mind and reproached the girl to remove them:

You want to be a Luyia? . . . Does your father have his teeth? Does your mother have her teeth? You want to do something forbidden [by refusing to have them out].

(*Dana okwer ni idwa bet jamua. . . . To wuor ni kod lake? Koso mer ni kod lake? Idwa timo tim ma kwero.*)

Moreover, in the 1930s and 1940s, most Luo youths—even those exposed to Christianity—had their teeth extracted. Auma explained, "I saw my age-mates with their teeth removed and I deemed it good for me, too, because it was still a Luo custom" (*Nene ka aneno jowadwa ma onag kor aneno beyona, nikech ne pod en chik Luo*). At the encouragement of her grandmother, Auma stole four *lando* and two *nela*[17] from her father and ran away to the home of her maternal uncle to have the operation performed. When she returned home, she took full responsibility for her act, saying it had been her decision alone. As the Roho congregation ruminated over whether to expel her, she told them, "I am a sinner, whatever you decide is my fate. For I have no say" (*An jaketho koro an gima uyie ema, du utimna nikech aonge gi duol*).

Auma maintains that finally an "answer came down from heaven" (*Koro ema ne polo oduoko wach*). The message indicated that the angel who guided Ludya (Auma's Anglican baptismal name) had separated from the Spirit and led the girl into sin. Therefore, she should discard the identity of Ludya, and the Holy Spirit would send another angel or companion to "help her work." Auma was thus baptized in the Roho church as Nereya and given a new guardian angel through the Spirit.

Thus, Nereya began a new life of religious dedication. She married, had children, and raised them in the Roho church. Not until she was nearly forty, however, did she discover her healing powers and become recognized as a doctor. She found her vocation in 1966, when traveling with her mother and Mariam Abonyo to retrieve the body of her father, Isaya Goro, who had died on a missionary trip to northeastern Tanzania. The journey to Rarenyo, the village where Goro died, took several days. The three women spent their first night in Makalda Munyu (Macalder mines) with Zakariah Oluk, Goro's godson, whose home lay near the border. On their arrival in Oluk's compound, the women had gone straight to his chapel and began singing, "Stand up Christian, look at your enemy!" (*Chung'i Jakristo, ne jasiki cha!*) Residents came running to see who was singing and joined the visitors in prayer. Everybody in Oluk's village had heard about the miracles that had taken place in Musanda and Ruwe and assumed that anyone from there must possess spiritual power. They thus appealed to the Musanda doctors (*laktache*) to heal those who were sick in the home.

Nereya claims that the invalids she and Miriam prayed for that night promptly recovered (*Ne walemo nigi, koro jogo ne dendgi oduogo aduoga maber kanyo*). The following morning, a number of women who were bewitched were brought to her:

> Thereupon, I began praying for them. Some of them had stomach worms due to demons [satans], and now vomited those things. One who had chest problems vomited foam as well as other things. They were then healed. I then took them outside, asked for a pot and led them to the river.

> (*Koro eka aketo gi gilemo. Koro ema moko nene oyie saitande mag kute kute ei gi, koro ng'ogo gigo. Wuon kor ni ng'ogo buoyo byuoyo, ma bende ng'ogo gik moko. Aye sano ema gichange. To agolo gi, to awacho ni miya uru ofuria, adhi atero gi e aora.*)

Nereya helped the women bathe and complete their cure, before she, Inondi, and Abonyo, accompanied by one of the women whose demons Nereya had exorcised, headed toward Rarenyo. Along the route was a place called Olando that contained a large Roho community.[18] The people of Olando had learned that some powerful healers from Ruwe would be passing through, and a large crowd had already gathered. The travelers felt obliged to stop, so they entered the grass-thatched Roho church there and began singing. Nearly all the villagers who followed them inside were "knocked down" by the Holy Spirit. Nereya prayed for many people that afternoon. In the crowd was a child medium. The angels spoke through her, foretelling what would take place at the funeral of Isaya Goro. "Wherever these people are going tomorrow," said the girl, referring to Nereya and her companions, "the angels will speak to them" (*Koro eka ging'iso weche, nu kiny unu dhi kucha to Malaika nowuo, owacho ni nyathi moro manyako*).

Nereya Auma was raised in Roho religion and therefore did not refer to her second baptism as a conversion (*lokruok*). She did indicate, however, that straying into traditional ways (due to Satan) and reentering the Roho faith was like joining the church from another denomination:

> Don't you see that you can pray in one denomination then when you join another denomination, you must be baptized. The Holy Spirit points out the sins you committed on the other side, yes, when you abandoned the work of God [i.e., in the previous denomination, or in Nereya's case, when she embraced Luo custom]. Then comes the answer that so-and-so should come and work, he/she had been [previously] won over because Satan had taken him/her astray, now he/she should work.

> (*Ok ine ka inyalo ga lemo e din moro, kendo ka idhi e din moro to kendo ibatisi. Roho ne owuoyo ni gima iketho kocha, ee, ha ne iweyo tich mar Nyasaye, koro mano ema ne oduok ni ng'ane mondo obi oti, nikech ng'ane ose lo, jachien oloyo bu odhi yore, ee, ng'ane mondo oti.*)

Taking a new name signified that Auma's old self, Ludya, as well as the latter's *juogi*, were gone. Like Daniel Otang'a's conversion, which entailed abandoning the traditional Luo harp, Auma's return to Holy Spirit religion involved eschewing customary rites and rejecting her desire to succumb to peer pressure. She could no longer define herself according to society's usual norms. Although this conversion-like experience was critical in Auma's life, she stressed that her self-realization as a healer took place gradually. She saw her ability to heal people as partly the result of her own perseverance and God's rewarding her "bit by bit" with increased power, and partly the product of others' recognition. In reflecting on her life, Auma posited the roots of her healing vocation in her childhood experience at the river. She did not actually become a *laktar*, however, until Tanzanians bestowed that role upon her: "The way that thing [being a *laktar*] began in me, specifically, [is that] I prayed for them and they now call me doctor" (*Kaka gino ne ochakore, kuom awuon wuon koro, alemo nigi koro mu giluonga ga ni laktar*). Nereya's brother, Meshak Ogola, was not aware of his sister's gradual personal or spiritual development prior to her trip to Tanzania. Instead, he thought his sister simply inherited their father's capacities upon his death. Not until Isaya Goro, the great preacher and healer, died, Ogola maintained, did Nereya gain the ability to perform that work:

> First she didn't have anything at all. [This was the case] for a long time, until the old man died. When the old man died, she went with them to [Tanzania]. Then when they came back they started calling her doctor.
>
> (*Mokwongo ne odhi ma ok obet gi gimoro amora, kuom ndalo mang'eny nyaka ne jaduong' otho. Ka ne jaduong' tho, nene giwuok kode ka gidhi kuro, koro eka ka giduogo to ochak luonge ni laktar.*)

Thus, for Meshak Ogola, his sister's leadership was not the culmination of many years of "working in the spirit" but had been automatically transferred to her by her father's spirit, irrespective of her own qualifications. These divergent interpretations again point to the inclination of men—when outlining religious biographies—to stress abrupt reversals, whereas women tend to stress continuity or the gradual development of faith—albeit punctuated by successive transformations—frequently expressed through images of work (*tich*).

These four conversion stories provide insight into differences in the way Roho men and women perceive the impact of religion on their lives. Collectively, these accounts follow a fairly conventional format, and, probably similar conversion narratives have been given by men and women belonging to any number of independent and perhaps even mainline denominations in Kenya. To determine whether these narratives contain any elements specific to Roho tradition would require further fieldwork. Likewise, to discover if the differences I have identified in men's and women's conversions are found in other Christian traditions would require a far broader comparative analysis than the scope of this study allows. Works by scholars on gender and conversion narratives (Brereton 1991) and on women's psychological and moral development (Gilligan 1982), however, suggest that there is ample material to warrant just such a study.

The next section considers women's reflections on the nature of the Spirit and their role as God's workers.

Work and Feeling Free:
Women's Perceptions of Life in the Spirit

Luo women living in the countryside work extremely hard. They are responsible for all the cooking and washing, fetching of firewood and water, and planting, weeding, harvesting, preparing, and storing of many crops. They bear the weight of numerous pregnancies and child care and are frequently pressured to generate supplemental income through selling surplus crops or manufacturing handicrafts. Only in cases of incapacitating illness or while paying visits on special occasions such as funerals does a Luo wife have a respite from this workload. Exhaustion, fevers, or mild injuries generally do not win a woman much assistance from her husband or male in-laws, although older children can be of great assistance, and cowives or sisters-in-law may lend a hand if they have time to spare. Since the colonial period, male labor migration has left women with more physical and agricultural work to perform than in earlier times (Stichter 1975–1976, 48–57; Hay 1982, 113). Tasks once classified as men's work have increasingly fallen on women's shoulders. Some men, when they are home, do take responsibility for the "nonroutine tasks of agriculture," such as building fences; others apparently feel no need to reclaim such chores, even when they are able. [19] Among the Luo, clearing the bush (*beto*), plowing (*pur gidhok*), and constructing granaries (*godero*), for example, were traditionally classified as men's tasks (*tije chwo*). Allocated to the husband in the past, these tasks are now often performed by his wives or, when resources permit, by hired male workers (Pala Okeyo 1983, 79).

The lives of rural Luo women, which have always entailed considerable labor, are thus increasingly dominated and defined by *tich* (work). This does not mean that women do not make time for socializing and friendship with other women. Market days, funerals, and church services afford excellent opportunities for such contact. Paying visits to friends and neighbors is another enjoyable pastime for both sexes, but men clearly have more free time to linger, to go for a drink, and to "discuss important issues" with kinsmen. [20] Women's casual conversation when they encounter each other along paths reflects the daily pressures they are under. [21] They are less likely than men to be met simply strolling together for recreation. Instead, they are usually in the midst of performing some errand or task: transporting water or firewood home, lugging the harvest in from their fields to be stored, carrying produce to market, or taking sick children to the dispensary or to a herbalist for treatment. That women are not very often apt to go for a "stroll" is, in part, due to the fact that a woman seen loitering along the pathways is stigmatized. Industriousness is a traditional virtue in Luo society—for both men and women—but the consequences of idleness tend to be more severe for women and girls.

The concept of work, I would suggest, is integral to the way in which Luo culture depicts and seeks to shape women. The notion of work is thus reflected in the way women conceive of themselves and their activity in the world, including their religious activity. [22] I noticed that women, far more often than men, evoked images of work when speaking of their involvement in the church. For instance, the late Turfosa Okoko, who lived in the Roho settlement at Mirunda from 1954 until her death in early 1993, maintained that during all those years she never considered leaving to return to her husband and six children in Uyoma. "If you are plowing," she said, "you don't look back." One might argue that Okoko was simply substituting an existence of drudgery and subservience at home with a more favorable, less exhausting type of work—one in which she labored in a supportive commune with other Roho adherents. Yet "God's work" (*tich Nyasaye*) has its own difficulties. The Roho ethos extends people's obligations beyond their own lineages and affines; for women, this means that the people they can be asked to support through their labor increases considerably. In addition, Roho teachings require that women bear problems with an equanimity and acceptance that surpasses that of their "unsaved" sisters. Ironically, this equanimity can be interpreted as both enslaving and empowering.

Anna Inondi, the wife of missionary Isaya Goro, was expected to welcome all visitors into her Christian home with a warm heart and an open hearth. Sick people, orphans, and converts from any region could come and expect to be taken care of for a period of time at the Goro compound. When harvests were good and her husband was around to help manage the additional dependents, things went well, but Inondi was often left alone for months at a time, with few resources and numerous mouths to feed, while her husband was away on missionary campaigns. "Truly in the name of God," she once exclaimed, "the way I cooperated (*wachung'*—lit., stood) with my husband, there isn't another couple who would have managed!" Inondi attributed her ability to live in peace—despite the additional responsibilities Isaya's vocation foisted upon her—to her participation in Roho religion:

> Even now, no woman would accept [those conditions]. As for me, if he wanted to go, I prayed for him, telling God to guide him well until he returns, and gave him the rope so that he could tie the community.[23] But the sick people remained here, the ones he brought here. I prepared them porridge; I cooked them ugali. Whoever arrived I looked after, even though I had to do it entirely on my own.

> (*Kata sani dhako dak yie da. To an ka ne odwaro dhi, alemo ne, ka awacho ni "Nyasaye ikonye wuoth maber nyaka oduogi." Kendo imiye tol ma onyalo tweyo go oganda. To an to ji odong' kani joma two, ma okel ka. Anudo ni nyuka atedo ne kuon. Kendo oganda ma donjo arango, to an ng'ato achiel hama.*)

Sometimes Inondi was so strapped that she denied herself and her own children food in order to serve the outsiders, a situation that she still described with a degree of bitterness, but with pride as well:

> When he [Isaya Goro] began to spread the word [of the Spirit], he captured the hearts of absolutely everyone with his behavior and his speech, such that he converted the country. All those people whom he brought [home], who stopped here, some stayed for three months, others for one month, another could remain for two months. But [you would not] hear a thing out of my mouth which could hurt them! That's why he converted the world. Even

now, if I went with you, and traveled with you, anyone who saw me would be like a person who sees God, because they would look at me and [see that] no matter what lifestyle a woman follows, I take her as a child whom I must love. I could deny my own child[ren], telling them, "Just keep quiet even if you are very hungry, you'll eat at another time." And then I would take the [visitors] from Tanzania and feed them.

(*Ka ochako dhi lando wachni, ne omako chuny ji tetete kuom timne, kod wuoyone osemiyo piny olokore. To kaka jogi duto ma nene okelo duto, ma onyono ka, moko tieko dweche adek, moko dweche achiel, moro chako tieko dweche ariyo. To rango, nuang'o gima owuok e dhoga ka ma chwany gi, ema omiyo oloko piny. Ma kata sani, ma ka awuok kata kodi, nu awuotho kodi, ng'ama onena to wad ma oneno Nyasaye, nikech giranga to chik ma mon ochung' kodo ma kata ni mani nyathine ema doher. Anyalo tuono nyathina maga gi awacho nu, ni ling'uru aling'a kata kech kayo u, ang'uru chiem saa moro, to akawo ma oa Tanganyika ema amiyo.*)

The contents of this testimony reveal the contradictory ramifications of life in the Spirit for many Roho women. On the one hand, Inondi implies that she put up with unreasonable demands, things that wives operating by usual norms would "not accept." That she never let a word of protest slip from her lips, that she "just kept quiet," indicates to her listeners that she considered the arrangement unjust, even exploitative.

On the other hand, like many pious Christians the world over, Inondi paradoxically finds such generous work transformative. Doing God's work does not render her meek or self-effacing. On the contrary, she openly takes partial credit for her husband's success and for the spread of the church throughout the country. She is confident that she is an exemplary person, claiming that her behavior perfectly mirrors God's love.

Inondi and others describe Roho life as liberating in a number of ways. They claim it gives them freedom (*thuolo*) from anxiety about sickness, death, loneliness, and the weight of responsibilities. Since she became a Roho adherent, for example, Inondi sees an improvement in her ability to cope with illness. She no longer worries herself over who may have bewitched her, nor does she blame God:

Now when I'm sick, I don't have bad thoughts, suspecting that a neighbor may have done something to me. I don't have bad thoughts. I don't think, "how my body hurts, yet God doesn't help me." I don't think that.

(*Koro an, kata atuoni, ok apar paro moro marach, kata kuom wadwa moro, ni chalo ni otima nadi. Kendo ok apar paro marach, to denda rama nadi mak Nyasaye konya ye, ok apar.*)

At a Roho funeral held for a young woman who died of a sudden illness in Ng'iya in May 1990, preachers likewise warned mourners against negative thinking.

They told people not to waste time suspecting neighbors of having caused the woman's death. A number urged their audience to accept God's will and not to fear the grave. The deceased woman's stepmother spoke with conviction:

> You shouldn't be filled with fright, for you know where Night[24] has gone. I am sure I know where Night has gone. I'm not frightened at all for one day I will also go there. And I shall go confidently without trepidation and without lamenting.
>
> (*To ok ibi bedo kod bwok moro, nikech ing'eyo kama Night odhiye. An gadier ni ang'eyo kama Night odhiye. Ok abi bwok kendo ok abi bedo gi luoro nikech an bende chieng moro achiel abiro dhi kuno. To nadhi gi chir maok aluor kend ok aywak.*)

Roho women speak of "feeling free" or "being at peace" as a result of learning to leave matters in God's hands. They describe coming to trust God during periods of hardship—particularly food shortages—as a liberating experience. When lacking food, Inondi would turn to God in prayer, saying, "My God, you are the owner who knows" (*Nyasacha, in iwuon ema ing'eyo*). She elaborated,

> If I find a little [food], and someone else manages to contribute a little, just enough for "moistening our spirits," then it is sufficient. I won't worry my heart wondering "what shall these people eat?"
>
> (*Ka ayudo matin, ng'ato oyud matin, mar bilo chunywa to bas. Ok aketo chunya mar paro ni to jogi tin ocham ang'o?*)

A number of *laktache* and other elderly Roho women spoke of the way in which the Spirit comforted and fortified them in their old age. For example, Turphena Ong'amba Asando, a lively senior member of a Roho congregation in Mombasa, stated that, after her husband died, she was profoundly disturbed and nearly died because nobody was caring for her, but now:

> It is the Spirit who takes care of me. Roho is my husband, my child, my father. . . . I don't have a single person [to support me]. I was in trouble but the Holy Spirit gave me the strength and now I am a person who walks around. If there were no Spirit, I would not be on this earth now.
>
> (*Ema Roho orita. Roho en ye chuora, to Roho en ye nythina, to Rohoni en ye wuora. . . . An aonge ng'ato kata achiel. An ne an e thagruok to Roho omiya an ng'ama otegno kendo an ng'ama sani an dhano mawuoth e wang piny. Dine bed ni onge Roho dak owutho e wang pinyni.*)

Such statements of faith reflect a type of spiritual growth and empowerment that may not be objectively measurable but that is nonetheless real and has manifest social and psychological ramifications. I choose to believe Roho women when they speak of the Spirit and "being in the power" (*e teko*) as transformative and freeing. Kelementina Abiero, a Masumbi *laktar* in her late fifties, described her experience of being overcome by the Holy Spirit:

> Those times when we are in/under the power . . . you perceive yourself rising, you feel weightless . . . you see angels and the light extremely clearly . . . then you see the source [lit., head] of the light, then the light itself.
>
> (*Seche ma wan e teko . . . ineno ka gima ichako dhi gimalo hama, koro iyot yot . . . ineno malaika ineno ler kabisa . . . aye to ineno wi ler hama aye to ineno ler.*)

The basic elements of Roho accounts of transcendent or ecstatic experience are fairly consistent with accounts from other Christian and Muslim mystical traditions. Members always speak of bright light and a sense of well-being. Some women encountered their deceased relatives or angels (generally taken as one and the same). A number stressed the ineffable quality of their experience and were reluctant to describe it, indicating that their experience was simply beyond this world; nothing could be compared with it.

Individuals generally perceive their ecstatic experiences as enabling them to perform important constructive acts, such as prophesy or healing. Joan Akello, after listening to Kelementina's testimony, expressed this notion succinctly, "Without seeing the light you cannot work" (*Ka ok ineno ler ok di ti*).

Thus, on a number of levels—spiritual, emotional, and psychological—Roho religion is an empowering undertaking for women. The implications of Roho religion for women's lives on the level of gender politics, however, are far more ambiguous. A number of Roho women, particularly older members, seem to perceive Roho religion as properly belonging to the female domain, a resource that is especially theirs. They express the belief that women are better suited to "take care of the Spirit" (*rito Roho*), for Roho requires someone who is loving and accepting. As mothers, they suggest, women have an inherent potential for unconditional love. "Even if your child is mad, is he/she not still from your womb?" a woman member once declared rhetorically. "Would you ever abandon such a child?"

According to dominant Luo ideology, women are, indeed, valued as comforting care givers, but they are also seen as being "like children." Luo men—Joroho as well as non-Rohos—do refer to women thus. Luo customary law also considers women children: "In a legal sense, women are minors all their lives, shifting only from the guardianship of their fathers to that of their husbands, and they are permanently disinherited" (Hay 1982, 113). Traditional cultural norms, customary law, and biblical literalism fuse within the institutionalized Roho church to legitimate women's secondary status. Moreover, women leaders often embrace this ideology vociferously in their preaching and in their personal interactions with younger women. Various senior Roho women spoke to me of their role in counseling wives how to live peacefully with their husbands. Consistently, they instructed other women to diffuse quarrels by playing the part of peacemaker. Common pieces of advice are that wives should never retaliate when abused by their husbands, they should serve meals promptly so as not to annoy their husbands, they should concur with their husbands' decisions and they should avoid feeling jealous of their cowives. In their instructive capacities, senior Roho women thus perpetuate the burdensome norms that they themselves feel so acutely.

However, when out of earshot of male officials, Roho women have, on occasion, been known to turn the societal hegemonic ideology on its head, describing grown men as "mere children." One Roho woman remarked that men have "low" minds and do not understand quickly. Inondi, perhaps the most outspoken because of her seniority, described men as fickle, cowardly, and lacking perseverance. The possibility that some Roho women secretly perceived themselves morally and spiritually superior to men—an assertion in the Roho context that entails a claim to a particularly potent kind of power—could be glimpsed in occasional fleeting instances. In responding to a question about dream visions, for instance, a *laktar* from Masumbi commented that men have far fewer visions than women because they neglect their prayers before going to sleep and are therefore not visited by the Spirit at night; all the women in the room concurred. Women's privately expressed frustration over pastors trying to curb their singing, the reenactment of the *mach* in which women marched with swords and killed men, and songs in which women boast of their courage are all veiled protests that indicate that women, while publicly supporting the church's official gender norms, do not fully endorse them.

Edwin and Shirley Ardener's writings on dominant and muted cultural models, like James Scott's notion of official and hidden social transcripts, provide us with a vehicle for understanding the contradictory character of Roho women's depictions of themselves and their roles. As a subdominant group within the church and within the larger Luo society, Roho women express their sense of their spiritual gifts and growth through dominant male terminology. As Shirley Ardener explains:

A society may be dominated or overdetermined by the model (or models) generated by one dominant group within the system. This dominant model may impede the free expression of alternative models of their world which subdominant groups may possess, and perhaps may even inhibit the very generation of such models. Groups dominated in this sense find it necessary to structure their world through the model (or models) of the dominant group, transforming their own models as best they can in terms of the received ones. (Ardener 1975, xii)

There is an uneasy "fit" between the nascent models of the subordinate group and the system of meanings available to them in the ideology of the dominant group. An observer can clearly see that, for Roho women, participation in religion entails a bold statement of self-confidence and liberation from some of society's imposed expectations, but the *ways in which women represent this empowerment* are obfuscating. For example, it is contradictory that Roho women describe their "freedom" in Roho as enabling them to perform the burdensome work assigned to their sex more easily and to endure insults without responding. Yet, this socially instilled model of the hardworking, obedient woman runs deep and has shaped the way in which Roho women view themselves. Subordinate groups do not merely *express* themselves through the dominant ideological paradigms provisionally, that is, in order to be "heard" (Whyte 1983, 181); they also, to some extent, subscribe to the official norms (Robertson 1987, 112).

Hymns: Women's Expressive Domain

Hymn singing is the special domain of Roho women. It constitutes the aspect of Roho liturgy and worship over which women exercise the most direct control. We can expect to find meanings and messages distilled in women's songs that are particularly theirs. Singing has always been an important activity in Luo communities. In the past, songs served to transmit the culture's normative values and history and also provided a vehicle for individual creativity and expression. As Ocholla-Ayayo has shown, praise or "virtue" songs were a favorite method for boasting of one's virtues (*pakruok*) (1976, 45–49). Largely a male practice, *pakruok* entailed boasting of one's strength, bravery, generosity, honesty, and so on. Often a man would commission a harpist (*jathum*) to be the preserver of his particular virtue song, which the harpist was paid to broadcast at social occasions such as dances and beer parties. Ocholla-Ayayo provides the following example of typical virtue song lyrics: "There are many wealthy men, but Onyango my friend is above them all" (*Jomoko moko mang'wony ka ring abula gi Onyango osiepa to oloyou*). Men also had special praise names, such as Iron Arm (*Thuon Bade Chuma*) or the Earth and Its Roof (*Piny gi Tate*), which no one else was allowed to claim (1976, 46–48).

Singing sometimes functioned as social censure. In addition to praising people of distinction, harpists used their art to condemn "thieves, lazy people, cowards and people with bad habits" (Odinga 1967, 9). A more informal type of admonishment was *huwege* songs composed in order to punish individuals who violated social norms. When a child was caught stealing food, for example, villagers would ridicule him in a song that would then spread quickly over the countryside. Just as praise names had a way of sticking with the owner, so were the shameful labels memorialized in catchy *huwege* tunes difficult for the culprits to shake. *Huwege* songs could thus have rather serious consequences for adults, affecting a person's marriageability or general reputation (Ocholla-Ayayo 1976, 66).

Finally, songs formed a critical aspect of Luo story telling and oral history. Every narrative had its accompanying song that punctuated the plot. Signature songs, as Onyango-Ogutu calls them, not only were helpful mnemonic devices but also had great emotional appeal: "The song can make more poignant a situation fraught with pathos; it can add spice and salt to a tale of merriment. The Luo *raconteur* knows well enough that music can leap the barrier of words and make a direct assault on the heart and senses" (Onyango-Ogutu and Roscoe 1974, 32).

These indigenous musical traditions have clearly shaped Roho singing. Songs performed during the *Sikukuu mar Rapar*, for example, contain elements of both signature and virtue singing. Referred to as "songs that tell the story" (*wende mag sigana*), these hymns transmit the fundamental drama of the *mach*. Like "signature" songs, the lyrics often make a direct appeal to emotions: "Oh! Oh! Terrible world! (*Uuwii! Uuwii! Piny lich!*) or "Horror! All our people are burning!" (*Wololoo! Yawa duto wang!*). At the same time, these songs glorify the virtues of Roho pioneers, employing *pakruok* conventions such as color codes to poetically convey an individual's special attributes. (See the Appendix to this volume.) Many story songs even conclude by praising current church leaders—male and female—for their generosity, kindness, goodness, and so on. Moreover, the individual worshiper's prerogative to jump up during a service and interrupt the speaker with a song glorifying God may derive from *pakruok* tradition. In *pakruok* practice, anyone could interrupt the harpist "in order to have his virtue-boasting heard" (Ocholla-Ayayo 1976, 45).

There is no categorical distinction between women's and men's songs in the Roho church. During church services, hymns are sung by the entire congregation. However, men tend to be more active in composing ballads and women tend to dominate in the so-called spiritual songs. For instance, men composed many of the *mach* story songs that I heard performed at the 1991 *Sikukuu mar Rapar* choir competition in Ruwe. These narrative songs, which draw so heavily on *pakruok* convention, may be a genre with which men are more comfortable. However, as I have stated, the distinction is not clear-cut. In Luo traditional culture, both sexes participated in *huwege* singing, and grandmothers, who told instructive stories in the *siwindhe* (girls' dormitory) at night, were as much masters of the signature songs as were men. According to Ocholla-Ayayo, Luo women did not have their own virtue names but boasted with their brothers', fathers', or (premarital) lovers' names (Ocholla-Ayayo 1976, 47). It appears that, as a rule, women did not participate as fully in *pakruok* as men. However, unmarried girls had their own musical tradition known as *oigo* singing, through which they could celebrate their qualities and individuality.

By at least the mid-1960s, *oigo* singing had died out. Henry Owuor Anyumba fortunately managed to collect a number of songs at that time from elderly

women who remembered them from their youth (Owuor Anyumba 1967, 50–
56). He states that the refrains of the songs have a high, repetitive, trilling quality,
like the chirping of the *oigo*[25] bird, for whom they are named. *Oigo* songs were
used in courting and conveyed a wide range of emotions from pride, to happiness, to melancholy. Girls would sing them as they walked together to the *simbas*
(bachelor huts) of their boyfriends and perform them at dances.

Owuor's description strongly suggests that certain aspects of the *oigo* tradition
may be very much alive in Roho women's singing of *wende mag Roho* (songs of
the Spirit). The sense of being controlled by a song emanating spontaneously
from within and the high pitch and rapid forcefulness with which a Roho female
cantor leads a "spiritual" hymn are consistent with *oigo* singing as Owuor
Anyumba characterizes it:

> The style of oigo singing is extremely distinctive. The singer trills in a bird-
> like voice and conveys an impression of being possessed by the stream of song
> within her, breathless and helpless. The emotions expressed are often sor-
> rowful and almost hysterical, yet the singer exults in her ability to sing
> endlessly like a bird. . . . [A girl's] singing is regarded as a good thing,
> especially when it is powerful—so that everybody can hear it—and persis-
> tent. As with a bird, singing appears to be the natural outpouring of the life
> force itself. The prestige of clan and family depended not only on the
> prowess of its young men but also on the zealous way in which its women
> represented its interests in song and dance. For a group of girls the oigo was a
> means of announcing their presence and of differentiating themselves from
> the older, married women; for an individual a way of expressing her idio-
> syncrasies. . . . The oigos are . . . more reflective and less excited than
> the insistent ree theme would suggest; they are simple, rather repetitive but
> nevertheless delightful tunes. (Owuor Anyumba 1967, 51)

The women who followed Mango and Lawi in the 1930s were primarily
young and unmarried. I have argued previously that, when these young women
marched over the countryside singing their crusading *askari* (soldier) hymns,
their expression was inspired both by *lang'o* ritual forms and by Christian revival-
ism. The *oigo* tradition—constituting part of a Luo woman's "cultural archive"
(Behrend 1990, 1)—may have been an influence as well. Roho oral history
documents the way in which women, in particular, announced their arrival in
new locales through song, much as girls used to announce their arrival at other
villages through loud *oigos*. Joroho see their hymns as direct, unexpected gifts
from heaven or the Spirit, not as pieces an individual intentionally composes.
Several women I knew recounted the experience of "being struck by the Holy
Spirit with a song." They woke up in the middle of the night singing something
they had never heard before. Much as *oigos* suggest the bubbling over of the life
force itself, Roho hymns convey the immanence of transcendent power.

Moreover, the older generation of Roho members tends to identify hymns by the names of their original "recipients," such as "Abisage's Song" or "Mariam's Song," a custom reminiscent of identifying a man by his virtue song or a girl by her favorite *oigo*. In the Mirunda branch of the Musanda Holy Ghost Church, two names are generally associated with Roho songs: that of the recipient and that of the heavenly bearer. For example, one hymn that children sang for me in 1990 in Mirunda was "brought" to Miriam Dibora Onyango in 1987 by the spirit of Elisha Otieno, who had died two years earlier. Members explained to me that when someone travels to heaven in a trance or is visited in a dream by an angel (the spirit of a relative or acquaintance), one is expected to "bring back something" from the encounter. One of the most convincing proofs of contact with heaven is music. As the closing verse of Otieno's hymn states: "The cassette recorders are playing sweet songs in heaven" (*Thumbe yuak giwer mamit ei polo*).

Culturally, the very act of singing with force and energy is a statement of collective power, women's pride, identity, and strength. The songs that Roho women receive from the Spirit are acknowledged even by outsiders to be characterized by particular beauty and poignancy. Although they attribute the origin of their music to the Spirit, women are nonetheless the special vehicles who allow others to hear the music of heaven. Through song and dance, they create an atmosphere conducive to ecstasy. Their music thus opens a channel of communication between the Spirit world and the gathering that facilitates the infusion of spiritual power into the community. It is no wonder that women resist male leaders' attempts to stifle or control their singing. Women seem to have no objection to pastors selecting the standard Christian hymns (*wende mag Nyasaye*) to be sung at the beginning of the service, but as the momentum of worship progresses, women consider it their prerogative to sing ecstatic songs (*wende mag Roho*) freely, as the Spirit moves them.

Given the Luo legacy of boasting contests carried out through song, Roho women have an opportunity during Roho festivals to articulate pride in themselves that they would not be able to do in everyday discourse. For example, one night during the 1991 *Sikukuu mar Rapar* celebrations in Ruwe, I witnessed a large group of women dance into Isaya Goro's compound beating drums and singing the refrain: "Women pray well, women pray better than [anyone else]" (*mon lamo berne, mon lamo berni*). They then laid greens and coins on the grave of Goro, singing their challenge louder and louder, before turning to dance their way to pay their respects elsewhere. Some Roho women clearly do think that they are more pious than many men and that their abilities to handle the Spirit surpass that of their male counterparts. Only through the lyrics of song, however, did I hear such sentiments clearly articulated collectively.

Other songs single out women as the primary bearers of religious power, keeping alive the memory of the part women played in establishing the Roho church. For instance, during the *Sikukuu mar Rapar*, a group of female elders was marching around the Roho churchyard, carrying sticks, and singing:

We are the children of the beginning of the power, (repeat)
(*Wan nyithind chakruok teko,*)

In Jesus' garden, all children are happy. (repeat)
(*E kombe mar Yesu, nyithindo duto mor.*)

Such lyrics, like those of the song "We are women of war, we are women of fire" (*Wan nyi kedo, wan nyi mach*), celebrate the historical role of Roho women as soldiers for the faith. Roho members do not distinguish between these hymns—what I would term "marching songs"—and other hymns inspired by the Spirit. However, the lyrics of the songs performed in drill formation are distinctive. They constitute a call to arms and contain images of battling for God, victory over opponents, and power. Roho missionaries sang these aggressive hymns while on the road and thus rendered their entrance into new communities more confident and impressive. Historically, we know, for example, that the Joroho used the hymn, "Stand up Christian, Look at Your Enemy" (*Chung'i Jakristo, Ne Jasiki Cha*) when embarking on proselytizing campaigns. Nereya Auma recalls that she, her mother, and two other women sang it when passing through Makalda Munyo on their way to Tanzania in 1966. It was this type of marching song that the Roho female *askeche* reportedly sang while drilling in Mango's compound in 1934. In the 1991 reenactment of the Musanda battle, the women soldiers sang these militant words "to encourage themselves" as they pretended to kill the Wanga warriors:

LEADER: Obworo, the lover of Mugunga,[26] wants some people to be killed.
(*JATELO: Obworo chot Mugunga dwa joma inego.*)

CHORUS: Someone bring me people to be killed so I can spear them.
(*JO-OLO: E ng'ato omiya joma inego atong'a.*)

As one stands watching these women miming acts of violence with mock weapons and listening to their aggressive songs, one is struck by the unusual overtones of their message, given the dominant Luo—and Roho—ideology, which casts women as quiescent. Through marching songs, Roho women envisage themselves as victorious warriors. These hymns convey an attitude of confident determination that is characteristic of Roho women's testimonies in general. The lyrics of their spiritual songs (*wende mag Roho*) tend to recapitulate other themes common to women's personal testimonies and conversion accounts. Consider the two beautiful hymns revealed to Abisage Muriro, "You Poor People" (*Un Jochan*) and "We Praise God's Love" (*Wapako Hera mar Nyasaye*). The first makes reference to the poverty many members endure and speaks of the inner transformation that the Roho faith can effect. The lyrics also carry a message of encouragement, stressing the need to persevere in prayer:

You poor people, don't stop saying the prayer that the Lord has left for you.
Don't grow tired, for even long ago [Jesus' disciples] did not accept his
    message.
Once [Roho] had come, we said the creed that changes the heart.
Let's sing that our helper has overcome death,
We too want to follow him with the everlasting power we have been given.

The remaining three verses develop the theological tenet of salvation through
Mango's death and mention the joy (*mor*) God has given his followers.[27] Muriro's
second hymn, "We Praise the Love of the Lord," contains the same salvational
theology. It stresses God's compassion, the unity of humanity, and, again, happiness in the Lord:

We praise God's love
For it unites people from all lands.
When he [Mango] comes we will proudly praise him,
The faithful followers of Israel.
When he returns we will rejoice, halleluia![28]

The theology conveyed in Muriro's hymns is indicative of Roho religion in
general. Her emphasis on love, unity, and perseverance, however, are somewhat
more characteristic of women's spirituality than that of men, which tends to
underscore truthfulness and productivity in the Lord. The hymn that angels
reportedly sang to Inondi and other women on their return from Musanda carries
the message of God's comfort, which is something women members, especially,
stress in their testimonies:

A person who trusts in one God
Will enter heaven with happiness,
And will remain there in heaven.
Even if you have no companions,
Don't think God isn't there.
He is near you and has not left you.[29]

Themes of comfort, divine love, God's concern for the poor, and the message
that we are all children of the Lord reappeared in the hymns women initiated
during the sabbath service at the 1991 *Sikukuu mar Rapar*. Hymns like "The
People of Odongo Are Working" and "Jesus Has Called You to Work for Him"
elaborated the view that religion is work, another notion women members frequently articulate.

Unfortunately, there are many Roho hymns whose origin will never be
known. Anna Inondi and her contemporaries could have named the original
bearers of most of these songs, but successive generations cannot. For today's
Roho members, the origin of all their music is the Holy Spirit. The identity of the

original human recipient is not very important; certainly, the gender of the bearer is not significant. Nevertheless, the few songs that we know to be composed by women and the hymns that women tend to select during the course of collective worship do appear to highlight those aspects of Roho spirituality and theology that women hold particularly dear.

To sum up, Roho women's hidden transcripts—or muted models of female assertiveness, power, and freedom—can be glimpsed in their songs. A theological perspective that takes God's love as its starting point, rejoices in Mango's salvational sacrifice, but also posits the need for people to persevere in doing God's work is expressed in these hymns. Women's foundational sense of themselves as strong spiritual and moral agents derives from a number of overlapping, highly expressive heritages, including virtue boasting, *oigo* singing, *lang'o*, and other *juogi* possession. Joroho reinterpreted these traditions in the light of charismatic Christianity and again in the light of the salvific Musanda event, which produced the model of the female soldier-martyr Turfosa Aloo.

In this mix of foundational influences, I wish to stress the importance of *lang'o* possession, at least for the older generation of Roho women. A form of ecstatic spirituality that has diminished in Luoland in recent decades, *lang'o* possession was still common in the 1950s, when today's elderly *laktache* were young women contributing to the genesis of Roho cultic practice. They were thus familiar with the *lang'o* prototype of a predominantly female cult, one in which women adepts outnumbered men by at least four to one (Owuor Anyumba [1954] 1971, 36). Henry Owuor Anyumba concludes that *lang'o* ceremonies made a twofold contribution to Luo society: (1) bringing the *juogi* nearer and (2) providing the community with the wonderful aesthetic experience of *lang'o* song and dance. With respect to the latter point, Owuor writes:

> I noticed that while the dances are going on a spectator becomes so much interested that he seems as if rooted to the ground; he is not aware of his neighbor, who is also abstracted. A similar effect is also seen in the dancers. They may dance for hours without stopping. It is not purely as a course of treatment that they do this. The expert does not compel any of them to dance; and also the non-jolango who may accompany an expert to the "return" ceremonies, also continue dancing, although they are not possessed. I think that it is the pleasure derived from the dance that makes them forget the time.
>
> This effect of the dance and song is not merely an attitude of the mind for in gracefulness and liveliness, and in the complete blending of the song and rhythm, I would consider the jalango dance as having no parallel in the Luo society. (Owuor Anyumba [1954] 1971, 40)

Founding Roho women clearly drew on the expressive musical tradition of *lang'o* and have preserved it within their church. Another legacy of *lang'o* practice that may have emboldened Roho women to express disaffection with existing hegemonies from time to time was the outspokenness of the *lang'o* "mother" or expert. Owuor Anyumba observes:

> We should also note that although the possessed person, sometimes tends to be rather imaginative and excitable, the speech of a jalango shows no sign of any kind of mental aberration. Their judgement is usually as sound as that of any ordinary person, and in some cases even better. Some of the experts that I interviewed, had a wonderful insight into human nature. This, plus a deep understanding of Luo customs (many of which are related to spirits in one way or another) makes a jalango a very logical critic of Luo affairs, and therefore very welcome in the society. ([1954] 1971, 41)

Again, Owuor's remarks can apply to many of the senior Roho *laktache* with whom I spoke.

Prophet Sarah and the Spirit Mother Church

Roho religion has afforded certain women an arena in which they have been able to influence people's lives profoundly. Although the process of institutionalization has gradually worked to "defeminize" authority in the Roho church, there is some evidence to suggest that the message of women's power has not been completely submerged. One phenomenon that I view as a surfacing of women's submerged charisma is the recent posthumous deification of Roho leader Sarah Agot of Mirunda, South Nyanza (1906–1986). Sarah Agot, who came to be known as Mama Jaote (Mother Prophet[30]) after her four-month stay in Musanda in 1935, attracted a large following during her lifetime. As indicated in chapter 3, she and her husband, Paul Odera, who had been a C.M.S. *padri*[31] before affiliating with the Musanda Holy Ghost Church, opened their home to the poor and the sick. Odera was even thrown in prison for allowing wives from other clans permanent refuge in his village, under the care of his wife.

According to local accounts, Sarah began showing signs of miraculous gifts as early as age two. Sarah's descendants have preserved a rich body of oral tradition that I did not have the opportunity to explore, yet I will mention two episodes in her life history that are critical to the way in which today's devotees interpret Prophet Sarah's mission on earth.

The first incident was a song Sarah received from the Holy Spirit shortly after Mango's death:

Yandi naselor Musanda, ere ng'ama mako wach?
I descended in Musanda, who is holding onto the word?

Kane mudho oimo piny duto, ere ng'ama yawo piny?
Darkness covered the whole world, who is lifting the darkness from the
    earth?

To Israel noyie an anyalo yawo piny.
And Israel consented, "I can open up/lift the darkness."

To ot noime malich, Yesu nobet gimor,
But the house covered him completely, Jesus rejoiced,

Teko duto mag polo noyiengini, atieko ruako osiepna,
The power of everything in heaven trembled, I welcomed my friend,

To ng'e uru gima nie piny, pinje duto magalo to gini yuag gi kanye,
But all you inhabitants of the earth should know, no part of heaven shall mourn,

To sulwe olwar Musanda, un nyithindo mor uru to piny otieko gik.
For a star has shone on Musanda, children rejoice, the world is coming to an end.

Agot, still an Anglican at the time, had not heard of Mango (Israel) or the massacre. The revelation of this song has thus been interpreted as her call to follow in Mango's footsteps. It grounds her firmly in his spiritual lineage; the same Spirit that descended in Musanda and empowered Mango made itself known directly to Sarah as well.

A later incident sets Sarah apart from her spiritual predecessors as the recipient of a subsequent, additional dispensation. This event reportedly occurred in November 1937. The Roho Mirunda community maintains that on the twenty-fifth of that month Jesus himself, accompanied by many angels, descended into the Odera compound and remained for twenty days, "teaching Sarah and the listeners hidden truths about God."[32] Many miracles and "wonders" reputedly took place during Jesus' visit, but most believers are reluctant to disclose these secrets to outsiders. However, a small contingent of Sarah's followers openly asserts that the truth Jesus revealed in Mirunda concerns Sarah's divine status:

> [Jesus] identified prophet Sarah saying she is the mother of all people and queen, forever separating her from her husband for life. He added that Sarah had been created from his own ribs by the father but that he himself had been created by the father from [the] father's ribs, being the first of all creations.[33]

This small segment of Agot's followers is led by Elijah J. O. Ayodo, a Luo man from Gem who joined the Musanda Holy Ghost Church in 1983 while working in Mombasa. Ayodo heard accounts of Sarah's amazing powers, so he traveled to Mirunda to see her himself. Over the course of several meetings with her, Ayodo began to view Sarah as a transcendent being. He came to believe that she was the Holy Spirit incarnate, come down to earth in her true feminine form. Through Sarah Agot, Ayodo and his supporters believe, the real nature of the Christian Trinity is finally made manifest: God the Father, Jesus the Son, and Sarah the

Mother Spirit. God's ultimate, complete manifestation in human form thus embraces both genders. Ayodo cites a multitude of biblical verses that, when deciphered according to his code, foretell God's final revelation in the person of Sarah Agot in South Nyanza. In explaining why God would choose to manifest himself through a woman, Ayodo refers to 1 Corinthians 1:27: "But God chose what is foolish in the world to shame the wise, God chose what is weak in the world to shame the strong." Ayodo elaborates:

> God does not want boasting. That is why he chose them [women] as his vessel. Women are low and hated for no reason. In fact they are good people. Very tender and good. But God chose them to be hated, because he hid in them. He didn't want people to see the brightness in women. He did this to shame the proud. [34]

In March 1990, authorities within the Musanda Holy Ghost Church rejected Ayodo's teachings about the divinity of Sarah and expelled him from the denomination. Ayodo therefore founded the Spirit Mother Church (S.M.C.) in Manyatta housing estate in Kisumu. In 1991, the church was still very small (no more than forty members) and was not registered with the government. It remains to be seen what will happen to the Spirit Mother Church if it survives. Ayodo, the current bishop, has voiced a preference for an organizational apparatus that promotes female leadership. He maintains that women are less biased in their interactions with others and thus make fairer leaders.

Conclusion: The Persistence of Awiti

How is one to interpret the deification of a female Roho prophet and the establishment of a church to glorify her? One could explain the Spirit Mother Church primarily in terms of the aspirations of Ayodo. One could interpret the S.M.C. as the attempt of a retired, lame railway worker to gain prestige by setting himself up as bishop of a fledgling congregation. A more generous view might even allow that Ayodo, clearly an individual with a passionate interest in religion and a dabbler in theology, established the S.M.C. as a way to pursue a lifelong avocation in his retirement. No doubt some such personal motivations are indeed at work. However, such an explanation ignores the factor of faith, the way in which Ayodo was moved by his encounters with Mama Jaote. He could easily have established his own branch on the basis of more egoistic criteria, yet it was his desire to bear witness to the divinity of Mama Jaote and his attempt to construct a theology congruent with that existential experience that prompted Ayodo's expulsion from the Musanda branch. Moreover, this belief that Sarah was the Holy Spirit incarnate does not seem to have originated with Ayodo. My understanding is that the notion has been circulating among those who knew Sarah for some time now, but that most have chosen to cultivate that belief privately rather than provoke a negative response from the Musanda Holy Ghost Church administration.

I would argue, alternatively, that the potential for a woman-centered charismatic theology has its roots in the *lang'o* cult tradition (and other *juogi* cults) as it has been reshaped by inspired Roho women. Although the autonomy of traditional female spirit possession and mediumship has gradually been stifled in the male-orchestrated process of institutionalization, the latent possibility for a resurgence of recognized female spiritual power remains, nonetheless, present. The discourse of contemporary Roho women, conflicted as it is, reflects the persistent strength of the model of the Roho *askari*, which in turn has roots in the model of the militant *Awiti nyar Lang'o*. Whether this model will become more muted over time or whether the experience of increasing gender subordination will cause women's hidden transcripts to achieve greater clarity until they erupt into the public domain remains to be seen. What is certain, however, is that, even in their silence, women see themselves as "the children of the beginning of the power." With this belief, they will never be thoroughly overwhelmed by conventions and institutional structures that privilege male authority.

CLOSING REMARKS

In August 1990, as our interview sessions were drawing to a close, Anna Inondi expressed relief. She was ill and had worried that she would die before leaving a record of "all that she had witnessed." Now, she remarked, her mind was spent and she felt free to "leave." Within a few weeks, Anna was bedridden, and in July 1991 she passed away.

As one of the last original Roho women soldiers, Inondi provided important information on the emergence of Holy Spirit religion in Ugenya. In three respects, her testimony, confirmed by the recollections of other church elders, provides a crucial counterweight to the record contained in colonial and missionary archives. First, the archival material depicts Roho "wenches" as ignorant and manipulated and thus fails to grasp the extent to which women were actively involved in the inception and survival of Roho religion. By giving Roho women pioneers names and identities, Inondi's account can be used to help produce a more balanced religious history of colonial Nyanza, a history that previously has featured almost exclusively men.

Second, the oral material presented in this study calls into question the usefulness of the dominant conceptual model of schism in understanding the emergence of independent churches in western Kenya. The schism model, as typically deployed in histories of East African independent churches, portrays mission churches as the repositories of normative Christianity. European missions are assumed to have set the standard, from which rebellious, innovative, African-led groups broke away. However, Roho elders' testimonies suggest that an already-indigenized charismatic Christianity, akin to that promulgated in grassroots Gandan "synagogi" in the late nineteenth century, had begun to take root in Nyanza well before European missionaries ever constituted a presence in the region. If there was any Christian norm in Nyanza during the first two decades of this century, it was this popular brand of indigenous Christianity. Indigenous charismatic Christianity developed alongside—and borrowed heavily from—*juogi* spirit possession. The many parallels between *lang'o* practice and that of the young, vow-taking Roho *askache* are but one example. In actuality, Christianity in rural Nyanza at this time was very open-ended, with few firm links to institutional hierarchies of any kind. I have argued that, in place of a model positing abrupt breaks and splits, we need a conceptual framework which accurately reflects the fluid character of Luo Christianity from 1900 through the 1950s.

The third important contribution that the testimony of Inondi and her Roho sisters makes to the historiography of religion in Nyanza concerns the wider issue of East African female spirit mediums and cultural change. Iris Berger has written on the predominance of women in spirit possession cults in the interlacustrine and Nyamwezi areas. She convincingly argues that the precolonial Cwezi, Emandwa, and Ryangombe cults, found in the Bantu cultural complex stretching from Buganda through Rwanda and Burundi to northwestern Tanzania, were all historically related (1976, 158). These cults had a number of deities in common and shared certain features, such as a focus on women's fertility, food taboos, esoteric languages, female itinerancy, and war regalia. All these aspects reappeared in the more militant spirit movements of the nineteenth century, like the Nyabingi cult. Female possession cults in the interlacustrine-Unyamwezi cultural complex, in fact, had strikingly similar counterparts among Nilotic societies to the east: the Acholi (Behrend 1990, 1991; Allen 1991; p'Bitek 1971, 106–120), Alur (Southall 1969), and Luo (Owuor Anyumba 1971, 1973, 1974; Whisson 1962; Stam 1910; Wipper 1977). Yet the possibility of religious interchange between these two large cultural regions has not been sufficiently explored. Tim Allen, building on parallels earlier noted by Aidan Southall, for example, has recently suggested that the Acholi Holy Spirit movement may have roots in Cwezi and other cults to the southwest (Allen 1991, 384). I would similarly like to underscore the need for scholars to position cults such as *lang'o* or Roho within the larger context of women's spirit mediumship in East Africa. In other words, we must extend our conceptual frameworks beyond ethnically defined regions or complexes.[1]

In addition, Anna Inondi's testimony and that of other Roho elders provide ample evidence of increasing marginalization of women within the church—a pattern that may be manifeseted in religious movements elsewhere in Africa. After Mango's death, Roho women exercised a great deal of freedom in the leadership roles they assumed. They founded congregations, served as pastors, and integrated older forms of female spiritual adepthood into their various ministries. In the 1960s, as we have seen, the confluence of a number of wider social, political, and economic trends made leadership positions within independent churches increasingly attractive and beneficial to literate Luo men. During this period, a process of state-prompted institutionalization was initiated, a process that privileged male authority and relegated women to limited, subordinate roles. The impact of Western-style institutionalization on Roho women was reinforced by a parallel process of indigenous routinization according to dominant Luo gender norms. In this latter process, women's autonomous ecstatic practices were all subsumed and "tamed" within the single role of the elderly healer (*laktar*), a contemporary version of the grandmotherly educator, or *pim*.

My findings on Roho religion span only sixty years or so, and the geographical scope of this study is, admittedly, microcosmic. The Roho church is a relatively small sect whose denominational reach has not extended much beyond the Luo

populations in Kenya, Uganda, and Tanzania. Yet, its pattern of institutionalization and the stifling impact this process has had on women's leadership appears
not to be unique.[2] I have attempted to point to a web of interconnections between
Roho religion and other indigenous, regional, and national movements. How
widely my defeminization model can be applied remains to be seen. It appears to
be illustrative of what has taken place within the Luo-based Legio Maria church,
in which women, until the late 1960s, said mass and administered the sacraments
but are now barred from doing so (Schwartz 1989, 65). In chapter 3, I listed
several other African independent churches whose histories, on the surface,
appear to suggest a gradual divestiture of women's authority over time, but each
case must be studied in its own context.[3] At the very least, the evidence gleaned
from discussions with elderly Roho women forces us to entertain the possibility
that the "ceremonial" character of female leadership in contemporary African
independent churches is not preordained. Such gender roles are not necessarily
intrinsic to the character of African spirituality but may, in fact, be the result of
identifiable historical factors and processes.

Finally, the testimony of Anna Inondi and her Roho sisters raises at once the
most difficult and most important issues facing the student of spirit possession: the
question of motivation. An exploration of this issue properly begins with
I. M. Lewis's work on women's ecstatic cults. In the mid-1960s Lewis's research
on the *zar* cult led him to develop his now classic theory of relative deprivation,
which he expounded in his 1966 article, "Spirit Possession and Deprivation
Cults" and his 1971 book, *Ecstatic Religion*. Lewis drew a distinction between
what he saw as a given society's "central morality code/cult" (generally controlled
by men) and its "peripheral" spirit possession cults. The former reinforced the
status quo, whereas the latter offered women—and other deprived individuals—a
means to manipulate oppressive situations to their advantage. A number of
subsequent studies of female spirit possession and mediumship in Africa have
developed variations of Lewis's basic utilitarian theory. In these works, women
are not necessarily seen to use spirit possession as leverage in their "sex war" with
men (Lewis 1966) but rather to gain advantage in struggles with other women
(Wilson 1967) or to achieve greater status and prestige generally (Berger 1976).

In the last decade, the sociological deprivation model has received increasing
criticism from scholars, primarily anthropologists, who call for a more nuanced,
multifaceted approach to possession.[4]

Susan Reynolds Whyte, for example, has pointed out that Lewis's designation
"peripheral" is biased, obscuring the fact that, from the perspective of women in
societies where possession cults are found, spirit religion is, in fact, central (1983,
181). Janice Boddy, in her eloquent interpretation of the *zar* cult in northern
Sudan, faults Lewis's deprivation hypothesis for its narrowness:

> Even granting that status may be a consideration in certain episodes of
> possession illness, the sociological argument cannot account for the *zar* in

its entirety. It glosses over the issue of belief and is therefore unable to explain or interpret possession forms (for example, the characteristics of spirits, and the nature and variety of possession symptoms) and processes (such as the reevaluation of one's past that acquiring a spirit entails). Such factors, however important to the possessed, are implicitly deemed incidental when the investigator's focus is competition. The social status model is unidimensional, at once too general in application and too narrow in concern to deal adequately with the complexities of *zar*. (1989, 139)

Boddy emphasizes both the expressive or "articulatory potential" of *zar* possession and its experiential aspect, which frees the imagination from "the fetters of hegemonic cultural constructs" and encourages transformative self-reflection (1989, 353–356). Boddy's interpretation thus builds on Vincent Crapanzano's notion of possession as a "cultural idiom" for articulating or rendering a "certain range of experience" meaningful (Crapanzano and Garrison 1977, 10). This range of experience can entail altered states of consciousness or the cathartic projection of emotions and needs, but the emphasis in the idiom model is always on the meaning that different cultures attach to these experiences. In Boddy's work, like that of Obeyesekere (1977) and Crapanzano and Garrison (1977), there is a recognition that possession experience can function as a kind of dynamic therapy, enabling the individual to realize a more fully integrated self. As such, Nils Holm has aptly characterized Crapanzano and the other authors represented in his collection as combining "a modified depth-psychology interpretation of possession with a social anthropological approach" (Holm 1981, 17).

Like Boddy, I have acknowledged a variety of dynamics at work in Roho religion. Indeed, women's testimonies make clear that what impels them to pursue the Roho life and the meaning they find therein are by no means uniform. I have acknowledged that by joining the Roho movement—particularly during the early period—women were able to achieve autonomy and mobility and to exercise leadership generally denied them in Luo society at that time. In later periods, emotional or psychological comfort offered by the Roho community, not to mention access to healing therapies, attracted others to the church. Ecstatic release and the joy and pride of self-expression through singing and dancing are clearly appealing elements of Roho religion for participants. None of these factors—or even all of them taken together—can, to my mind, however, offer a satisfactory explanation of women's involvement.

Any multidimensional approach to cultural phenomena ultimately emphasizes some aspects over others. Throughout this study, I have chosen to underscore the element of faith or religious commitment. To my mind, this factor offers us the best key for unlocking the dynamic character of Roho women's lives. It is women's faith in the Holy Spirit's special relationship with Mango's community, faith in their own identity as inheritor's of Turfosa Aloo's bravery, and faith in God's love that gives meaning to their experiences of being "in the power."

Moreover, I have argued that the benefits women gained through affiliation with the Roho movement were, in many instances, counterbalanced by resulting hardships and that it was the resiliency of members' faith that enabled the church to survive difficult times. Academic studies of religious movements in Africa frequently overlook this factor of personal religious commitment, yet this component, with its inherent directedness, above all else accounts for Roho women's continued membership.

I have also argued that the energy Luo women devote to ecstatic religions such as Roho derives, in part, from the legacy of spirit possession practice, which in traditional culture was primarily a female undertaking. Thus, we find that women's deeper identities are bound up in the symbol clusters of *juogi* possession, which female Joroho have, in turn, adapted and developed within their church. Given that Roho religion provides an arena in which women have managed to keep alive their integrity as spiritual agents, it is also a likely repository for women's "muted models" and "hidden transcripts" (S. Ardener 1975; Scott 1990). As male officials seek to place increasing constraints on Roho women's religious expression, it may well be that the latter's latent assertiveness will eventually erupt into the public domain. The future, of course, has yet to unfold. One can be sure, however, that Roho women will continue to take pride in themselves and find fulfillment as participants in Mango's *singruok* (covenant) and as upholders of his code.

This study should be taken as part of a more general argument for the role of religious experience and belief as a motivating force behind people's individual and collective actions. Through this glimpse into Roho women's lives and words, I hope the reader will be persuaded as to the depth of their commitment to "live in the Spirit." As Drid Williams remarked in her study of British Carmelite nuns, "Can they really be explained adequately under the rubric of generalizations about social phenomena such as struggle against the natural environment, or individual biological survival, economic deprivation, frustration, repression, and so on?" (1975, 123). Material interests, struggles against inequalities, and escape from the alienating weight of daily routines cannot explain the essence of the Roho movement. Faith goes beyond such significant secular realities. Whether it sustains contemplatives in their search for the infinite God or emboldens village women to spread the healing power of the Spirit, faith motivates souls and shapes human practice, to which it gives meaning, hope, and transcendence.

APPENDIX

A Roho Ballad (*Wer Sigana*)

Sung by the Arum church choir from Kapisul, Abach, during the *Sikukuu mar Rapar*, January 21, 1991.

JO-OLO:
We mondo ang'isu da uling' thi ka iparo jalamo,
Odongo nokelo Roho, ma JaMusanda kawango owang'o. (repeat)
Wiu kirwil, wadwa paro Mango, Odongo jakonywa,
Gima pod wawuoro ni Lawi Obonyo rateng'[a] onindo. (repeat)
CHORUS:
Let me tell you, you should be quiet as you remember the faithful,
Odongo brought the Spirit, the man from Musanda was burnt by the
    Wanga. (repeat)
Do not forget, we want to remember Mango, our helper,
And what causes us to wonder is that Lawi Obonyo, the dark/black one, died
    [lit., sleeps]. (repeat)

JAKWANO:
Yaye Odongo Mango
SOLOIST:
Oh, Odongo Mango
JO-OLO:
Odongo Mango JaMusanda ne okelo Roho,
Ndalo mochwere ma ne okwong nyuol kuom Joluo. (repeat)
CHORUS:
Odongo Mango, man from Musanda, brought the Spirit,
The everlasting, which first appeared [lit., was born] among the Luos.
    (repeat)

JAKWANO:
Isaya oyoro
SOLOIST:
Isaya made his way through

a. According to traditional *pakruok* (virtue boasting) convention, *rateng'* (black) symbolizes bravery (Ocholla-Ayayo 1976, 47).

211

JO-OLO:
Isaya oyore thimbe madongo motamo wang' ji,
Wathagore ma nyaka namba oromo pinywa. (repeat)
CHORUS:
Isaya made his way through wildernesses that had overwhelmed others,
We struggled until the emblem [S †] filled our country. (repeat)

JAKWANO:
Turfosa Aloo
SOLOIST:
Turfosa Aloo

JO-OLO:
Turfosa Aloo, koda Persila ne oting'o tonge,
Mi gikedo lweny ma iro odum to mach bende liel. (repeat)
CHORUS:
Turfosa Aloo, along with Persila, carried spears,
Then they fought the battle; the smoke billowed and the fire blazed. (repeat)

JAKWANO:
Oloo, wuon Awuor
SOLOIST:
Oloo, father of Awuor

JO-OLO:
Oloo, wuon Awuor, ne gikelo Roho kuom jarateng' to piny ne ok oyie,
Omiyo jogo owang'e kendo ne giyiko Odongo Kakamega. (repeat)
CHORUS:
Oloo, father of Awuor, they brought the Spirit among the blacks, but the
    country did not accept it,
Therefore those people burnt him, moreover, they buried Odongo in
    Kakamega. (repeat)

JAKWANO:
Nyithiwa
SOLOIST:
Our children

JO-OLO:
Nyithiwa, paruru Oktoba e wang'e hik piero aboro
Barnaba bende owewa; wana chom kure ka jogo oduogo? (repeat)
CHORUS:
Our children, remember it was the month of October exactly, in the year
    [19]80,
When Barnaba left us. Now where shall we turn if those people [i.e., the
    enemy] come back? (repeat)

JAKWANO:
Pate wa duto

SOLOIST:

All our pastors

JO-OLO:

Pate wa duto notimo neno kar adiera,

Laktare duto notimo neno ma wawinjo te: (repeat)

Kweri ma wuod Aringo; Okiri ma wuodi Goyo; Omunga ma wuodi Asiso; Ndolo Matthayo ne ni kanyo; Hundho Kojowa Ree; Odiero min Musa be onindo. (repeat)

CHORUS:

All our pastors have borne witness to the whole truth,

All doctors have borne witness such that we have heard it all: (repeat)

Kweri, son of Aringo; Okiri, son of Goyo; Omunga, son of Asiso; Nodlo Mathayo was there; Hundha, from the home of Ojowa "Ree"; Odiero, mother of Musa, died as well. (repeat)

NOTES

Introduction

1. Ojolla mission, located fifteen miles northeast of Kisumu, was established in 1906 by a Mill Hill priest named Grimshaw. The site, at an elevation of approximately 4,200 feet, was chosen in hopes that its climate would prove healthier for European missionaries than the "pestilentious" port of Kisumu (Burgman 1990, 33).

2. See Whisson 1962, 3–8, for more information on varieties of Luo spirits.

3. *Juok nam* (lake spirits), *juok Mumbo* (spirits of the huge serpent Mumbo), and *juok yie* (canoe spirits) are examples of common "free" powers—that is, spirits that are not circumscribed by lineage and can strike anyone.

4. Henry Owuor Anyumba's writings should be consulted for information on the particular possession symptoms and cultic practices associated with various *juogi* ([1954] 1971, 1973, 1974).

5. As of 1972, 89 percent of Luos were Christian (Barrett 1982, 434).

6. See chapter 1, note 1.

7. The Holy Spirit Church of East Africa (H.S.C.E.A.) is a Luyia-based denomination that evolved from a 1927 revival within the Friends mission at Kaimosi, led by Yakobo Buluku (Anderson 1971, 14–19).

8. In remarks delivered at a Comparative Studies in Religion panel at the American Academy of Religion meeting in San Francisco in November 1992, Karen McCarthy Brown argued that adopting neutrality—*epoche*—is fine when analyzing religious texts. However, when dealing with people, *epoche* is, in fact, "passive-aggressive." Brown emphasized the need for trustworthiness when studying other people's religions and cultures. She pointed out that trustworthiness sometimes entailed financial assistance, although this fact is not talked about enough by fieldworkers. See also her remarks on her longtime friendship with Vodou priestess Alourdes (Mama Lola) (Brown 1991, 1–20).

9. This term is borrowed from the title of Godfrey Lienhardt's festschrift volume, edited by Wendy James and Douglas H. Johnson (1988).

Chapter 1

1. Accurate statistics on participation in independent churches are very difficult to come by. Zadock Ochoma, the general secretary of the Ruwe Holy Ghost Church, explained that their annual report of 1989 documented a total membership of forty-six thousand. At that time, the denomination comprised three hundred sixty-two churches or "worship centers," but within a year ten new congregations had already been added. The size of these local congregations fluctuates from year to year, and many do not keep up-to-date rolls. The majority of the Ruwe Holy Ghost congregations are in Kenya; approximately thirty are in Tanzania, and ten are in Uganda. Vastly different

figures appear in Barrett's *World Christian Encyclopedia* (1982, 436), which lists the Ruwe and Musanda denominations as having five thousand members each, and the Cross Church claiming fifteen thousand. Unfortunately, I could not obtain statistics on the latter two denominations myself, but Barrett's figures nevertheless seem unduly low. For one thing, Barrett does not mention Roho congregations outside Kenya, yet all three denominations have active communities among the Ugandan and Tanzanian Luo. In the late 1960s, Perrin Jassy identified between ten to seventeen Musanda Holy Ghost congregations in the Tanzanian district of North Mara alone, as well as six to seventeen affiliated with the Holy Cross branch (or Roho Musalaba) (1973, 97). By contrast, Ochoma's membership figures appear to be inflated. Because each of the three hundred sixty-two churches on his list can actually be located, and because roughly 75 percent of the Roho worship services I attended had between thirty and sixty people present, I would offer, instead, the extremely rough estimate of between sixteen and twenty thousand active members belonging to the Ruwe Holy Ghost Church. The Musanda branch is, at this point, less well organized and smaller, whereas Roho Musulaba (based in Kabondo) is reputedly larger than the other two. We may conclude that the people involved in the three main denominations linked to Mango's Roho movement number somewhere between fifty and seventy-five thousand. This figure does not include, however, the membership of many smaller, unregistered Roho churches such as Roho Fweny, whose sizes are impossible to estimate without further fieldwork.

2. *Sikukuu* is a Swahili word that has gained wide currency throughout Kenya even in places where Swahili is rarely spoken. *Sikukuu* (*Siku* means "day"; *kuu* means "major" or "big") connotes a holiday or festival that occurs at the same time every year. The phrase *mar rapar* is Dholuo, meaning, literally, "for remembrance."

3. While conducting research among members of the Ruwe Holy Ghost Church, I was frequently urged to attend the reenactment of the Musanda fire so that I could see "how it really happened." It was, indeed, during the *Sikukuu mar Rapar* that I was struck by how well established the oral tradition had become. For example, when distributing written copies of the report I had compiled, one middle-aged member (someone too young to have been an "eyewitness" in 1934) told me that I had "left out a certain part" about the smoke billowing "like a snake" out of Mango's house. In addition, when the news circulated that I was recording the history of the church, one young man from Manyatta parish in Kisumu town presented me with his own hand-written version of the sequence of events, including a profile of all the Roho "pioneers." His brief account is on the whole consistent with the information I had received from my main informant, Anna Inondi, an elderly women who had joined Mango's movement in the early 1930s. A less detailed, but again quite consistent handwritten history was given to me by a young man from South Nyanza who had recorded the words of his grandmother, once an active Roho member. Finally, General Secretary Zadock Ochoma provided me with his own written version of Roho church history.

4. During the colonial period, Kenya was divided into provinces which were, in turn, subdivided into administrative districts, locations, and sublocations. Although in many instances the boundaries have been redrawn, this basic territorial organization remains.

5. KNA (Kenya National Archives). DC/NN10/1/1: Acting Provincial Commissioner to District Commissioner, April 8, 1931; ibid., April 21, 1931; Ogot 1971, 97.

6. E. S. Atieno-Odhiambo (1973, 8) succinctly describes how Owen attacked the

"audacity" of other missionaries who presumed to speak on behalf of Africans, while he at the same time "translated himself into the native's *alter ego.*"

7. KNA. DC/NN10/1/1: To the district commissioner of North Kavirondo from Owen, A. E. Pleydell and A. J. Leach, n.d.

8. CMSA (Church Missionary Society Archives). (G3A5/O 1933/#178) Original Papers, Owen to Pitt Pitts, October 25, 1933.

9. KNA. DC/NN10/1/1: To Colonel Anderson, district commissioner January 1934. The "agreement" mentioned refers to a document signed by Mango and four other Kager in which they promised to abide by certain rules established by the Wanga authorities. These rules included Mango's individual promise "to confine himself entirely to Church and other work connected with his calling as given him by Archdeacon Owen and the Bishop" (KNA. DC/NN10/1/1: one-page agreement, 10 April 1933). It is this rule—which is actually no. 3, not no. 4—that Owen cites.

10. Ibid.

11. KNA. MSS/21/1: Owen Papers (M937/Box 1, Acc 8301–8301/5), letter to Pitt Pitts, February 1, 1934. In the conclusion of this lengthy letter, Owen recapitulates his impression of Mango's political motives: "I think that there can be no doubt that underlying the apparently purely religious character of this movement there was a desire on the part of Alufayo and Lawi to strengthen their position in Bantu territory."

12. CMSA. Original Papers (G3/A5/O 1933/#178), Owen to Pitt Pitts, October 25, 1933.

13. Atieno-Odhiambo prints a portrait of Owen as preoccupied with maintaining "his" natives' devotion and confidence (1973, 7–8).

14. KNA. DC/NN10/1/1: "Report on the Disturbances at Musanda in Wanga," by district officer, Captain Hislop, February 9, 1934, p. 5; see also letter cited in note 7, p. 2; and letter cited in note 8, pp. 3, 10.

15. CMSA. Owen to Pitt Pitts, October 25, 1933.

16. Ibid.

17. Ibid.

18. Strayer documents how East African missionaries in the early 1900s frequently discouraged the education of African women and girls (1978, 81–91). See also Stock (1899, 367–369).

19. The apprehension that wives and family life would distract men from mission duties was reflected in C.M.S. policy regarding married couples. In the 1870s, married people were not admitted to the society's missionary training program; C.M.S.-trained missionaries were supposed to go into the field single. (University graduates and others who were accepted for immediate service were exempt from the rule.) After a year, if society-trained volunteers chose to marry, they were permitted to do so, and their wives could join them. In 1889 this rule was made even more stringent to the effect that all volunteers—university graduates included—had to serve a minimum of three years in the field before getting married. That way, a man would know the rigors of missionary life and would better be able to determine whether his fiancée possessed the "spiritual and missionary qualifications" necessary to undertake such a life (Stock 1899, 356). Yet, for several decades, the belief that single men make the most effective missionaries prevailed. Beidelman suggests this attitude was largely due to the fact that the presence of wives and children violated missionaries' romantic visions of their exciting crusade in the Dark Continent, much as "women threatened American men's enchantment with the early frontier" (Beidelman 1982, 12–13). For another example of missionary feelings about the negative impact of wives on East African mission stations, see Greaves 1969, 29.

20. For example, Archdeacon Owen objected to female representation on African church councils, calling instead for "separate men's and women's councils, with the former having the final say" (Strayer 1978, 81). One legacy of this segregationist pattern of mission church governance has been the persistence of mothers' unions—or comparable women's groups—in many Kenyan independent churches today and the continued exclusion of women from important administrative councils.

21. On the alleged "communal enjoyment of women" in Mumboism, see Wipper 1977, 54; Nyangweso 1930, 14. On the reported "sexual perversions" of men and "luscious young girls" involved in Ishmael Noo's Anglican revival movement, see Welbourn and Ogot 1966, 30–32.

22. See A. M. Elverson, *A Cast-Away in Kavirondo* (London: Church Missionary Society, 1920), a little propaganda book condemning the horrors of a Luo girl's life and appealing to ladies in England for help in the missionary effort.

23. At one meeting, for example, Owen called on male Christians to lend their wives more assistance in household chores, at least on Sunday. According to his own report, "One man got up and voiced the feeling of the men saying, 'We have had to pay cattle for our wives, why should we help them?'" (Richards 1947, 32).

24. See KNA MSS/21/1: Owen Papers (M937/Box 1, Acc 8301–8301/5), memo on forced labor dated December 24, 1920, and letter addressed to "Arthur" dated December 5, 1923. See also Rev. H.D. Hooper's memo, April 29, 1921.

25. Spirits are traditionally believed to hover in the corners of roofs.

26. Traditionally, the chest (*kor*) was believed to be a favorite seat of possessing *juogi* (Owuor Anyumba [1954] 1971, 10). For a discussion of the various "body areas" of Legio Maria members affected by spirits, including the Holy Spirit, see Nancy Schwartz 1989, 231–234.

27. Mango's son Ibrahim, bishop of the Musanda Holy Ghost Church, contests the claim that the Spirit entered Ruwe before it possessed Mango. Alfayo Odongo Mango is, indeed, seen by many believers as God's special messenger—the very first to bring the Spirit to Africans. Regional and denominational rivalry may also be at play here. Bishop Ibrahim O. Mango wrote: "I do not have anything to say on the Holy Spirit first appearing in Ruwe in 1912 as I have not heard of it. If there was anything at all at that time then it must have been people converting to Christianity—Not [the] Holy Spirit" (personal correspondence February 13, 1991).

28. Marching in drill formation is common in many independent churches in western Kenya. A number of Kenyans have suggested to me that this widespread practice is a legacy of Salvation Army influence. The paramilitary rituals of the Salvation Army were, indeed, very popular—particularly in Luyia country—and no doubt did influence the evolution of Christian ritual in that region. However, the Salvation Army did not enter Kenya until 1921 (Barrett et al. 1973, 249). The use of militaristic hymns and slogans had been adopted by some early Anglican congregations at least a decade earlier.

29. In 1902, Nyanza became part of the Kenya Protectorate (established in 1895). The Anglican missions in that region, however, remained within the Ugandan diocese until 1921, when they were transferred to the diocese of Mombasa. Some historians have argued that the liberal policies of the Uganda diocese, coupled with Kavirondo's distance from Mengo, the diocesan headquarters, contributed to the early emergence of independent Christianity in the region (see Welbourn and Ogot 1966, 21–24).

30. Stock 1899, 453; Pirouet 1978, 25.

31. Ibrahim Owuor Mango, personal interview, July 17, 1990.

32. For an overview of the Kager clan's unsuccessful attempts from 1913 to 1917 to get the boundary changed, see Ogot 1971, 97–98 and Nundu 1982.

33. KNA. DC/NN3/2/18: "Notes on a Baraza held at Matungu on 13-12-31." Chief Mulama recalls the establishment of the South Ugenya–Buholo boundary by Spencer. In the same file, see Spencer's handwritten letter to Colonel Anderson (dated January 30, 1932) on the subject.

34. Spencer's letter of January 30, 1932.

35. Haggai Nundu sets Mango's year of birth at 1890 (1982, 24). However, 1884 was the date given by the Ruwe church elders and was not contested by Mango's son, so it is the one I have used here.

36. KNA. MSS/21/1: Owen Papers (M937/Box 1, Acc 8301–8301/5), letter to Colonel Anderson, November 20, 1931.

37. It is highly unusual and, as Ogot acknowledges, "contrary to Luo custom," for a man to take his brother's wife while the latter is still living. Moreover, what is even more difficult to understand is that Mango reportedly "took the matter somewhat lightly." None of my informants mentioned this event to me, nor did I ask Bishop Ibrahim Mango about it directly.

38. Abigael Atieno died in the late 1960s; Salome Ndiany and Fibbi Adhiambo are both married and living in Seme; Jacob Konya, the eldest son, passed away in the early 1970s. As Ogot points out, both of Mango's sons were public figures in Kenya. Jacob Konya was the first African to become assistant superintendent of the Railway Training School in Nairobi and the first African to serve on the Kitale Municipal Board as director of social services. Ibrahim Owuor worked with the East African Railways, was active in the trade union movement, and served as president of the Kenya Federation of Labor (Ogot 1971, 110). In his retirement, Ibrahim Owour Mango has returned to Musanda and is currently the bishop of the Musanda Holy Ghost Church.

39. H. R. Mudany, "Rev. Alfayo Odongo Mango." I was unsuccessful in obtaining this paper.

40. Mango's physiological response to seeing the Christian books for the first time is entirely in keeping with Luo cultic forms of the eighteenth and nineteenth century. Illness, epileptic seizures, stomach pains, and temporary insanity are all standard features of an individual's initial reaction to a supernatural entity that will later claim that person in some way. Mediums or healers generally underwent such physical stress just prior to their initiation into the cult of a particular deity. See Owuor Anyumba 1973, 1974, Abe 1978, and Whisson 1962, 12–13.

41. Ruwe elders claimed that the mud church was constructed in 1914. Mango's son set the date later, at 1918. A more likely date is 1912 because the Reverend Walter Chadwick, who arrived at Butere in that year, was the one to notice Mango's initiative and send him to school at Maseno in 1913. A point on which all my sources agree is that Mango's thatched church was later burnt by the Wanga, and he was encouraged by the missionaries to replace it with a brick one. Thus, according to Bishop Ibrahim Mango, his father erected a permanent church on the same site in 1928. The brick foundation was still visible at the base of St. Paul's church in 1991.

42. Ibrahim Owuor Mango made a sharp distinction between Butere, which was "the main center for Anglican missionaries," and Maseno, which was a "school for education, not for missionaries." As we have seen, Butere became a mission site in 1912, when "the Uganda C.M.S. accepted the request of the Kenya Government to open a school and mission for the 'Bantu Kavirondo'" by sending Walter Chadwick and several Baganda assistants (Ogot 1971, 93). For Luo Anglicans living in Wanga,

Buholo, and Marama, their pastorate headquarters was Butere—in the heart of Wanga country. Yet, according to Ibrahim Owuor Mango, they were frequently sent to Maseno to obtain their education with other Luos. Maseno, the oldest C.M.S. station in Nyanza, was the pastorate headquarters for the "Nilotic Kavirondo," or Luos.

43. It should be noted that Roho elders such as Inondi still recall the names—and often the personalities—of the Anglican missionaries to Nyanza during the colonial period. They are remembered as teachers, superiors, and adversaries with whom Mango dealt. Inondi remembers Chadwick as the missionary in charge when Mango first began praying with people under trees and in the thatched church. Mango's son recalled that Pleydell baptized his father at Maseno. (Pleydell was nicknamed Orengo by the local community because he always carried a fly whisk [*orengo*] with him wherever he went. This fact also appears in Ogot 1971, 94 and Nundu 1982, 24). It is remembered that Chadwick was killed in the war (he "had been taken to go pray for the soldiers") and that Bwana Leech (known as Alich or Alichi by Luos) was in charge of Butere pastorate when Mango constructed the permanent brick church. In fact, it was Leech who encouraged him to use brick, after the original building had been burned down. Anna Inondi explained that at the time Leech was pastor in Butere, Archdeacon Owen was in Maseno. When asked whether she knew who the bishop (who resided in Uganda) was, she replied, "In those days we did not know. We only knew our archdeacon, because the bishops' names were difficult to remember" (*Ndalono nene pok wakia. Ndalo cha nene achidcon ema wa thoro ng'eyo ahinya nikech bishope go bende nyinge gi nene tek mako*). The bishops were merely names to people. In some of the accounts given by second- and third-generation Roho members, the white players in the story are confused; in one instance, Owen becomes the district comissioner, for example.

44. My informants indicated that the congregation in Alego Nyadhi was one of the "twelve small churches" Mango was in charge of as a catechist.

45. Many rural Kenyan churches lack benches. When chairs are present, they are generally used by the men. Women are expected to bring mats to sit on.

46. *Gitin'gore malo* (They held themselves above) was the phrase used.

47. The Spirit's promise to Mango to return constitutes a well-known segment of oral tradition. Roho members tend to put this promise into their own words. For example, a middle-aged Roho pastor at Ruwe named Daniel Were phrased it thus: "I have come to visit you but have found that you are not yet mature. You cannot take care of the sheep properly. You cannot make people's hearts/souls well. I am going, but I'll return. (*Abiro limi to anuango kapod iyom. Ok inyal rito romena maber, pod ok du los chuny ji maber. Adhi to anachakaduogi.*) Note that Were's version places the emphasis on Mango's immaturity, whereas Inondi's statement stresses the immaturity of his followers. Were interjected the thought that the Spirit spoke these words to Mango during his initial vision in Alego. He prefaced these words of Mango's by saying, "There is also a place where it said" (*bende nitie kama nene owachne*), indicating that he was sure of the statement but did not know exactly where it occurs in the narrative. I have stuck with Inondi's sequence because she was actually present in Alego at the time.

48. Presumably Mango was leery of provoking the kind of animosity Ibrahim Osodo and his group had experienced at Ruwe.

49. KNA. MSS/21/1: Owen Papers (M937/Box 1, Acc 8301–8301/5), letter to Pitt Pitts, February 1, 1934.

50. Even today, this is a common sermon theme at funerals. There is still a tendency in many rural Luo communities to attribute death to malicious intent,

primarily witchcraft. People thus continue to remind each other that this cannot be the case, for death is natural.

51. Ibrahim Owuor Mango, personal communication, February 13, 1991.

52. Letter to Pitt Pitts, February 1, 1934.

53. B. A. Ogot (1971, 100) places the Evison affair in 1932. According to archival records, the hiring of Evison occurred in 1931 and was a primary cause for Mango's eviction in April 1932.

54. Katar Singh, the truck driver employed to transport Evison and the elders to the boundary, subsequently reported the meeting to local authorities (KNA. DC/NN10/1/1).

55. KNA. DC/NN10/1/1: Acting provincial commissioner to the district commissioner, April 8, 1931 (ref. no. NZA/LND. 2/2/2/3/4).

56. KNA. DC/NN10/1/1: Acting provincial commissioner to the district commissioner, April 21, 1931 (ref. no. LND. 2/2/2/3–7).

57. KNA. DC/NN10/1/1: Handwritten memo from Thompson (provincial commissioner) to Anderson (district commissioner), September 21, 1931.

58. KNA. DC/NN10/1/1: District commissioner to the acting provincial commissioner, April 24, 1931 (ref. no. 899/LND. 13/3).

59. See note 57.

60. Canon Leech was the missionary who took charge of Butere in 1921 when Owen moved to Maseno. Ogot describes Leech as "a sensitive and eccentric cleric who shunned politics and public affairs." He spoke Dholuo and was generally well liked by the Luo community in North Nyanza (Ogot 1971, 98).

61. KNA. DC/NN10/1/1: District commissioner to Leech, April 24, 1931 (ref. no. 905/MISS. 20/7).

62. KNA. MSS/21/1: Owen Papers (M937/Box 1, Acc 8301–8301-5), letter to District Commissioner Colonel Anderson, November 20, 1931. See also Owen's recommendations to the Land Enquiry Commission, September 2, on the same microfilm.

63. The Kager were willing to grant that some of the land they inhabited was Wanga land. A memo in February 1932 states: "The Kager admit that their people living in Manga and Butere areas are tenants (jobedo) but they insist that those living under Osundwa in the localities of Lisaya Musanda, Lihonji, Madungu and Tingari are the rightful owners" (KNA. DC/NN10/1/1: Provincial commissioner to the district commissioner, ref. no. LND. 2/2/2/3/23).

64. KNA. DC/NN10/1/1: The district commissioner to the provincial commissioner, February 10, 1932 (ref. no. 128/LND. 13/3/A).

65. KNA. DC/NN3/2/18: Notes on the Baraza held at Matungu on December 13, 1931. See also the District Annual Report, 1931, pp. 4–5 (KNA. DC/NN1/12).

66. KNA. DC/NN10/1/1: Petition addressed to his excellency, August 18, 1932. In addition to calling for a review of the administration's land rights policy and the return of all exiled Ugenya, the association requested that Shadrack (Awelu) Omolo be appointed the "sole leader in all matters affecting (the) Ugenya Kager tribe." It also requested that all Luo officials and elders appointed by the government "at the instigation" of Mumia be replaced by individuals from the Ugenya Kager tribe.

67. KNA. DC/NN1/1/13: North Kavirondo District 1932 Annual Report, 4.

68. Ibid., 5

69. KNA. DC NN10/1/1: Document dated April 10, 1933 (ref. no. LND. 13/3/H).

70. KNA. DC/NN10/1/1: "Petition of the Ugenya Kager peoples" to the provincial commissioner of Nyanza (undated).

71. KNA. DC/NN10/1/1: District commissioner, Kakamega, to the provincial commissioner, September 7, 1933 (ref. no. 947LND. 13/3/A).

72. *Askari* is a general term encompassing many types of armed officials or guards: military soldier, policeman, tribal retainer, watchman.

73. KNA. DC/NN10/1/1: "Report on the Disturbances at Musanda in Wanga North Kavirondo, in January 1934" by Captain Hislop, February 9, 1934.

74. The leading role that the Luo schoolteacher Daniel Musigo (or Daniel Muzigo Oludhe) assumed in opposing Mango's Roho movement is corroborated by Ogot 1971, 104–105.

75. It should be noted that Odongo, as well as other Kager leaders, had likened tenancy (the lives of *jodak*) to slavery. *Wasumbni* is a variant of *misumbeni*, the standard Luo term for slaves.

76. Grace Clarke translates *osodo* as "hopping," but Inondi suggested that *osodo* was a particular type of locust, saying "that was when the locusts of the *osodo* type were here" (*ma nene bonyo mag osodo ochung'ye ka*).

77. *Harambee* (pulling together) was the motto of Kenyatta's presidency and referred to the cooperative self-help model of development. *Nyayo* (footsteps) is President Moi's motto, signifying his plan to follow in the path of Kenyatta, building on the *harambee* ethos. The cry of *Umoja!* (Unity!), which one often hears at state ceremonies and rallies, conveys the ideal of a strong nation, devoid of tribal divisiveness.

78. KNA. DC/NN1/1/13, 1932 North Kavirondo District Annual Report, 3; Wagner [1949] 1970, 81, 84, 96–99.

79. KNA. DC/NN10/1/1: Memo to the provincial commissioner in Kisumu from the district commissioner of North Kavirondo, April 9, 1932.

80. "Report on the Disturbances."

Chapter 2

1. In his "Brief History of the Beginning of Ruwe Holy Ghost Church," Zadock Ochoma writes that Lawi started preaching when the missionaries transferred Mango to Mombasa (i.e., to attend seminary). "At the time he (Mango) was transferred to Mombasa, his relative, Lawi Obonyo, a Carpenter, also received God's message and started straight away preaching the Gospel in areas as far as Alego, where through God's power [he] did Miracles by healing the sick, dead, and cripples that drew a large crowd of believers to follow him wherever he was going to conduct prayer.

"When Mango reached Musanda from Ulumbi, he found Lawi was fully equipped by the Holy Spirit. They joined each other and started praying seriously with the people who always gathered at his home." (Spelling and punctuation corrected).

2. *Kuon* is the Luo term for a stiff porridge made from corn, millet, or sorghum flour. Known as *ugali* in Swahili, this paste constitutes the staple dish for many ethnic groups in Kenya.

3. In Dholuo, the words for "cowife" and "jealousy" are the same: *nyiego*. Inondi's aside suggests that in the past, bouts of spirit possession may have been commonly associated with rivalry between cowives, evidence that might support I. M. Lewis's controversial claims (1966, 1971). This issue bears further research, however.

4. An *olang'* is not exactly a bell, but "a piece of metal which is beaten and used as a bell for calling people" (Clarke's *Luo-English Dictionary*).

5. Australian C.M.S. missionary Fanny Moller arrived in Ng'iya in 1923 and immediately founded a school for girls that has evolved into the famous Ng'iya Girls School (Ogot 1971, 102).

6. Canon Pleydell (also known as Orengo), Mango's former teacher from Maseno who moved from Maseno to head the new mission at Ng'iya in 1921 (Ogot, 1971; CMSA G3/A5/ O/1933, Owen's letter to Pitt Pitts, October 25, 1933).

7. *Chunye ochot* unambiguously means "he/she is dead" (Clarke's *Dictionary*).

8. *Chuny* means "liver" or "heart," which in Luo thought is associated with the spirit or soul of the individual. Missionaries thus translated "Holy Spirit" as *Chuny Maler*. Similar to our wide use of the word *heart* in expressions relating to character, there are many Luo expressions in which *chuny* designates disposition or conscience, such as *chunye osea* (he has lost courage) and *chunye pek* (he is heavy of heart). When Luos speak of losing consciousness, they might say *chuny odhi mabor* (the soul has gone far).

9. The well-founded fear on the part of Joroho that the authorities would accuse them of utilizing "traditional medicine" (*yath*) for destructive purposes was expressed in Lawi's later refusal to report to the district officer following a revival meeting. Owen wrote: "Lawi was invited to ac[c]ompany the lads to the District Officer, but declined on the ground that he would be accused of employing 'medicine' to produce the condition in which the lads were" (KNA. DC/NN0/1/1).

10. Luos traditionally wore *tigo* (beads) for ornamentation, but they also often used them to conceal charms known as *ris*, which were strung around the waist.

11. On *chira* in Luo culture, see Wilson 1961, 104–105. Meshak Ogola, an elder at Ruwe, likens *chira* to AIDS.

12. KNA. DC/NN10/1/1: Memo to D.C. Col. Anderson from Owen, entitled "Re. Rev. Alufayo Odongo, Musanda," January 17, 1934. See Also KNA. MSS/21/1: Owen Papers (M937/Box 1, Acc. 8301-8301/5), letter to Pitt Pitts February 1, 1934.

13. Owen to Pitt Pitts, October 25, 1933.

14. Ibid.

15. Ibid.

16. KNA. DC/NN10/1/1: To the district commissioner of North Kavirondo, from Owen, Pleydell, and Leech, n.d.

17. Owen later learned that the official he assumed to be the A.D.C. (assistant district commissioner?) was in fact the district officer for Central Kavirondo, Armitage.

18. Owen to Pitt Pitts, October 25, 1993.

19. "Report on the Disturbances."

20. Letter to Pitt Pitts, February 1, 1934.

21. Ibid.

22. Letter from Owen, Pleydell, and Leech, n.d.

23. "Report on the Disturbances," 2.

24. Ibid.

25. Letter to Pitt Pitts, February 1, 1934. This alternative spelling of Alfayo Odongo's name appears in many administrative documents as well.

26. Letter from Owen, Pleydell, and Leech, n.d.

27. Anna Inondi claimed that this service took place in January, but both Ibrahim Mango's testimony and Owen's letters confirm that it occurred on December 17.

28. Ibrahim Owuor Mango confesses that he himself did not pass Lawi's test. Mango thinks that Lawi objected to his English-style schoolboy haircut. The Roho view holds that true Christians are not supposed to "beautify" themselves. Owen recorded that Alfayo "publicly disowned his two sons, Yakobo, an old Maseno boy, and Ibrahim, at present a pupil at Maseno, because they refused to join the sect" (letter to Pitt Pitts, February 1, 1934.). Today, Ibrahim Mango is the bishop of a major Roho denomination. As a Maseno student, however, Ibrahim Mango would not have been

permitted by his Anglican schoolmasters to join a movement such as Roho. He explained that he was not inclined to join his father's religion, which would have entailed abandoning his education.

29. Ibid.

30. Ibid.

31. Harrison Kojunju's written history also identifies the service in which Lawi "was given the clothes" and then baptized people as "the beginning of the division." According to Kojunju's text, however, it was Lawi who "told Odongo to remove the clothes for [Lawi] wanted to baptize," and Odongo obeyed him.

32. Owen's letter to Pitt Pitts, February 1, 1934.

33. Ibid., 7. Owen describes how the district commissioner sent tribal retainers "to secure our people in the use of the building."

34. "Report on the Disturbances," 3.

35. *Jokorwach* "tell what has happened as well as what will happen" (*gikoro gima ose timore, kata gimo biro timore*).

36. "Report on the Disturbances," 3.

37. Owen's letter to Pitt Pitts, February 1, 1934, 6.

38. Ibid.

39. The phrase *nwang'o lwedo* literally means "to receive the hand," referring to the fact that the act of confirmation is achieved when a member of the clergy lays hands on the head or shoulders of the candidate.

40. We cannot be sure of when this event took place. When asked, Anna Inondi stated that Barnaba's resurrection occurred in December. However, she was certain that it, together with the *nwang'o lwedo*, happened after the group was barred from Musanda Luo, a ruling made on January 6.

41. Anna Inondi comments that this was the same technique European missionaries employed when first spreading the gospel. "[Mango's disciples] were going to call their brothers. Alfayo wanted them to come in order that they be told something, otherwise they might later ask themselves why they had not given the news [i.e., why they had been excluded]. Is this not how the whiteman also came to give us the word of God?" (*Gidhi luongo jowadgi, Alfayo nene dwaro ga ne mondo obi owach nie jogi, nikech chieng' nigi wach ne wachni nene dak ng'isgie. Ok e kaka nene ja rachar bende obiro ng'iso wa wach Nyasaye?*)

42. Inondi explains that people feared that the Joroho wanted captives and that "the Holy Spirit which had entered us would enter them" (*nene giluo ni roho ma omako wa no biro mako gi*).

43. Owen's letter to Pitt Pitts, February 1, 1934.

44. Jeremiah Ogutu, who was a child staying in Mango's compound at the time of the massacre, tells a different version of "the bright light" incident. He claimed that when the kerosene ran out, Lawi prayed. He then informed the Joroho that some kerosene could be found on the slope of Musanda Luo hill, if only they would go and pray under the large fig tree there. A number of the adults followed his instructions but returned empty-handed. Then Lawi took all the children to the hill, where they encircled the tree and knelt. Lawi dug a shallow hole in the ground and placed a small dish (*tawo*) in the center. He instructed the elder children to collect four banana leaves and arrange them near the base of the tree, sloping into the pot. He then asked each child to say a prayer. As they did so, the banana leaves became wet and then filled with kerosene, which flowed into the pot. Lawi presented the children before the rest of the community: "We didn't go to the shops . . . if it (the kerosene) lights, then the children have more power than you; they are the ones who will build the church with

twelve doors." (*To ok wadhi e duka . . . ka oliel, to nyithindo oloyo u gi teko; nyithindo ema noger koro kanisa ma dho ode apar kod ariyo.*) The current Ruwe Holy Ghost headquarters church has twelve doors and is said to have been built according to Lawi's prophesy.

Anna Inondi disputed Jeremiah Ogutu's story. At one point, she said that "he was just a child at the time and didn't know anything" (*nene en nyathi ndalo no, ok nene ong'eyo gimoro*). Inondi stressed the fact that she was an adult at the time and had seen the light with her own eyes and that the light was "truly different from that shed by kerosene" (*opogore kod mafuta adier*). The elders at Ruwe sided with Inondi and saw Ogutu's assertion as an attempt to claim importance and to put his voice on my cassette. Jeremiah Ogutu was born around 1926 and is currently an elder in the Ruwe Holy Ghost Church.

45. Anna Inondi and Daniel Were drew a connection between this exchange and Mango's land dispute with the colonial administration. Initially, Mango had refused to sign a paper giving him tenant status (*keto seyi mar jadak*), saying that he would rather "kill the whole world" (*daneg piny mangima*) than acknowledge himself a land client. However, Mango later relinquished his claim to his land, indicating that he was no longer interested in "the reign of Caesar's people" (*loch mar Jokaisar*). He was now committed to gaining power in the heavenly realm.

46. Like Mango, Oloo finally signed a statement accepting the official label of "tenant," which enabled him to return home a year later. Oloo had originally migrated into the area from Sakwa. My informants pointed out that the Kamlwang' are the clan of the former Kenyan vice president and protest politician, Oginga Odinga.

47. Johana Omina stated that most of Mango's followers did not know why Lawi had ordered them to beat Oloo. They simply followed Lawi's command and later came to realize that they had been testing the mettle of their new king. Henry Osodo, one of my research assistants, explained that the revelation about the African king and the prophesy of future death and suffering for the Joroho were somehow contingent on each other. As he put it, "The two prophesies were given equal weight." If the promise of a black ruler were, indeed, to come true, then there would have to be pain as well. The fact that Elijah Oloo endured the pain and came through it victorious was a harbinger of the future of the Roho community and Africa in general.

48. The sticks (*runge*) were not simply carried like rifles for effect, for they were, in fact, the weapons of the small Roho army. "They were guns" (*ne gin bunde*), Inondi asserts.

49. One interpretation I received was that each color represented one of the three races: blue symbolized African people, red the Asians, and white the Europeans. The message was that each community would have its "own authority" (*loch margi*).

50. According to Zadock Ochoma, people had tried to fetch Oloo's wife to fill the role of queen, but her father prevented her from coming (see note 55). Other Ruwe Roho elders simply said that she was afraid and ran away.

51. See chapter 4 for more on the secret Roho language.

52. *Nyaldiema* is severe diarrhea caused by cholera. By giving his spear the name of this dreaded disease, the owner was implying that death would come quickly to whomever it struck.

53. According to Hislop's report, this event occurred on January 19.

54. Owen's letter to Pitt Pitts, February 1, 1934.

55. Zadock Ochoma states Isaya Goro's visit to Lazaro Gombe's home occurred on January 15, for he asserts a direct connection between the confrontation there and the

crowning of *Kingi* Elijah Oloo, which occurred on January 16. Oloo knew in advance that he was going to be installed and wished to have his wife installed alongside him as queen. However, Oloo's father-in-law had caught wind of the fact that plans to attack Iwinda were brewing, and he didn't want his daughter to die. Therefore, he prevented her from going there by shutting her in a house guarded by several strong men, one of whom was Lazaro Gombe. Isaya was one of those sent to get Oloo's wife. When he reached the house where she was sequestered, Goro tried to force his way in and was consequently speared in the chest by Gombe.

56. The widespread perception among non-Rohos in the area, even today, is that Mango's people stole a bull and that this act precipitated the fighting that led to his death.

57. KNA. DC/NN10/1/1: minutes from Hislop's "Enquiry under the Collective Punishment Ordinance, 1930," 2.

58. Ibid., 4, 11.

59. Archdeacon Owen, by contrast, appears to justify the actions of the "two pagan Bantu": "It is reported that these two men had been intimidated by Lawi previously and told that they must either join them or clear out, that they could not be allowed to defile the place with their presence." He makes no mention of their drunkenness (letter to Pitt Pitts, February 1, 1934).

60. Owen referred to him as "one of Lawi's men, who had seceded from us" (letter to Pitt Pitts, February 1, 1934).

61. Hislop's "Enquiry," 10.

62. Owen (letter to Pitt Pitts, February 1, 1934) called Turfosa Aloo "an elderly woman," something never mentioned to me by Roho members.

63. This hymn was not original. It had been sung in Anglican churches in Mango's area. Several Joroho explained to me that, in singing the words "You love all people," Mango was asking God to help his followers and forgive their sins. "Just as Jesus said, 'They don't know what they are doing, be merciful to them, forgive them'" (*Kaka Yesu bende ne wacho ni gikia gima gitimo, ngwon nigi, we nigi*).

64. The tunnel of smoke enabling the Joroho to escape has become a canonical piece of the Roho story. Young Harrison Kojunju, a first-time pilgrim to Ruwe and Musanda in 1991, wrote in his outline of the history of the church that when Mango's house was ablaze, God "made a miracle by making a path through the smoke" (Kojunju n.d., 2).

65. Minutes from Hislop's "Enquiry," 2.

66. The account given to me by members of the Ruwe Holy Ghost Church did not contain this episode.

67. Minutes from Hislop's "Enquiry," 6.

68. When Roho members speak about the death of their founder, in conversation or in sermons, they generally stress the fact that Mango did not run but chose to stand still, bravely accepting his fate. In one of my interviews with a group of four church elders, Anna Inondi tried to make the point that Mango had no choice. "Even if he ran out [of the house] he would still be in trouble. . . . Moreover, [the Wanga] were waiting for him at the door" (*Ne oringo to ong'e ni en e tabu, kata oringo kato owuok pod nobed e tabu. . . . To kendo iye no to gikiye e dho ot*). Whenever Anna tried to make that point, another elder, Johana Omina, who had also fought in "the war," would correct her, "No, just say it like this" (*Da, wach awach kama*). Then, he would proceed to insist that Mango could have run if he had chosen to do so. "No, that person was simply brave on his own" (*Aa, ng'at cha nene odhil odhila owuon kende*). In other

words, other elders wished to view their founder not as an unwilling, trapped victim but as a self-sacrificing martyr.

69. Inondi's account also maintains that Lawi's killer was a left-handed person (*ng'at ma racham*), but she could not recall his name.

70. My informants had no idea why the Wanga had cut out Lawi's tongue.

71. Hislop prepared a map to accompany his eleven-page report. Unfortunately, it is so faint and smudged as to be entirely unreadable.

72. Hislop's "Enquiry," 7.

73. The chief's camp was located at Ambira. It is possible that, in commanding Mango's corpse to rise, Owen's intent was to dispel any beliefs the onlooking Joroho might have as to Mango's ability to self-resurrect.

74. Lawi's son actually escaped at the last minute but was so badly burned that he died a short distance from the house. Owen reported that the charred remains of Odongo and Enoka's son "were found in the smoking hut under a pile of smouldering thatch" (letter to Pitt Pitts, February 1, 1934).

75. Hislop's "Enquiry," 7.

76. An exception is David Barrett who states—correctly, in my opinion—that Mango himself never actually left the Anglican church. According to Barrett, Mango received a vision in 1916 "commissioning him to begin the Roho (Holy Ghost) movement which remained inside the church for eighteen years" until after his death in 1934, whereupon his followers seceded to establish a distinct church (1968, 10, 258).

77. Ogot states that these particular events occurred during 1932, but administrative records make clear that they all transpired in 1933. See KNA. DC/NN10/1/1.

78. KNA. DC/NN10/1/1: Memo to D. C. Col. Anderson from Owen headed "Re. Rev. Alufayo Odongo, Musanda."

79. Hislop corroborates this claim in his report: "A name came into use for those people who followed Lawi; they did not actually adopt this name themselves, but it was used conveniently by most people. The name was JO-ROHO MALER, (a mixture of Kiswahili and Luo) meaning the people of the Holy Spirit" ("Report on the Disturbances, 2").

80. Okite 1973, 118.

81. Sundkler 1976, 1961; Barrett 1968, 270.

82. Terence Ranger (1986, 37).

83. Ugenya historian Haggai Nundu claims that "Opere" was Father "Brandisman" (1982, 24). Actually, the priest's name was Brandsma, and he established a Catholic mission station at Mukumu near Kakamega in Luyia country in 1906. However, mission historian Hans Burgman states that Brandsma was nicknamed Otwala when he lived among the Luo in Ojolla. It was Father Bouma who was known as Opere Oboma. Ojolla came to be known as Kotwala after Father Brandsma, and the Catholics of Ojolla were called Jokotwala. Burgman states that this label remained in use for many years (1991, 41,36).

84. See Mrs. Owen's description of the numerous "tree congregations" started by local evangelists in Butere (Richards 1947, 12). See Pirouet (1978) on the proliferation of *synagogi* (small reading houses) in Uganda in the 1890s (25–26) and of the large number of "private churches" by the Teso country as early as 1909 (183).

85. Hislop's "Enquiry," 2.

86. I suspect that Tim Allen's findings on the transethnic continuity between possession cults in northern and southern Uganda might extend beyond the border (1991, 384).

87. See also Owuor Anyumba ([1954] 1971).

88. Interestingly, these islands, where George Pilkington had his mystical experience, were important traditional cultic centers (Kenny 1977, 721).

89. Mr. Nundu had not heard of Ibrahim Osodo and his small charismatic group in Ruwe (personal communication, September 14, 1990).

90. The Nomiya Luo Mission Church was not registered with the state until 1914 (Whisson 1964, 154).

91. The word is from *mi'raj* in Arabic, which means ladder but has come to refer to literature pertaining to the Prophet's heavenly ascent.

92. Hislop's "Report on the Disturbances," 1.

Chapter 3

1. Ibrahim Mango recalls that authorities detained the Joroho in Silvan Nyamogo's *boma*. When Ibrahim spotted his mother, Rael, he ran toward her, but armed guards stopped him. At this point, Ibrahim began crying. Owen saw him crying and ordered the soldiers to allow him to speak with his mother.

2. This rumor still exists among some non-Roho members in the area.

3. KNA. DC/NN10/1/1: "Report on the Disturbances," 8.

4. KNA. DC/NN10/1/1: The district commissioner, Kakamega, to the provincial commissioner, Kisumu, dated February 9 (ref. n. 249/LND 13/3/A).

5. KNA. DC/NN10/1/1: "Enquiry under the Collective Punishment Ordinance 1930," by Sd. F. D. Hislop, February 26, 1934, 3, 12.

6. KNA. DC/NN10/1/1: The district commissioner, Kakamega, to the provincial commissioner, Kisumu, dated March 5, 1934 (ref. no. LND. 3/3/A).

7. KNA. DC/NN10/1/1: "The Collective Punishments Ordinance 1930: Order," dated March 14, 1934, signed by Governor J. Byrne.

8. KNA. DC/NN10/1/1: The colonial secretary to the provincial commissioner of Nyanza, dated March 26, 1934, headed "Collective Punishment—North Kavirondo."

9. KNA. DC/NN10/1/1: Personal letter from E. L. S. Anderson to the provincial commissioner, dated April 16, 1934 (ref no. LND. 13/3/A).

10. Ogot 1971, 108. See also KNA. DC/NN10/1/1: Letter from District Commissioner Henderson to Acting Provincial Commissioner of Nyanza, dated June 25, 1935 (ref. no. 368 Land/13/3 a); KNA. DC/NN10/1/3: agreement signed by District Commissioner Pedraza and Akunda, Ogumbo, and Nahunje, dated November 22, 1940 (ref. no. LND. 13/3/A).

11. Ogot, 1971, 107.

12. "Report on the Disturbances," 3.

13. Ibid., 8.

14. KNA. DC/NN3/2/18: "Précis of Recent Events in Wanga North & South, 1929–1935," by District Commissioner of North Kavirondo E. L. B. Anderson, dated September 21, 1935.

15. Islam has had more of an effect on the development of independent Christianity in western Kenya than scholars have generally acknowledged. Islam thrived in the busy trading center of Mumias—the home of the paramount Wanga chief. According to colonial records, in 1926, an anticolonial "Mohammedan movement" spread rapidly through North Kavirondo District. Its agents preached that "Mohammed or some other chosen of Allah would soon arrive to exterminate all infidels." Its adherents believed that the Europeans would be forced off the land, the inevitable upheaval ending in a new age of Islamic supremacy (KNA. DC/NN10/1/2: "The Mohammedan

Movement in North Kavirondo"). As we have seen, Johana Owalo, founder of Nomiya Luo, the first Luo indigenous church movement, had at one time been a Muslim and integrated Islamic practices into his new faith (Whisson 1962, 25). When I asked Anna Inondi about the similarity between her prayer schedule in those days and that of the Muslims, she stated that there was no connection. Although some of her relatives through marriage, such as Fadmullah Obadha, had ties with Mumia's family and were Muslim, she claimed that she was not familiar with their practices. I take her response as consistent with the emphasis members of independent churches place on the uniqueness of their ritual practice.

16. In Musanda, the Joroho used to wake at 2 A.M. (*saa aboro mar otieno*) and pray until 8 A.M. (*saa ariyo mar okinyi*). Then they would eat breakfast. In the morning, children marched in drill formation and sang Christian songs; later, the adults did the same before they returned to lengthy afternoon prayers.

17. Elders recounted an incident that suggests the district administration had spies keeping an eye on the Roho enclave. When the delegation arrived at district headquarters, they discovered that the district commissioner, having heard that trouble was brewing, had already sent an *askari* (policeman) to Ruwe to investigate. Because the men did not meet the agent on the road, the district commissioner concluded that his employee had dallied or taken an unauthorized detour and thus promptly sacked him.

18. When a *bondo* (gum tree) falls, people rush to collect its milky sap, which is an excellent adhesive used especially in affixing wooden handles to iron implements. The proverb indicates that luck or good fortune has befallen someone.

19. KNA. DC/NN 10/1/1: Letter to the provincial commissioner from E. L. B. Anderson, dated April 16, 1934, 1.

20. Ibid.; see also "Précis of Recent Events."

21. KNA. PC/NZA 1/29: Annual report, 1934 by C. Tomkinson, 7.

22. When Inondi recounted this experience, she did not use the word *dream* (*leko*) but stressed repeatedly that she saw (*neno*) Mango clearly and that he was setting an example (*mafuano*) in carrying out the dirt. When I asked whether others had witnessed his return, she responded, "You know, seeing (a vision) is given to one person" (*Ing'e, neno imiyo ng'ato achiel*).

23. In Luo homesteads, kitchens are small huts separate from the main eating and sleeping quarters.

24. Until recently, one could easily distinguish members of Musanda-derived denominations from other spirit groups because their *namba* or emblem included the letter S affixed to the left side of the cross. Various Joroho interpret the meaning of this S differently. Many would accept the association of Mango's epithet Israel with the S. Bishop Ibrahim Owuor Mango of the Musanda Holy Ghost Church confirmed this interpretation of the S but said that the significance of the cross definitely did not have anything to do with the way in which Lawi died. An elderly member of a Musanda Holy Ghost Congregation in Ng'iya told me that † was actually a T and thus the emblem singnified *sand gi temo* (suffering and temptation). Perrin Jassy's informants in Roho churches in North Mara indicated that S did indeed stand for *sandruok*, which she defines as redemption, but also means suffering or affliction (Perrin Jassy 1973, 195). Ogot maintains that the S "probably means Singruok, which is the Luo word for 'oath'" (Ogot 1971, 109), but has also come to mean "covenant" in Roho theology. While the S has been the distinguishing feature of "Mango's people," the cross has nevertheless always held pride of place in Roho regalia and decor. The newest set of uniforms worn by high-ranking church officials in the Ruwe Holy Ghost Church omits the S altogether.

25. We know that many charismatic Christian groups in Nyanza at this time dressed in white. It was therefore not an unusual color for the Joroho's robes. Moreover, in traditional Luo culture, the color white symbolized purity. It was also associated with spirits (*juogi*). People believed that *juogi* were white and liked only "white things to be given to them" (Owuor Anyumba [1954] 1971, 9; Whisson 1962, 13).

26. KNA. DC/NN10/1/1: The district commissioner of North Kavirondo (Kakamega) to the Acting provisional commissioner of Kavirondo (Kisumu), memo entitled "Ref. Safari Diary of Mr. A. K. Rice D.O. in S. Wanga, November 26–29 and the D.C.'s Comments Thereon," dated January 11, 1935 (ref. no. 23 LND.13/3/A).

27. Nereya Auma, the *laktar* who told this story, used angels (*malaika*) and the Holy Spirit (*Roho Maler*) interchangebly, something my informants did frequently. Thus, at this particular point, she stated: *Bas, ne malaika ooro wach, Roho owacho ni dhi uru urom nigi gine, kanye cha Simenya* (Then the angels sent a message, the Spirit said, "Go and meet those people at Simenya").

28. Esta Songa dispensed of the shards, a spiritually risky task.

29. The Roho missionaries discovered that Barnaba had planted some traditional magical herbs (*yien*), thus unwittingly exacerbating the misfortune.

30. The Seventh-Day Adventist church was, and still is, very strong in South Nyanza. The local preachers were no doubt annoyed that the Roho outsiders from North Nyanza had come to proselytize in what they considered their territory.

31. Esta Songa recalled the opening words as something like: *E kore kenda kore mamori*, but indicated that she was not sure because it was a long time ago and people do not sing such songs any more.

32. While I was visiting Ibrahim Mango in January 1991, two Legio Maria members from South Nyanza appeared at Mango's gate, saying they had been ordered in a dream to travel to that home. On another occasion, an elderly Roho woman in Ruwe commented that traveling in vehicles was not an effective way to proselytize, for the sound of the motor drowned out the voice of the Spirit directing one into homes along the way.

33. They fought together in the First World War. Magak was a sergeant in the King's African Rifles (see KNA. PC/NZA1/29: Provincial Commissioner's Annual Report for 1934, 16).

34. KNA. DC/NN10/1/3: Memo entitled "WATU WA ROHO" from Provincial Commissioner Fazan to the district commissioner, Kisii, dated May 9, 1941.

35. KNA. DC/NN/1/22: The 1940 District Annual Report of North Kavirondo, by District Commissioner R. Pedraza.

36. KNA. DC/NN10/1/3: One page of handwritten notes, signed by the district commissioner, dated May 31, 1941.

37. KNA. DC/NN10/3: A handwritten memo in Swahili from Chief Murunga to the district commissioner.

38. If one wishes to explore the truly new, innovative religions in East Africa, Hannah Kinoti insists, one should look at the evangelical "house churches" springing up throughout urban centers, at the recent appearance of New Age religion, or at the growing Islamic revival movements (personal communication, March 1991).

39. Jules-Rosette has found that among the Apostles of John Maranke (Bapostolo) certain women have the authority to arrange marriages between church members, and they do so within special ceremonies held solely for that purpose. Women are also the primary healers in Bapostolo churches, again transmitting their knowledge to apprentices in specially designated training sessions. Similarly, in the Nigerian Church of the Lord Aladura, the healing clinic run by women is kept distinct from the large Sunday

service led by male clergy. Both Bapostolo and Aladura women adepts act as midwives, using their spiritual power and expertise during an event that is outside the male domain (Turner 1967, 115, 151–154; Jules-Rosette 1979, 135–136).

40. The words of the lustral prayer can vary. *Laktar* Joan Akello of Masumbi described the procedure she follows: "Oh Son of God, I want to drive away the evil spirits. Help me to chase them, because I don't have the power; the power is yours." (*A Wuod Nyasaye, adwaro kwongo jachien. Konya kuongo, nikech aonge kod teko; teko nikuomi.*) After reciting these words, she drives the demons away by facing the door, clapping and shouting, "Get out, get out!" (*Ogole, ogole*). She concludes the purification rite by kneeling and saying, "Our God, you see that if I want to do your work, I am unable. You are the owner of the power; you help me to work so that I am able, in the name of Christ our Lord, Amen." (*Nyasachwa, ineno ka adwaro tiyo tichni, an ok anyal. Inie wuon teko; ikonya tich kuona anyal, e nying Kristo Ruodwa, Amin.*)

41. This ceremony is clearly connected with the traditional rite known as *Golo-Kwer*, which marked a newborn baby's first exposure to the outside. Ocholla-Ayayo writes, "It was on that day that an animal was slaughtered for the mother, after what the Luo call *Golo-Kwer* ("removing the forbidden") (1976, 181). Roho ritual often combines this older custom with baptism.

42. The Joroho are known for their nice songs: I have heard outsiders comment on the particular beauty and originality of Roho melodies.

43. These hymns sometimes appear in widely circulated hymnals such as *Wende Luo* (Church of the Province of Kenya, 1970).

44. Rosalind Hackett has pointed out that in the early 1990s, the elderly Christina Abiodoun regained prominence among Cherubim and Seraphim churches, exercising leadership in mending rifts among the movement's leaders (personal communication, November 1992). This fact suggests that the processes of institutionalization that have worked to marginalize women are not irreversible.

45. During the long intervening period between 1916 and 1933, Mango turned away from charismatic religiosity. He spent a lot of time away from home. He traveled throughout eastern and central Nyanza in his capacity as deacon, attended conferences in Nairobi, and studied theology for two years in Mombasa. In 1932, he was exiled from Musanda by the government because of his involvement in highly volatile inter-ethnic land disputes. When the district commissioner and the Local Native Council finally permitted him to return to his native locale in April 1933, Mango discovered that many of his parishioners had turned against him because of his confrontation with the colonial administration. Roho members maintain that, throughout his travels, Mango was privately cultivating his relationship with the Holy Spirit and waiting for the right moment to reveal himself as God's messenger to the blacks.

46. See Archdeacon Owen's letter to C.M.S. General Secretary Pitt Pitts, October 25, 1933 (CMSA. Original Papers [G3A5/O/1933/#178]).

47. This fact is repeatedly impressed on younger converts by the senior women members. In January 1991 Julia Aor, the elderly wife of the now deceased bishop of the Ruwe Holy Ghost Church, stood and addressed the congregation, saying, "I rejoice that Alfayo Odongo died for me. Before his death, I was unable to walk in the light. Now I can. Through Alfayo, women are now allowed to preach, something that was not permitted before."

48. For more on Sarah Agot, see chapter 5.

49. For example, widows of childbearing age are not allowed to enter the front portion of the church at the Ruwe denominational headquarters until they have remarried.

50. A shift to a predominantly male priesthood similarly occurred within the Legio Maria, another indigenous Luo-based church in western Kenya. In her in-depth study of the movement, Nancy Schwartz observes: "Although women did act as priests, saying mass, hearing confession, and administering the sacraments at the start of Legio, the church began to end what one informant called 'this system' in the late 1960's. While a small number of women reportedly continued to say mass as visiting priests at a few Legio churches, and more often in their own homesteads or those of other Legios, into the 1970's, the last date at which my informants could, or would, recall a woman saying mass was around 1974" (1989, 65). I would venture that some of the same factors facilitating the ascendancy of a male hierarchy in the Roho church similarly facilitated a return to the patriarchal Catholic model in the Legio church, but the issue, of course, bears further research.

51. See Igor Kopytoff's discussion of the Kita ritual among the Suku of south-western Zaire as the "residue" of a revitalization cult that failed to modify its claims along the more humbler plane necessary for routinization (1980, 204–206).

52. Fearn (1961, 212) mentions the Co-operative Societies Ordinance of 1945. It is not clear whether my Roho informants were referring to this ordinance and were confused about the date or had a different ordinance in mind. At any rate, they did not feel any pressure to register their denomination until the late 1950s.

53. When I was in the field during 1990–1991, it was still not uncommon to hear Roho elders in Siaya and Ugenya speak of "going to school" (*wadhi skul*) when going to church to worship. The practice of erecting churches cum schools on one's property was by no means peculiar to the Joroho but was a standard feature—and an important modus operandi—of the spread of Christianity first in Buganda and in Nyanza. See Stock 1899, 453; Pirouet 1978, 25; and Willis (1916) quoted in Welbourn and Ogot 1966, 24–25.

54. Terence Ranger (1983, 225) sees the pattern of young migrants who return home and "establish themselves as catechists" as largely an attempt to "outflank" their elders by manipulating colonially invented tradition to their own advantage. People began this practice and carried it out most easily during the early colonial period.

55. Ruwe Roho officials report that Oginga Odinga left the church in 1966, the year he resigned as Kenyatta's vice president and quit the ruling party (KANU) in order to form an opposition party, the Kenya People's Union (KPU).

56. Also, Syprose H. Odero, personal communication, May 1, 1990.

57. E. S. Atieno-Odhiambo points out that *juogi* are associated with every object and being. "*Juogi* exist in everything that is. Every individual has his own *juogi*, and it is noteworthy that both malevolent and positive *juogi* exist in the same indi-vidual. . . . Every tree has got its own *juogi*. Collectively *juogi* may belong to a phenomenon as *juogi mumbo*, which reside in the lake; *obongo, juogi rege*, which reside in or possess bangles made from ivory; *juogi munde* which possess ironworkers; *juogi nyalolwe*, which possess healers. The soil has its own *juogi*, and a very potent force it is" (1970, 15).

58. Owuor Anyumba posits the origin of Lang'o possession in turn-of-the-century battles with the Nandi or Kipsigis but indicates that in the popular mindset *lang'o* spirits are also identifed with the Maasai (1974, 2). Ocholla-Ayayo corroborates this fact, saying that *Juok Lang'o* is believed to reside "in the distant steppe-forest of Maasai-land" (1976, 174).

59. See Whisson (1962, 6) for a similar description of the treatment a newly possessed *jalang'o* received at the home of an expert.

60. Owuor Anyumba indicates that *lang'o* experts were often critics of Luo affairs

and thus "very welcome in society." The tension between the normative ancestral cult and possession cults such as Lang'o was thus considered healthy ([1954] 1971, 41).

61. Personal communication, March 1, 1991

62. This comment, I am quite sure, contained a veiled critique, either of the then elderly Ruwe Roho bishop who was too sick to minister but would not resign or of the Kenyan president who refused to relinquish power.

Chapter 4

1. Joroho consider Jesus a *mzungu* (European) and not one of their own.

2. According to Marie-France Perrin Jassy, Roho congregations in Tanzania tell a slightly different version of the Musanda event and have a theology that—at least in the early 1970s—was decidedly Christocentric, unlike that of the Kenyan Roho church. She claims that, for Tanzanian Joroho, Mango and Lawi were "prophets chosen by God to lead them to salvation and martyrs for their faith. But they have never been compared to Jesus, who remains the source of salvation" (1973, 114).

3. On June 5, 1990, I listened to a discussion about Mango's status between Zadock Ochoma, then secretary of the Ruwe Holy Ghost Church, and Daniel Ogusu, a member of the African Israel Church Nineveh (A.I.C.N.) and director of the Theological Education by Extension program (T.E.E.) for the Organization of the African Independent Churches (O.A.I.C.). Ogusu told Ochoma that other Christians criticized Roho members, claiming that they prayed to Alfayo Odongo Mango as Jesus. "Is this true?" Ogusu asked. Ochoma explained that the Joroho did not confuse Mango with Jesus, for Mango was "the one who came after Jesus, fulfilling the promise of Jesus. He was the Comforter Jesus had promised." Ogusu then stated that he chose to view the founders of African independent churches—such as Kivuli, the founder of the A.I.C.N.—as prophets. To this, Ochoma responded that he saw Mango as "more of a Spiritual Father."

4. Roho myths and exegesis show that members consider Jesus and his legacy as insufficient and lacking in spiritual power. There is continuity between this notion and what was embraced by Johana Owalo's Nomiya Luo religion, which preceded Mango's movement. In a more detailed version of the visionary journey quoted in chapter 2, Owalo reported that when in heaven he "saw the Holy Spirit coming out of the mouth of God like smoke, but that there was *no such Spirit* coming from the mouth of Jesus" (Whisson 1962, 24; italics mine).

5. See Grace Clarke, *Luo-English Dictionary*.

6. Hobley cites instances of killing a goat to compensate for a broken taboo (1902, 31) or to "avert ill luck" (32), killing a sheep and feeding portions to one's enemy in a peacemaking ceremony (34) and, "making a feast" and throwing bits of meat to the four directions as "propitiatory offerings" to the spirits (1903, 343). Northcote comments that Luos worship the sun and make offerings "at all important occasions in their daily life." These offerings, concludes Northcote, are not made with any hope of "obtaining positive benefits" but simply to appease the sun, who is basically "malignant" (1907, 63).

7. This stereotype was later challenged by a number of East African scholars, and the debate over whether a Supreme Power—however conceived—ever existed in traditional Luo belief has dominated much subsequent discussion of Luo religion (Ogot 1961; Hauge 1974, 98; Ocholla-Ayayo 1976, 170; P'Bitek 1979, 70–79; Ogutu 1987; Atieno Odhiambo 1989, 16–25).

8. For instance, like Evans-Pritchard, Hans-Egil Hauge distinguishes between

public (or collective) and private (or personal) sacrifices (1974, 106–108). Hauge does not, however, assume that all sacrifices directed to spirits were implicitly made to God (*Nyasaye*) as well. On those occasions when sacrifices were made "simultaneously to both the dead and to Nyasaye," he argues, it was to "ensure that [Nyasaye] will give the departed person strength and power to carry out what he is being asked to do" (1974, 11). Ocholla-Ayayo upholds this basic distinction between God-directed sacrifice and sacrifices made to spirits but acknowledges that, in practice, the distinction between the two types is often obscured (1976, 170).

9. Ocholla-Ayayo maintains that in traditional Luo cosmology, the land of the dead was not in the sky, but "below the sea or below the earth" (1976, 171). There are conflicting findings on this point. It is certain that, by the turn of the century, notions about a celestial afterlife were current, perhaps partly the result of the Chieng' (Sun) possession cult.

10. Among the Nuer, for example, the idea is conveyed in concept of *kok* (ransom), in which a precious object or an animal is given as return for the well-being of the sacrificer (Evans-Pritchard [1956] 1977, 222–225).

11. Roho sermons and prayers occasionally refer to the Musanda martyrs as "the nine nations" (*oganda ochiko*). *Oganda* can mean "crowd," "multitude," "tribe," or "nation." The appellation may have been inspired by frequent mention of tribes (*ogendeni*) in the Old Testament that are identified in terms of specific eponymous ancestors, such as the twelve tribes of Israel, associated with the descendants of Israel's (Jacob's) twelve sons. The Joroho are fond of highlighting the parallel between themselves and the peoples of ancient Israel, with whom God also made a covenant. Perhaps to speak of the original Roho martyrs as "tribes" or "nations" is to elaborate on this symbolic parallel. Indeed, the reference must be metaphorical because most of the nine who died in the 1934 fire were young, unmarried, and childless. They can hardly, therefore, be viewed as actual progenitors.

12. Nancy Schwartz informed me that members of the Legio Maria church have also asserted a special relationship between themselves and certain famous Luo natural monuments such as *Kit Mikayi*.

13. Elijah Oloo was not from the Kager clan, as were most Luo agitators in Wanga. He belonged to the Kamlwang' clan and reportedly migrated from Sakwa.

14. I owe the latter insight to discussions with Robert Fatton and Joseph Hellweg.

15. It is common practice in Kenyan churches for lay members to lead the congregation in prayers and songs while waiting for the clergy to arrive.

16. In Luoland generally, any type of ankle-length gown worn by men is referred to as a *kanzu*, after the traditional white outer garment worn by Muslim men on the Swahili coast.

17. There is a growing attempt within the Ruwe Holy Ghost Church to clothe people of the same rank uniformly. Roho pastors dress much like Anglican clergy, wearing a black cotton cassock, white surplice, and a thin black stole. Their costume does not include the traditional white "dog collar," however. Instead, two small, bright red crosses are appliqued on either side of the collar, identifying the wearer as a member of the Roho clergy. In the months following Mango's death, Barnaba Walwoho received a vision containing the basic design of Roho ritual garb. According to Anna Inondi's account, the Holy Spirit delineated three simple costumes: one for laywomen, one for laymen, and one for pastors. Since then, Roho attire has become increasingly complex and differentiated, commensurate with the proliferation of offices as the denomination has grown. Today people serve as *laktache* (healers), *jopuonj* (teachers), *joote* (apostles or messengers)—leaders of men, women, and youth,

respectively—choir directors, treasurers, secretaries, and so on. Each of these roles requires its own distinctive costume. Moreover, within each role are rankings such as senior, junior, and assistant. Such differences in rank are often indicated by colored bars or patches sewn onto the shoulder, lapel, or front of the garment.

Religious garb is not cheap. I was told that clergy ordained in 1991 had to raise 3,000 Kenyan shillings (at that time, approximately $136 U.S., or the cost of a local cow) to pay for their robes. However, from the Roho point of view, proper ritual dress is simply requisite. The rite of ordination is realized in handing a set of new robes to the pastor by the bishop. Once ordained, a pastor cannot baptize or bless when clothed as a layman. In such a state, his acts would be considered ineffectual and illegitimate. Many Roho women indicated that the crosses on their headscarves facilitate the entry of the Holy Spirit into the bodies of the wearer and ward off evil forces. Clothed in white, members consider themselves dressed like the angels or ancestors in heaven.

18. The general content of the *Nzari Mbethi* closely resembles that of the congregational confession recited by members of the mainline Church of the Province of Kenya (C.P.K.). However, when one translates the *Nzari* into Dholuo and compares it with the Luo version of the C.P.K. confession currently in use, one finds notable differences in wording. (See Church of the Province of Kenya, *Kitap Lamo, Book of Common Prayer with additional Services and Prayers in Dholuo*, Nairobi: Uzima Press, 1976, 2.) It is possible that we have preserved in the *Nzari Mbethi* an earlier form of the confession, as disseminated by Anglican missionaries in the 1930s or 40s. Although Anglican liturgies—not to mention Luo translations of the Bible—have undergone a series of published revisions since the 1930s, the *Nzari*, so far as I know, has never been intentionally altered. Because the *Nzari* is disseminated primarily via oral transmission (a number of Rangeng'a's handwritten texts remain, but few people have access to them), changes in the written Book of Common Prayer (*Kitap Lamo*) would not have affected the *Nzari*. The *Nzari* translates into more simple, colloquial Luo than the Luo used in the current (C.P.K.) Confession. The same holds true for the *Rosi Somp Mpaik* (Lord's Prayer) and the *Njonzari Osheu* (Apostles' Creed). It is also possible that Paulo Rang'eng'a and other Roho founders may have rendered the substance of the Anglican Confession into their own words. If, in fact, we discover that the Joroho have retained an older form, it would be consistent with what has occurred in the Legio Maria church, a prominent Luo Catholic independent church. Whereas the Catholic church has revised its liturgy, the Legio mass preserves portions of the Roman Catholic liturgy as it was preached in Nyanza by Catholic missionaries in the late 1950s.

19. I have divided Luo phrases (in this case *wase/timo*—"we have/done") into syllable clusters consistent with their rendering in Dhoroho manuscripts, as opposed to the way they would appear in standard written Luo (i.e., *wasetimo*).

20. The correct spelling of this word should be *mowinjore*, meaning "which ought." However, the original word in the Dhoroho manuscript, *sinjewimpu*, lacks the consonant *nd*, which is the code for *n*, according to the key provided me (see "Note on the Roho Lituigical Language" in the appendix to this volume). Nonetheless, it is clear from the context that *mowinjore* is what is meant. The same is true for *wijore* in the following line.

21. The Luo syllable *en* here is meaningless, but that is how the Dhoroho word *und* translates. Perhaps there is an error or omission in the original manuscript.

22. The Joroho believe that the first covenant privileged the Europeans and the second privileged the Asians (see earlier in this chapter).

23. The continuity between *lang'o* spirit possession and possession by the Holy

Spirit in Roho churches is marked. Compare this 1991 Roho sequence with Henry Owuor Anyumba's following description of a nighttime ceremony he observed in the early 1950s marking the return of a newly initiated *lang'o* adept to her home: "Usually nearly every space in the room is filled with the spectators. The song and the playing of the rattle become even more lively. The dance now includes the local jolango as well. Amid the vigorous dancing, some of the jolango fall down into a wild state accompanied by sharp excited sounds—that is speaking in tongues. (In some cases, I was told, foam comes from the mouth of the fallen person.) The other people do not mind: They continue dancing. With the Mumbo and Wagande types the dancers accompany the experts' song with grunt like sounds (personated from the chest) at regular intervals. The jolango of the Chieng, as we have seen, shout the shio!, hee! Hoo!, hai! all at once, making it nearly impossible to hear anything else" (Owuor Anyumba [1954] 1971, 22).

24. Rang'eng'a's Dhoroho manuscript trails off at this point. The version currently recited in Ruwe services includes the following few final phrases shown here. An alternative ending was appended to the Rang'eng'a manuscript in pen by Meshak Ogola in 1991. It reads as follows:

> *Cheche vumpinjo choso mpodh ndechudh thnijig nde chaise. Nzetende to nze-tende. Osend.*
>
> *(Kiki terowa kama mach nikech dwong ni kuomi higni gi higni. Amin.)*
>
> (Don't carry us to hell [lit., fire] because greatness is yours forever and ever. Amen.)

25. I do not yet know who composed this hymn, but it can be found in one of the handwritten manuscripts attributed to Paulo Rang'en'ga. The congregation today sings the song almost exactly as it appears in that manuscript; they have changed only a few suffixes.

26. The following version of the Roho creed—the one Ruwe Roho members currently recite—is probably very close to, if not identical with, the original because, like the Lord's Prayer and confession, the language is far more simple than the form used in the C.P.K. today. Unfortunately the written original, if there ever was one, does not appear in the collection of prayers, hymns, and biblical passages that were scripted in Dhoroho by Paulo Rang'eng'a and his colleagues in the 1930s and 1940s. Again, I have provided Luo and English translations.

27. Rael Oloyo, Odongo Mango's widow, continued to be active in the Roho movement after her husband's death. The Joroho often invoke the names of their deceased members, both male and female. Founders, as well as the martyrs of the *mach*, are believed to be heavenly mediators. They frequently appear to living members of the community in dreams or visions, and their memories are kept alive in songs.

28. *Mwakedogo* is probably a distortion of the Swahili adjective *dogo* (small). The Joroho here seem to be using *mwake* (his/hers/its—animate) as an adjectival prefix.

29. I was told by everyone that the Dhoroho word *cher* means *ee* (yes) in Dholuo. Letter for letter, however, *cher* translates into *kil* in Dholuo, which is used in neither Luo nor Swahili greetings. At present, I cannot explain how *cher* has come to mean "yes" in Dhoroho.

30. This question-and-answer format is a convention used widely in classrooms, churches, and outdoor gatherings throughout Kenya. Usually the audience is simply expected to demonstrate their attentiveness by repeating the word or phrase the speaker has just uttered. Sometimes, using the specific inflection reserved for this particular rhetorical technique, the speaker will pause midsentence and wait for the listeners to produce the correct word. Preachers and teachers can utilize this technique when they

sense they are losing their audience. The method generally works to stimulate people's interest, at least temporarily.

31. A reference to the nine people who died as a result of the attack made on Alfayo Odongo Mango's compound on January 20, 1934, who are metaphorically seen as the progenitors of the current generations, or "nations," of believers. As we have seen, only four actually burned to death on that night: three children—Joel Owino, Zadok Aol, and Persila Adongo—in addition to Mango himself. Salome Omondi died two days later as a result of burns sustained in the *mach*. The others—Turfosa Aloo, Isaka Obayo, Musa Muga, and Lawi Obonyo—died from spear wounds. That all nine martyrs are popularly remembered as dying in the flames suggests, to my mind, the strength of the sacrificial fire in Luo religious imagination.

32. This hymn appears in the Anglican hymnal *Wende Luo* produced by the Church of the Province of Kenya. It has a more conventional structure than many of the Roho original hymns, consisting of five verses and a two-line refrain that is repeated twice after each verse.

33. People from a number of Roho congregations have made the distinction between *wende mag Roho* (songs of the Spirit) and other Christian hymns. *Wende mag Roho* are fast-paced songs to which the drum can be beaten and which lend themselves to dancing. In the Mirunda parish of the Holy Spirit Church of East Africa, I once heard a *padri* admonishing the whole congregation—and the women in particular—for sluggish singing. "The Holy Spirit came with dancing and drums! The Holy Spirit came with many different things such as prophesy. You people, this is your work! But you people don't want to answer; you don't want to dance. The only time you should be seated is when praying. Otherwise, when singing, stand up!" The connection between being filled with the spirit, prophesy, and dancing is stressed. It is during the long repetitive songs—a single phrase can be repeated forty or fifty times—accompanied by drums that people most frequently fall into trance or become possessed. The Ruwe parish was the only Roho congregation I came across that did not permit drums inside the sanctuary. (During the big celebration of *Sikukuu mar Rapar*, however, members from other congregations around the country did bring and use their large drums during services inside the Ruwe church.)

34. *Mirembe* is a greeting of ambiguous origin. Grace Clarke's *Luo-English Dictionary* defines the word as a noun meaning "Peace. (a salutation, greeting. It may most likely be borrowed from the Bantu people south-west from Shirati, who use the word extensively.)" Stafford's grammar also defines the word as a noun meaning "Peace" but says it is "old-fashioned." In some Luo-English dictionaries, the word does not even appear (*Dholuo Grammar*, St. Joseph's Society, Mill Hill Society, Kisumu: Kisumu Stores, n.d.). In Luoland, I have only heard *Mirembe* used as a greeting in charismatic independent churches. It could be an adaptation of the Luyia salutation *Mulembe*. It is also possible that *Mirembe*, which is a greeting in Luganda (also meaning "Peace"), was introduced into western Kenya churches by Baganda missionaries during the East African Revival in the 1940s or perhaps even earlier. An earlier origin is indeed suggested by the answer I received when I asked Roho church members why they used a Bantu greeting in addressing fellow Joroho; the word *Mirembe* does "not belong to any tribe"; it is the universal language of Christianity. It has been used since the time of Adam and Eve; the word "came directly from God." This explanation suggests that the greeting may have been part and parcel of the charismatic Christian religion as it first appeared in Luoland between 1910 and 1920.

35. The particular preacher quoted here uses the names of three founders in greet-

ing his audience: Odongo, Lawi, and Turfosa. In Ruwe, it is also common for members to use just two collective appellations, one derived from a male name (generally Alfayo/Odongo) and one derived from a female name (generally Turfosa/Aloo). The epithet *"joka-so-and-so"* appears in other Luo-based churches. For example, Nancy Schwartz says that *joka-Mama* (referring to the Virgin Mary) and *joka-Baba* (referring to Baba Ondeto, the now deceased head of the Legio church) are common terms of address among the Legio Maria, along with many other epithets derived from both male and female spiritual heroes. Schwartz points out that these terms are not gender-specific in designation. All Legios are *joka-Mama*, regardless of their sex. Members of the Roho church would likely agree that they are all *joka-Turfosa*, whether male or female. Yet, I also contend that the simultaneous, ritualized use of male-derived and female-derived terms is consistent with the way the Roho church (like Luo society) structures itself—segregated but inclusive. Many students of independent Christianity have noted the existence of parallel gender hierarchies within churches. Schwartz likewise cites one Legio member as saying: "As Baba Ondeto has his priests is like how Mama [the Virgin Mary] has mothers. They are her government" (1989, 68).

36. Ruwe is in Ugenya location in Siaya District; although Musanda actually lies just over the district border, Alfayo's home is associated with Ugenya in the minds of members of the Ruwe Holy Ghost Church.

37. See previously in this chapter for the remaining lyrics.

38. The speaker was referring to Musa Ochieng, the bishop at the time. His ability to claim classificatory kin ties to a number of the Roho pioneers probably increased his status in the eyes of the congregation. Indeed, church members who are lineal descendants of the core group of Roho founders do hold a revered position within the contemporary Roho community. The people whose parents and grandparents participated in the 1934 battle or witnessed the *mach* (regardless of whether they were among the actual martyrs) distinguish themselves by wearing the S † insignia on the right side of their uniforms rather than on the left, as everyone else does. Although Christian conversion is the modus operandi for denominational growth, the principle of patrilineage, so basic to Luo society, also seems to be operative in the way in which the community structures and conceives of itself as a collectivity.

39. Roho Christians, especially women members, often elaborate on the theme that the Holy Spirit gives strength to endure hardship and to avoid quarrels. See chapter 5.

40. The four songs were (1): *Ji Duto mag Piny onego unego* (All the killers of the world have been killed), (2) *Ang'o motimore ka Odongo Mango?* (What happened in the home of Odongo Mango?), (3) *Oseyawo, oyawore* (It has opened, it is opened), and (4) *In e wuon lamo Oloo, Odongo loyo lweny* (You are the father of worship, Oloo, Odongo wins the battle).

Chapter 5

1. Themes of reversal are characteristic of many prophetic movements during the colonial period (Wipper 1977, 44; MacGaffey 1983, 18, 208).

2. See Clarke's *Luo-English Dictionary*.

3. Since the publication of Bengt Sundkler's *Bantu Prophets* in 1948, scholars of African Christianity have drawn attention to the high degree of "religious mobility" in many African countries. Sundkler lamented the frequency with which South Africans switched churches, which, he argued, led to a sad "spiritual vagrancy," resulting in "the emergence of leaderless groups that float around, as it were, temporarily lacking

connexion with any church and in search of some leader to whom to give allegiance" (1961, 166–167). For James Kiernan, however, the staying power of such grassroots "bands" constitutes the very strength and essence of South African Zionism (1976, 357). A number of scholars have argued that we need a different conceptualization of conversion to understand the fluidity of church affiliation and membership in Africa (Hackett 1989, 347–355; Olupona n.d.). For an important debate on the nature of religious conversion in Africa, see Robin Horton's "African Conversion" (*Africa* 41, 2 [1971]:85–108), Humphrey Fisher's critique of Horton's intellectualist theory in his essay "Conversion Reconsidered" (*Africa* 43, 1 [1973]:27–40), followed by Horton's response to Fisher, "On the Rationality of Conversion" (*Africa* 45, 3 [1975]:219–235; 4, 373–399) and finally Fisher's belated rejoinder, "The Juggernaut's Apologia: Conversion to Islam in Black Africa" (*Africa* 55, 2 [1985]:151–173). See also MacGaffey 1983, 14–21.

4. *Wopnjiw*, the word for "teacher" in Dhoroho, is the encoding of *Japwonj*, spelled with a *w* as opposed to the modern spelling, which uses a *u* (*Japuonj*).

5. *Maranda* generally means "primitive." However, an apparently older usage refers to the male custom of dressing "in skins and feathers to look like a fighting hero" during funerals and perhaps other gatherings (Oomo quoted in Schwartz 1989, 618).

6. A *poko* is a small earthen dish that forms the top part of a bong or hookahlike instrument used in smoking hemp.

7. Phesa Ogido, son of Oure, was working with Otang'a on the farm of a European settler in Kitale. Phesa (whose wife stayed on the estate as well) was the "house boy"; Otang'a was the "shamba boy" (gardener); and a third man, Onyango Sauri, was the cook. At some point, Otang'a's employer died, but his widow kept the three servants on to look after the property while she was away working with a Nairobi publishing house. Her employees thus had more freedom than many Africans working on settlers' farms.

8. A Swahili word meaning "traditional, local, native."

9. A *dindo* is a short spear whose shaft and head are made of one piece (Clarke's *Luo-English Dictionary*).

10. In describing his hairstyle, Otang'a used the word *boya: Ndalo no apidho, gimoro ne ilouongo ga chon ni "boya" wich ne apidho wiya kabisa ma ka aywayo to gik mana kae.* (In those days I cultivated something which used to be called *boya*; I really took care of my head so that if I stretched a piece [of hair] it would reach here [his cheek].)

11. A family's normal response to such fits would have been to take the child to an *ajuoga* (diviner-doctor) for treatment. However, according to custom, the nature of Omina's birth prohibited him from being taken to healers. Omina was born after a succession of siblings who had died. A child born to a woman who has lost her previous child or children was symbolically "discarded" by the roadside at birth. An old woman (notified in advance) would "happen upon" the "abandoned" baby in the road and would carry the baby to its mother, pretending to impose this "stranger" infant upon the mother for safekeeping. According to Omina, such children were treated differently from other children. Their hair was never cut (Omina received his first haircut in school), and it was taboo to take them to *ajuoke*.

12. See Ocholla-Ayayo for reference to the importance of the beer party as an arena in which male virtues were celebrated and reaffirmed (1976, 45–57).

13. Even outsiders appreciate this aspect of Roho Christianity. A Luo Anglican pastor once commented that he was most impressed by the honesty and sincerity in the Roho community.

14. Achola Pala Okeyo (1980, 191) points out that a Luo woman often endures a bad marriage rather than lose access to her children and to land.

15. *Washington Post,* "Third World, Second Class: Women in the Village," February 15, 1993, A33.

16. Research conducted by the Ojolla Secondary School Cultural Club in 1983 indicated that fourteen had been the average age for tooth extraction (1983, 35). Hauge found it to be ten years of age (1974, 14); Roscoe states simply that it occurred at puberty (1915, 283). Sometimes six teeth were extracted, sometimes four. In the early 1900s, teeth removal was the central act in the Luo rite of passage. Youths who had undergone the procedure recuperated together for four days, during which they were instructed in clan customs by elders. Afterward, they were honored with gifts and could no longer sleep in their parents' houses. Roscoe indicates that girls' puberty rites were similar but included scarification of the back and sides. As Christianity took deeper root in Kenya in the 1930s and 1940s, so did missionaries' denunciation of teeth extraction and other forms of bodily marking. People who wanted it performed had to sneak off for the procedure, for it was no longer a central institution, although many—particularly the older generation—continued to value it. Whenever I asked about this erstwhile custom, I received the same explanations as Hauge: it enabled Luos to distinguish their dead from the corpses of other tribes in warfare; when lockjaw struck, victims could still be fed through the gap in their teeth; and, most important, it served to prepare children for the pains of adulthood.

17. I was told that a *lando* was a 10-cent coin used during the colonial period. A *nela* was a small coin with a hole in the center.

18. Perrin Jassy lists the congregation at Olando, Tanzania, as the oldest and largest in the district, boasting a big church building (1973, 173). Inondi asserted that Isaya Goro was the missionary responsible for converting the people there.

19. LeVine and LeVine (1966, 13–15), quoted in Stichter 1975–1976, 49.

20. To my knowledge, no study of visiting patterns among the Luo has been conducted. My generalizations here are tentative, based simply on my own impressions, drawn from a total of more than three years living and working in rural Nyanza. Stichter (1975–1976, 48) cites Norman Humphrey's 1947 study on Maragoli and Marama, which indicated that a man's main work was completed by noon, whereas his wife worked the entire day, as well as Gunter Wagner's observations to the same effect.

21. The pressing reality of household and farm chores constantly intruded on my formal interview sessions with Roho women. As a result, my interviews with women frequently had to be divided into a number of shorter sessions extending over several days or weeks. By contrast, only rarely did my male Roho informants express a need to cut short my questioning in order to go carry out some task.

22. Ivan Karp has pointed out that among the Iteso—a para-Nilotic group who neighbor the Luo in Busia district—spirit possession ritual is defined as "work for women." Karp argues that just as women's agricultural labor "brings to fruition" the land that men have cleared and "tamed," so too does women's involvement in possession rites—which entail wearing fertility objects and symbols of sexual conjunction— "produce the conditions for orderly reproduction." Women, he suggests, are mediators, both in their agricultural work, in which they mediate between nature and culture, and in their ritual work, in which they mediate between spirits of the dead (*ipara*) and living households or lineages. In the latter activity, they draw on the energy or power of spirits to produce progeny (Karp 1989, 102–104). It is possible that similar significances attached to women's traditional possession practices among the Luo, but further research needs to be done.

23. Anna was probably speaking metaphorically. Rope imagery occasionally appears in Roho prayers to convey unity: "Join us together in a rope of togetherness" (*Iriwowa e tol mar achiel*), prayed a Masumbi *laktar* in 1990 upon the entry of visitors into the room. Rope imagery is also used by Luo charismatic Christians to describe the bond between divinity and the world. For example, when describing his church's historical relationship with the Luyia-based Roho church founded by Yakabo Buluku, one Roho elder depicted a kind of tug-of-war between the two groups and the Spirit. The Holy Spirit told Buluku, "Pray hard because the rope has been placed before you to pull." Buluku and his followers gathered in his home to pray, while Odongo Mango and his community prayed in Musanda. Finally, the Spirit told Buluku, "You have not prayed hard enough; some other people have pulled the rope. So you will be punished because you have been lax." By outdoing their rivals in prayer, Mango's followers thus won direct access to the Spirit. This conceptualization is probably rooted in older Luo cosmology. One Luo myth states that God once threw a rope down to earth to request that a sacrifice to be sent up. A number of messengers failed to deliver the offering, so God cut the rope and punished humanity by forcing them to work for their livelihood (Hauge 1974,36; Onyango-Ogutu and Roscoe 1974, 43–44). Regional cultic forms also invoke rope imagery. For example, the gargantuan python divinity, Mumbo, was depicted by devotees as standing erect in the middle of Lake Victoria, his tail in the water, his head in the clouds, reconnecting the two realms. (The word for "python" in Luo is "rope of the forest" [*tond bungu*]) (Whisson 1962, 12–13; Nyangweso 1930, 13–17; Wipper 1977, 48–49.)

24. The deceased's real name was Mary Atieno, but everyone called her Night, the English translation for *Atieno*. Night's death was particularly anxiety-producing for her relatives. A young woman in her early twenties, Night should have been married. That she was still living in her natal home at the time of her death was considered "very bad," a failure on the part of her father, whose responsibility it was to arrange for her marriage. Night had given birth to an illegitimate son, who subsequently died, a fact that may have hindered her finding a suitable husband. According to Luo custom, Night could not be buried within her father's *boma*. A mature daughter no longer rightfully belongs to her father but should be part of another man's home. Luos believe that the souls of such single women, interred betwixt and between the home and the outside, are restless. Their spirits can be particularly bitter and vengeful, so relatives take extra measures to appease them. I learned of these beliefs while attending Night's funeral. They are corroborated by Michael Whisson, who recounts a case of an unmarried, nubile woman relentlessly haunting the man responsible for her death. "Such was the punishment for wasting the fertility of a woman," Whisson concludes (1962, 5).

25. An *oigo* bird is a blue-breasted waxbill (Clarke's *Luo-English Dictionary*).

26. Different names were inserted as the two lines were repeated over and over.

27. See chapter 4 for the rest of the verses and the original Luo lyrics.

28. See page 154 for all the Luo lyrics and translations.

29. See earlier in this chapter for Luo lyrics.

30. *Jaote* means "messenger" or "apostle" (as in the twelve *joote* of Christ). Members of the Roho churches also apply the term to persons who receive visions, foresee the future, and serve as mouthpieces for the Holy Spirit or God—that is, prophets. Sarah's followers who speak English give her the title of Prophet, so I have done the same.

31. I do not know Odera's official rank within the Anglican church before he

joined the Roho denomination. Like Mango—who was ordained only as a deacon—Odera was known as *padri* (pastor) to the members of his congregations.

32. This quote is taken from page 5 of the pamphlet *Revelation about the Holy Spirit*, printed by Elijah J. O. Ayodo, dated June 21, 1990.

33. Ibid.

34. Personal communication, November 8, 1990.

Closing Remarks

1. For example, Berger recounts that a Nyabingi priestess known as Rutajirakijuna was greeted as royalty with "hand clapping" (1976, 177). Roho members similarly do not shake hands, but greet through clapping, a practice entirely alien to Luo custom. Some members have explained that this practice reflects a desire to avoid pollution. ("You never know what sin another person may have just committed with his hands.") Others have indicated that the origin of Roho hand clapping was a secret, known only to a few. Could the hand-clapping custom reflect broader cultic influences? It is a possibility worth pursuing.

2. Ibid. on the Nyabingi cult. I. M. Lewis has similarly hypothesized that women's spirit-possession cults may frequently be "co-opted by the male establishment," yet "women seem to have played a major, if much ignored, role in religious change and innovation" (1971, 157).

3. Rosalind Hackett, author of *Religion in Calabar* (1989), has questioned the applicability of my model to certain women-founded independent churches in West Africa. For example, she points to the important role that aging Nigerian prophetess Christina Abiodoun has recently played in reuniting several antagonistic factions within her Cherubim and Seraphim Society. Hackett also suggests that the process of institutionalization in South African Zionist churches has not had the same kind of negative impact on women's leadership within the movements (remarks delivered at the American Academy of Religion meeting in San Francisco in November 1992).

4. For a recent critical overview of theories of possession from an anthropological perspective, see Ivan Karp (1989, 90–98).

REFERENCES

Abe, T. 1978. "A Preliminary Report on Jachien among the Luo of South Nyanza." Discussion Paper No. 92. Nairobi Institute of African Studies. Unpublished manuscript.

Allen, Tim. 1991. "Understanding Alice: Uganda's Holy Spirit Movement in Context," *Africa* 61,3:370–399.

Anderson, W. B. 1971. "Children of Jakobo," *Risk* 9,3:14–19.

Ardener, Edwin. 1975. "Belief and the Problem of Women," in Shirley Ardener (ed.), *Perceiving Women*, 1–17. London: Malaby Press.

Ardener, Shirley. 1975. "Sexual Insult and Female Militancy," in Shirley Ardener (ed.), *Perceiving Women*, 29–53. London: Malaby Press.

Atieno Odhiambo, E. S. 1970. "Some Aspects of Religious Activity among the Uyoma Fisherman: The Rites Connected with the Launching of a Fishing Vessel," *Mila* 1,2:14–21.

———. 1973. "A Portrait of the Missionaries in Kenya before 1939," *Kenya Historical Review* 1,1:1–14.

———. 1989. "The Hyena's Dilemma." Unpublished manuscript.

Awn, Peter J. 1983. *Satan's Tragedy and Redemption: Iblis in Sufi Psychology*. Leiden: E. J. Brill.

Ayodo, Elijah J. O. 1990. "Revelation and the Holy Spirit." Unpublished manuscript.

Barrett, David B. 1968. *Schism and Renewal in Africa: An Analysis of Six Thousand Contemporary Religious Movements*. Nairobi: Oxford University Press.

———. (ed.). 1982. *World Christian Encyclopedia*. Nairobi: Oxford University Press.

———, George K. Mambo, Janice McLaughlin, and Malcolm J. McVeigh (eds.). 1973. *Kenya Churches Handbook*. Kisumu: Evangel Publishing.

Beattie, John. 1980. "On Understanding Sacrifice," in M. F. C. Bourdillon and Meyer Fortes (eds.), *Sacrifice*, 29–44. London: Academic Press for the Royal Anthropological Institute of Great Britain.

Beetham, Thomas A. 1973. "Co-operation Between the Churches," in David B. Barrett et al. (eds.), *Kenya Churches Handbook: The Development of Kenyan Christianity 1498–1873*, 149–153. Kisumu: Evangel Publishing House.

Behrend, Heike. 1990. "The Holy Spirit Movement and the Forces of Nature in the North of Uganda (1985–1987)." Unpublished manuscript.

———. 1991. "Is Alice Lakena a Witch? The Holy Spirit Movement and Its Fight against Evil in the North," in Holger Bernt Hansen and Michael Twaddle (eds.), *Changing Uganda: The Dilemmas of Structural Adjustment and Revolutionary Change*. London: James Currey.

Beidelman, T. O. 1982. *Colonial Evangelism: A Socio-Historical Study of An East African Mission at the Grass Roots*. Bloomington: Indiana University Press.

243

Berger, Iris. 1976. "Rebels or Status-Seekers? Women as Spirit Mediums in East Africa," in Nancy J. Hafkin and Edna G. Bay (eds.), *Women in Africa: Studies in Sociology and Economic Change*. Stanford, Calif.: Stanford University Press.

————. 1981. *Religion and Resistance: East African Kingdoms in the Precolonial Period*. Annales 105. Tervuren, Belgium: Musée Royal de l'Afrique Centrale.

p'Bitek, Okot. 1971. *Religion of the Central Luo*. Nairobi: East African Literature Bureau.

Bloch, Maurice. 1974. "Symbols, Song, Dance and Features of Articulation: Is Religion an Extreme Form of Traditional Authority?" *Archives Européennes de Sociologie* 15:51–81.

———— and Jean H. Bloch. 1980. "Women and the Dialectics of Nature in Eighteeenth-Century French Thought," in C. P. MacCormack and M. Strathern (eds.), *Nature, Culture and Gender*, 25–41. Cambridge: Cambridge University Press.

Boddy, Janice. 1989. *Wombs and Alien Spirits: Women, Men and the Zar Cult in Northern Sudan*. Madison: University of Wisconsin Press.

Breidenbach, Paul. 1979. "The Woman on the Beach and the Man in the Bush: Leadership and Adepthood in the Twelve Apostles Movement of Ghana," in B. Jules-Rosette (ed.), *The New Religions of Africa*, 99–115. Norwood, N.J.: Ablex.

Brereton, Virginia Lieson. 1991. *From Sin to Salvation: Stories of Women's Conversions, 1800 to the Present*. Bloomington: Indiana University Press.

Brown, Karen McCarthy. 1991. *Mama Lola: A Vodou Priestess in Brooklyn*. Berkeley: University of California Press.

Burgman, Hans. 1990. *The Way the Catholic Church Started in Western Kenya*. London: Mission Book Service.

Carrasco, David. 1987. "Star Gatherers and Wobbling Suns: Astral Symbolism in the Aztec Tradition," *History of Religions* 26,3:279–294.

Christ, Carol P. 1991. "Mircea Eliade and the Feminist Paradigm Shift," *Journal of Feminist Studies in Religion* 7,2:75–94.

Church of the Province of Kenya. 1970. *Wende Luo*. Nairobi: Uzima Press.

————. 1976. *Kitap Lamo: Book of Common Prayer with Additional Services and Prayers in Dholuo*. Nairobi: Uzima Press.

Clarke, Grace. n.d. *Luo-English Dictionary*. Kendu Bay: East African Publishing.

Cohen, David W. 1985. "Doing Social History from Pim's Doorway," in Oliver Zunz (ed.), *Reliving the Past: The Worlds of Social History*, 191–235. Chapel Hill: University of North Carolina Press.

———— and E. S. Atieno Odhiambo. 1989. *Siaya: The Historical Anthropology of an African Landscape*. London: James Currey.

Comaroff, Jean. 1985. *Body of Power, Spirit of Resistance: The Culture and History of a South African People*. Chicago: University of Chicago Press.

———— and John L. Comaroff. 1991. *Of Revelation and Revolution: Christianity, Colonialism and Consciousness in South Africa*. Chicago: University of Chicago Press.

Crapanzano, Vincent and Vivian Garrison. 1977. *Case Studies in Spirit Possession*. New York: Wiley.

DeWolf, Jan J. 1983. "Dini ya Msambwa: Militant Protest or Millenarian Promise," *Canadian Journal of African Studies* 17:265–276.

Driberg, J. H. 1923. *The Lango: A Nilotic Tribe of Uganda*. London: Unwin.

Eliade, Mircea. [1954] 1974. *The Myth of the Eternal Return or, Cosmos and History*. Princeton, N.J.: Princeton University Press.

———. 1957. *The Sacred and the Profane: The Nature of Religion*. New York: Harcourt Brace Jovanovich.

Elverson, A. M. 1920. *A Cast-Away in Kavirondo*. London: Church Missionary Society.

Evans-Pritchard, E. E. 1949. "Luo Tribes and Clans," *Rhode-Livingstone Journal* 7:24–40.

———. 1950. "Ghostly Vengeance among the Luo of Kenya," *Man* 50:86–87.

———. 1950. "Marriage Customs of the Luo of Kenya," *Africa* 20,2:132–142.

———. [1956] 1977. *Nuer Religion*. Oxford: Oxford University Press.

Fabian, Johannes. 1971. *Jamaa: A Charismatic Movement in Katanga*. Evanston, Ill.: Northwestern University Press.

Fatton, Robert, Jr. 1992. *Predatory Rule: State and Civil Society in Africa*. Boulder, Colo.: Lynne Rienner.

Fearn, Hugh. 1961. *An African Economy: A Study of the Economic Development of the Nyanza Province of Kenya, 1903–1953*. London: Oxford University Press.

Fernandez, James W. 1978. "African Religious Movements," *African Review of Anthropology* 7:195–234.

———. 1982. *Bwiti: An Ethnography of the Religious Imagination in Africa*. Princeton: Princeton University Press.

Fisher, Humphrey. 1973. "Conversion Reconsidered," *Africa* 43,1:27–40.

———. 1985. "The Juggernaut's Apologia: Conversion to Islam in Black Africa," *Africa* 55,2:151–173.

Gilligan, Carol. 1982. *In a Different Voice: Psychological Theory and Women's Development*. Cambridge: Harvard University Press.

Glickman, Maurice. 1974. "Patriliny among the Gusii and Luo of Kenya," *American Anthropologist* 72,2:312–317.

Greaves, L. B. 1969. *Carey Francis of Kenya*. London: Rex Collins.

Gwassa, C. G. K. 1972. "Kinjikitile and the Ideology of Maji Maji," in T. O. Ranger and I. N. Kimambo (eds.), *The Historical Study of African Religion*, 202–217. Berkeley: University of California Press.

Hackett, Rosalind I. J. 1989. *Religion in Calabar: The Religious Life and History of a Nigerian Town*. New York: Mouton de Gruyter.

Hartmann, H. 1928. "Some Customs of the Luwo (or Nilotic Kavirondo) living in South Kavirondo," *Anthropos* 23:263–275.

Hauge, Hans-Egil. 1974. *Luo Religion and Folklore*. Oslo: Universitetsforlaget.

Hay, Margaret Jean. 1976. "Luo Women and Economic Change during the Colonial Period," in Nancy J. Hafkin and Edna G. Bay (eds.), *Women in Africa: Studies in Social and Economic Change*, 87–109. Stanford, Calif.: Stanford University Press.

———. 1982. "Women as Owners, Occupants, and Managers of Property in Colonial Western Kenya," in Margaret Jean Hay and Monica Wright (eds.), *African Women and the Law: Historical Perspectives*, 110–123. Boston University Papers on Africa, 7.

——— and Sharon Stichter (eds.). 1984. *African Women South of the Sahara*. London: Longman.

Hinfelaar, Hugo. 1991. "Women's Revolt: The Lumpa Church of Lenshina Mulenga in the 1950s," *Journal of Religion in Africa* 21,2:99–129.

Hobley, C. W. 1902. *Eastern Uganda*. Occasional Papers no. 1. London: Anthropological Institute of Great Britain and Ireland.

——. 1903. "Anthropological Studies in Kavirondo and Nandi," *The Journal of the Anthropological Institute of Great Britain and Ireland* 33:325–359.

——. 1929. *Kenya: From Chartered Company to Crown Colony*. London: Witnerby.

Holm, Nils G. (ed.). 1981. *Religious Ecstasy*. Upsala: Almqvist and Wiksell.

Hopkins, Elizabeth. 1970. "The Nyabingi Cult of Southwestern Uganda," in Robert I. Rotberg and Ali A. Mazrui (eds.), *Protest and Power in Black Africa*. New York: Oxford University Press.

Horton, Robin. 1971. "African Conversion," *Africa* 41,2:85–108.

——. 1975. "On the Rationality of Conversion," *Africa* 45,3:219–235.

Humphrey, Norman. 1947. *The Liguru and the Land: Sociological Aspects of Some Agricultural Problems of North Kavirondo*. Nairobi: Government Printer.

Jacobs, Janet L. 1991. "Gender and Power in New Religious Movements: A Feminist Discourse on the Scientific Study of Religion," *Religion* 21:345–356.

James, Wendy and Douglas H. Johnson (eds.). 1988. *Vernacular Christianity*. Occasional Papers No. 7. Oxford: JASO.

Jayaratne, Toby Epstein, and Abigail J. Stewart. 1991. "Quantitative and Qualitative Methods in the Social Sciences," in Mary Margaret Fonow and Judith A. Cook (eds.), *Beyond Methodology: Feminist Scholarship as Lived Research*. Bloomington: Indiana University Press.

Johnson, Benton. 1992. "On Founders and Followers: Some Factors in the Development of New Religious Movements," *Sociological Analysis* 53:S1–S13.

Johnson, Douglas Hamilton. 1980. "History and Prophesy among the Nuer of the Southern Sudan." Ph.D. dissertation, University of California, Los Angeles.

Jordanova, L. J. 1980. "Natural Facts: A Historical Perspective on Science and Sexuality," in C. P. MacCormack and Strathern (eds.), *Nature, Culture and Gender*, 42–69. Cambridge: Cambridge University Press.

Jules-Rosette, Benetta. 1975. *African Apostles: Ritual and Conversion in the Church of John Maranke*. Ithaca, N.Y: Cornell University Press.

——. 1979. "Women as Ceremonial Leaders in an African Church: The Apostles of John Maranke," in Benetta Jules-Rosette (ed.), *The New Religions of Africa*, 127–144. Norwood, N.J.: Ablex.

——. 1987. "African Religions: Modern Movements," in Mircea Eliade (ed.), *The Encyclopedia of Religion*, 1:82–89. New York: Macmillan.

Karp, Ivan. 1989. "Power and Capacity in Rituals of Possession," in W. Arens and Ivan Karp (eds.), *Creativity of Power: Cosmology and Action in African Societies*. Washington, D.C.: Smithsonian Institution Press.

Kenny, Michael G. 1977. "The Powers of Lake Victoria," *Anthropos* 73:717–733.

Kenyatta, Jomo. 1965. *Facing Mount Kenya: The Tribal Life of the Gikuyu*. New York: Vintage.

Kiernan, J. P. 1976. "Prophet and Preacher," *Man* (N.S.) 11:356–366.

King, Kenneth. 1971. "A Biography of Harry Thuku," in Kenneth King and Ahmed Salim (eds.), *Kenya Historical Biographies*, 155–184. Nairobi: East African Publishing.

Kinyanjui, Elijah. 1973. "The Rise and Persecution of the Aroti Prophets, 1927–1948," in David Barrett et al. (eds.), *Kenya Churches Handbook*, 124–127. Kisumu: Evangel Publishing House.

Kirwen, Michael C. 1979. *African Widows: An Empirical Study of the Problems of Adapting Western Christian Teachings on Marriage to the Leviratic Custom for the Care of Widows in Four Rural African Societies.* Maryknoll, N.Y.: Orbis.

Knappert, Jan. 1967. *Traditional Swahili Poetry: An Investigation into the Concepts of East African Islam as Reflected in the Utenzi Literature.* Leiden: E. J. Brill.

Kojunju, Harrison Migiko. n.d. "The Beginning of Ruwe Holy Ghost Church of East Africa." Unpublished manuscript.

Kopytoff, Igor. 1980. "Revitalization and the Genesis of Cults in Pragmatic Religion: The Kita Rite of Passage among the Suku," in Ivan Karp and Charles S. Bird (eds.), *Explorations in African Systems of Thought.* Bloomington: Indiana University Press.

Lehman, Dorothea. 1963. "Women in the Independent African Churches," in Victor E. W. Hayward (ed.), *African Independent Church Movements,* 65–69. Edinburgh: Edinburgh House Press.

LeVine, Robert A. and Barbara B. LeVine. 1966. *Nyasongo: Gusii Community in Kenya.* New York: Wiley.

Lewis, I. M. 1966. "Spirit Possession and Deprivation Cults," *Man* (N.S.) 1,3:307–329.

———. 1971. *Ecstatic Religion: A Study of Shamanism and Spirit Possession.* London: Routledge.

Lienhardt, Godfrey. 1961. *Divinity and Experience: The Religion of the Dinka.* Oxford: Clarendon.

Lindholm, Charles. 1990. *Charisma.* Cambridge: Basil Blackwell.

Lonsdale, J. M. 1970. "Political Associations in Western Kenya," in Robert I. Rotberg and Ali A. Mazrui (eds.), *Protest and Power in Black Africa,* 589–638. New York: Oxford University Press.

MacGaffey, Wyatt. 1983. *Modern Kongo Prophets: Religion in a Plural Society.* Bloomington: Indiana University Press.

Mambo, George K. 1973. "The Revival Fellowship (Brethren in Kenya) in Kenya," in David B. Barrett et al. (eds.), *Kenya Churches Handbook,* 110–117. Kisumu: Evangel Publishing.

Mbiti, John S. 1973. "Diversity, Divisions and Denominationalism," in David B. Barrett et al. (eds.), *Kenya Churches Handbook,* 144–148. Kisumu: Evangel Publishing.

A Member of St. Joseph's Society, Mill Hill. n.d. *Dholuo Grammar.* Kisumu: Kisumu Stores.

Muigai, Githu. 1989. "Women and Property Rights in Kenya," in Mary Adhiambo Mbeo and Oki Ooko-Ombaka (eds.), *Women and Law in Kenya,* 113–122. Nairobi: Public Law Institute.

Northcote, G. A. S. 1907. "The Nilotic Kavirondo," *Journal of the Royal Anthropological Institute of Great Britain and Ireland* 37:58–66.

Nundu, Haggai Opondo. 1982. *Nyuolruok Dhoudi mag Ugenya.* Nairobi: Kenya Literature Bureau.

Nyangweso [pseud.]. 1930. "The Cult of Mumbo in Central and South Kavirondo," *Journal of East African and Ugandan Natural History* 38:13–17.

Oakley, Ann. 1981. "Interviewing Women: A Contradiction in Terms," in Helen Roberts (ed.), *Doing Feminist Research.* London: Routledge and Kegan Paul.

Obbo, Christine. 1980. *African Women: Their Struggle for Economic Independence.* London: Zed Press.

Obeyesekere, Gananath. 1977. "Pychocultural Exegesis of a Case of Spirit Possession in Sri Lanka," in Vincent Crapanzano and Vivian Garrison (eds.), *Case Studies in Spirit Possession*. London: Wiley.

Ochieng, J. O. 1973. "The Nomiya Luo Church," in "The Story of My Church: An Anthology of Congregational Histories from Kenya." A collection of unpublished research papers. Nairobi: Department of Philosophy and Religious Studies, University of Nairobi

Ochieng, William R. 1971. "The Biography of Yona Omolo," in Kenneth King and Ahmed Salim (eds.), *Kenya Historical Biographies*, 74–89. Nairobi: East African Publishing.

Ocholla-Ayayo, A. B. C. 1976. *Traditional Ideology and Ethics among the Southern Luo*. Uppsala: Scandinavian Institute of African Studies.

Ochoma, Zadock. n.d. "A Brief History of the Beginning of Ruwe Holy Ghost Church in Western Kenya between 1916 and 1934." Unpublished manuscript.

———. 1991. "Some Corrections." Unpublished manuscript.

Odinga, Oginga. 1967. *Not Yet Uhuru: The Autobiography of Oginga Odinga*. London: Heinemann.

Ogot, Bethwell A. 1961. "The Concept of Jok," *African Studies* 20,2:123–130.

———. 1967. *History of the Southern Luo*. Nairobi: East African Publishing.

———. 1971. "Reverend Alfayo Odongo Mango 1870–1934," in Kenneth King and Ahmed Salim (eds.), *Kenya Historical Biographies*, 98–111. Nairobi: East African Publishing.

Ogutu, Gilbert E. M. 1987. "Culture and Language in the God Talk," in Robert P. Scharlemann and Gilbert E. M. Ogutu (eds.), *God in Language*, 90–99. New York: Paragon House.

Ojolla Secondary School Cultural Club. 1983. *A Brief Introduction to Luo Traditional Culture*. Kisumu: Ojolla Secondary School.

Okite, Odhiambo W. 1973. "Politics of Africa's Independent Churches," in David B. Barrett et al. (eds.), *Kenya Churches Handbook*, 118–123. Kisumu: Evangel Publishing House.

Okot p'Bitek. 1971. *Religion of the Central Luo*. Nairobi: East African Literature Bureau.

Olupona, Jacob K. n.d. "Continuity and Change in Conversion: A Study of Religious Change in Ondo-Yoruba Society of Southwestern Nigeria." Unpublished manuscript.

Ominde, Simeon H. [1952] 1977. *The Luo Girl: From Infancy to Marriage*. Nairobi: East African Literature Bureau.

Omoyajowo, J. Akinyele. 1982. *Cherubim and Seraphim: The History of an African Independent Church*. New York: NOK Publishers International.

Onyango-Ogutu, B. and A. A. Roscoe. 1974. *Keep My Words: Luo Oral Literature*. Nairobi: East African Publishing.

Otto, Rudolf. [1923] 1950. *The Idea of the Holy*. Oxford: Oxford University Press.

Owen, W. E. 1933. "Food Production and Kindred Matters amongst the Luo," *Journal of the East Africa and Uganda Natural History Society* 49–50:235–249.

Owuor Anyumba, Henry. [1954] 1971. "Spirit Possession Among the Luo of Central Nyanza." Kampala: East Africa Institute of Social Research.

———. 1967. "Luo Songs," in Ulli Beier (ed.), *Introduction to African Literature: An Anthology of Critical Writing*. London: Longman.

————. 1973. "The Historical Dimensions of Life-Crisis Rituals: Change and the Mechanism of Juogi Experience." Unpublished manuscript.

————. 1974. "The Historical Dimensions of Life-Crisis Rituals: Some Factors in the Dissemination of Juogi Beliefs among the Luo of Kenya up to 1962." Unpublished manuscript.

Pala Okeyo, Achola. 1980. "Daughters of the Lakes and Rivers: Colonization and the Land Rights of Luo Women," in Mona Etienne and Eleanor Leacock (eds.), *Woman and Colonization: Anthropological Perspectives*. New York: Praeger.

————. 1983. "Women's Access to Land and Their Role in Agriculture and Decision-Making on the Farm: Experiences of the Joluo of Kenya," *Journal of Eastern African Research and Development* 13:69–85.

Palmer, Susan J. and Frederick Bird. 1992. "Therapy, Charisma and Control in the Rajneesh Movement," *Sociological Analysis* 53:S71–S85.

Parsons, Talcott and A. M. Henderson, eds. and trans. [1947] 1964. *Max Weber: The Theory of Social and Economic Organization*. New York: Free Press.

Paus, Ansgar. 1989. "The Secret Nostalgia of Mircea Eliade for Paradise: Observations on the Method of the 'History of Religions,'" *Religion* 19:137–149.

Peel, John D. Y. 1968. *Aladura: A Religious Movement among the Yoruba*. London: Oxford University Press for the International African Institute.

Penner, Hans. 1986. "Structure and Religion," *History of Religions* 25,3:236–254.

Perrin Jassy, Marie-France. 1973. *Basic Community in the African Churches*. Maryknoll, N.Y.: Orbis.

Pirouet, M. Louise. 1978. *Black Evangelists: The Spread of Christianity in Uganda 1891–1914*. London: Rex Collings.

Potash, Betty. 1978. "Some Aspects of Marital Stability in a Rural Luo Community," *Africa* 48,4:380–396.

Ranger, Terence. 1983. "The Invention of Tradition in Colonial Africa," in Eric Hobsbawm and Terence Ranger (eds.), *The Invention of Tradition*, 211–262. Cambridge: Cambridge University Press.

————. 1986. "Religious Movements and Politics in Sub-Saharan Africa," *African Studies Review* 29,2:1–69.

Rasmussen, Ane Marie Bak. 1995. *A History of the Quaker Movement in Africa*. London: British Academic Press.

Rawcliffe, D. H. 1954. *The Struggle for Kenya*. London: Victor Gollancz.

Ray, Benjamin C. 1971. "'Performative Utterances' in African Ritual," *History of Religions* 13,1:16–35.

————. 1987. "Stonehenge: A New Theory," *History of Religions* 26,3:225–278.

————. 1991a. *Myth, Ritual, and Kingship in Buganda*. New York: Oxford University Press.

————. 1991b. "The Koyukon Bear Party and the 'Bare Facts' of Ritual," *Numen* 38,2:151–176.

Rennie, Bryan S. 1992. "The Diplomatic Career of Mircea Eliade: A Response to Adriana Berger," *Religion* 22:375–392.

Richards, C. G. 1947. *Archdeacon Owen of Kavirondo: A Memoir*. C.M.S. Literature Society. Nairobi: Highway Press.

Roberts, Andrew D. 1970. "The Lumpa Church of Alice Lenshina," in Robert I. Rotberg and Ali A. Mazrui (eds.), *Protest and Power in Black Africa*. New York: Oxford University Press.

Robertson, Claire. 1987. "Developing Economic Awareness: Changing Perspective in Studies of African Women, 1976–1985," *Feminist Studies* 13,1:97–135.

———— and Iris Berger (eds.). 1986. *Women and Class in Africa.* New York: Africana Publishing.

Robins, Catherine. 1979. "Conversion, Life Crises and Stability in the East African Revival," in Benetta Jules-Rosette (ed.), *The New Religions of Africa*, 185–202. Norwood, N.J.: Ablex.

Roscoe, John. 1915. *The Northern Bantu: An Account of Some Central African Tribes of the Uganda Protectorate.* London: Frank Cass.

Rudolph, K. 1989. "Mircea Eliade and the 'History' of Religions," *Religion* 19:101–127.

Ryba, Thomas. 1991. "Review Article: The Separation of Religious Studies and the Social Sciences," *Religion* 21:93–97.

Schwartz, Nancy L. 1989. "World without End: The Meanings and Movements in the History, Narratives and 'Tongue-Speech' of Legio of African Church Mission among Luo of Kenya." Ph.D. dissertation, Princeton, N.J., Princeton University.

Scott, James C. 1985. *Weapons of the Weak: Everyday Forms of Peasant Resistance.* New Haven, Conn.: Yale University Press.

————. 1990. *Domination and the Arts of Resistance: Hidden Transcripts.* New Haven, Conn.: Yale University Press.

Segal, Robert A. 1989. *Religion and the Social Sciences: Essays on the Confrontation.* Atlanta: Scholars Press.

———— and Donald Wiebe. 1989. "Axioms and Dogmas in the Study of Religion," *Journal of the American Academy of Religion* 57,3:591–605.

Shimanyula, James Bandi. 1978. *Elijah Masinde and the Dini ya Musambwa.* Nairobi: Transafrica.

Shipton, Parker. 1984a. "Strips and Patches: A Demographic Dimension in Some African Land-Holding and Political Systems," *Man* 19:613–634.

————. 1984b. "Lineage and Locality as Antithetical Principle in East African Systems of Land Tenure," *Ethnology* 23:117–132.

————. 1988. "The Kenyan Land Tenure Reform: Misunderstandings in the Public Creation of Private Property," in R. E. Downs and S. P. Reyna (eds.), *Land and Society in Contemporary Africa*, 91–135. Hanover, N.H.: University Press of New England.

Smith, Jonathan Z. 1978. *Map Is Not Territory: Studies in the History of Religion.* Leiden: E. J. Brill.

————. 1987. *To Take Place: Toward a Theory in Ritual.* Chicago: University of Chicago Press.

————. 1990. *Drudgery Divine: On the Comparison of Early Christianities and the Religions of Late Antiquity.* London: School of Oriental and African Studies.

Southall, Aidan. 1969. "Spirit Possession and Mediumship among the Alur," in John Beattie and John Middleton (eds.), *Spirit Mediumship and Society in Africa.* New York: Africana Publishing.

————. 1970. "Rank and Stratification among the Alur and Other Nilotic Peoples," in Arthur Tuden and Leonard Plotnicov (eds.), *Social Stratification in Africa*, 31–46. New York: Free Press.

Stafford, R. L. 1967. *An Elementary Luo Grammar with Vocabularies.* London: Oxford University Press.

Stam, N. 1910. "The Religious Conceptions of the Kavirondo," *Anthropos* 5:359–362.

Stamp, Patricia. 1991. "Burying Otieno: The Politics of Gender and Ethnicity in Kenya," *Signs* 16,4:808–845.

Stichter, Sharon. 1975–1976. "Women and the Labor Force in Kenya 1895–1964," *Rural Africana* 29:45–67.

Stock, Eugene. 1899. *The History of the Church Missionary Society: Its Environment, Its Men and Its Work*, Vol. 3. London: Church Missionary Society.

Stocking, George W. 1987. *Victorian Anthropology*. New York: Free Press.

Strayer, Robert W. 1973. "Missions and African Protest: A Case Study from Kenya 1895–1935," in Robert W. Strayer, Edward I. Steinhart, and Robert M. Maxon (eds.), *Protest Movements in Colonial East Africa: Aspects of Early African Response to European Rule*. Syracuse, N.Y.: Syracuse University.

———. 1978. *The Making of Mission Communities in East Africa: Anglicans and Africans in Colonial Kenya 1875–1935*. London: Heinemann.

Suchman, Mark C. 1992 "Analyzing the Determinants of Everyday Conversion," *Sociological Analysis* 53:S15–S33.

Sudarkasa, Niara. 1986. "'The Status of Women' in Indigenous African Societies," *Feminist Studies* 12,1:91–103.

Sundkler, Bengt G. M. [1948] 1961. *Bantu Prophets in South Africa*. London: Oxford University Press. [first published by Lutterworth Press]

———. 1976. *Zulu Zion and Some Swazi Zionists*. London: Oxford University Press.

Sytek, William. 1972. *Luo of Kenya*. New Haven, Conn.: Human Relations Area Files.

Toren, Christina. 1988. "Making the Present, Revealing the Past: The Mutability and Continuity of Tradition as Process," *Man* (N.S.) 23:696–717.

Turner, H. W. 1967. *African Independent Church*, Vols. 1 and 2. Oxford: Oxford University Press.

Turner, Victor. 1974. *Dramas, Fields and Metaphors: Symbolic Action in Human Society*. Ithaca, N.Y.: Cornell University Press.

Valk, John. 1992. "The Concept of the Conincidentia Oppositorum in the Thought of Mircea Eliade," *Religious Studies* 28:31–41.

Wagner, Gunter. 1939. *The Changing Family among the Bantu Kavirondo*. London: International Institute of African Languages and Cultures.

———. [1949] 1970. *The Bantu of Western Kenya*. London: Oxford University Press.

Walker, Sheila. 1979. "Women in the Harrist Movement," in Benetta Jules-Rosette (ed.), *The New Religions of Africa*, 87–97. Norwood, N.J.: Ablex.

Wallis, Roy. 1982a. "Charisma, Commitment and Control in a New Religious Movement," in Roy Wallis (ed.), *Millenialism and Charisma*, 73–140. Belfast: Queens University Press.

———. 1982b. "The Social Construction of Charisma," *Social Compass* 29,1:25–39.

Welbourn, F. B. and B. A. Ogot. 1966. *A Place to Feel at Home: A Study of Two Independent Churches in Western Kenya*. London: Oxford University Press.

Werblowsky, R. J. Zwi. 1989. "In Nostro Tempore: On Mircea Eliade," *Religion* 19:129–136.

Were, Gideon. 1967. *A History of the Abaluyia of Western Kenya, c. 1500–1930*. Nairobi: East African Publishing.

Whisson, M. G. 1961. "The Rise of Asembo and the Curse of Kakia." Unpublished manuscript.

———. 1962. "The Will of God and the Wiles of Men: An Examination of the Beliefs concerning the Supernatural Held by the Luo with Particular Reference to their Function in the Field of Social Control" (East African Institute of Social Research, Makerere University College. Kampala). Unpublished manuscript.

———. 1964. *Change and Challenge*. Nairobi: Christian Council of Kenya.

White, Landeg. 1987. *Magomero: Portrait of an African Village*. Cambridge: Cambridge University Press.

Whyte, Susan Reynolds. 1983. "Men, Women and Misfortune in Bunyole," in Pat Holden (ed.), *Women's Religious Experience: Cross-Cultural Perspectives*, 175–192. Totowa, N.J.: Barnes and Noble.

Williams, Drid. 1975. "The Brides of Christ," in Shirley Ardener (ed.), *Perceiving Women*. London: Malaby Press.

Wilson, Gordon. 1961. *Luo Customary Law and Marriage Customs*. Colony and Protectorate of Kenya.

Wilson, Peter J. 1967. "Status Ambiguity and Spirit Possession," *Man* (N.S.) 2, 3:366–378.

Wipper, Audrey. 1977. *Rural Rebels: A Study of Two Protest Movements in Kenya*. Oxford: Oxford University Press.

Wright, Sue Marie. 1992. "Women and the Charismatic Community: Defining the Attraction," *Sociological Analysis*. 53:S35–S49.

INDEX

Abiero, Kelementina, 193
Abiodoun, Christina, 102, 243n.3
Abonyo, Mariam, 89, 90, 177, 186, 187
Abudha, Amelea, 43, 50
Abwodha (Buholo clan ringleader), 61, 62, 78, 79, 80
ACC (African Church Council), 25, 27
Adere, Persica, 90, 92, 94, 105
Adhiambo, Elizabeth, 79
Adhiambo, Fibbi, 20, 219n.38
Adhiambo, Mariam, 104
Adongo, Persila, 48, 67, 68, 237n.31
Agot, Sarah, 105, 106, 107, 113, 136, 139, 202–4
Ajanja, Roslida, 91, 105
Akeich, Morris, 130
Akello, Joan, 193
Alego, 6, 13, 17, 18, 22, 36–37, 40–43, 46–48, 72, 82, 90–91, 138–39, 162
Allen, Tim, 73, 98, 207
Aloo, Turfosa, 68, 119, 201, 210
death of, 63, 67, 237n.31
as leader of the Roho women soldiers, 57, 103
references to during 1991 *Sikukuu mar Rapar* service, 138, 139, 162, 163, 166, 167, 169
Amis, Patricia, 43, 46, 86, 90
Anderson, E. L. B., 29, 30, 32, 80, 81, 83, 95
Anglican missionaries 5–7. *See also* Owen, Walter Edwin
Anyama, Norah, 105
Anyango, Nora, 32, 91
Aol, Zadok, 67, 68, 237n.31
Apostles' Creed (*Njonzari Osheu*), 151–52

Arathi, 76
Ardener, Edwin and Shirley, 194
Arinda, Daudi, 41, 83
Asando, Turphena Ong'amba, 192
Askari (pl., *askeche*), 8, 32, 50, 53, 60–63, 87, 117, 139, 167, 197, 205
Atieno, Abigael, 20, 219n.38
Atieno, Mary ("Night"), 241n.24
Atieno Odhiambo, E. S., viii, 6, 38, 99, 114, 138
Auma, Nereya, 90, 183–88, 199
Awanda, Elias, 30
Awelu, Shadrack, 29
Ayodo, Elijah J. O., 26, 49, 203–4

Barrett, David, 227n.76
Beecher, Reverend (missionary), 28
Beidelman, Thomas O., 70
Berger, Iris, 98, 108–9, 207
p'Bitek, Okot, 124
Biuru Ire Yesu Jakony (Come to Jesus the Savior), 148–49
Boddy, Janice, 209
Bouma (Catholic priest), 70, 227n.83
Briscoe (doctor), 67
Brown, Karen McCarthy, 217n.8
Buluku, Jakobo (Jacob Muruku), 74, 95–96, 165
Burns, George, 25
Byrne (colonial governor), 80

Celebration of Remembrance. *See Sikukuu mar Rapar*
Chadwick, Walter, 5, 14, 21, 26
Chaza, Mai (Mother), 102
Cherubim and Seraphim Society, 248n.3
Chilson, Arthur, 74

253